UNDERSTANDING HUMAN SEXUALITY IN JOHN PAUL II'S THEOLOGY OF THE BODY

UNDERSTANDING HUMAN SEXUALITY IN JOHN PAUL II'S THEOLOGY OF THE BODY

An Analysis of the Historical Development Of Doctrine in the Catholic Tradition

JOHN SEGUN ODEYEMI

CITI OF
BOOKS

CITIOFBOOKS, INC.
3736 Eubank NE Suite A1
Albuquerque, NM 87111-3579
www.citiofbooks.com
Hotline: 1 (877) 389-2759
Fax: 1 (505) 930-7244

Ordering Information:

Quantity sales. Special discounts are available on quantity purchases by corporations, associations, and others. For details, contact the publisher at the address above.

Printed in the United States of America.

ISBN-13:   Softcover   978-1-960952-80-6
                eBook   978-1-960952-81-3

Library of Congress Control Number: 2023912934

DEDICATION

In honor of my dearly beloved parents on the 50th anniversary of their marriage, (October 30th, 1965 – October 30th 2015) Richard Tunji and Agnes Morolayo Odeyemi. I thank you for your many years of sacrifices for us your children and many, many extended family members and friends. Thank you for your forthrightness, fortitude, love of God and dedication to family.

&

In ever loving memory of "a man for all seasons", **The Very Reverend Father Neil McCauley** of the Diocese of Pittsburgh, USA.

> Born: Nov. 22, 1939
> Ordained to the Catholic Priesthood: May 14, 1966
> Entered Eternal Life: June 28, 2014.

A man who showed me through the simplicity of his own life and service, how to be a servant to God's people through acts of kindness and to be a brother to other priests in such a selfless manner.

ACKNOWLEDGEMENT

"Levabo oculos meos in montes; unde veniet auxilium mihi? Auxilium meum a Domino, qui fecit caelum, et terram" – Ps. 121:1

I thank the almighty God and Father, creator, He who makes all things possible. I thank Jesus who redeemed us with His unfailing love. I thank the Holy Spirit who inspires goodness and continues to lead us into all truths. I thank the blessed Mother of God whose love for me is undeniable.

To my local ordinary, Most Rev. Ayo Maria Atoyebi OP, my brothers of the diocesan Presbyteral family of the Catholic Diocese of Ilorin, Nigeria. To my family; my dad and mum, my older sister, Tina Olaoye, my younger sisters, Pauline Odeyemi and Angelina Salako, my two brothers, Emmanuel and Peter Odeyemi and their families, sincere thanks for your prayers, moral support and unflagging encouragement.

To Duquesne University of the Holy Spirit, especially the faculty members of the department of theology. Special recognition must be accorded Prof. George Worgul Jnr, who admitted me into the program and who was my chair of theology for three years. Dr. Marie Baird, a most capable and energetic director of doctoral program in theology, Dr. Maureen O'Brien, immediate past Chair of theology, Dr. Elizabeth Agnew Cochran, Rev. Dr. Gregory I. Olikenyi C.S.SP my first and second readers respectfully and members of my dissertation committee.

To our beloved 'elder' Rev. Dr. Eugene Elochukwu Uzukwu C.S.SP and 'senior brother' Dr. Marinus Iwuchukwu, current chair of theology at Duquesne University. And also to Rev. Dr. Paulinus I. Odozor of Notre Dame University.

I am eternally grateful for the fraternal charity and support of Very Rev. Fathers Louis Vallone, Carmen D'Amico, who both have been truly a source of inspiration and encouragement all through the good and not so great moments of this journey. Very Rev. Frs. Ezekiel Ade Owoeye, Anthony Taiye Fadairo, and Frs. Anselm Jimoh Ph.D, Francis Adedara Ph.D, Emmanuel Ogundele Ph.D, Stephen Ogumah (Ph.D ABD), Msgr. Paschal Nwaezeapu and so many others too numerous to mention. And to some of the many people sent by God to give me a helping hand all through this journey, morally, spiritually and financially; Grandma Jean Szermer (who turns a 100 years old on May 19, 2016), my friends Bernadette and Gary Butler, whose friendship and support over these years has never once waivered, Michele Fagan, Irene Lahr, Dr. Yinka Aganga Williams, Andrew and Diana James, Toritseju Omaghomi (Doctoral student at University of Cincinnati, Ohio), Mr. Cyril Okolo and family. And all the good people of St. Benedict the Moor Church, Church of the Epiphany, St. Mary of Mercy, St. John of God Parish and Our Lady of the Miraculous Medal, all Churches within the diocese of Pittsburgh where I have had the good fortune of serving the people of God in the last couple of years. To my fellow travelers on this wonderful journey; Mark Otwein Ph.D, Rufus Burnett Jr. Ph.D, Ximena DeBroeck (ABD), Martin Ahiaba (ABD), Fr. Emmanuel Ahua C.S.SP (ABD), Joyce Konigsburg (ABD), Fr. Cajetan Anyanwu CMF (Doctoral Candidate), Fr. Felix Onyebuchi Okeke (Doctoral Candidate). My gratitude goes to Mr. Don Ross and his family. Don provided technical support and his family made me welcome in the home. And to everyone else who in one way or another 'pushed' and 'nudged' me when I was tired, slow or became lethargic, to all of you I extend my sincere appreciation and extend God's abundant blessings in all things and in all ways.

Finally, and to all who in so many different ways push me to be the best version of myself and to live and act *In persona Christi Capiti*, may God bless you all.

John Segun Odeyemi

Table of Contents

DEDICATION v

ACKNOWLEDGEMENT.. vii

FOREWORD xi

INTRODUCTION 1

CHAPTER ONE

THE ROLE OF ENCYCLICALS IN DEVELOPING CHURCH DOCTRINE 19

    The Encyclical Tradition in Historical Review 22

    Summary.. 65

    Conclusion 67

CHAPTER TWO

JOHN PAUL II'S THEOLOGY OF THE BODY: AN OVERVIEW 69

    Faith and Love in St. John of the Cross 78

    John Paul II's Biblical and Exegetical Foundations.......................... 90

    "Male and Female, He created them": The Genesis Account 94

    The Matthew 5:27-28 Account: In the light of The Sermon

        on the Mount 99

    The Marriage of the Lamb: TheEphesians 5:21-33 Account 103

    Sexuality and Marriage in John Paul II's Theology of the Body: 106

    Critical Evaluations of John Paul II's Theology of the Body.................. 110

    Conclusion 124

CHAPTER THREE

NATURAL LAW, CONTEMPORARY THINKING, AND MARRIAGE

    AS A BASIC GOOD... 126

    German Grisez, John Finnis and the NNLT School 149

    Critique of NNLT 157

    Conclusion 169

CHAPTER FOUR

INTERACTIONS: SOME CONTEMPORARY THINKERS ON

    SEXUALITY AND MARRIAGE... 175

    John S. Grabowski... 175

    Lisa Sowle Cahill... 189

    Amber Mercy Ewudziwa Oduyoye 216

    Conclusion 224

CHAPTER FIVE

ENGAGING VARIOUS CONTEXTS FOR CONTINUED THEOLOGICAL
AND PASTORAL IMPLICATIONS...225

The Development of Doctrine...226

Condomized Sex within Sacramental Marriage 238

Same Sex Unions 264

Matter and Form: A Hypothetical Frame Work 271

Faith, Tradition and Traditioning the Faith.................................278

Amoris Laetitia: A Case for Development in Doctrine. 283

Conclusion 293

GENERAL CONCLUSION.. 297

Bibliography 311

Encyclicals and Other Church Documents 324

FOREWORD

Understanding Human Sexuality in John Paul II's Theology of the Body: An Analysis of the Historical development of Doctrine in the Catholic Tradition, is the title of the book by Rev. Fr. John Odeyemi, a priest of the Diocese of Ilorin – Nigeria, well known to me since his early childhood in Ilorin, where I used to be a young bishop in the 1980s. This book is a work of great courage and faith. This is a work of courage because many theologians and authors tend to avoid the subject of the book as unpopular subject, leaving people open to taking positions that would be considered "politically correct". They would therefore prefer to deal with topics that do not demand taking any clear position on highly controversial issues. Fr. Odeyemi believes that we cannot avoid taking on such complex matters, which call for clarity and commitment. He did not close his eyes to the realities of the modern world, which he has encountered head-on in his many years of studies and pastoral apostolate in the United States of America. He was able to see the truths of the faith in the evolving changes of our modern life. Change without a firm root in a solid unchanging point of reference leads to an aimless and lost humanity. His work is therefore a great service to keeping the Church of our days on an even keel, in the high tempests of change around us.

"The West has lost the golden thread that binds us to God, Creation, and each other. Unless we find God again, there is no hope of halting our dissolution." This is a line from a recent New York Times bestseller, *The Benedict Option: A Strategy for Christians in a Post-Christian Nation,* authored by American journalist Rod Dreher. Many secular newspapers and magazines and Christian blogs have reviewed the book because of its far-reaching proposals for the recovery of the lost values of Western culture. Interestingly, it is not only Dreher who is entertaining deep fears and anxiety about the future of the West's political and cultural life. Many scholars and astute observers of contemporary culture are raising concerns about the ever-widening gap between religious truths and secular thought on different aspects of today's ethical and moral issues. This widening gap often takes the form of insidious, relentless attack on the moral teachings of the Catholic Church by advocates of secularism and relativism; and the battleground for this culture war is the family.

When John Paul II was elevated to the papacy, he unveiled a series of reflections on which he had worked for some time. He gave these in the form of weekly general audiences between 1979 and 1984. These talks became known as "The Theology of the Body" and have had a growing impact on Christian thinking about what it means to be embodied as male or female. Rooted in Scripture, the central insight of St. John Paul II is that God intends for sex to express the mutual self-giving of a man and woman joined in marriage. Rather than use others for mutual gratification alone, he points out that the Bible exhorts us to experience the joys of physical union as a sign of the deeper spiritual union of marriage. In the Biblical view, human love is not a lifelong search for someone to gratify one's personal needs, but a genuine friendship that may find physical expression in a sacramental commitment respecting the dignity of both partners.

Reflecting on the Genesis accounts of creation, Pope John Paul II underscored the way in which the body reflects or expresses the person. The human person discovers his dignity through his body and its capacity to express his ability to think and to choose, unlike the animals, who lack this ability (cf. Genesis 2:19-21). However, John Paul II understood the impact of sin on the human body. The fall brings about a series of ruptures within the person, radically diminishing the body's capacity to express reason and freedom. It introduces alienation and a struggle for control into the relationship of male and female, distorting their relationships in marriage and in human society (cf. Genesis 3:16). And it devastates the human sexual drive, redirecting it from an impulse toward life-giving interpersonal union between covenantal partners to a desire to use and exploit others for personal satisfaction.

Today, postmodernity has destabilised the concept of family defined as a community constituted by the covenant of a man and a woman in the framework of marriage and comprising children who are offspring of their union. It has broken this "single model" of the family, which it claims limits the individual's "possibilities to choose," and promoted an enlarged concept – the diversity of family forms – a concept, which celebrates the individual's "freedom to choose." According to this new ethic, those who live together and arbitrarily define themselves as family, accepting a mutual commitment to the wellbeing of the other, must be equally respected as basic unit of society, as family. Amidst this post-modern confusion, Catholic moral teaching points in a different direction. In teaching and preaching the Gospel of Life, the Church holds that God has created the human person to share in his own blessed life and that it is only in seeking this God that the human person can find ultimate happiness and fulfilment. Thus, any post-modern, secularist construct that undermines the divine origin and destiny of the human person can only lead to doom.

In this book, Father Odeyemi takes a long journey to the heart of the Catholic tradition on matters relating to Christian morality and works his way to the contemporary situation. Taking Pope St John Paul II's *Theology of the Body* as a trusted guide, he explores the history of the development of doctrine of marriage and sexuality in the Catholic tradition and uses that as a launch pad for addressing the grievances of postmodern culture against Catholic moral theology. He conducts this discussion with full grasp of current philosophical, anthropological and sociological data from secular voices, while not ignoring the voice of the Church. His is a highly commendable effort to bridge 2000 years of unchanging Catholic doctrinal and moral teaching on marriage and human sexuality in one piece. Beneath the simplicity of his writing style lies a methodical, systematic and orderly presentation of arguments.

It takes breathtaking courage for a theologian to enter into this "volatile" dialogue on marriage and human sexuality in the Catholic tradition in a post-modern secular society that rejects truth, beauty and goodness. Thus, Father Odeyemi has done us a world of service in promoting John Paul's magnificent celebration and eloquent defence of the human person as a being created in the image of God. Fr. Odeyemi is turning out to be one of the now many theologians and thinkers from Africa who are patiently and humbly expressing the truth of our faith in the midst of the so-called "modern and civilized" Western society. This may seem a thankless task, swimming against the current, sometimes welcome but most often unwelcome. Whether rejected, ridiculed or simply ignored, this is a task that must be done, not only in the name of Mother Africa, but above all in the service of the Church of God all over the world.

+ John Cardinal Onaiyekan
Archbishop of Abuja, Nigeria

INTRODUCTION

The Church is *Ad Gentes*, a Church on mission to the nations of the world, a Church confronted by a mainly liberal-secularist, hedonistic, materialistic, anti-authority and postmodern reality. This is a Church that carries a message that is ancient, yet ever new, and which she must always make new. This Church has a divine mandate to communicate this message to a new age, an age of unbelief. In the face of the contemporary societal all permissive, pleasure seeking cultures, mostly the ethical aspect of religious faith, especially, the Christian faith seems to keep becoming more and more an unachievable utopia and pipe dream. The excessive individualism, claims to personal rights, liberty and freedom makes orthodox Christian faiths suspect and unpopular. The space of encounter becomes even more difficult to navigate when legislations in the political sphere pass into law acts that are totally at variance with the tenets of religious faith. Carson Holloway in his book, examining the impact of John Paul II's theology on the dignity of the human person and secular liberalism,[1] states that liberal modernity looks like a direct reaction to traditional premodern political thought; individual interest against the classicist medieval belief in communities oriented towards the common good achieved by a life of moral nobility and virtue.

Holloway's work gives me a template on which the foundational thesis of my work is based; the understanding of the background and turning point in modern western European and American socio-

---

1   Holloway uses the term 'liberal modernity' to connote the intellectual, political and philosophic movement characteristic of the last recent centuries initiated by Thomas Hobbes and carried on by other political thinkers who focus on the idea of personal self-preservation and material wellbeing, especially as this thinking has impacted the political evolution of the western hemisphere to date. Cf. Carson Holloway, *The Way of Life: John Paul II and the Challenge of Liberal Modernity* (Waco Texas: Baylor University Press, 2008), 3ff

cultural and political systems and its impacts on the moral tradition of Christianity. In contrasting John Paul II's understanding of human dignity in *Evangelium Vitae*, common good and acknowledgement of God as basis for the welfare of the human race against modern liberalism's hedonistic individualism, shows that modern extreme liberalism invariably leads to tyranny. This Holloway claims was already present in the work of Thomas Hobbes, later expounded and elaborated on by John Locke, David Hume, the American founding fathers and the declaration of independence, and the political articulations of M. de Tocqueville for a modern account of democracy. Due to globalization, this experience is no longer limited to the societies of the global west. It is gradually impacting and becoming entrenched in other cultures of developing and fledgling democratic systems around the globe. Through technology (especially media), politics, trade and the global market, the world has become the proverbial 'global village.' According to Holloway, John Paul II's critique is directed at the philosophic modern liberal project also known as the enlightenment on which contemporary democratic systems are built. Holloway notes that out of the enlightenment movement was born all of the totalitarian and murderous institutions of the twentieth century which are commonly traced to European philosophical enlightenment.

Holloway notes that in contrast to the negative aspect of the enlightenment and the tyranny born of it, John Paul II teaches that humanity fully realizes its potentials in the vocation to love and serve each other rooted in the self-sacrifice of Christ. In this account, John Paul II is of the opinion that modern enlightenment rejected the notion of love and service of one another thereby rejecting Christ. In which case, the enlightenment's rejection of Christ " 'opened' up a 'path' that would lead towards the devastating experiences of evil which were to follow – that is to the unheard of disregard for human dignity manifested by the 'ideologies of evil'... Enlightenment's novel contribution, it would seem, was to turn the dismissal of love into a public philosophy, and therefore to lay the intellectual and moral foundations of the culture of death that has emerged in the societies erected on Enlightenment principles. "[2] This is what John Paul II refers to as 'The Culture of Death', the rejection of love, the repudiation of

---

2 Holloway, Ibid., 146

God as the ultimate source of the supreme good and as the provider of all morals laws and their objective validity. John Paul II pays particular attention to the radical re-orientation of philosophy by Rene Descartes away from the idea of God as the supreme and self-sufficient being, grounds for all created being "and to a concern with the thinking subject or with the 'content of human consciousness.' This turn - which is evident in Descartes's celebrated point of departure, 'I think, therefore, I am', "[3] *(corgito ergo sum)* influenced modern European liberalism and philosophy which morphed into a science of pure thought and on this rests a public morality of utilitarian foundations which reduces morality 'enlightened self-interest'.[4] It is this kind of fragmentation and separation in the society that inadvertently engendered the clash between religious claims and humanistic autonomy propounded by modern liberal political philosophies.

A good number of studies and polls carried out in the western hemisphere within the last decade show a sharp drop in the number of people who claim affinity to the Christian faith. Church attendance has declined notably, and among those who attend, the number of those who adhere to magisterial and doctrinal authority have also dropped most significantly. The reality of the situation, based on every observable social and cultural trend shows a widening gap between Church authority and the faithful, it shows also that this chasm will continue to expand. Winfried Aymans, in her Introduction to her edited volume titled, *Eleven Cardinals Speak on Marriage and the Family: Essays from a Pastoral Viewpoint,* avers, "The notion that prevail, on the one hand, in secular society and those that result, on the other hand, from the Church's faith have drifted apart, and, because of this,

---

3   Ibid.

4   Some thinkers accept liberal humanism because they see in religion some moral unwholeness, for instance after the world wide large scale of terrorists attacks, they argue that religion "inspires an irrational fanaticism that leads to violence. " But Holloway postulates that, "Examining such events in a different light, however, we might equally contend that they demonstrate society's real need for the morality of love that John Paul II offers.... Events like those of September 11 surely demonstrate that the world remains a very dangerous place- in which, we might add, people are moved to violence not only by religion, but also by national or ethnic solidarities or economic interests, sometimes invoking religion as a convenient justification rather than responding to it as the genuine motivation.

problematic situations and conflicts are increasing. "[5] Experientially, questions of sexual morality, marriage and family life are the mostly contested areas. Sex, marriage, family have become new areas given new definitions and newer understanding. Traditional understanding keeps evolving and from one culture to another, varying contexts continue to brew varied interpretations. For instance, Aymans notes that despite renewed efforts by the Church to close the widening gap between ecclesiastical and secular approach to these issues, "The two sets of arrangements have drifted apart, nonetheless, and the main starting point of that trend was the ever increasing frequency of civil law divorces. "[6] Aymans opines that the very idea of marriage and family life are no longer unambiguous in contemporary societies to the point where they have become dubious. For this reason, Aymans concludes "... it is all the more necessary for the teaching of Jesus Christ not to come into question and for Church teaching, unabridged, to find its indubitable expression in our days as well. "[7]

This project therefore focuses on exploring the theological underpinnings by which secularists accuse the Church of been unable to develop with the contemporary age. In this work, I intend to argue that in the conversation between secular voices and the magisterium of the Roman Catholic Church, the accusation leveled against the Church on her position on human sexuality as patriarchal, archaic, unchanging, callous and outdated is not accurate. Drawing on John Paul II's "Theology of the Body " as a frame work for current magisterial position on human sexuality, which in itself relies heavily on magisterial tradition of papal doctrinal encyclicals, and the Natural Law Theory, I will argue that there are developments in doctrine appropriate to the nature of doctrine, since doctrines are specific responses at particular times, carried on into the future, depending on what questions are raised. I consider taking this position timely and necessary since within the various dialogues or disputations on this issue, the two sides of the debate seem to have come to an impasse. The ongoing conversation between the orthodoxy of the Catholic Church

---

5   Winfried Aymans, ed., *Eleven Cardinals Speak on Marriage and the Family: Essays from a Pastoral Viewpoint* (San Francisco: Ignatius Press, 2015), viii

6   Aymans, Ibid. vii

7   Ibid.

and what John Paul II refers to as "postmodern secular humanism[8] "and "ethical relativism of liberal society "[9] need to refocus on the high and major points of the conversation, and more so look at the Church's logic, tradition, consistency and the history of the development of its doctrines over time. I intend to engage these two sides, to consider in what ways the Church's magisterial tradition respond to concerns raised by critics, while looking at exploring how current magisterial and doctrinal position attempts to address contemporary problems such as sexuality within sacramental marriage, the use of contraceptive devices as a therapeutic means for discordant couples, and the acceptance to sacramental and ecclesial communion of same sex friendships.

---

8   Since the industrial revolution, the Church has had to respond to new waves of liberal modernity which challenges the authority of the magisterium. John Paul II's vast works is seen to be in tension with this "postmodern secular humanism ", making him often times target of criticism as an implacable enemy of development. Richard Spinello surmises that the John Paul II understood modernity but disagreed with liberal thinkers like Locke and Kant who failed to develop an appropriate anthropology to ground the rights of the individual which they claim to focus on. He states thus "The primary problem in modern and postmodern culture is that.... Modern humanity becomes easily entangled in foggy doubts and stands on the precipice of a desolate nihilism.... Modern man has lost sight of the provident Creator, seduced into thinking he is the center of the universe .... By philosophers such as Freud, Sartre, and Marx who promise temporal bliss through pleasure, unfettered freedom, or an egalitarian utopia. " Richard A. Spinello, *The Encyclicals of John Paul II: An Introduction and Commentary* (New York: Rowman & Littlefield Publishers Inc., 2012) pp. ix-xi In most of John Paul II's works, he thematizes a philosophical and anthropological approach which puts into consideration an integral vision of the human person, a fight against modern skepticism and practical atheism which challenges moral truth. Vincent Twomey in his work clarifies further that the kind of postmodern secular humanism that is referred to here is understood as "traditional and objective morality on the one hand and progressive or evolutionary and subjective morality on the other hand. Those who reject traditional morality accordingly believe more or less in the evolution of moral values, namely that they must change with the times.... John Paul II.... attacked some of the fundamental assumptions of modern civilization... the denial, both theoretical and practical, of the existence of God. It is one of the basic presuppositions of secularization. The denial of God in turn produces anthropology – that is, a view of what it is to be human – which is at variance with the religious view.... Such an anthropology in turn gives rise to a view of morality which radically departs from classical morality, both pagan and Christian. (cf. D. Vincent Twomey. Moral Theology after Humanae Vitae: Fundamental Issues in Moral Theology and Sexual Ethics. (Dublin: Four Court Press, 2010) Pp. 18-19 Twomey states further that this kind of new morality created individuals who rebel against any kind of social discipline and external compunction. "He seeks not mechanism but freedom, and his hostility to marriage springs from a romantic idealization of sex and a desire to free his emotional life from all constraints. " (Ibid. Pp. 24-5)

9   John Wilkins, ed., *Considering Veritatis Splendor* (Cleveland, Ohio: The Pilgrim Press, 1994), p. x

This work will be reviewed from the standpoint of history and the development of doctrine within the Roman Catholic tradition. There is no doubt that the Church's magisterium in its doctrinal teachings especially when it broadly affects human sexuality has faced major opposition from within and outside the Church. There are many who argue that the Church's position has become antiquated, a fossil of a historical past now outmoded.[10] This situation calls for a renewed effort at re-evaluating and understanding the Church's pedagogical, epistemological and hermeneutical methodology. Subsequently, I hope this work may provide an essential foray into the history of the development of doctrine of marriage and marital sexuality generally in the Church. Such an examination, relying on, John Paul II's philosophical and theological scholarship on human sexuality in his *Theology of the Body*[11] should provide a foundational understanding of marriage in our (post)modern context. Lastly, I aim to construct a dialogical scheme between the historical voice of the Church, current secular arguments and the Church's magisterial position.

In this work, in an attempt to provide some clarifications on the question at hand, methodologically, the entire project is sectioned into a broad introduction, five chapters and a section containing the conclusion to the entire text. Chapter one examines and studies the encyclical tradition of papal teachings on family, marriage and various aspects of human sexuality. This section helps to clarify a historical time line of a hundred years at the turn of the century up to date of consistency in doctrine and needed adaptations as theology evolved and understanding grew. In Chapter two John Paul II's Theology of the Body which is the main frame and reference for the entire project is reviewed mostly from the aspects where a theological anthropology of marriage, family life and sexuality are dealt with. John Paul II's 'body theology' is arguably seen as the most contemporary encapsulation of magisterial position presented from a philosophical, phenomenological, spiritual, scriptural and theological perspectives. John Paul II's

---

10   This view remains till today and is often employed as a reaction against Catholic ethical hermeneutics. More will be said on this issue when considering the import of modern pastoral and ethical encyclicals.

11   From this point on, it will be referred to as *TOB* for Theology of the Body and JPII for John Paul II..

'theology' is essential to the work because it takes into consideration various sociological and contemporary problems that this work aims to proffer some resolutions to. The natural law theory is an essential component of Catholic moral theology and ethics. Therefore, in the third chapter both a historical and critical analysis of the natural law is explored to provide a tradition that dates back to scholasticism of one of the major arguments proposed by the Church and most attacked in modern times as insufficient for making moral judgements. Within this chapter, the development of the theory which is re-baptized as the new natural law theory by its proponents is also reviewed. Germain Grisez *et al*, built a new theory that is purely philosophically argued without theism with the aim of making the natural law theory tenable to a wider public that is mostly made up of non-theists. Having established these foundations, in the fourth chapter, various voices are engaged who contribute to the conversation on marriage, family life and human sexuality. John Grabowski's covenantal theology presents a perspective that is mostly scripturally based. Lisa Cahill presents a Catholic theological and ethicist's perspective with particular attention to gender issues. The 'Just Love' of Margaret Farley is essential for a critical re-reading of Catholic moral theology in its tradition. Farley's insight is invaluable as she is recognized by many as a thinker of commendable clarity in the area of moral epistemology, ecumenism, feminism and generally questions about human sexual ethics. And finally, the indispensable voice of Mercy Amber Oduyoye, womanist, ecumenist, ethicist and woman African theology; Oduyoye has been at the fore front of these various theological enterprise for over four decades. Her versatility and African perspective provides an important addition to a necessary critical engaging of contemporary thinkers. In the final and fifth chapter, situating the idea of a development in doctrine as a reality, the idea of development viewed from the prism of 'tradition' and continuous 'traditioning' will be explored. In the light in which doctrine as tradition that is continually traditioned is understood, two questions that are of utmost importance for contemporary theology and pastoral consideration are put in play. First the question of discordancy of sacramentally married persons and the possibility of permitting condomized sexual encounter in such cases. Second, the status of same sex unions to be recognized as sacramental marriage. These two example are used to situate the idea of 'matter and form' which is considered in the following section. The argument simply is that there are doctrines that by their very nature are unchangeable (usually referred to as dogma), and there are some doctrines that can accommodate renewal or re-interpretation. In this way, this work concludes that doctrines can change in as long as it does not contradict its divine origin, transmission and consistency within the Church's universal mandate. If this position is understood, then the accusation that the Church is archaic and outmoded is no longer valid. More importantly, this work proves its thesis. To back up this claim, *Amoris Laetitia* of Pope Francis is reviewed not essentially in what it argues for or against, but as a model from which a clear understanding of the process of the development in doctrine within the Roman Church unfolds and evolves.

Within contemporary (post)modern hermeneutics of theological discourse, current theological works no longer rely solely on the traditional Aristotelian/Thomistic deductive method but rely also on the inductive, experiential and historically conscious method. This project will incorporate inductive reasoning particularly in the final chapter which considers specific contemporary moral questions to approach general doctrinal reasoning which will be hermeneutical, contextual and practical. The complexity of the subject matter requires a dialogical and cross fertilizing of differing theological and non-theological positions. The methodology adopted for this work takes into account the historical, revisionist, contemporary, philosophical and anthropological foundations of the Church's understanding of marriage, the natural law theory and human sexuality. The focus is to engage the key points and arguments posited by the Church within a historical timeline as expounded in official documents and doctrinal teachings. To review main line scriptural, traditional, philosophical and theological points that upholds the Church's position while allowing contemporary scholarly voices from within and outside the Church to question these ecclesiastical doctrinal pre-suppositions. This is the reason why the notion of "a history of development of doctrine " is utilized to delineate and expound on the idea that the Church's magisterial position is not necessarily rigid, static or inscribed in stone. Even though the doctrine remains constant, it also has evolved as it is evident in JPII's *TOB* and within the corpus of most of the encyclicals that will be reviewed in this work. It should be pointed out that the development in doctrine referred to is not in any way directly affective on the core of doctrine but as a response to shifts and changes in sacred tradition, culture, time and society.[12]

To approach the fundamental question of my thesis, I appropriate and borrow the idea of "matter" and "form" in the sacramental theology of the Church as a metaphor, an analytical tool, to explain the converging point of disagreeing positions. I suggest that to understand possible changes or shifts on doctrinal position on human sexuality can be better explored borrowing the idea of matter and form from liturgical theology. The matter and form position as a metaphor helps to delineate the difference between theological essentials and its incidentals, its subjective and objective nature. Therefore, we can trace shifts in the teachings in the areas of conjugality between married couples, leading to raising further specific questions about discordant couples and even the question of same sex unions. My conclusion is to insist that the core of doctrine does not change because of its normativity but incidentals that are contemporary challenges needs the attention of the magisterium, theologians and secular society to study and dialogue carefully with mutual respect, in a listening environment, to give answers that are ethical and respect human beings and leads to life. In this essay, my direction is to look back into history so as to evaluate the present, and possibly put a spotlight on the possibilities that lies ahead as the conversation between the Church, theologians and secular society continues. Current interest shown in JPII's *TOB* requires that we mine and milk its riches in an effort to respond to the various questions that challenges Christian sexual ethics today. By engaging JPII's anthropological-philosophical and theological method,

---

12   In Jan Hendrik Walgrave's seminal work titled *Unfolding Revelation: The Nature of Doctrinal Development*, supports this position by positing that development of doctrine is the efforts of the church to consistently try to fit the expressions of faith into contemporary patterns of thought, retouching, recreating and guiding the progressive movement of Christian belief by which faith is constantly and continuously reincarnated in human culture and giving it new meaning within a developing human history. Jan Hendrik Walgrave, *Unfolding Revelation: The Nature of Doctrinal Development* (Philadelphia: The Westminster Press, 1972), p. 41

the post Vatican II Church is challenged to take another look at how contextual problems challenge traditional hermeneutics of the Church.

The post synodal Church is well aware of these problems, and states unambiguously,

> .... There should be no conflict between the Church's divinely given teaching authority and the conscience of the faithful Catholics. God does not contradict Himself. Neither can the Church's teaching on morality be reduced to one theological opinion among others. Such a view undermines the claim that the spirit guides the Church. Binding on theologians as much as on any other member of the faithful, the authoritative teaching of the Church determine the limits within which moral theologians is to develop a deeper understanding of the principles underlying the Church's teaching, to expound the validity and obligatory nature of the precept it proposes, to offer guidelines based on this precepts and principles, to help solve new moral dilemmas created, for example, by cultural changes and the advances in technology, and to demonstrate the connection of these principles and precepts with one another and their relationship with man's ultimate end.[13]

The fathers of the synod on the family, in their final report[14] to the Holy Roman Pontiff, Pope Francis, strongly and carefully, without equivocations from the very first paragraph of the report make allusions to Christ's words about marriage in Mark 10 and Mathew 19, these texts make immediate reference to the first two chapters of Genesis. While this position resonates with the traditional position as the biblical texts on which heterosexual and Christian monogamous marriage rests, it

---

13   Veritatis Splendor #10

14   This is the final report by the bishops of the synod on the family titled, "XIV Ordinary General Assembly: The Vocation and Mission of the family in the Church and the Contemporary World, " Vatican City, published 24th Oct, 2015, accessed Jan 30th, 2016, http://www.vatican.va/romaan_curia/synod/documents/rc_synod_doc_20151026_relazione-finaale-XIV- assemblea_en.

also argues against those who see creation story in the Genesis account as some simple story modern people can no longer belief in. The synod Fathers referencing a homily by Pope Francis asserts,

> God did not create us to live in sorrow or to be alone. He made men and women for happiness, to share their journey with someone who complements them, [...]. It is the same plan which Jesus presents [...] summarized with these words: 'From the beginning of creation [God] made them male and female; for this reason, a man will leave his father and his mother and cleaves to his wife and they become one flesh. So they are no longer two but one flesh' (*Mk* 10:6-8; cf. *Gen*1:27; 2:24). " God "joins the hearts of two people who love one another, he who joins them in unity and indissolubility. This shows us that the goal of conjugal life is not simply to live together for life, but to love one another for life! In this way Jesus re-establishes the order which was present from the beginning. [...] only in the light of the folly of the gratuitousness of Jesus' paschal love will the folly of the gratuitousness of an exclusive and life-long conjugal love make sense.[15]

Aware of contemporary liberal secularism and in response to the major shifts in society, the synod Fathers acknowledge these changes but reiterate,

> We are aware of the major anthropological cultural changes today which have an impact on all aspects of life. We remain firmly convinced that the family is a gift of God, the place where he reveals the power of his saving grace. Even in our day, the Lord calls a man and a woman to marry, abides with them in their life as a family and offers himself to them as an ineffable gift. "The Church is called to scrutinize the signs of the times, interpreting them in the

---

15   *Homily at the Opening Mass of the Synod,* 4 October 2015, #2

light of the Gospel. Thus, in language intelligible to each generation, she can respond to the perennial questions which people ask about this present life and the life to come, and about the relationship of the one to the other. We must therefore recognize and understand the world in which we live, its explanations, its longings, and its often dramatic characteristics " (cf. *GS*, 4).[16]

The Fathers affirm further,

In today's society, we observe a multiplicity of challenges which manifest themselves to a greater or lesser degree in various parts of the world. In different cultures, many young people demonstrate a resistance in making definitive commitments in relationships, and often choose to live together or simply to engage in casual relationships. The declining birth rate is a result of various factors, including industrialization, the sexual revolution, the fear of overpopulation, economic problems, the growth of a contraceptive mentality and abortion. Consumerism may also deter people from having children, simply so they can maintain a certain freedom and life-style. Some Catholics have difficulty in leading a life in keeping with the Catholic Church's teaching on marriage and the family, and in seeing, in such teaching, the goodness of God's creative design for them. The number of marriages taking place in some parts of the world is declining, while separations and divorces are not uncommon.[17]

After a careful expounding on contemporary problems, the fathers of the synod turn their attention to a bigger perennial problem which the

---

16   XIV Ordinary General Assembly, Ibid. #5

17   XIV Ordinary General Assembly, Ibid. #7

Church faces by a redefinition of marriage by civil society. The fathers state their understanding and position thus,

> Today, a very important cultural challenge is posed by "gender" ideology which denies the difference and reciprocity in nature of a man and a woman and envisages a society without gender differences, thereby removing the anthropological foundation of the family. This ideology leads to educational programmes and legislative guidelines which promote a personal identity and emotional intimacy radically separated from the biological difference between male and female. Consequently, human identity becomes the choice of the individual, which can also change over time. According to our faith, the difference between the sexes bears in itself the image and likeness of God (*Gen*1:26-27). "This tells us that it is not man alone who is the image of God or woman alone who is the image of God, but man and woman as a couple who are the image of God. Modern contemporary culture has opened new spaces, new forms of freedom and new depths in order to enrich the understanding of this difference. But it has also introduced many doubts and much skepticism. [.] The removal of the difference [...] is the problem, not the solution " (cf. Pope Francis, *General Audience*, 15 April 2015).[18]

The synod Fathers, referencing Pope Francis' encyclical, *Laudato Si*, calls attention to "the family, which as a part of a significant human ecology, should be adequately protected (cf. John Paul II, *Centesimus Annus*, # 38). Through our family, we belong to the whole of creation; we contribute in a specific manner to promoting ecology.... In the family we first learn how to show love and respect for life; we are taught the proper use of things, order and cleanliness, respect for the local ecosystem and care for all creatures. In the family we receive an integral

---

18   Ibid. #8

education, which enables us to grow harmoniously in personal maturity " (cf. also LS, 213).[19] Careful note is made for a consistent ethic in human ecology and as it relates to cosmological ecology. Adequate care and concern must be extended to the elderly, widowed, dying, persons with special needs, the unmarried, migrants, refugees, the persecuted, those with unique cultural or social challenges, children, women, men and young people. The Fathers, in their report continue,

> The great values of marriage and the Christian family are a response to the search inherent in human existence, even at a time characterized by individualism and hedonism. People ought to be received with understanding and sensitivity to their real-life situations and to learn how to continue their search for meaning in life. Faith inspires a desire for God and to feel fully part of the Church, even in those who are experiencing failure or are in very difficult situations. The Christian message always contains the reality and dynamics of mercy and truth, which converge in Christ: "The Church's first truth is the love of Christ. The Church makes herself a servant of this love and mediates it to all people: a love that forgives and expresses itself in the gift of oneself. Consequently, wherever the Church is present, the mercy of the Father must be evident " (*MV*, 12) .... Everyone needs to be understood, bearing in mind that situations far from the life of the Church are not always desired; oftentimes, they are created, and, at times, simply endured. From the vantage point of faith, no one is excluded: all are loved by God and are important in the Church's pastoral activity.[20]

The report gives extensive and carefully worded pastoral guidelines to problems, old and new which family life and marriages continue to struggle with. Parts II and III of the report shines a light on the re-

---

19   Ibid. #15

20   Ibid. #34

examination and expounding on questions of pre-marital catechesis, the actual celebration of marriage, the initial and early years of marriage and family life. The Fathers of the synod includes in the larger ecclesial family the importance of priestly formation and of all other pastoral agents. The Fathers also restated the consistency of the magisterial position of fecundity and generativity in marriage and the training and raising of children. Keeping in line with the Church's sacred doctrinal tradition, the value of human life in all its stages; from conception to its natural end is once again upheld. And in situations where couples are unable to conceive and have their own biological children, adoption and foster parenting are recommended as a Christian good and solution.

In the section where the Synod fathers respond to the complexities of contemporary culture/society, they give pastoral guidelines for bishops, pastors and pastoral agent on how to guide people who are divorced, people who cohabit, and people who are married civilly and not sacramentally, or who are in a mixed marriage situation or a marriage with disparity of cult. The Fathers reminds all, that, the Church *"lovingly shares the joys and hopes and the sorrows and anxieties of every family."* For the Church, staying close to the family as a companion on the journey means to assume an attitude which is wisely nuanced. Sometimes, staying close and listening in silence is needed; at other times, moving ahead and pointing the way; and at still other times, the appropriate action is to follow, support and encourage. "The Church will have to initiate everyone — priests, religious and laity — into this 'art of accompaniment' which teaches us to remove our sandals before the sacred ground of the other (cf. *Ex.* 3:5). "[21] On the question or the possibility of seeing same sex unions as marriage, the synod Fathers states,

> The Church's attitude is like that of her Master, who offers his boundless love to every person without exception (cf. *MV*, 12). To families with homosexual members, the Church reiterates that every person, regardless of sexual orientation, ought to be respected in his/her dignity and received with

21   Ibid. #77

respect, while carefully avoiding "every sign of unjust discrimination " (Congregation for the Doctrine of the Faith, *Considerations Regarding Proposals To Give Legal Recognition To Unions Between Homosexual Persons*, 4). Specific attention is given to guiding families with homosexual members. Regarding proposals to place unions of homosexual persons on the same level as marriage, "there are absolutely no grounds for considering homosexual unions to be in any way similar or even remotely analogous to God's plan for marriage and family " (*ibid*). In every way, the Synod maintains as completely unacceptable that local Churches be subjected to pressure in this matter and that international bodies link financial aid to poor countries to the introduction of laws to establish "marriage " between people of the same sex.

The report relies foundationally on sacred scripture and tradition. While nuancing the works of Vatican II, the report makes copious references to the encyclical traditions of Popes Paul VI, John Paul II, Benedict XVI and Francis I. The report makes clear connections by establishing their conclusions as consistent with previous traditions and recent teachings to show fidelity in continuity. The Fathers propose journeying together in solidarity with reliance on the Eucharist as the food for the Church, preempting the eternal banquet where Christ the bridegroom will host his bride, the Church to an eternal banquet.

The report of the synod father reiterates the responsibility of the Church to divine revelation held in apostolic trust and tradition. At the same time acknowledging the need to be present to, and walk with women and men of our time. And through the Holy Spirit remain true to what has been handed down to the Church. It is this parallel state of encounter between the religious and the secular in a shared space that this book will attempt to explore and speak to. Perhaps by some divine intervention, there can be some resurgence in the practice of the Christian faith in the global west in the future. But in the interim, the interplay between societal ethical mores and the Church's ethical traditions will have to continue to exist in a shared space, unfortunately, it seems, in a mutually exclusive way. If the Church sees divine revelation as ontological truth demanding total self-submission, adherence and obedience, and society lay claim to absolute autonomy, the impasse remains as a wall of separation.

Rev. John 'Segun Odeyemi Ph.D.
Duquesne University,
Pittsburgh, PA
May, 2016

CHAPTER ONE

THE ROLE OF ENCYCLICALS IN DEVELOPING CHURCH DOCTRINE

The encyclicals of the Roman pontiffs are of the utmost importance to this work. The Church claims that the Popes enjoy a divine teaching authority, which they exercise when issuing encyclicals among the other means by which they exercise their teaching authority. The original texts of an encyclical are written in Latin and published in the *Acta Apostolicae Sedis*, a monthly journal published by the Roman Curia. Through the use of encyclical letters, the Pope exercises his Petrine ministry of teaching. The Catholic Encyclopedia clarifies:

> It should be noted that encyclicals pertain per se to the Pope's exercise of his ordinary magisterium.... The contents of an encyclical are presumed to belong to the ordinary magisterium unless the opposite is clearly manifested.... While encyclicals are not of themselves infallible pronouncements, and although their teachings are subject to change, Catholics are nevertheless obliged to assent to their doctrinal and moral content... this assent must be not merely a respectful silence, but a true internal... assent of the intellect to the doctrines precisely as they have been proposed.[22]

Encyclicals are official Church documents written in the form of a formal letter addressed to the entire Church: "Christ has entrusted the Pope with a teaching authority whose purpose is to foster the unity of faith, safeguard the understanding of truth and build up ecclesial communion... characteristically denotes the communion of faith

---

22   *New Catholic Encyclopedia*, 1ˢᵗ ed., s.v. "encyclical. "

and charity that exists among various 'Churches' that is, among the various communities that make up the Church. "[23] The encyclicals are fashioned traditionally after the example of the epistles of the apostles in the early Church, which are contained in the canons of the New Testament of the Bible.

Because encyclicals have various forms and uses, they are placed in a hierarchical level of importance.[24] They are generally divided into three major categories: doctrinal, social, or exhortational.Most of the encyclicals under consideration in this work will be doctrinal ones (there is one exception, an apostolic exhortation).Michael J. Miller distinguishes between "two kinds of doctrinal encyclicals ...; first are those which deal with particular points of Catholic doctrine in a general way. While undoubtedly conditioned by the theological climate of their age, these encyclicals are primarily aimed at a serene exposition of Church teaching.... Second are those doctrinal encyclicals which more explicitly involve the Pope's responsibility to safeguard the integrity of the apostolic deposit of faith. "[25] By defending the authenticity of the apostolic faith and Church doctrine, the Pope also defends the right of the people of God to receive the teachings of the Church in their

---

23   Paul VI, General Audience, Aug. 5, 1964, *The Encyclicals of John Paul II*, J. Michael Miller, ed. (Huntingdon, Indiana: Our Sunday Visitor, Inc. 1996), 10.

24   *Papal or apostolic constitutions* are generally used for doctrinal or disciplinary pronouncements. Bulls are official documents by which dioceses are erected, saints canonized, and dignitaries appointed. *Encyclicals* are given as instructions on doctrinal or moral matters; *rescripts* are given to grant favors or dispensations or to bestow privileges based on a previous request; and *decrees* establish papal authority over juridic persons or places. A *motu propio* is an instruction or guideline given personally by the pope to assist in the development of a particular teaching, mostly for particular Churches. Cf. Ann Fremantle, ed., *The Papal Encyclicals in Their Historical Contexts* (New York: New American Library Publishers, 1956), 25-26.

25   Miller, *Encyclicals John Paul II*, 13-14.

purity.[26] The encyclicals which will be under consideration in this work were issued between 1880 and 1995 within the pontificates of four Popes.Even though they were issued at different times and for different historical situations, one easily grasps a sense of consistency and a certain kind of flexible fluidity within the tradition.[27]

This historical review is undertaken to study the relationships between one encyclical and another, to establish that they build on each other, and to establish the continuity of doctrine from one generation to another.Additionally, it will reveal how the Church attempts to address social problems as they arise in different historical and social contexts. This historical review is essential to the entire argument upon which this work relies: that is, that the Church must maintain doctrinal truth and, at the same time, be willing to see where doctrine can develop within the frame work of both the immutability of ontological and doctrinal truths, and the signs of the times.

---

26   Here, we must necessarily consider the question of papal authority, which is exercised collegially with the bishops and the entire Church to preach the gospel, administer the sacraments, and serve the Church in unity. When the Pope teaches *ex cathedra*, he exercises his ministry on behalf of the Church with a "charism of the Holy Spirit which protects the Church from error when he solemnly defines a matter of faith and morals.... Definitions of the pope are 'irreformable by themselves (*ex sesse*) and not by reason of the agreement of the Church (*non autem ex consensu ecclesiae*). " Infallibility, as this doctrine is known, does not apply to non-infallible teachings (such as those from the encyclical letters under consideration in this chapter). Infallible papal teachings must also be understood to enjoy a divine authority which requires "religious allegiance of will and intellect " (*Dogmatic Constitution on the Church*, #25). Cf. Richard McBrien, *Catholicism*, Vol. 2 (Minneapolis: Winston Press, 1980), 840-841. This must be understood differently when the Church teaches infallibly through the ordinary and universal magisterium. In which case, a teaching is infallible because the pope does not teach from the chair of Peter (*ex cathedra*) but acts in collegiality with all the bishops of the church around the world, teaching definitively and authoritatively as successors of the apostles. (The encyclical *Evangelium Vitae* of JPII is an example of a teaching that is infallible from an ordinary and universal magisterial position.)

27   Urbine and Seifert state that papal and Church documents, beginning with *Arcanum*, is the way the Church has responded to the "philosophical systems arising from the post-reformation era, and particularly those of the enlightenment. The emphasis on the empirical sciences led to a denial of God and organized religion and to the rise of a purely secular vision of human destiny. The resulting rejection of any religious vision led to the denial of the authority of the Church in the area of marriage and family life. The Church's response led to Vatican I and subsequent official statements. " Cf. William Urbine and William Seifert, *On Life and Love: A Guide to Catholic Teaching on Marriage and Family* (Mystic, CT: Twenty Third Publications, 1996), 1-2.

The Encyclical Tradition in Historical Review

Leo XIII penned *Arcanum Divinae Sapientiae* (an encyclical letter on Christian marriage) published on February 10, 1880. This encyclical was a response to the question of the separation of Church and state in Italy at the time, and the question of who has the overall authority to legislate over marital issues, the civil government or the Church.28 The encyclical insists on the divine origin of marriage, over which the Church is naturally empowered to have jurisdiction rather than the State. The pope established very early in this letter that Christ entrusted the continuance of his work to the Church by restoring to order what might have become deranged in society or what might have fallen into ruin.[29] Leo XIII drew attention to the initial corruption of marriage in both Jew and Gentile society wherein it became lawful for men to have more than one wife and to put their wives away by a writ of dismissal, thereby creating polygamy and divorce. The pope wrote that "all nations seem, more or less, to have forgotten the true notion and origin of marriage, and thus everywhere, laws were enacted with reference to marriage, prompted to all appearance by State reasons, but not such as nature required.[30]

The pope next mentions the subjugation of women by men as society's projection of confusion over the "mutual rights and duties of husbands and wives,"[31] noting that "nothing could be more piteous than the wife, sunk so low as to be all but reckoned as a means for

---

28   Urbine and Seifert, *On Life and Love*, note that the direction of Leo XIII's *Arcanum* was ground breaking because of its efforts to respond to social conditions of married people of the time. They note that *Arcanum* preceded *Rerum Novarum* (The Condition of Labor) by eleven years. Leo XIII started the work of a first unified Code of Canon Law which was completed during the papacy of Benedict XV. In the new code, four chapters are dedicated to summarizing key juridical concerns about marriage. Canons 1012-1057 codify general provisions for marriage, sacramental impediments to marriage, valid consent and form for marriage, and the dissolution, separation, and convalidation of marriage. (cf. 7-8) Urbine and Seifert further note that *Arcanum* is the first in a series of papal teachings that will focus on marriage and family life as a reaction against a fast-growing, worldwide trend that questioned the authority of the Church over marriage.

29   *Arcanum*, #2.

30   *Arcanum* #7. From this section of the encyclical, Leo XIII starts to allude to the natural as always a backdrop to Roman Catholic ethics.

31   Ibid.

the gratification of passion, or for the production of offspring. "[32] Leo XIII went on to promote the sacramental and monogamous nature of Christian marriage when he stated "that Christ our Lord raised marriage to the dignity of a sacrament.... And that in a wondrous way, making marriage an example of the mystical union between Himself and His Church, He not only perfected that love which is according to nature but also made the naturally indivisible union of one man with one woman far more perfect through the bond of heavenly love. "[33] This union, in the teachings of Leo XIII, is not only open to the propagation of the human race, but also to the bringing forth of children for the Church and for upholding the ideals of the human and Christian family.

In *Arcanum*, Leo XIII states succinctly that the attack on marriage, started by the "archenemy of mankind " is carried on today "because very many imbued with the maxims of a false philosophy and corrupted in morals, judge nothing so unbearable as submission and obedience; and strive with all their might to bring about that not only individual men, but families, also...indeed human society itself....may in haughty pride despise the sovereignty of God. "[34] By so doing, society deprives marriage of its natural holiness, transferring it to civil jurisprudence where laws affecting marriage are made indirect contradiction to what the Church holds as impediments to marriage. Relying on the apostolic tradition of several popes before him, Leo XIII in *Arcanum* admonishes,

> Let no one, then, be deceived by the distinction which some civil jurists have so strongly insisted upon.... the distinction, namely, by virtue of which they sever the matrimonial contract from the sacrament, with intent to hand over the contract to the power and will of the rulers of the State, while

32   Ibid.

33   *Arcanum*, #9. Leo XIII based this teaching on the normativity of scripture and the Pauline text of Eph. 5:25-32.

34   *Arcanum*, #16. Leo XIII explicitly clarified, "Again in the very beginning of the Christian Church were repulsed and defeated, with the like unremitting determination, the efforts of many who aimed at the destruction of Christian marriage, such as the Gnostics, Manicheans, and Montanists; and in our own time Mormons, St. Simonians, Phalansterians, and communism. "

reserving questions concerning the sacrament of the Church.A distinction, or rather severance, of this kind cannot be approved; for certain it is that in Christian marriage the contract is inseparable from the sacrament, and that, for this reason, the contract cannot be true and legitimate without being a sacrament as well.For Christ our Lord added to marriage the dignity of a sacrament; but marriage is the contract itself, whenever that contract is lawfully included.[35]

Central to the Pope's argument in *Arcanum* is the idea that the Church's divine mandate over contracting marriage can never be strictly under the powers of the State.He argues that such usurpation by the State can only bring calamity and great evil, as unhallowed marriages could never be the source of any fruitful benefit to the individual or the public. Under the counsel of God,marriage "strengthens the union of hearts in the parents; to secure holy education for the children; to temper the authority of the father by the example of the divine authority; to render children obedient to their parents...."[36] Consequently, he states further, "when the Christian religion is rejected and repudiated, marriage sinks of necessity into the slavery of man's vicious nature and vile passions, and finds but little protection in the help of natural goodness. "[37] Though secular society and governments clamor to exclude God and the Church, they cannot provide a remedy for moral corruption,which is spreadingwidely. Such corruption, the Pope claims, is evident in unfaithfulness in marriage and weakened mutual kindness between spouses, the breakdown of families resulting in divorce, and the improper discipline and education of children; and the dignity of womanhood is lessened when women are cast aside after having been abused as sex slaves.

Leo XIII summarized the overall effect thus: "Since, then, nothing has such power to lay waste families and destroy the mainstay of kingdoms as the corruption of morals, it is easily seen that divorces are

---

35   *Arcanum*, #23.

36   Ibid., #26.

37   Ibid., #27.

in the highest degree hostile to the prosperity of families and States, springing as they do from the depraved morals of people, and, as experience shows us, opening out a way to every kind of evil-doing in public and in private life. "[38]

The encyclical condemns any novelties within secular and religious cultures that accept any form of marriage outside of monogamy: marriage as a union between one man and a woman. The encyclical posits that modernity, as represented by liberal secularists, is wrong in trying to usurp the natural rights of the Church to legislate on marriage, thereby attacking the foundations of the true human family as ordained by God.[39]

Leo XIII acknowledges the distinction that exists between religious and civil authority and the necessity for each to be free and remain unhindered in its spheres. He asserts, however, that it is in the interest of common good that some form of union and accord should exist between them, for "the intellect of man is greatly ennobled by the Christian faith, and made better able to shun and banish all error.... "[40] Following earlier magisterial tradition, Leo XIII concludes that "if there be any union of a man and a woman among the faithful of Christ which is not a sacrament, such union has not the force and nature of proper marriage; that, although contracted in accordance with the laws of the State, it cannot be more than a rite or custom introduced by civil law...[;] further... that no power can dissolve the bond of Christian marriage whenever this has been ratified and consummated...[; and] that the doctrine and precepts in relation to Christian marriage... tend no less to the preservation of civil society than to the everlasting salvation of souls. "[41]

Theodore Mackin, who critiques Leo XIII's *Arcanum* on various levels in his seminal work *Marriage in the Catholic Church: The Marital Sacrament*, pointed out that prior to the publication of *Arcanum*, Leo

---

38   Ibid., #34.

39   Claudia Carlen, ed., *The Papal Encyclicals*, Vol. 2 (Wilmington, NC: McGrath, 1981), 1878-1902.

40   *Arcanum*, #36.

41   Ibid., #40, 41, 45.

XIII had published two[42] earlier letters on marriage which could be seen as preliminary drafts for *Arcanum*. Mackin notes that the Pope grounds the origin of marriage in God, based on "the historical factuality of the first two chapters of Genesis as the source of his information.And unembarrassedly combined the creation poem of Genesis 1.... with the garden narrative of Genesis 2.... "[43] Second, Mackin criticizes *Arcanum* by stating that Leo XIII's biblical exegesis is inadequate whereby he establishes the permanent and unitive traits of marriage and shows Christ raising marriage to sacramental status:

> When Leo gets explicitly at the sacramentality of marriage, we note his going decisively to a kind of predication with which he only dallied earlier in the encyclical.It is a kind which he avoided when writing in detail about innumerable degradations that marriages suffered during the four millennia between creation and the ministry of Christ.There he recorded the fate of marriages in their historical concreteness, in the misery of wives in real life.But here as he begins his reflections on the sacrament, he recedes into abstractions; he writes about "marriage. "And this leads into an at least *prima facie* inexactness, since he stays in his abstraction to say that Christ raised "marriage " to the dignity of a sacrament, not that he made the marriages of his Christian followers sacraments.[44]

Mackin suggests that this exegesis fails because Leo XIII, when naming the precise agency of Christ in raising marriage to the sacramental level, fails to cite any references from the synoptic tradition.According to Mackin, Leo XIII "turns instead to the Pauline tradition, to the *loci*

---

42   Theodore Mackin, *Marriage in the Catholic Church: The Marital Sacrament* (Mahwah, NJ: Paulist Press, 1989), 520. The two letters are *Quod Apostolici* Dec 28, 1878, and Leo XIII's letter to the Italian Bishops of the Piedmont of June 1, 1879. According to Mackin, these two letters were very much a précis, a preliminary draft of what Leo XII would say in *Arcanum* eight months later.

43   Ibid., 521

44   Ibid., 522

classici in 1 Corinthians 7 and Ephesians 5: 21-33. "[45] Based on the text from Ephesians 5, Leo XIII situates the duties of the spouse, seeing the husband as ruler in his family and head of his wife, the wife is subject to him not as a servant but as a companion. Mackin argues that in this analogy "the husband is the image of Christ while the wife is that of the Church. "[46] In doing so, "Leo referees the details and the meaning of the metaphor to the spouses in 'marriage' not with deontological valence, but unhesitatingly with ontological. That is, he does not say that the husband *ought* to be guide to his wife as a head is to the body, but that the husband simply is head to his wife—husband in abstraction to wife in abstraction. The result is an ideal construct, and the metaphor has been turned into the reality. "[47] Therefore, historically, Leo XIII argues that marriage is not a product of the semi-deliberate evolution of social structures or the capitalist society's economic arrangement and its tyranny against women. Rather, marriage is of a divine origin which from the beginning "has foreshadowed the becoming man of the word of God and its end product of an image of the mystical marriage of Christ and the Church. Marriage taken abstractly this way becomes universal. " Mackin argues further that in asserting that "any marriage of two Christians is a sacrament.... Leo feels no unease and suspects no anomaly in saying that 'the form and figure' in a marriage's imaging the mystical marriage of Christ and the Church is a contract. "[48] Despite the critique, Mackin agrees that *Arcanum* is in agreement with the traditional magisterial position on marriage.

Mary Shivanandan points out that *Arcanum* is interesting because it lays out two aspects essential to a personalist view of marriage without ever using the word "person "[49]:the sacramentality and contract form of marriage, which ground *communiorum personarum*. She states that Leo XIII was responding to the neo-liberalism of nineteenth century Europe, which centered on individualism; the new scientific ways of the Enlightenment, which explained better the meaning of sex; and the

45   Ibid.

46   Ibid.

47   Ibid.

48   Ibid., 523

49   Mary Shivanandan, *Crossing the Threshold of Love: A New Vision of Marriage* (Washington DC: The Catholic University of American Press, 1999).

new market economy, which redefined new gender roles in the public sphere.In this secular context, this encyclical was promulgated so as to prevent marriage (as a sacrament) from becoming secularized.

Pope Pius XI published *Casti Connubii* (On Christian Marriage) on December 31, 1930, fifty years after *Arcanum.*In this encyclical, which is said to have closely echoed the Council of Trent, Pius XI attempts to speak to humanity at the dawning of a new age with new ideas about marriage and family life.It is generally accepted that this encyclical was also a response to the Lambeth Conference of 1930,in which the Anglican Church broke ranks with the orthodox position on contraception by agreeing to its use in limited circumstances.[50] This encyclical is also seen as a reaction against the widespread socialist and communist philosophies that were gaining ground after the economic depression following World War I.[51]

In *Casti Connubii*, Pius XI copiously references *Arcanum* and endorses again magisterial and papal tradition on the subject of marriage and sexuality. He focuses on five issues: (1) the sanctity of marriage, (2) the opposition to eugenics, (3) re-clarification of the Church's position on artificial birth control, (4) the purpose of sexuality, and (5) the continued insistence on the prohibition of abortion.Pius XI states that "the dignity of chaste wedlock " must be renewed by the Church's speaking for the dignity of marriage. His argument is based on the "immutable and inviolable fundamental doctrine " that matrimony was instituted as God's law, which cannot be subject to any

---

50   From article 15 of the Anglican Lambeth Conference of 1930, 193 prelates voted in favor of and published the following statement against 67 other prelates who voted against the new position: "Where there is clearly felt moral obligation to limit or avoid parenthood, the method must be decided on Christian principles. The primary and obvious method is complete abstinence from intercourse (as far as may be necessary) in a life of discipline and self- control lived in the power of the Holy Spirit. Nevertheless, in those cases where there is such a clearly felt moral obligation to limit or avoid parenthood, and where there is a morally sound reason for avoiding complete abstinence, the conference agrees that other methods may be used, provided that this is done in the light of the same Christian principles. The conference records its strong condemnation of the use of any methods of contraception control from motives of selfishness, luxury, or mere convenience."

51   Urbine and Seifert, *On Life and Love*, 27. For further readings on the historical climate of the time and commentaries on the entire encyclical, cf. Walter J. Handren, *No Longer Two: A Commentary on the Encyclical* Casti Connubii *of Pius XI* (Westminster, Maryland: The Newman Press), 1956.

human decree or contrary pacts, even by the spouses themselves.[52] To this sanctified state of life comes the gift of propagation of progeny, their proper education,[53] and "the blessing of conjugal honor which consists in the mutual fidelity of the spouses in fulfilling the marriage contract.... "[54]

The encyclical contrasts two "evils " that oppose the benefits of matrimony. First, it maintains that offspring must be seen as a gift of life and not a burden.[55] Therefore, any deliberate means of frustrating ability of the conjugal act to generate life is to be branded grave sin. Second, tampering with human life in the womb is equally forbidden.[56] The encyclical calls this "direct murder of the innocent " and denounces eugenic laws made at the time against those whom society deems "unfit " to marry and have children.Pius XI clarifies, "Finally, that pernicious practice must be condemned which closely touches upon the natural right of man to enter matrimony but affects also in a real way the welfare of the offspring. "[57] He goes further, "For there are some, over solicitous for the cause of eugenics, who not only give salutary counsel for more certainly procuring the strength and health of the future child—which, indeed, is not contrary to right reason—but put eugenics before aims of a higher order, and by public authority wish to prevent from marrying all those whom, even though naturally fit for marriage, they consider, according to the norms and conjectures of their investigations, would through hereditary transmission, bring forth defective offspring. "[58]

Casti Connubii expresses the true meaning of conjugality within Christian marriage as intrinsically tied to procreation while acknowledging as licit a sexual encounter that is unitive.Seen from its volitive perspective, it should be viewed from the "chaste honor

---

52   *Casti Connubii*, #5.

53   Ibid., #11-15.

54   Ibid., #19.

55   Ibid., #53-62.

56   Ibid., #63.

57   Ibid., #67.

58   Ibid., #68.

existing between man and wife, the due *subjection*[59] of wife to husband, and the true love which binds both parties together. "[60] The encyclical calls on the Bishops and upon Catholic Action (a lay organization) around the world to join hands in fighting tendencies that destabilize marriages, family life, the protection of unborn life and whatever promotes abortion.[61]

In critiquing Pius XI's *Casti Connubii*, Mackin states that Pius XI substantially continues in the *Arcanum* tradition with further, more exact, and more inclusive details than did his predecessor. For Mackin, the first area for substantial improvement is a reworking of and improvement on the Church's approach to the anthropology of marriage, where hitherto in its juridical definition it had simply joined "contract" to sacrament. Pius XI's anthropology of marriage, according to Mackin, is "crucial because from this it follows that marriage's natural indissolubility has a holding power greater than only the demands of marriage's nature. "[62] In making this bold move, Pius XI alludes to Ephesians 5: 21-23 and to Christ's words in one of the synoptic gospels, "Therefore they are no longer two but one flesh " (Mk. 10:8), in this way making more explicit what makes marriage a sacrament.[63] Pius XI in stating the structure of this new anthropology relies again on Ephesians 5, insisting that whereas the husband is the head and ruler of the household, the wife must live in *subjection and obedience*. This does not take away her freedom, which is found in the fact that she is the heart in the marriage of which the husband is the head.

---

59   Emphasis mine, because the use of the word 'subjection' has been used by various groups to suggest patriarchy without reference to how it is interpreted in the same text. Pius XI clarifies in article #76 of the same encyclical that "[t]his equality of rights, which is so exaggerated and distorted, must indeed be recognized in those rights which belong to the dignity of the human soul and which are proper to the marriage contract and inseparably bound up with wedlock. In such things undoubtedly both parties enjoy the same rights and are bound by the same obligations; in other things there must be a certain inequality and due accommodation, which is demanded by the good of the family and the right ordering and unity and stability of home life. "

60   Ibid., #72

61   Anne Freemantle, ed., *The Papal Encyclicals in Their Historical Context: The Teachings of the Popes from Peter to John XXIII* (New York: Mentor-Omega, 1963), 239.

62   Mackin, *Marriage in the Catholic Church*, 524-5

63   It is important to note that "mutual help " is broadly used: it includes conjugality, the raising of offspring, and partnership of life.

As previously mentioned, this sacramental marriage is indissoluble by any State powers and not even by the will of the couple because it is ordained as a sacrament by God. Finally, an indissoluble marriage as the consummated, sacramental union of two Christians is based on the traditional teaching of the Church that Christian marriage images the union of Christ and his Church, which can never be dissolved.

In response to Pius XI's teaching on the connection between the indissolubility of marriage and consummation, Mackin opines that "Pius does not offer to explain the ontological link…. Nor does he explain how the consummation brings the imaging to its fullness."[64] Mackin then points out what he refers to as "an overall ambiguity " created by this document.He holds as suspect the idea that the conjoining in a sacramental marriage of two Christians images the union of Christ and the Church.[65] Mackin further argues that such exhortation is pointless if the dereliction from that which is exhorted were not possible.Otherwise, "Pius implies clearly enough that even without their actually imaging, in their conduct, the union of Christ and the Church, the marriage of Christian spouses nevertheless does this imaging."[66] He surmises that it will be difficult for others to detect this imaging and wonders for whom the sacrament is a sign of Christ's presence in the world.

Mary Shivanandan's critique is mainly from the perspective of gender equality.She disagrees with the application of the legal language of "contract " over "covenant " and the over emphasis on the superiority of the male over the inferior role assigned to the woman, as well as withthe application of the analogy of Christ and his spouse the Church without reference to Christ who gave himself up for his spouse.She argues further that Pius XI "specifically did not propound a personalist view of marriage but [that] all the elements are implicit, the necessity of a transcendent relationship to God, self-determination and self-possession, openness to communion of person and to parenthood."[67] Shivanandan's point being that the idea of covenant makes male

---

64   Ibid., 527.

65   Ibid., 528.

66   Ibid.

67   Shivanandan, *Crossing the Threshold*, 198.

gender superiority over the female inadmissible as an argument. And that in Pius XI's *Casti Connubii*, the idea of 'personalism', even if not intentional on the part of Pius XI, gives foundation to expounding equality of both persons entering into a marriage covenant as equal in gender and personhood.

Daniel Callahan in a journal essay critiques both *Casti Connubii* and *Humanae Vitae* from the standpoint of the magisterial refusal to acknowledge a sociological need to re-evaluate contraception and abortion.He premises his critique with the idea that conflicts on the Church's position on questions of sexual doctrine and practices have overshadowed more serious dogmatic conflicts like questions about the Trinity, the Incarnation, and papal infallibility and so on.He continues that questions of sexual ethics embody the new conflict that endangers ecumenical work. The Catholic hierarchy has also been seen by some as an obstacle to governments' efforts in family-planning programs, changes in abortion laws, and the availability by choice of contraceptive devices.These issues are a cause of discord even within the Catholic Church itself.

Callahan argues that Pius XI's position on contraception as "intrinsically evil " and insistence on the "rhythm " method and abstinence demonstrates that "the papal argumentation tended to rely heavily on the language of natural law philosophy, "[68] thus implying that the teaching on contraception is not viewed as a sectarian Catholic teaching but as applicable for all peoples.On this basis, the Catholic Church opposes all laws and policies which support contraception. Callahan concludes his critiques by citing two adverse effects of this encyclical.First, "the difficulties encountered by Catholic couples in trying to make the 'rhythm' method work effectively, together with their understandable reluctance to embrace abstinence, meant that a faithful adherence to the papal teaching imposed great, and in many cases insuperable, burdens on them. "[69] Secondly, Pius VI's teaching, Callahan believes, afforded some theologians an opportunity to successfully create "a theological line of attack on papal teaching

---

68   Daniel Callahan, "Contraception and Abortion: American Catholic Responses, " *Annals of the American Academy of Political and Social Sciences*, Vol. 387, *The Sixties: Radical Change in American Religion*, (Jan. 1970): 110.

69   Ibid., 112.

"[70] by elevating what Pius XI referred to as the "secondary ends" of the marital act to a position of parity with the primary end, which is procreation.

In Carl Reiterman's essay, he suggests that the real issue is an internal controversy within a Church faced with an accelerated social shift.Initially between theologians, the controversy expanded, seeming to pit the clergy and struggling married members of the Church against traditional Catholic dogmas. In conclusion, he summarizes the situation thus:

> The internal dissension we have outlined has been viewed in the light of a clash between the ideals established by the allegedly immutable dogmas of the Church, as defended predominantly by the clergy; and the practical problems of the laity.The conflict has centered on the question of whether or not the regulation of family size is morally permissible and, if so, by what means.It is clear that, whatever may be the status of the dogmas, the manner in which they are expressed and defended has undergone considerable modification....[71]

Reiterman succinctly concludes:

> It is apparent that the confrontation between immutable dogma and the rapidly changing contemporary world is severely challenging the adaptive powers of the Church.This may have encouraged contemporary efforts to examine a fundamental base of the Catholic birth control doctrine—the natural law arguments.... Difficulties—both theological and practical—will always remain.To face the former, to question, to reformulate, is not to abandon tradition or admit to error; it is simply to acknowledge the wonderful

---

70   Ibid.

71   Carl Reiterman, "Birth Control and Catholics, " *Journal for Scientific Study of Religion* 4, no. 2 (1965): 232.

depth of reality and the limits of the human mind. There is nothing sacrosanct, however, about this or that formulation of natural law.[72]

Susan Ross, in reacting to Pius XI's *Casti Connubii* encyclical, suggests an approach to the encyclical that includes a critical appraisal of the contemporary Catholic theology of marriage with attention to questions of body and gender. While crediting Pius XI for moving away from the "predominantly juridical and reductionist language for marriage found in canon law and in the manuals of moral theology, "[73] she contends that even though Pius XI provided a more personalist approach, the overall teaching still relied heavily on the traditional scholastic conception of marriage.Ross avers that this move was met by opposition from traditionalists in the Church. Pius XI realized that to present a more positive view of the body and sexuality, especially within the fast-changing social and cultural milieu, was of the utmost importance.According to her, this body/personalist approach served as a pivot between the Church and the world.

Ross argues further that the insistence on Natural Law Theory, "with its reliance on an ahistorical and, critics claimed, 'physicalist' view of the person, failed to take into account the subjective and 'personal' character of the human. "This situation persists, according to Ross, because marriage theologically is a primary, if not central, metaphor for the Church. From the covenant between Yahweh and Israel,to the Pauline Christ and his bride the Church, this marital parallel is continually drawn.She posits that this metaphor remains necessary because "gender relationships and sexuality were and are primary loci for establishing and maintaining power in the Roman Catholic Church. "Ross insists that this dynamic in Catholic marriage theology represents the hierarchical authority as symbolized and exercised.

Ross surmises thus:

---

72   Ibid., 233.

73   Susan A. Ross, "The Bride of Christ and the Body Politic: Body and Gender in Pre-Vatican II Marriage Theology, " *Journal of Religion* 71, no. 3 (1991): 345-7.

The hierarchical relationship of husband and wife was symbolic of the Church's own hierarchical structure. The masculine power of the clergy to lead and instruct the feminine and receptive laity was supported by this "gendered" theology of marriage. Therefore, the "degendering" of this theology reconceived relationships between men and women, clergy and laity: no longer hierarchical, but free and mutual. The threat to the Church was clear.

Paul VI's ***Humanae Vitae*** of July 25, 1968, remains perhaps the most controversial of the Catholic Church's encyclicals especially because it forcefully denounces the use of contraception as "intrinsically evil, " arguing that it violates the very purpose and nature of the sexual act, consequently violating the dignity of the human person. *Humanae Vitae* re-affirms previous encyclicals regarding the aspects of married love, conjugality within marriage, and responsible parenthood, and supports the total rejection of any form of artificial birth control. The encyclical states that,

> …. any direct interruption of the generative process already begun, even if for therapeutic reasons, are to be absolutely excluded as licit means of regulating birth; sterilization whether perpetual or temporary, in either the female or male, and any action which either in anticipation of the conjugal act, or in the accomplishment of it, or in the development of its natural consequences, proposed whether as an end or as a means, to render procreation impossible is illicit.[74]

Even though Paul VI continues in the apostolic tradition of his predecessors, the volatility of public response was strong. Vatican II had just taken place, with what many perceived to be a more progressive and less conservative and traditionalist approach to Church teaching. Paul

---

74   Paul VI, *Humanae Vitae: Encyclical Letter on the Regulation of Birth*, #14, published 1968, accessed June 1, 2015, www.vatican.va/holy_father/paul_vi/encyclicals/documents/hf_p-vi_enc_25071968_humanae-vitae_en.html

VI's rejection of the majority opinion of the Pontifical Commission on Birth Control that had been setup by his predecessor was seen as authoritarian.[75]

The encyclical's first sentence states its overarching view: "The transmission of human life is a most serious role in which married people collaborate freely and responsibly with God the creator. "[76] "Collaboration, " as used by Paul VI, connotes a responsible acceptance of working with Divine Providence, without any arbitrary choices on the part of the human agent which may seem to interfere with God's design.Paul VI acknowledges the reality of the married state when he states, "[Marriage] has always been a source of great joy to them, even though it sometimes entails many difficulties and hardships. "[77] The pope recognized changes that continually takes place in society and which challenges married people, such as demographic problems of over population, causing greater economic and educational demands; a very important new understanding of the dignity of women in the society;

---

75   John XXIII had established a commission in 1963 to advise him on the question of contraception and population as a response to the availability of oral contraception. The committee was still meeting when John XXIII passed away while sessions of Vatican II were still in progress. Paul VI was elected the next Pope and he expanded the Commission to fifty-eight members from its original six, which now included lay men and women from the scientific/medical fields, married couples, theologians, and bishops. It is generally argued that the work of this Commission forms a large part of the drafting of the last document of Vatican II titled *Gaudium et Spes* #47-52, which focuses on the nobility of marriage and responsible parenthood. The question of the licit or illicit forms of contraception was reserved to Paul VI. In May 1966, shortly after the close of Vatican II, the Commission presented its findings to Paul VI, in which it approved by a majority the possibility of the use of contraception by married couples in certain cases. The minority also issued its own statement to counter the majority report. It would take another two years of consultations and study before *Humanae Vitae* was issued, which definitively disapproved of any hormonal anti-ovulants used for contraceptive purposes. Because of the lack of consensus between the two factions of the commission, Paul VI states that what is true yesterday will be true today and true in the future. Therefore towing apostolic tradition is the best way to go rather than change revealed truths of the sacred scriptures. It must be stated also that this Commission was acting in a consultative role to the Pope, who was not under obligation to accept the outcome of either minority or majority reports. (Cf. article #6 of *Humanae Vitae* for the Holy Father's explanation for rejection of the Majority Report as not "definitive or absolutely certain, " and that some of its conclusions were at variance with "the moral doctrine on marriage constantly taught by the magisterium of the Church. ")

76   Paul VI, *Humanae Vitae*, Introduction, published 1968, accessed June 1, 2015, http://www.vatican.va/holy_father/paul_vi/encyclicals/documents/hf, #1

77   Ibid.

the true meaning of conjugality in marriage; and the relationship of conjugal acts to love.Paul VI insists that despite a "most remarkable development....in man's stupendous progress in the domination and rational organization of the forces of nature to the point that he is endeavoring to extend this control over every aspect of his own life— over his body, over his mind and emotions, over his social life, and even over the laws that regulate the transmission of life. "[78] All of these, for Paul VI, raise the following questions: "Would it not be right to review the moral norms in force till now, especially when it is felt that these can be observed only with the gravest difficulty? " Further, "could it not be accepted that the intention to have a less prolific but more rationally planned family might transform an action which renders natural processes infertile into a licit and provident control of birth? "And finally, "whether, because people are more conscious today of their responsibilities, the time has not come when the transmission of life should be regulated by their intelligence and will rather than through the specific rhythms of their own bodies? "

To be able to respond to these questionsadequately, Paul VI clarifies that the Church's magisterium has the competency to interpret the natural moral law.Based on this, the encyclical is directed at clarifying the question of human procreation, a mission that humanity is called to in both its natural and earthly aspects and its supernatural and eternal aspects.These, he avers, transcend specific disciplines, such as biology, psychology, demography, or sociology.Married love, therefore, is revealed in its true nature and nobility because it takes its origin from the God who is love.This married love among baptized Christians is sacramental, fully human, an act of free will, faithful and exclusive until death, and fecund.It is this kind of married love that Paul VI argues must give birth to responsible parenthood: "In a word, the exercise of responsible parenthood requires that husband and wife, keeping a right order of priorities, recognize their own duties towards God, themselves, their families and human society. "[79] In referring to the natural law, Paul VI writes, "The Church, nevertheless, in urging

---

78   Ibid. #2

79   Paul VI, *Humanae Vitae*, #10.

men to the observance of the precepts of the natural law, which it interprets by its constant doctrine, teaches that each and every marital act must of necessity retain its intrinsic relationship to the procreation of human life. "[80]

The foregoing, therefore, becomes the logical background for Paul VI to ground his teaching on the unlawful means of birth control:

> Therefore, we base Our words on the first principles of a human and Christian doctrine of marriage when We are obliged once more to declare that the direct interruption of the generative process already begun and, above all, all direct abortion, even for therapeutic reasons, are to be absolutely excluded as lawful means of regulating the number of children. Equally to be condemned, as the magisterium of the Church has affirmed on many occasions, is direct sterilization, whether of the man or of the woman, whether permanent or temporary. Similarly excluded is any action which either before, at the moment of, or after sexual intercourse, is specifically intended to prevent procreation—whether as an end or as a means. Neither is it valid to argue, as a justification for sexual intercourse which is deliberately contraceptive, that a lesser evil is to be preferred to a greater one.... Though it is true that sometimes it is lawful to tolerate a lesser moral evil in order to promote a greater good, it is never lawful, even for the gravest reasons, to do evil that good may come out of it.... Consequently, it is a serious error to think that a whole married life of otherwise normal relations can justify sexual intercourse which is deliberately contraceptive and so intrinsically wrong.[81]

Paul VI clarifies that the Church does not "consider illicit the use of those therapeutic means necessary to cure bodily diseases, even if

---

80   Ibid., #11

81   Ibid. #14

a foreseeable impediment to procreation should result there from—provided such impediment is not directly intended for any motive whatsoever."[82] Therefore, "the Church teaches that married people may then take advantage of the natural cycles immanent in the reproductive system and engage in marital intercourse only during those times that are infertile, thus controlling birth in a way which does not in the least offend the moral principles...."[83]

Reflecting on the consequences of a contraceptive culture, Paul VI warns of three consequences: (1) that the practice of methods of artificial birth control could easily open wide the way for marital infidelity and the general lowering of moral standards; (2) that a man who grows accustomed to the use of contraceptive methods may forget the reverence due to a woman, and disregarding her emotional and physical equilibrium, reduce her merely to an instrument of his own desires while no longer considering her within a sacramental frame work as a partner who needs care and affection; and (3) that careful consideration is given to the danger of public authorities having legislative power over this matter as they care little for the precepts of the moral law. The Pontiff warns as to the limits of the control humanity has over itself, stating that "…. unless we are willing that the responsibility of procreating life should be left to the arbitrary decision of men, we must accept that there are certain limits, beyond which it is wrong to go, to the power of man over his own body and its natural functions—limits, let it be said, which no one, whether as a private individual or as a public authority, can lawfully exceed."[84]

Paul VI then turns to the concerns of the Church and reasons for publishing *Humanae Vitae*:

> It is to be anticipated that perhaps not everyone will easily accept this particular teaching. There is too much clamorous outcry against the voice of the Church, and this is intensified by modern means of communication. But it comes as no surprise to the Church that she, no less than her divine Founder, is

---

82   Ibid., #15.

83   Ibid., #16.

84   Ibid., #17.

destined to be a "sign of contradiction. "She does not, because of this, evade the duty imposed on her of proclaiming humbly but firmly the entire moral law, both natural and evangelical.

Since the Church did not make either of these laws, she cannot be their arbiter—only their guardian and interpreter.It could never be right for her to declare lawful what is in fact unlawful, since that, by its very nature, is always opposed to the true good of man.

In preserving intact, the whole moral law of marriage, the Church is convinced that she is contributing to the creation of a truly human civilization.She urges man not to betray his personal responsibilities by putting all his faith in technical expedients.In this way she defends the dignity of husband and wife.This course of action shows that the Church, loyal to the example and teaching of the divine savior, is sincere and unselfish in her regard for men whom she strives to help even now during this earthly pilgrimage "to share God's life as sons of the living God, the Father of all men. " [85]

The encyclical concludes by issuing pastoral directives to the entire Church to recognize this encyclical as a "promulgation of the law of God Himself, " which requires from "men and women, from families and from the human family, a resolute purpose and great endurance " which makes periodic continence and self-discipline possible, and can create an atmosphere favorable to the growth of chastity so that true liberty may prevail over license and the norms of the moral law may be fully safeguarded. The Pontiff then appeals to public authorities not to accede to legislation which introduces practices opposed to the natural law of God for marriage and family life.To scientists, Christian couples, doctors and nurses, family apostolates, the bishops of the Church, the pope called for a unified voice that condemns contraceptive culture

---

85   Ibid., #18.

and abortion and calls for a renewed respect for human life, marriage, and the education of offspring.

As noted already, this encyclical and Paul VI met with public outcry and critique.Some bishops and a good number of theologians in Europe and America openly either tried to soften the perceived harshness of the encyclical or outright oppose it in public dissent.The critique of *Humanae Vitae* continues to this day, mostly along the same broad lines of argumentation.For example, Charles Curran's critique of this encyclical offers the standard objections.His work points out the basic criticisms of Paul VI's *Humanae Vitae*.[86]

The first area of difficulty in the encyclical, Curran says, is the questionableappeal tonatural law.Revisionists argue that there are weaknesses in the philosophical aspects of the natural law in the traditional manuals employed by Paul VI.They argue that Paul VI's approach to and use of natural law accept a classicist worldview that does not make room for historical consciousness, and accepts and absolutizes the physical aspect of the human act without consideration for the truly holistic person. In addition, the nature and finality of the sexual faculties are overly emphasized, whereas relationships and the person are not sufficiently taken into consideration.For Curran, historical consciousness gives pride of place to the human subject, who is a knower and an acting person, embedded in history and culture. The shift, therefore, is from the classicist method to the historical

---

86   Charles Curran is perhaps the foremost moral theologian who has critiqued encyclicals and magisterial positions from a revisionist/liberal perspective. Curran's critique of John Paul II's moral theology is documented in a major monograph penned by Curran. Curran's insights are invaluable to the encyclicals and the sexual, marital and family life they envision. Curran's work, even though a critique, inadvertently provides me with material to support the notion that there has always been development of doctrine within the tradition but these developments did not affect the core of doctrine. For instance, as Curran is quick in many of his works to point out that for the greater part of the Church's history, marriage was not accorded a sacramental character. That it was not until Trent that the requirement for a priest to be present as a witness for the Church at a marriage was instituted or that the spouses are the celebrants of their own sacrament. Another shift is often referenced by Curran is to point out that there was a time when the Church saw marriage as a contract but now the language has changed to covenant. And in the area of marital conjugality, there was a time when marital intercourse was understood as geared towards procreation and control of 'concupiscence.' But with the acceptance of the rhythm method by Pius XII, the sex act was opened up for mutuality and communion of the spouses outside of the intention to procreate. Any serious study in the area of Catholic sexual ethics and tradition necessarily must take Curran's contribution to the field into consideration.

consciousness which is flexible and open to change and development. In Curran's words, manualistic natural law employed deductive syllogism as its method, which "claims that the conclusion is just as certain as the premises, provided the logic is correct. "[87] Herein, the end of the deductive and syllogistic method is certitude.On the other hand, historical consciousness applies an inductive method, which considers many aspects of any one particular act, thereby affecting the application of the old natural law argument.According to Curran, the old manuals assume a monolithic natural law theory which can be applied deductively across the board to moral problems. An insistence that the natural law is eternal, immutable, and unchanging and that its conclusions are always certain becomes a problem in itself because it contradicts the reality of Catholic teachings on specific moral questions, such as slavery, defendants' right to silence, usury, and even the understanding of the ends of marriage in the ways it has currently been re-arranged.

Curran takes up the issue of physicalism.Here Curran refers to "the a priori identification of the human moral act with the physical or biological aspect of the act.... In sexual ethics there exists an a priori identification of the physical structure with the moral aspect of the act. "[88] Curran argues that one of the main problems here is the traditional understanding of and reliance on Aquinas and the use of "Ulpian's " understanding of Natural Law Theory as that which nature teaches all animals and humans.Even though Aquinas distinguishes between the natural law of humans based on pure reason versus the natural law in animals, this anthropology ended up creating two layers in the human person: a bottom layer common to humans and animals alike and a top layer which is unique only to humans.Curran then questions, "Why should the physical structure of the marital act always be morally obliging? Why cannot human reason interfere with the physical structure of the act for a proportionate good? "[89] In which case Curran takes the position that "[a] more personalist or relational anthropology does not absolutize finality of the faculty itself.The sexual faculty or

---

87   Charles E. Curran, *Catholic Moral Theology in the United States: A History* (Washington, DC: Georgetown University, 2008), 103.

88   Ibid., 104.

89   Ibid., 105.

power exists in light of the total person and the person's relationships."[90] Therefore, and according to Curran, "for the good of the person or the good of the marriage, one can and should interfere with the sexual faculty or power."[91]

Two other equally difficult problems from *Humanae Vitae*'s use of Natural Law Theory must be noted—namely, the question of absolute moral norms and intrinsically evil acts. Even though revisionists are not opposed to absolute moral norms and acts that are intrinsically wrong, yet they argue that "actions that are described only in terms of the physical aspect or structure are neither necessarily always wrong nor intrinsically evil."[92] The revisionists defended their arguments based on their understanding of proportionalism, as represented mostly by the moderate proportionalism of Richard McCormick. According to Curran, McCormick "recognizes his own position as avoiding the two extremes of absolute deontology, as found in the Catholic manualist tradition and in Germain Grisez, and absolute consequentialism, as identified with Joseph Fletcher and some utilitarians. His moderate teleology sees the role of consequences as necessary but not sufficient for determining the morality of actions."[93] McCormick's moderate proportionalism relies on three foundational assumptions. First, there must always be a proportionate reason to justify any moral act; one must not knowingly choose a wrong option. Second, the basic goods are themselves incommensurate, and third, there can be no establishment of a hierarchy or order among the basic goods.[94]

Even though the encyclical *Humanae Vitae* continues to receive negative critique, a few voices see its value and support it. Mary Shivanandan, relying largely on John Paul II's writings and support for the encyclical, posits among other positive remarks that even though the language of *Humanae Vitae* uses the term "human" rather

---

90   Ibid.

91   Ibid.

92   Ibid., 106.

93   Ibid., 107.

94   Ibid., 108. According to Curran, proportionalism is no longer very consequential in contemporary theological conversation; newer approaches have taken its place. However, proportionalism was an option for its time, and it did try to extend development in the thinking of the traditional manualist approach to natural law theory.

than "personal " when referring to the conjugal act, the encyclical emphasizes a communion of being and an integral understanding of the person.This analysis develops the concept of love understood as a reciprocal gift of persons, understood from revelation and theology as an anthropology which is profoundly personalistic.She further clarifies that this anthropology of the person-subject within the principle of totality is a question of this specific man or woman who in their sexual nature have a common object, which is the body.She avers, "Only an integral vision of man can serve as a basis for ethics.When this is ignored, the body comes to be looked at exclusively in the somatic dimension to be manipulated technologically, as in the case of contraception. "[95] She then traces a connection betweenHumanae *Vitae* and *Gaudium et Spes*as well as John Paul II's Wednesday catechesis which gave birth to his *Theology of the Body*.She surmised that in this encyclical, "[t] he integral vision of man ... is a 'vision of faith,' which views man's natural and supernatural destiny in the light of revelation.It penetrates the search for the truth about man himself. "[96]

She sees the encyclical as a bold defense of the dignity and sacredness of human life, an appeal for responsibility in sexual relationships within marriage, especially in the face of contemporary problems of artificial birth control.She also sees Paul VI's insistence on the competence of the magisterium to teach in the areas of Christian ideals of conjugal love as promoting responsible parenthood within an integral vision of the human person. She points out that the Pope recognizes also the responsibility of spouses in conscience to be able to determine the number of children they intend to have and their spacing.Within the purview of Paul VI, the encyclical *Humanae Vitae*gives directives as for what may be considered licit or illicit as means of regulating birth while also proposing pastoral directives to support human dignity and Christian values.

In John Paul II's Synodal exhortation, ***Familiaris Consortio*** (The Christian Family in the Modern World), promulgated on November 22, 1981, he develops the Church's position on marriage as family life noting that this institution currently faces an attack from modernity

---

95   Shivanandan, *Crossing the Threshold*,115-6.

96   Ibid.

which attempts to deform its nature and character. In the very opening lines of the document, JPII states, "The family in the modern world, as much as and perhaps more than any other institution, has been beset by the many profound and rapid changes that have affected society and culture."[97] He points to signs of a

> ...disturbing degradation of some fundamental values; a mistaken theoretical concept of independence of spouses in relation to each other: serious misconceptions regarding the relationship of authority between parents and children; the concrete difficulties that the family itself experiences in the transmission of values; the growing number of divorces; the scourge of abortion; the evermore frequent recourse to sterilization; the appearance of a truly contraceptive mentality.[98]

JPII points to the roots of these phenomena as "a corruption of the idea and the experience of freedom, conceived not as a capacity for realizing the truth of God's plan for marriage and the family, but as an autonomous power of self-affirmation, often against others, for one's selfish well-being. "[99]

In an attempt to respond to these phenomena of which the pope speaks, the 1980 Synod of bishops, in line with previous episcopal synods, pointed out ways by which it could catechize and bring to full human and Christian maturity the Christian family. They claimed that an educated Christian community and family help people to discern justice, interpersonal relationships and their own individual vocations in life. For the Synodal fathers, the task ahead was to help humanity to recapture the ultimate meaning of life and its fundamental values. The bishops insist that

---

97   John Paul II, *Familiaris Consortio: Apostolic Exhortation* (On The Christian Family in the Modern World), Published on Nov. 22, 1981, accessed August 15, 2015, www.vatican.va/apost_exhortations/documents/hf_jp-ii_exh_19811122_familiaris-consortio_en.html, #1.

98   Ibid., #6.

99   Ibid.

[o]nly an awareness of the primacy of these values enables man to use the immense possibilities given him by science in such a way as to bring about the true advancement of the human person in his or her whole truth, in his or her freedom and dignity. Science is called to ally itself with wisdom.... Modern culture must be led to a more profoundly restored covenant with divine Wisdom.Everyman is given a share of such Wisdom through the creating action of God.And it is only in faithfulness to this covenant that the families of today will be in a position to influence positively the building of a more just and fraternal world.[100]

Familiaris Consortio recalls the grounds by which God instituted marriage and family: God created human beings in His own image and likeness, bringing us into existence through love and calls us to love.For this reason, love is the fundamental and perennial vocation of every human person.This invitation to God's love is expressed either in marriage or in a life of virginity or celibacy; in either instance, its proper form is an actuation of a most profound truth about humanity as created in the image of God and called to love.In the exhortation, JP II surmises,

Consequently, sexuality, by means of which man and woman give themselvesto one another through the acts which are proper and exclusive to spouses, is by no means something purely biological, but concerns the inner most being of the human person as such.It is realized in a truly human way only if it is an integral part of the love by which a man and a woman commit themselves totally to one another till death.The total physical self-giving would be a lie if it were not the sign and fruit of a total personal self-giving in which the whole person, including the temporal dimension, is present; if the person were

---

100   Sean O'Riordan, "The Furrow, " *The Synod on the Family* 31, no. 12, 1980, 775-77.

to withhold something or reserve the possibility of deciding otherwise in the future, by this very fact he or she would not be giving totally.[101]

JPII states that this kind of totality of self-giving in conjugal life demands responsible fertility which truly can be found only in marriage where spouses freely and reciprocally give of each other exclusively. This kind of self-giving according to JP II, is free and "far from being restricted by this fidelity, [the person] is secured against every form of subjectivism or relativism and is made a sharer in creative Wisdom."[102] The family's mission and role in the world is to represent its dynamic and existential nature as a community of life and love, which it must safeguard, reveal, and communicate to the world by being at the service of life, form a community of persons, participate in the integral development of society, and share in the life and mission of the Church.[103]

This document focuses on the ideals of a truly Christian family life and marriage, at the same time re-stating the Church's opposition to artificial birth control and abortion.[104] The bulk of the exhortation is devoted to articulating the ideals of marriage as a sacrament, noble and indissoluble, the need for prayers and self-giving of spouses, and the education of offspring. The exhortation concludes by rejecting as illicit any other form of unions outside of what it has enumerated.[105]

In John Paul II's **Veritatis Splendor** (The Splendor of Truth), published August 6, 1993, the Pope approaches the foundations of Catholic moral teaching from a theological and philosophical

---

101   Ibid., #11.

102   Ibid.

103   Ibid., #17.

104   Ibid., #30: "Thus, the Church condemns as a grave offense against human dignity and justice all those activities of government or other public authorities which attempt to limit in any way the freedom of couples in deciding about children. Consequently, any violence applied by such authorities in favor of contraception or, still worse, of sterilization and procured abortion, must be altogether condemned and forcefully rejected. Likewise to be denounced as gravely unjust are cases where, in international relations, economic help given for the advancement of peoples is made conditional on programs of contraception, sterilization and procured abortion. "

105   Ibid., #86.

standpoint. This encyclical, at the time was regarded as the official, most comprehensive and up-to-date teaching on moral theology in the Catholic tradition. It has an introduction, three chapters, and a conclusion. In the introduction, JPII states that his reason for writing the encyclical is to react against a crisis in fundamental moral theology. He notes that within the Christian community, the church is faced not only with dissent but also by "an overall and systematic calling into question of traditional moral doctrine, on the basis of certain anthropological and ethical presuppositions. At the root of these presuppositions is the more or less obvious influence of currents of thought which end by detaching human freedom from its essential and constitutive relationship to truth. "[106] In the post-conciliar Church, the pope declares his intention as "clearly setting forth certain aspects of doctrine which are of crucial importance in facing what is certainly a genuine crisis, since the difficulties which it engenders have most serious implications for the moral life of the faithful and for communion in the Church, as well as for a just and fraternal social life. "[107] To do justice to this issue, the pontiff proposes, "to set forth, with regard to the problems being discussed, the principles of moral teaching based on scripture and the living apostolic tradition, and at the same time to shed light on the presuppositions and consequences of the dissent which that teaching has met. "[108]

This encyclical aims at establishing the relationship between Christian faith and morality, faith being what we believe in our hearts and morality being that which determines how, as influenced by faith, we make choices with our wills. JPII identifies the authenticity of Christian morality only if it is based on "Truth "—that is, on Christ who is the truth.[109]

The three chapters of *Veritatis Splendor* present three themes under which JPII discusses the role of the Church in teaching authoritatively concerning morals. The first chapter bears the title "Teacher, what

---

106   John Paul II, *Veritatis Splendor* [The Splendor of Truth] (Vatican City: Libreria Editrice Vaticana, 1993), #4.

107   Ibid.

108   Ibid., #5.

109   John A. Hardon, *Catechism on the Splendor of Truth* (Bardstown, KY: Eternal Life Publications, 1996), 4.

must I do? " and is an in-depth commentary on the question the rich young man asks Jesus in the Gospel of Matthew (19: 16-21). With this text, JP II emphasizes the existential significance of the question, which is asked with a presupposition that there is a nexus between moral good and the ultimate destiny of every human being.JPII concludes that this question in itself is "a religious question… the goodness that attracts and at the same time obliges man has its source in God, and indeed is God himself. "[110] Here JPII lays out the doctrinal position of the Church on some "fundamental questions regarding the Church's moral teaching, issues being debated by ethicists and moral theologians, while responding also to erroneous views from principles of a moral teaching based upon scripture and tradition. "[111] JPII argues that the answer to the young man's question "can only be found by turning one's mind and heart to the 'One' who is good…, [which] ultimately means to turn towards God, the fullness of goodness. "[112] God has answered this question, the pope says, by creating human beings and ordering them with wisdom and love through a law inscribed in their hearts (Rom. 2:15), the "natural law " infused by God at creation, as a way of understanding what must be done and what must be avoided. In the history of the Israelites, God gave them the Decalogue, linking it to the new covenant revealed and communicated in Jesus. The Ten Commandments of God, given through Moses,are contrasted with the Sermon on the Mount, which JPII understands as making

> a close connection … between eternal life and obedience to God's commandment… From the very lips of Jesus, the new Moses, man is once again given the commandments of the Decalogue…. The commandments are linked to a promise.In the Old Covenant the object of the promise was the possession of a land…. (cf. Deut. 6:20-25).In the New Covenant the object of the promise is the "kingdom of Heaven. "[113]

---

110   Ibid., #9.

111   Ibid.

112   Ibid., #9; see also #11, 12.

113   Ibid., 12.

JPII expatiates further that the commandments of the Decalogue are rooted in the commandment expressing "the singular dignity of the human person ":

> The different commandments of the Decalogue are really only so many reflections on the one commandment about the good of the person, at the level of the many different goods which characterize his identity as a spiritual and bodily being in relationship with God, with his neighbor, and with the material world… The commandments of which Jesus reminds the young man are meant to safeguard the good of the person, the image of God, by protecting his goods.[114]

The precepts of the Decalogue couched in the negative form, "thou shall not, " express the need always to safeguard human goods and values.Here again, the pope re-enunciates the entire Catholic moral tradition.JPII will return again and again to this crucially important point in this encyclical, especially while discussing intrinsically evil acts, asserting that if there were no absolute moral norms excluding intrinsically evil acts, the human person would have no truly inviolable rights.In the Sermon on the Mount, Jesus extends and re-interprets the law and the prophets by bringing out their fullest meaning (cf. Mt. 5:17): that certain specific kinds of human behavior are incompatible with the Christian way of life.Furthermore, Christ has handed authority to his disciples and their successors to interpret "authentically " the word of God either in written form or in transmission by tradition, which is also known as the Church's living tradition.[115]

The second chapter is titled "Do not be conformed to this world. " Its main theme is that there is no absolute conflict between human freedom of choice and the moral law because the moral law, which has God as its author, does not contain an arbitrary legalism designed to impinge on human freedom.Rather, moral laws contain truths meant to help people in making morally sound choices.JPII's focus was to

---

114   Ibid., #13.

115   Ibid., #26-7.

articulate a proper understanding of the nature of true autonomy proper to human beings as against moral theories that uphold human freedom with subjectivistic notions that human beings determine the moral order.[116] In line with Augustine, Aquinas, and Vatican II, in articles #38-45, JPII insists that "the moral law has its origin in God and always finds its source in him... by virtue of natural reason, which derives from divine wisdom; it is a properly human law."[117] In reaction to Catholic theologians who criticize the traditional conception of the natural law as "physicalistic" and "biologistic," the pope argues that this sort of position "does not correspond to the truth about man and his freedom."[118] In article # 53, JPII repudiates as relativistic the view that because of human historicity, moral norms are not immutable but change under every varying historical and cultural situation. JPII opines that this is incompatible with Christ's teaching and the idea of the immutability of revealed truths.

JPII then offers a brief reflection on "conscience and truth." For him, conscience is not a decision on how to act or not act in a given situation, it is a *practical judgement* "which makes known what one must do or not do, the proximate norm of personal morality, the capacity to disclose the truth about moral good and evil, the truth indicated by divine law, the universal and objective norm of morality."[119] The pope opposes those who attempt to make "pastoral solutions" on the norm of an individual conscience in its process of making a moral judgment, to justify a hermeneutic in which the conscience is in no way compromised in every case, by any kind of negative precept.[120]

---

116   Ibid., #35-7.

117   Ibid., #40.

118   Article # 46 states, "The alleged conflict between freedom and law is forcefully brought up once again today with regard to the natural law, and particularly with regard to nature. Debates about nature and freedom always marked the history of moral reflection: they grew especially heated at the time of the Renaissance and the Reformation.... Our own age is marked, though in a different sense, by a similar tension. The penchant for empirical observation, the procedures of scientific objectification, technological progress and certain forms of liberalism have led to these two terms being set in opposition, as if a dialectic, if not an absolute conflict, between freedom and nature were characteristic of the structure of human history."

119   Ibid., #60-3.

120   Ibid., #56.

Contrary to this position, the pope asserts that the conscience is not a "creative" decision but rather a judgment drawn from moral truth.[121]

Concerning the relationship between free choices of specific kinds of acts and the fundamental option to choose for or against God, for or against truth, these are choices that determine the person and shapes the individual's entire moral life. While condemning a theology that seeks to separate the person from an act, he affirms that, "to separate the fundamental option from concrete kinds of behavior means to contradict the substantial integrity or personal unity of the moral agent in his body and in his soul."[122] He goes on to state that the choice of freedom acknowledged in Christianity as fundamental moral choice-making is "the decision of faith, of the obedience of faith (Rom. 16:26)...by which man makes a total and free self-commitment to God, offering the full submission of intellect and will to God as he reveals."[123] The pope points out that "the morality of the human act depends primarily and fundamentally on the 'object' rationally chosen by the deliberate will."[124] We do know that "there are objects of the human act which are by their nature 'incapable of being ordered' to God because they radically contradict the good of the person made in his image."[125] He then concludes this section by repudiating consequentialism and proportionalism as flawed moral theories which are opposed to divine revelation and magisterial authority.

In the third and final chapter, titled "Lest the cross of Christ be emptied of its power," the pope lays out a catechesis for returning to Jesus and His Gospel in order to live by and hand on the moral truths taught by the Church as a moral teacher. This responsibility is more for teachers and priests, and especially for bishops, to whom the encyclical is specifically addressed. In this section, JPII insists that true human freedom is possible only when it is linked to Christ, who is truth revealed, and to the truth that Christ reveals in the "law" written naturally in the human mind. In the relationship between

---

121   Ibid., #65.

122   Ibid.

123   Ibid., #66.

124   Ibid., #78.

125   Ibid., #80.

human freedom and truth, he states that "the crucified Christ reveals the authentic meaning of freedom; he lives it fully in the total gift of himself and calls his disciples to share in his freedom. "[126] JPII insists that the intimate, inseparable unity of faith and morality is one acute pastoral concern in the face of contemporary growing secularism, where faith is separated from morality. He calls for a rediscovery of the authentic reality of the true Christian faith, which cannot be reduced to a set of mere propositions accepted intellectually but the newness of faith, which has the power to judge and can prevail in all cultures.

Authentic faith according to JPII, possesses a moral content, which calls for a commitment to observing the commandments of God, a faith which must bear fruit in works of "charity and of the authentic freedom which is manifested and lived in the gift of self even to the total gift of self, like that of Jesus. "[127] In concluding this third section, JPII, refuting those who raise the objection that the Church is too rigorous and unrealistic when it insists on absolute moral norms prohibiting intrinsically evil acts, JPII responds that there is an absolute need for God's grace to live a morally upright life. Alluding to the witness of martyrs, he states further, "The unacceptability of 'teleologism,' 'consequentialism,' and 'proportionalist' ethical theories, which deny the existence of negative moral norms regarding specific kinds of behavior, norms which are valid without exception, is confirmed in a particularly eloquent way by Christian martyrdom. "[128]

Addressing the socio-economic and political realms, JPII illustrates and expounds further in these words:

> These norms in fact represent the unshakeable foundation and solid guarantee of a just and peaceful human coexistence, and hence of genuine democracy which can come into being and develop only on the basis of the equality of all its members, who possess common rights and duties. When it is a

---

126   Ibid., #85.

127   Ibid., #88-9.

128   Ibid., #90.

matter of the moral norms prohibiting intrinsic evil,
there are no privileges or exceptions for anyone.[129]

Two short sections in Chapter 3 are devoted to addressing pastors, theologians, and bishops of the Church, urging them to recognize their "grave duty " to instruct the faithful about the commandments and practical authoritative norms declared by the Church. The theologians are called to develop a better articulation of the Church teachings by "expounding the validity and obligatory nature of the precepts it proposes, demonstrating their connection with one another and their relation to man's ultimate end. "[130] He condemned "dissent, " which he sees as a

> form of carefully orchestrated protests and polemics carried on in the media... opposed to ecclesial communion and to a correct understanding of the hierarchical constitution of the people of God.... The Church's pastors have the duty to act in conformity with their apostolic mission, insisting that the right of the faithful to receive Catholic doctrine in its purity and integrity must be respected.[131]

Finally, in this encyclical, John Paul II argues that the content of divine revelation contains "a specific and determined moral content, universally valid and permanent, "[132] which the Church's magisterium has competence to interpret and teach. He argues that the faith at the turn of the third millennium faces "a crisis of truth "[133] which, according to him, has the most serious implications for the people's moral lives, for the Church, and for a just and fraternal social life. The focus of John Paul II in *Veritatis Splendor* was particularly on the dignity of the human person from conception to natural death. Using

---

129   Ibid., #96.

130   Ibid., #110.

131   Ibid., #113.

132   Miller, *Encyclicals John Paul II*, 651.

133   Ibid.

scriptures copiously, referencing Aquinas and Augustine, he argues his position on the basis of the natural moral law.[134]

Charles Curran's critique of JPII's *Veritatis Splendor* is of primary theological significance.He acknowledges JPII's insistence and emphasis on the primacy of Christ as "the truth " in considering human morality.However,Curran disagrees with him because JPII, in his encyclical,does not develop human sources of truth but actually excludes them.According to Curran, "one might explain the tension or the inconsistency about common human sources of truth…. but still one would expect documents coming from the Catholic tradition to explicitly recognize and develop both faith and reason as sources of truth…. "[135] Curran continues further to say that JPII in *Veritatis Splendor* seem to fail to recognize truth as an analogous concept but persistently uses truth in the univocal sense.For Curran, there necessarily exists a significant difference between truths and faith regarding existential questions. In addition, because there is significant differentiation between specific truths of moral questions and truths about the ultimate meaning of human existence, Curran states "Catholic tradition has often used casuistry as a way of trying to deal with specific moral issues, thus showing how important it is to consider all the details of the situation. "[136] Curran cites also what he calls "the age old epistemological problem—what is truth and how do we know truth? "[137] For Curran, JPII approaches this question from a classicist notion of truth:that it exists and is knowable by all.

---

134   In this section on *Veritatis Splendor* and for this summary, I am indebted to William E. May's essay "Pope John Paul II, Moral Theology, and Moral Theologians," in *Veritatis Splendor and the Renewal of Moral Theology*, eds. Augustine DiNoia and Romanus Cessario (Chicago: Midwest Theological Forum, 1999), 211-240; William E. May, "Veritatis Splendor: An Overview of the Encyclical, " *Communio: International Catholic Review* 21 (Summer 1994): 229-51.

135   Charles E. Curran, *The Moral Theology of Pope John Paul II* (Washington, DC: Georgetown University Press, 2005), 25.

136   Ibid., 33.

137   Ibid., 34.

Curran also disagrees with JPII's exegetical work in *Veritatis Splendor*, stating that while the encyclical relies heavily on scriptures to defend its thesis, it distorts them.[138]In the story of the rich young man in Matthew 19 that JPII uses to start the encyclical, Curran argues that it ismisapplied because the story deals with riches, not with a universal call to Christians to obey precepts from the Old Testament.Curran further argues that JPII distorts the true meaning of Christian morality as it is found in scripture by insisting on obedience to commandments. For Curran, morality as portrayed in the scriptures is more than this; he asserts that "morality involves a change of heart, conversion, response to the loving God, and the virtues, attitudes, and dispositions that characterize the Christian person. "[139] Curran also disagrees with the pope's use of scripture in an attempt to ground his philosophical and ethical concepts, especially because these were unknown in biblical times.Curran asserts, "*Veritatis Splendor* explicitly uses scripture to support the notion of intrinsic evil proposed by the contemporary hierarchical magisterium in its arguments against proportionalism and consequentialism.But scripture does not know any of these concepts. "[140] He also critiqued JPII's appropriation of the text of Ephesians 5:21- 33.Curranargues that this text represents householdsas they were structured in biblical times.However, JPII uses this text in an attempt to ground equality in mutual subjection out of respect for Christ.For Curran, "such an interpretation seems to go against the very words used by the biblical author. "[141]

Gilbert Meilaender wrote an essay that addresses *Veritatis Splendor* from what he called a "Reformation perspective. "To explore this

---

138   Ibid., 52.

139   Ibid.

140   Ibid., 53.

141   Ibid., 55. Curran as a revisionist critiques magisterial positions because he believes that these teachings are very legalistic in nature and are based on antiquated ethics borne of the manualist system. Curran thus challenges magisterial positions to become more aware of people's lived experience. It should be mentioned that, sometimes, Curran seems to miss the entire point of John Paul's *Theology of the Body* in its anthropology and phenomenology as solely focusing on a personalist approach to sexuality, marriage and family lie ethics.

dimension, he appropriates Karl Barth's[142] explanation of the story of the rich young ruler in contrast to the way JPII explicates this text. Meilaender argues that the question under investigation played a significant role in the history of the split of the Western church in the Middle Ages.Meilaender opines that JPII seems to translate the rich young man's story to mean that the performance of good acts and adherence to the Decalogue constitutes the indispensable condition and path to everlasting life.He claims that JPII's perspective could be admissible as a description of one way towards fellowship with God and not simply a condition of it.From a Reformation perspective, therefore, "the language of „*conditions*' in these contexts risks undercutting the centrality of grace in the journey towards God. "[143] According to Meilaender, JPII's exegesis seems to offer the power of grace apart from pardon, a grace that seems not to accept human weakness and sinfulness. In this case, there is a rejection of theReformation understanding of faith as *fiducia* where going to Christ even in sin makes one right with God.He summarizes his critique of *Veritatis Splendor* by acknowledging that it speaks a theological language of Christian ethics which keeps the language of faith in the vision of the reformation alive and makes possible a conversation born of current theological existence.He concludes his essay by stating,

> Against that emphasis on the soul-making power
> of deeds, spoken entirely alone, spoken apart from

---

142   Karl Barth's exegesis explains the story of the rich young man as coming into the "sphere " of Jesus where all are invited either in obedience or disobedience. The directive of Jesus to the rich young man to go and sell, give and come follow him brought a new awareness to the disciples who had done this but now understand the lure of riches and what they had given up; here, according to Barth's explanation in Meilaender's essay, "the apostles themselves stand on the edge of the abyss of disobedience. " Here, then, we find what he considers the distinguishing contrast to JPII's exegesis: "With no clear distinction remaining between the obedient and the disobedient, with both constantly standing on the edge of an abyss they cannot cross, Jesus can only be the one who is for both. " Structurally therefore, Barth's exposition focuses not just on the rich young mans as JPII does, but also on the disciples, the obedient and the disobedient. Gilbert Meilaender, "*Veritatis Splendor*: Reopening Some Questions of the Reformation, " *The Journal of Religious Ethics* 23, no. 2 (1995): 231.

143   Meilaender, "*Veritatis Splendor*, " 229.

an unconditional promise of acceptance to the disobedient in their disobedience, the reformers— whether correctly discerning the nature of late medieval Catholicism or not—spoke a message not just of *sola gratia* but of *sola fide.*If V*eritatis Splendor* grasps—albeit a bit haltingly in places— the importance of *sola gratia*, it fails to enunciate clearly the *sola fide.*It is necessary, therefore, to reassert against its pattern of thought the centrality of the language of faith for Christian life.[144]

In ***Evangelium Vitae***(The Gospel of Life), promulgated November 25, 1995, John Paul II insists on the traditional Catholic position concerning the value of human life and its inviolability: "The gospel of life is at the heart of Jesus' message.... It is to be preached with dauntless fidelity as "good news " to the people of every age and culture. "[145] This encyclical is unique because it is given as part of the aftermath of a special consistory of cardinals held in Rome between April 4 and 7, 1991, and in collegial consultation with bishops from all around the world.This collegial act on the part of JPII gives this

---

144   Ibid., 237.

145   ohn Paul II, *Evangelium Vitae* [The Gospel of Life] (Vatican City: Liberia Editrice Vaticana, 1995), #1. This point is made further in article #2 thus: "Man is called to a fullness of life which far exceeds the dimensions of his earthly existence, because it consists in sharing the very life of God. The loftiness of this supernatural vocation reveals the greatness and the inestimable value of human life even in its temporal phase.... It remains a sacred reality entrusted to us, to be preserved with a sense of responsibility and brought to perfection in love and in the gift of ourselves to God and to our brothers and sisters.... Every person sincerely open to truth and goodness can, by the light of reason and the hidden action of grace, come to recognize in the natural law written in the heart (cf. Rom. 2:14-15) the sacred value of human being to have this primary good respected to the highest degree. Upon the recognition of this right, every human community and the political community itself are founded... believers in Christ must defend and promote this right.... This saving event [the incarnation] reveals to humanity... the incomparable value of every human life. "

encyclical a greater force in the unified voice of the Church's hierarchy and magisterial authority.[146]

In the first part of this encyclical, JPII refers to and explicates various biblical texts to support the biblical injunction against the taking of human life.He uses these texts to affirm the injustices of abortion, euthanasia, and the death penalty.He argues that this teaching is "based on the natural law, upon the written word of God and transmitted by the Church's tradition as taught by the ordinary and universal magisterium. "[147] The encyclical touches on capital punishment; ecological concerns; society and its contemporary wish to improve efficiency and productivity over family life and human life values; the tendency to see the sick, the weak, and the poor as expendables; and "the education of teenagers in the proper understanding of sex. "[148] He also calls on the mass media to be serious and responsible in how they present the positive values of sexuality and human love, insisting on "a scrupulous concern for factual truth... to combine freedom

---

146   It is important to note this section because though JPII claims ordinary and universal magisterium by acting collegially, he does not claim papal infallibility; but *ipso facto*, this encyclical's position on murder, directly willed abortion, and euthanasia enjoys infallibility of the ordinary and magisterial kind. The Congregation for the Doctrine of the Faith (CDF) under Cardinal Ratzinger affirms this; moreover, *Lumen Gentium* #25 from the post synodal documents of Vatican II states clearly, "...Individual bishops do not enjoy the prerogative of infallibility; they nevertheless proclaim Christ's doctrine infallibly whenever, even though dispersed through the world, but still maintaining the bond of communion among themselves and with the successor of Peter, and authentically teaching matters of faith and morals, they are in agreement on one position as definitively to be held. " (For further reading on this topic, see Francis Sullivan, "The Doctrinal Weight of Evangelium Vitae, " *Theological Studies* 56, no. 3 [1995]: 560-565.)

147   Ibid., #62.

148   JP II, in line with his position broadly on the question of human sexuality, has the following to say to the young people of the world who form the greater part of the demography of those who face the new culture of "free sex " and the culture of death: "In particular, there is a need for education about the value of life from its very origins.... Sexuality which enriches the whole person 'manifests its inmost meaning in leading the person to the gift of self- love.' The trivialization of sexuality is among the principal factors which have led to contempt for new life. Only a true love is able to protect life. There can be no avoiding the duty to offer, especially to adolescents and young adults, an authentic education in sexuality and in love, an education which involves training in chastity as a virtue which fosters personal maturity and makes one capable of respecting the 'spousal' meaning of the body. " *EV* #97.

of information with respect for every person and a profound sense of humanity. "[149]

The encyclical focuses on the gift of human life as a sharing in the divine life of God and on the necessity of holding human life sacred, especially that of the weak, the defenseless, and the unborn.[150] The encyclical calls attention to "scientific and systematic threats" against life, asking that everyone respect, love, protect and serve every human life because the "value at stake is one which every human being can understand by the light of reason"[151] and is "written in the heart of every man and woman. "[152]

Abortion, the killing of innocent human life, and euthanasia are central to the entire text while an explanation of the Christian message, a new culture of life, and the biblical injunction "Thou shalt not kill" are presented as panaceasfor the present day culture of death and threats to human life.John Paul II asserts that humanity needs to return to building a civilization at the service of life, a duty binding on the Church and on all sectors of society.*Evangelium Vitae* issues a vigorous challenge to the various political systems around the world to

---

149   Ibid., #98.

150   JPII continues in article #3 by establishing the different factors in the society mitigating the preservation and respect for the inviolability of human life, stating succinctly thus, "Today this proclamation is especially pressing because of the extraordinary increase and gravity of threats to the life of individuals and peoples, especially where life is weak and defenceless. In addition to the ancient scourges of poverty, hunger, endemic diseases, violence and war, new threats are emerging on an alarmingly vast scale... new prospects opened up by scientific and technological progress... at the same time a new cultural climate... broad sectors of public opinion justify certain crimes against life in the name of the rights of individual freedom, and on this basis they claim not only exemption from punishment but even authorization by the State, so that these things can be done with total freedom and indeed with the free assistance of health care systems... In such a cultural and legislative situation, the serious demographic, social and family problems which weigh upon many of the world's peoples and which require responsible and effective attention from national and international bodies, are left open to false and deceptive solutions, opposed to the truth and the good of persons and nations. The end result of this is tragic: not only is the fact of the destruction of so many human lives still to be born or in their final stage extremely grave and disturbing, but no less grave and disturbing is the fact that conscience itself, darkened as it were by such widespread conditioning, is finding it increasingly difficult to distinguish between good and evil in what concerns the basic value of human life. "

151   Ibid., 101.

152   Ibid., 29.

the inviolability of human life, the grave moral evil of euthanasia and abortion.[153]

Evangelium Vitae is a follow up to *Veritatis Splendor* in its use of biblical sources, its resorting to the natural law argument and strong condemnation of direct killing, direct abortion, and euthanasia; thus, one clearly sees a hermeneutic of continuity. JPII recognizes that in the widely diversified and pluralistic society common to most modern societies, an appeal to natural law is the only possible route to getting civil laws enacted which will not endorse abortion, euthanasia, or any other unjust taking of human life.

In critiquing *Evangelium Vitae*, Curran presents the encyclical as a flash point of tension and inconsistency. He opines that "the pope insists

---

153   JPII focuses on the perennial problem of democracy in a secularized world and how it responds to ethical questions:

... in the democratic culture of our time, it is commonly held that the legal system of any society should limit itself to taking account of and accepting the convictions of the majority... Consequently, when establishing those norms which are absolutely necessary for social coexistence, the only determining factor should be the will of the majority, whatever this may be... As a result we have what appears to be two diametrically opposed tendencies....in carrying out one's duties the only moral criterion should be what is laid down by the law itself. Individual responsibility is thus turned over to the civil law, with a renouncing of personal conscience, at least in the public sphere. At this basis of all these tendencies lies the ethical relativism which characterizes much of present-day culture. There are those who consider such relativism an essential condition of democracy, in as much as it alone is held to guarantee tolerance, mutual respect between people and acceptance of the decision of the majority, whereas, moral norms considered to be objective and binding are held to lead to authoritarianism and intolerance.

But it is precisely the issue of respect for life which shows what misunderstandings and contradictions, accompanied by terrible practical consequences, are concealed in this position... Everyone's conscience rightly rejects those crimes against humanity of which our century has had such a sad experience. But would these crimes, cease to be crimes if, instead of being committed by unscrupulous tyrants, they were legitimized by popular consensus? Democracy cannot be idolized to the point of making it a substitute for morality or a panacea for immorality.... The basis of these values cannot be provisional and changeable "majority " opinions, but only the acknowledgement of an objective moral law which, as the "natural law " written in the human heart, is obligatory point of reference for civil law itself. If, as a result of a tragic obscuring of the collective conscience, an attitude of skepticism were to succeed in bringing into question even the fundamental principles of moral law, the democratic system itself would be shaken in its foundations, and would be reduced to a mere mechanism for regulating different and opposing interests on a purely empirical basis.... The legal toleration of abortion or of euthanasia can in no way claim to be based on respect for the conscience of others, precisely because society has a right and the duty to protect itself against the abuses which can occur in the name of conscience and under the pretext of freedom. EV # 69-71.

on the tectonic struggle between truth and error, between the culture of life and the culture of death.But the encyclical then claims that its teachings opposing direct killing, direct abortion, and euthanasia are based on natural law with its emphasis on human reason common to all. "[154] Curran claims that the references to the Natural Law Theory are similar all through the text with no proof to how JPII develops to any depth this argument.As in all other JPII's doctrinal encyclicals, he relies heavily on scripture with constant references to both the Old and New Testaments.Curran states "the frequent headings and subheadings in the text invariably contain a scriptural citation together with a short description of the matter to be treated.... The scripture citations are often proof texts used to affirm a particular point that is not all that clearly present in the original scriptural text. "[155] According to Curran, from the perspectiveof theological method, JPII employs a consistent Christology from above.Depending mostly on Johannine writings, the pope provides nine citations in order to ground his argument that life originates from the being of the Father.

Additionally, Curran critiques the eschatology of *Evangelium Vitae* as not being consistent with the eschatology in JPII's other encyclicals. Curran thinks that JPII's eschatology in *Evangelium Vitae* completely lacks the basic transformationalist motif common to his earlier works. Curran surmises that JPII spends too much time, fourteen paragraphs, dealing with the negative factors that spawn the culture of death, and then assigns two paragraphs to presenting the positive signs in support of the culture of life.Therefore, it seems, "the pope has allowed his rhetoric and his concentration on two controversial issues to replace the eschatology that has consistently developed elsewhere. "[156]

On the question of the viability of the fetus in its mother's womb, Curran asserts that until the twentieth century, which constitutes very recent history in the Church, delayed animation was the popular theological position and leaning, to which JPII makes no allusion. Curran points to two questions when it comes to the viability of the embryo and its abortion: first, that concerning the status of the

---

154   Curran, *Moral Theology*, 25-6.

155   Ibid., 146.

156   Curran, *Moral Theology*, 148-9.

embryo-fetus after conception and, second, the resolution of conflict. Within this question, he believes, there is the need to understand the idea of direct and indirect actions, which the encyclical did not clarify. For instance, direct abortion by the very nature of the act or the intention of the agent aims at killing the fetus either as a means or as an end. Curran argues that "as in the question of killing, direct abortion is always wrong, but indirect abortion *(killing)* maybe permitted."[157]

Curran's critique then engages one of the dynamic and dialectical developments in Catholic moral theology within the last century. Curran argues,

> Note that here again the problem of physicalism occurs—the moral concept of directness is based on the physical structure or causality of the act. Catholic theologians who accept the theory of proportionalism maintain that direct killing understood as the physical causality of the act is not necessarily always morally wrong. The "direct—indirect" solution to conflict situations is based on one philosophical approach (the twentieth century neoscholastic) that is not accepted even by all Catholic theologians. Because the teaching that direct abortion is always wrong is not as certain as John Paul II implies, he definitely goes too far in quoting from Paul VI "that this tradition is unchanged and unchanging."[158]

Curran goes on to critique *Evangelium Vitae* on what he sees as JPII's unequal treatment of an identical issue. Concerning abortion, JPII pays compassionate attention to the circumstances that force women at times to seek abortion to protect their health or to protect the living standards of their family. However, in the case of suicide, Curran argues that JPII insists that suicide is always as morally objectionable as murder, though the pope acknowledges there may be circumstances in which a difficult life situation influences a person to commit suicide,

---

157   Ibid., 152.

158   Ibid., 153.

thereby "lessening or removing subjective responsibility. "[159] Curran says when the pontiff then speaks about abortion, he never mentions the possibility of "lessening or removing subjective responsibility. "[160]

On euthanasia, Curran argues again that the pope does not do enough to ground his argument. Curran states, "Condemnation rests on the definition of direct killing as an act that by the intention of the agent or the nature of the act aims at death either as a means or an end, as distinguished from indirect killing. "[161] The difference therefore in Curran's thinking between euthanasia and indirect but permissible killing in the pope's presentation is not based on scripture or even the incomparable value of human life but purely on JPII's philosophical understanding of the difference between acts of omission and acts of commission. Curran submits that "specific teachings condemning direct killing, direct abortion, euthanasia, and suicide simply repeat what has been frequently proposed by the papal magisterium in the past. "[162] However, he agrees that JPII's treatment of capital punishment in this encyclical is "definitely new and different " wherein the pope clarifies that "punishment exists to redress the violation of personal and social rights, to defend public order, to ensure people's safety and to furnish rehabilitation of criminals. To achieve this purpose, the extreme case of capital punishment can be justified only in cases of absolute necessity. "[163]

On JPII's use of magisterial tradition, Curran states that it is in this encyclical that JPII cites sources from tradition more than in any other encyclical. Curran alludes to the third chapter of the encyclical wherein Gregory of Nyssa, John Damascene, the *Didache*, the letter of Pseudo- Barnabas, Augustine, Aquinas, and Alphonsus Ligouri are all cited. Also, JPII frequently had recourse to previous papal teachings, documents of Vatican II, and the *Catechism of the Catholic Church*.

---

159   Ibid., 153.

160   Ibid.

161   Ibid., 154.

162   Ibid., 155.

163   Ibid.

Summary

This entire chapter has been devoted to studying the encyclical tradition that deals with sexual ethics, marriage, the dignity of human life (especially the unborn) and the related ethical questions from a contemporary perspective. The overriding aim is to situate material from these encyclicals in order to demonstrate a development in the Church's doctrinal tradition. Vitaliano Gorospe[164] in a journal essay situates this type of development within four periods in history: the first is between 50 and 450 AD, at which point the view of Clement of Alexandria held sway, that within marital intercourse, procreation must be the one and only intention of the spouses. In the second period, from 450 to 1450 AD, St. Augustine's view that the only justification for sexual intercourse is for procreation and controlling of concupiscence was prevalent. This view was held by the Church for over a thousand years. According to Gorospe, the third period 1450-1750 marked a period of both innovation and preservation of the Church's teaching, relying heavily on Augustine's anti-Manichean position and the Church's ruling against contraception. The fourth period, situated between 1750-1965, marked the beginning of a slow shift in Pius VI's *Casti Connubii* where for the first time in the known history of Christian doctrine, the Church acknowledged and stated that marital sexual intercourse has several purposes: first and most important, that sexual intercourse between spouses is to foster love and their marital unity and then for the rearing of offspring. This position was reiterated by the second Vatican Council and has marked current magisterial position as can be seen in many doctrinal documents of contemporary times.

That there is development in doctrine is therefore true, no matter how slowly the wheels of change may turn. In Gorospe's view, moral rules are always a response to practical questions and that always, in different cultures and times "[t]he Church will be developing traditional values, while changing old norms."[165]

---

164   Vitaliano R. Gorospe, S.J., "The Church and the Regulation of Birth: After *Humanae Vitae*," *Philippine Studies* 17, no. 3 (1969): 557.

165   Gorospe, "The Church, " 566.

Theodore Mackin's work is helpful in understanding the timeline of how specifically each of these encyclical builds on the previous to establish development in doctrine and the idea of the Church coming to a better understanding while growing with the signs of the times. He asserts that in the nineteenth century, even though the magisterial position on marriage and relevant questions surrounding it were doctrinal, they were yet largely apologetic. They were written and published to combat secularist claims that marriage is merely a social institution with no sacramental or divine dimension. This idea, for example, is the focus of Leo XIII's 1880 *Arcanum Divinae Sapientiae*. Then in the twentieth century, the first major document that followed up *Arcanum* was Pius XI's *Casti Connubii* in 1930, which was a response to the massive moral disillusionment in Europe after the First World War. Pius XI extended the understanding of Christian marriage by establishing that men and women create their own marriages by making of themselves a self-donation one to the other. This self-donation in love takes on a greater meaning because the spouses minister the sacrament to one another. According to Mackin, Pius XI in his encyclical "brought the human and the divine elements in the sacrament closer together than any of his predecessors had ever done."[166] Within this history, even though mentioned briefly in this text, the Fathers of the Second Vatican Council, in their *Pastoral Constitution on the Church in the Modern World*, innovated by stating further that spousal self-gift is a covenant, a primary sanctifying of grace which binds the spouses to one another and to God. They also moved away from the claim that procreation and nurture are the primary ends of marriage. Children are therefore the natural fruits of a fecund love in a sacramental union.

Paul VI in *Humanae Vitae*, responding to the question of contraception insisted that marital love must be fruitful because "God who awakens and animates it in the spouses does so with his own essentially fruitful love."[167] Therefore, any form of artificial contraception before, during or after the conjugal act is sinful. Following the 1980 synod of bishops on the family, John Paul II published his apostolic exhortation *Familiaris Consortio*, which is unique because he

---

166   Mackin, *Marriage in the Catholic Church*, 570.

167   Ibid., 572.

takes into cognizance the experiences and understanding of couples who are already living the sacramental life of marriage as essential for building a new vision of the theology of marriage. Following the teaching of Paul VI, the exhortation states that "[b]ecause God is essentially an act of love... [t]his same creative love has produced the human race and draws human beings together.... This condition is realized most vividly in marriage, because in order to be creative, human love, because it is embodied, must be sexual... The marital sacrament in its fullest expression and in its primary meaning is life in family. "[168] In Mackin's opinion, the revision most relevant for this period is the identification of the spouses' exchange of covenantal commitment by which they create their own marriage, the personal exchange of the gift of the self, one to the other. We find supporting documents in *Veritatis Splendor*, where moral theology challenges the "crisis of truth" which endangers the moral life and fraternal social co-existence. *Evangelium Vitae* then reiterates the values of human life, establishing the Church's position on abortion and euthanasia in a response to the modern day culture of death.

Conclusion

The strength and true genius of the Catholic Church remains in its ability to stand against the tides of time and perceived popular opinions, to uphold as the truth what Christ teaches and is upheld by apostolic tradition, such as rights and duties, liberty, law, truth and freedom with a basis in objective truth as revealed at different epochs of the Church's history. According to Anthony Lusvardi, the Church is committed to this stance because "[a] threat to the moral law is a threat to freedom.... John Paul offered a spirited defense of both of

---

168   Ibid. Mary Shivanandan's work says of JPII's *Veritatis Splendor*, "John Paul II has greatly expanded the Church's understanding of marriage in his development of marriage as a communion of persons and the theology of the body, showing how contraception denies the nuptial meaning of the body and fragments the communion of persons.... The interplay of experience, the human science, and biblical and philosophical reflection has enabled John Paul II to place in a whole new context the Church's perennial teaching on the inseparable connection between the procreative and unitive dimensions of conjugal love. " *Crossing the Threshold*, 205, 207.

these commitments—to freedom and to truth—in *Veritatis Splendor*."[169] Perhaps in the pursuit of this objective, any change that is needed for doctrine to develop and to answer modern questions happens very slowly so that the Church is able to listen to the Holy Spirit and so that her doctrines may remain one and the same with the gospel of Jesus Christ, truly offering freedom and truth.

---

169   Anthony S, Lursvardi,   "The Law of Conscience: Catholic Teaching on Conscience from Leo XIII to John Paul II, " *Logos: A Journal of Catholic Thought and Culture* 15, no. 2 (2012): 13-41

CHAPTER TWO

JOHN PAUL II'S THEOLOGY OF THE BODY: AN OVERVIEW

In the previous chapter, I reviewed the encyclical tradition in an attempt to gain an understanding of the historical and theological development of doctrine via papal encyclicals. We turn now to John Paul II's *Theology of the Body*, which representsthe contemporary and standard position of the Catholic Church on the question of human sexuality, presenting human beings as embodied persons living within the matrimonial covenant. This chapter will focus on how John Paul II's *Theology of the Body* affects and contributes to our understanding of what is essentially doctrinal in the marriage between a man and his wife, their sexuality as married persons, and some of the hermeneutical underpinnings of how John Paul arrived at and presents this teaching to the Church and society.

The *Theology of the Body (TOB)*, as JPII envisioned it and presented it to the Church, is regarded by many as a *tour de force* in contemporary Catholic philosophical and theological thinking on the question of human sexuality. The original texts of *TOB* are 129 papal general audiences and catechesis held between September 5, 1979 and November 28, 1984. JPII used the tradition of the Fathers as his foundation but only as a source of departure as he avoids past suspicion of the body to create a new way of looking at the body: it is "a sign and instrument of the same message of our salvation in Christ...human embodiment and the call of man and woman to unite in 'one flesh' signifies and foreshadows the mystery of Christ (see Eph. 5:31- 32)."[170] JPII approaches *TOB's* catechesis in the first part of his work as a question of embodiment, male and female, as a basis for his theological

---

170   Christopher West, *Theology of the Body Explained: A Commentary on John Paul II's "Gospel of the Body "*(Boston: Pauline Books and Media, 2003), 2.

anthropology.[171] In the second part, JPII addresses how humanity can successfully live out the truths about itself. In this work, he describes the human body as the locus of a pre-eminent and primordial sign of a reality which is not merely a biological organism, but also a locus of a spiritual and divine mystery.[172]

Michael Waldstein opines that the greatness of JPII's *TOB* is in

> … his concern for spousal love in the larger context of his concern about our age, above all for the question of scientific knowledge and power over nature, that is, the characteristically modern question of "progress " …. John Paul II sees…the quest for freedom, with "owning and controlling " one's own body… he sees such individual autonomy (which is the only freedom [Margaret] Sanger speaks about, exactly like Descartes and Kant) as standing in the service of a still greater kind of freedom, 'the freedom of the gift.'[173]

Mary Shivanandan pursues the same line of thinking when she argues that there is a conflict of ideas between modern civilization and the Catholic sexual ethics tradition which JPII represents. For her, JPII's central focus on the person and family as argued in *Humanae Vitae* and as JPII clarifies in his 1991 "Letter to the Families " is to show "how the family is placed at the center of the great struggle between good

---

171   "Hence, John Paul's Theology of the Body is much more than a reflection on sex and married love. Through the lens of marriage and the 'one flesh' union of spouses the Pope says we rediscover 'the meaning of the whole of existence, the meaning of life.' (Oct. 29, 1980) Christ teaches that the meaning of life is to love as he loves (Jn. 15:12) One of the Pope's main insights is that God inscribed this vocation to love as he loves in our bodies by creating us male and female and calling us to become 'one flesh' (Gen. 2:24). " Christopher West, *Theology of the Body for Beginners: A Basic Introduction to Pope John Paul II's Sexual Revolution* (West Chester, Pennsylvania: Ascension Press, 2004), 2.

172   Christopher West clarifies this point further by stating, "Christ's mission is to restore the order of love in a world seriously distorted by sin. And the union of the sexes, as always, lies at the basis of the human 'order of love.' " Therefore, what we learn in the Pope's theology of the body is obviously "important in regard to marriage and the vocation of husbands and wives. " However it "is equally essential and valid for the understanding of man in general. " Ibid., 2.

173   John Paul II, *Man and Woman He Created Them: A Theology of the Body* (Boston: Pauline Books & Media, 2010), xxiii.

and evil, between life and death, between love and all that is opposed to love. "[174] Referencing JPII's work, she states,

> Only if the truth about freedom and the communion of persons in marriage "can regain its splendor" can the "civilization of love," which is the essence of culture, replace the "civilization of use." Contemporary society has elevated scientific and technological progress in a one-sided way that results in a utilitarian approach to the person. In such a society the "woman can become an object for man, children a hindrance to parents, the family an institution obstructing the freedom of its members. "[175]

The *TOB* of JPII responds to this modernist interpretation of the ontological reality of what it means to be embodied and the integrality of human sexuality.

JPII's purpose in the catechesis was to provide a modern conceptual frame work to re- articulate and present a hermeneutic of continuity which, rather than merely defending the spousal meaning of the human body in its gender differentiation, responds to the questions about the person in contemporary times; who are we, why are we here, what does it mean to be enfleshed, why are we male or female, etc.? These questions were pursued as an integral vision of the human person in *Humanae Vitae*, where Paul VI locates this integrality in the two inseparable meanings of the conjugal act, the unitive and the procreative. As a follow-up, the over-arching aim of JPII in *TOB* is to develop further the spousal meaning of the body in the teachings of Jesus, who went back to the beginning.[176] This he approaches in three ways: first, he addresses God's original plan from the very beginning, in the present

---

174   Mary Shivanandan, *Crossing the Threshold of Love: A New Vision of Marriage in the Light of John Paul II's Anthropology* (Edinburgh: T&T Clark Ltd, 1999), 117.

175   Ibid., 117.

176   Going back to "the beginning" is essential to understanding the entire Catholic doctrine on marriage and the insistence that marriage will always be located within the gender differentiation of a man and a woman. In Jesus' teaching, going back to the intention of the creator clarifies and leaves no doubt that any cultural or popular sub culture cannot distort the intentions of the creator from the very beginning.

struggle against concupiscence, and in the hope for future fulfilment at the resurrection. Second, he studies the spousal meaning through the sacrament of love and the language this love speaks as an effective sign of this sacrament. Third, he shows conclusively that just like *Humanae Vitae*, *TOB* is asking modern minds to re-read the language of the body in its freedom, consisting mainly of love, which gives of its own freedom to the other, truthfully.[177]

JP II's work is divided into two broad parts with sub-sections in which he thematically setsout a map for a new way to understand the human body, its sexuality, marriage, and the human person's being in God. JPII invites his readers to see in the incarnation of Christ and his body on the cross the meaning of the gospel, of being in the body of Christ as the justification for a "theology of the body. "[178] From the original "nakedness " of Adam and Eve, the incarnated Christ reveals himself to humanity. According to JPII, the body represents the original "sign " of God's own mystery whereby what is visible makes known the invisible.[179] In this way, he links anthropology and

---

177   Michael Waldstein summarizes this position thus: "There is a main argument that runs through *TOB*. It is enriched by many subthemes, but it is in itself clear and simple. What is at stake in the teaching of *Humanae Vitae* about the inseparability of the unitive and procreative meaning of the conjugal act is nothing else than 'rereading [it] the "language of the body " in truth' (*TOB* 118:6). John Paul II developed the concept 'language of the body' and 'rereading [it] it in truth' in the section of the sacrament in the dimension of sign (*TOB* 103-16). The whole argument preceding *TOB* 103 can be understood as providing the foundation on which the concept of 'rereading the "language of the body " in the truth' can be understood. The key concept in this foundation is 'the spousal meaning of the body.' It is this meaning that is reread in the truth when man and woman engage in authentic sexual intercourse. " From Waldstein's introduction to John Paul II, *Man and Woman*, 120.

178   West, reflecting on this point, argues thus: "When it comes to religion, people are used to an emphasis on the spiritual realm. However, many people are unfamiliar, and sometimes even uncomfortable, with an emphasis on the body. For John Paul II, this is a false divide. Spirit certainly has priority over matter. Yet the *Catechism of the Catholic Church* teaches that '[a]s a being at once body and spirit, man expresses and perceives spiritual realities through physical signs and symbols'…. Many think Christian teaching considers their spirits to be 'good' and their bodies to be 'bad.' Such thinking couldn't be further from an authentic Christian perspective! The idea that the human body is 'bad' is actually a heresy… known as Manicheanism. " *TOB for Beginners*, 3.

179   Ibid., 53. On page 5, West also asserts, quoting JPII, "The body, in fact, and it alone is capable of making visible what is invisible: the spiritual and divine. It was created to transfer into reality of the world, the mystery hidden since time immemorial in God, and thus to be a sign of it (Feb. 20, 1980). "

theology in an organic manner. He introduces the analogy of spousal love to elucidate divine mystery. According to Christopher West, this "nuptial mystery provides a lens through which we view and penetrate the most important theological and anthropological truths of faith. "[180] West clarifies further, "We can see the fundamental importance of the nuptial mystery by looking at the signs of the Old and New Covenants. "[181] In the resultant primordial sacrament of nuptial communion, man and woman participate in God's life and love which the "original temptation " debased and ruptured in the harmony of humanity's body and soul, humanity and the mystery of God.

Humanity Through the History of Creation to Redemption in John Paul II's Theology of the Body

Original Humanity	Fallen Humanity	Redeemed Humanity	Glorified Humanity
Before the Fig Leaves Gen 1 & 2	Entrance of the Fig Leaves Gen 3:7	Beyond the Fig Leaves Matt 22:30	Covered with the garments of right- eousness
The Original State: Bodies made into the image and like- ness of God.	The Fall: Corrupted Bodies	The Body of Christ and His Cross / His Redemption	Future Hope: Glorified Bodies

In this way, the human body is seen by JPII, in a sense, as a sacrament but not simply within the traditional classification of seven sacraments. It is sacramental in a more generic way as "a sign that makes visible the invisible mysteries of God, " a material way of encountering the spiritual, thus making the human body the crown of God's creation.[182] On these grounds, West offers further insight on how the Pope's thinking develops further: "Christianity is the religion of God's union with humanity. It's the religion of the word (who is pure spirit) made flesh. In the body of Jesus, 'we see our God made visible and so are

---

180   Ibid., 54.

181   Ibid. For instance, the blood from Abraham's circumcision foretold the blood of Christ's body on the cross and his Eucharist.

182   West points out that the sacramental practices of the Catholic faith makes it sensual and fleshy because in the sacraments we encounter God in bodily senses: "through bathing the body with water (baptism); anointing the body with oil (baptism, confirmation, holy orders, anointing of the sick); eating and drinking the Body and Blood of Christ (Eucharist); the laying on of hands (holy orders); confessing with our lips (penance); and the unbreakable joining of man and woman in 'one flesh' (marriage). " Ibid., 4.

caught up in love of the God we cannot see.' "[183] In this way of seeing the body as a primordial sacrament in and of itself, a "theology of the body " is born. It is in this sacramental imagining that the mystery of the "communion of persons " draws our attention to yet another reality. God is an eternal communion of persons bound by love where the Father begets the Son, and the Son responds in love by giving himself back to the Father. This co-relation generates the Holy Spirit who "proceeds from the Father and the Son. " It is this Trinitarian love that is extended to humanity, which according to West, makes our male and female-ness. "In this way, sexual love becomes an icon or earthly image in some sense of the inner life of the Trinity. "[184]

Christ thus calls humanity to reclaim the mystical meaning of nuptial love and communion, which is revealed in the proper ordering of our sexual bodies and realized only through the dynamism of the incarnation. JPII's *TOB* is "an extended commentary on this fundamental truth: Christ fully reveals man to himself through the revelation-in his body-of the mystery of divine love. "[185] West posits that *TOB* is also a reaction to "the subjective turn in modern philosophy[186] and the massive shift of Western cultures from religion to science which demands a new synthesis of the faith to which the contemporary world can relate... a bold philosophical project to integrate the faith with insights of the modern philosophy of consciousness, without sacrificing anything essential to the traditional philosophy of being. "[187] At this point, JPII embraced phenomenology by approaching the reality of things as they are experienced, thereby making room for

---

183   Cf. 1 Jn. 4:20.

184   Ibid., 8–9.

185   John Paul II, *Man and Woman*, xxviii.

186   "The human family is facing the challenge of a new Manichaeism, in which body and spirit are put in radical opposition... This neo-Manichaean culture has led for example, to human sexuality being regarded more as for manipulation and exploitation than as the basis of that primordial wonder which led Adam on the morning of creation to exclaim before Eve: 'This at last is bone of my bones and flesh of my flesh' (Gen 2:23). " Ibid., xxiv.

187   Ibid., 55.

"subjective experience. "[188] West believes that JPII's acknowledgement of subjectivism within an objective or realist philosophy, avoids the pitfalls of objectivizing rigorism and subjectivizing relativism.

West succinctly summarizes the main thrust of JPII's *TOB* thus:

> Its first step consists in unfolding the teaching of Jesus about the spousal meaning of the body (in its three dimensions: in God's original plan "from the beginning "; in the present struggle with concupiscence; and in the future fulfillment by the resurrection). Its second step consists in observing how this spousal meaning functions in the great sacrament of love, particularly in the language of the body that is the effective sign of this sacrament. Its third step consists in showing that *Humanae Vitae* simply asks men and women to reread this language of the body in the truth.[189]

Many argue and subscribe to the view that *TOB* is written as a re-affirmation of Paul VI's *Humanae Vitae*[190] yet JPII's "philosophical

---

188   John Hamlon argues against any question of whether JPII was a phenomenologist or not by stating, "JPII realizes that....phenomenology captures the attention of modern man. It speaks to people of our age with conviction and force that even the system of St. Thomas Aquinas does not approach.... Wojtlya and the Lublin/Cracow school were to employ the essential discoveries of phenomenology in the service of faith without sacrificing objective ethical principles and the teachings of the Church. We are persons because we are like God, made in God's image.... The truth that we are created in the image of God is both subjective and objective. It saves the subjective insight of the phenomenologist without losing the objectivity of the gospel.... His philosophical insight when applied to the truths of the faith, produce a new theological synthesis. The unifying element in this synthesis is the individual subject— the human person—created by God in His own image and redeemed by Christ. JPII is teaching the world a new presentation of the faith. Most significantly, he has developed a new theology of the body and a theology of the family. " John S. Hamlon, *A Call to Families: Study Guide and Commentary for Familiaris Consortio* (Collegeville, MN: Human Life Center, 1984), x-xii. For further readings on the aspects of JPII's use of phenomenology, cf. Kenneth L. Schmitz, *At the Center of the Human Drama: The Philosophical Anthropology of Karol Wojtyla/Pope John Paul II* (Washington DC: The Catholic University of America Press, 1994); John Paul II, *Man and Woman*; and Rocco Buttiglione, *Karol Wojtyla: The Thought of the Man who Became Pope John Paul II*(Wm. B. Eerdmans Publishing, 1997).

189   John Paul II, *Man and Woman*, 124.

190   One of the main goals of the theology of the body is the defense of Paul VI's encyclical *Humanae Vitae*. The defense must be seen in the context of John Paul II's

project proves more fruitful....[A]s a corrective to antiquated explanations of sexual ethics that were often impersonal, legalistic, and authoritarian, John Paul II's theological pedagogy of the body provides a winning personalistic affirmation of Humanae Vitae. "[191] JPII adopts the theology of spousal love from St. John of the Cross and builds a new pedagogy around it, thereby creating a fresh perspective on what had hitherto been looked upon as sinful and disgraceful. JPII grounds *TOB* on a correct understanding of three fundamental questions about sexuality and sex; first, to avoid the traditional excessive distinction between "eros " and "agape " since in JPII's view, "erotic tension and sexual enjoyment are essential parts of spousal agape.[192] Through such tension and enjoyment, the human body speaks the spousal gift of self in sexual intercourse. "[193] Second, he advocates for an appreciation of the goodness of sexual pleasure as against the traditional Manichaean annihilation of the body or the toleration of sex on the grounds of need or necessity only. For JPII, "the sexual revolution does not sufficiently appreciate the value and beauty of sex. It deprives sex of its depth by detaching it from the spousal meaning of the body. It favors the sexual lie, in which the language of radical gift is overlaid by the contrary language of individual autonomy and the use of persons for pleasure. "[194] He emphasizes the goodness of sexual pleasure as belonging "by its deepest and innermost nature to the dynamism of radical gift between man and woman. "[195]

JPII ascribes two vocations to the Christian life: marriage and virginity/celibacy both are geared towards realizing the profound reality of being created in the image and likeness of God. JPII sees in the celibate vocation a free self-gift also for the sake of the kingdom,

---

defense of the ordinary human experience of love and it reasonableness. The teaching of *Humane Vitae*, as John Paul II understands it is based on the spousal meaning of the human body, that is, on the God-given power of the body to be a sign of the radical gift of self between man and woman. Cf. John Paul II, *Man and Woman*, xxv.

191   Ibid., 56.

192   In the encyclical *"Deus Caritas Est"* of Pope Benedict XVI, this theme is picked up again and better light is shed on the theological import of erotic love.

193   John Paul II, Man and Woman, 125.

194   Ibid., 126.

195   Ibid., 127.

a sign that the body, whose end is not the grave, is directed towards redemption by Christ and glorification. Therefore, "[t]he idea of virginity or celibacy as an anticipation and eschatological sign derives from the association of the words spoken... in the conversation with the Sadducees, when he proclaimed the future resurrection of the body. "[196] JPII teaches that the state of virginity prefigures the eschaton where people will no longer be given in marriage (Mt. 22:30, Lk. 20:34, Mk. 12:25, 1Cor. 15:28). Christopher West clarifies this line of thought thus: "Christian celibacy, therefore, is not a rejection of sexuality. It points to the ultimate purpose and meaning of sexuality... [an] anticipation of the heavenly reality, the 'marriage of the lamb'... Christian celibacy reveals that the ultimate fulfilment of solitude is found only in union with God. "[197] This is what the Church calls the consecrated life of avowed celibacy or virginity, which in and of itselfalso is a call, alongside marriage, a vocation to love and the gift of the totality of the self.In this case there is no reciprocal human giving of the self in return. This self-gift in celibacy/virginity is never to be construed as "a lack but as an overflowing plenitude of love. Christ, the son and the bridegroom, reveals in his own flesh that virginity is the highest summit of the spousal meaning of the body itself.... "[198]

Carl Anderson and Jose Granados adapt what they call "the threefold pattern " of the body to see how celibacy or consecrated life is constitutive of the Jesus' mission. First,we see in the life of Christ that he himself embraced

> ... the virginal meaning of the body with his exclusive dedication to the Father's will... Second point... [:] it is not that Christ... fulfils ordinary earthly marriage by transforming it into a sacramental image of his spousal relation with the Church. The Son, in other words, is also the bridegroom who generates, and unites himself to,

---

196   John Paul II, *The Theology of the Body: Human Love in the Divine Plan* (Boston: Pauline Books and Media, 1997), 264.

197   West, *TOB for Beginners*, 66.

198   Carl Anderson and Jose Granados, *Called to Love: Approaching John Paul II's Theology of the Body* (New York: Doubleday, 2009), 217.

the Church on the cross. Third and finally, Christ's spousal union with his Bride is supremely fruitful; through baptism, Christ begets sons and daughters for the Father from the womb of the Church. "[199]

The final section on virginity closes with a reflection on Mary's virginity as a model for consecrated living. Her virginity also plays out in filiation through the conception of the son, in nuptiality both in the sense of birth and at the foot of the cross; she is truly mother because from her womb came forth son who is the salvation of the world. JPII includes the experience of people who various situationsmust live the single life. They are to find a home in the Church and their place around the table where they participate in the triple pattern of being a child of God, spouse of Christ (as members of the Church), and possibly parents at some stage.

Most of those who undertake the study of JPII's theology broadly will agree with Christopher West when he concludes, "We have not fully penetrated the teachings of John Paul II if we have not penetrated his theology of the body. "[200] The published works, encyclicals and apostolic letters of JPII illustrate that the pontiff grounded his philosophical and theological thinking using *TOB* as the starting point with great implications for his pontificate and legacy.

Faith and Love in St. John of the Cross

A twenty-one-year-old Karol Wojtyla in 1941 met and became friends with a layman, Jan Tyranowski, who became a mentor and spiritual guide and who introduced the young Karol to the works of St. John of the Cross. Because of the German invasion of Poland

---

199   Ibid., 218-9. The writers explain that the consecrated life is a gift that manifests the true face of humanity's original solitude which is characterized by the face of the son. In the fulfilment of the original unity, the consecrated person is called like Christ, who is the bridegroom and embodies the totality of the meaning of self-giving. Consecrated persons therefore configure themselves to Christ by living out the spousal love of Christ, sharing in his compassion and in the hopes and struggles of their brothers and sisters. They emphasize the "spiritual fatherhood/motherhood " which Pauline theology sees as fruitful; it is not sterile or purely ethereal but flowers in a sense also according to the nuptial meaning of the body.

200   West, *TOB for Beginners*, 5.

and the suppression of the Catholic Church at this time, young Karol enrolled and started his studies for the priesthood in the underground seminary.[201] In order to get a better grasp of St. John of the Cross, Karol Wojtyla learned Spanish to be able to read the mystic in his original language. This marked the beginning of a lifelong study of John of the Cross which, in turn, markedthe future pope's vision and theological understanding of life, love, and truth. At the age of twenty-eight, now a priest, Karol Wojtyla wrote his dissertation on the understanding of faith in St. John of the Cross under the direction of the renowned spiritual theologian at the Angelicum, Reginald Garrigou-Lagrange. Wojtyla's central thesis concerned faith as a means of union between humanity and God.

Mary Shivanandan notes that Wojtyla's dissertation on faith in St. John of the Cross marked the beginning of his developing an analytical and methodological approach to moral theology that would be reflected even in his later works as Pope John Paul II. It is also in this dissertation that Wojtyla starts to develop the ideas on original solitude, the person, and love. Shivanandan elucidates this point further:

> In analyzing both faith and love in St. John's writing, Wojtyla gains a clearer understanding of the relation of the person, especially his will and intellect, to God and to the union with God in love. In virtue of its relation to the intellect, faith possesses an essential *likeness* to God because faith makes God known to the intellect in a way in which no created thing can do. The *union* with the supernatural being of God is brought about and increased through grace and love. It gives a "new birth." St. John applies the word "transformation" to this process. Love determines the degree of transformation, and

---

201   John Paul himself chronicles the history of these parts of his development in *Gift and Mystery: On the Fiftieth Anniversary of my Priestly Ordination* (New York: Doubleday Publishers, 1996).

progress in love depends on uniting the will to God. Wojtyla comments how much more vividly the truths of speculative theology can be expressed by someone who has actually experienced them.[202]

Shivanandan therefore concludes that Wojtyla "learns from St. John of the Cross the essential character of love, which is to subject the lover to the beloved. It is a union of likeness effected by love. Love operating in the will draws the whole person to the object loved. "[203]

Even though Wojtyla was deeply influenced by John of the Cross, in his later development his attraction to psychology, phenomenology, and anthropology helped him to create a vision of man which is personal and at the same time mystical. JPII's personalist view cuts broadly across his moral theology but especially in the way he approaches human sexuality and marriage.[204] JPII sees humanity's relationship as this one

---

202   Shivanandan, *Crossing the Threshold of Love*, 19.

203   Ibid.

204   *The Jeweler's Shop* is a play the young priest Karol Wojtyla wrote as a meditation on the sacrament of matrimony, passing on occasion into drama (the play's official subtitle). In this play, one begins to get a glimpse of Karol Wojtyla's thoughts about marriage and human sexuality. Boleslaw Taborski, who translated the 1992 English edition from the Polish writes articulately in his introduction of the young playwright and author, "The timeless, nonlinear structure of *The Jeweler's Shop*, connected as it is with the author's unique imagery and oblique way of reasoning, makes for complexity. But on another level it is simple enough. The three parts of the play deals with three couples, married or about to be married, loving each other in the present, or having loved each other in the past, their histories are intertwined... The Jeweler stands for the durability of the sacrament of marriage. He not so much sells as dispenses his wedding rings and refuses to take them back when they are no longer wanted, if both the marriage partners are still alive... He writes with insight and at times with great power, about human love; love that has survived the grave... love that has withered and died... love budding out of complexes, doubts and uncertainties... There are no easy solutions, there is no happy ending. But there is hope, if only we can reach out of ourselves, see the true face of the other person, and hear the signals of a love that transcends us. To this state of mind and heart we are not browbeaten but invited.
    "*The Jeweler's Shop* seems to me a significant link between the future Pope John Paul II's writings on ethics (*Love and Responsibility* among them), on the one hand, and his poetry on the other. It combines the elements of a treatise with rich poetic imagery and inner dramatic development. It is the work of a man in whom unbending principles are connected with boundless forbearance and understanding for people. Here, too, out of the chaos created by our human loves, hates and weaknesses, he gently points the way in the right direction. " Karol Wojtyla, *The Jeweler's Shop: A Meditation on the Sacrament of Matrimony, Passing on Occasion into Drama*, trans. Boleslaw Taborski(San Francisco: Ignatius Press, 1992), 18-19.

person in a mystical union with Godbecause God cannot be understood or known as an object, but as a person which comes into being through mutual self-donation. In Wojtyla's philosophical and anthropological theology, the subjective aspect of faith in relation to experience remains objective in its subjectivity completely. Shivanandan clarifies this point further by stating, "As a person, man, too, cannot be objectivized.... Neither must he be treated simply as an object."[205]

Waldstein opines that to understand JPII's philosophical and anthropological theology is to understand the triangle thesis of John of the Cross that has remained the depth and structure of JPII's understanding of the person based on a Trinitarian personalism.[206] The foundation to this Carmelite Trinitarian personalism Waldstein calls "The Sanjuanist Triangle." Characteristic to this triangle, Waldstein points out, first, love as self-giving; second and paradigmatically, this self-giving is vivified in spousal exchange between a man and a woman; and third and finally, the trinity is an archetype which exemplifies the love between two human persons which derives from imitation and participation in divine self-gift. Waldstein, in reflecting on JPII's catechesis on this Trinitarian/spousal self-exchange as gift, maintains,

> When there is union of love, the image of the beloved is so sketched in the will, and drawn so intimately and vividly, that it is true to say that the beloved lives in the lover and the lover in the beloved. Love produces such likeness in this transformation of lovers that one can say each is the other and both are one. The reason is that the union and transformation of love each gives possession of self to the other and each leaves and exchanges self for the other. Thus, each one lives in the other and is the other, and both are one in the transformation of love.[207]

This spousal self-giving in John of the Cross is equated with and analogous to JPII's interpretation of the carnal and physical sexual

---

205   Ibid., 22.

206   Waldstein in JPII, *Man and Woman*, 34.

207   Ibid., 30.

consummation aspect of human spousal self- giving within marriage. Waldstein restates it thus: "The defining element of 'spiritual marriage,' according to this text is the total surrendering of the self-possession of each to the other, analogous to the consummation of love by sexual union in marriage. "[208] He later says, "The fullest, the most uncompromising form of love consists precisely in self-giving, in making one's inalienable and non-transferable 'I' someone else's property. "[209] JPII's works, especially his books *Love and Responsibility* and *Man and Woman He Created Them,*and the encyclicals *Familiaris Consortio* and *Evangelium Vitae,*offer the analogy of the "gift of self " that echoes John of the Cross as well as the Vatican II document *Gaudium et Spes.*

In his philosophical, anthropological, and theological works,JPII constantly returns to sacred Scripture, the Fathers, sacred Tradition, and St. John of the Cross. In a more modern context, the pontiff's affiliation with phenomenology and his engaging of Kant and Max Scheler gives his writing a greater dimension in which to engage a doctrine going through development.

In JPII's use of phenomenology, he examines the natural and everyday experiences of life as phenomena, the reality of things as they are, a way in which the links between objective reality and subjective experience, ethics and anthropology, truth and freedom, God and man are reconfigured to present a new philosophical, theological, and anthropological methodology. George Weigel, in his commentary on JPII's *TOB* writes,

> With human experience as a point of departure,
> Wojtyla gains a much needed and traditionally
> neglected perspective in the interior life of the human
> person. He discovers in the subjectivity of man's
> inner world a unity with the objectivity of man's
> outer world. By analyzing this unity, he can confirm
> objective truths while avoiding "objectivizing "
> abstractions. He demonstrates that the Church's

---

208   Ibid., 31.

209   Ibid.

vision of man is not foisted him from "the outside,
" but corresponds to his self- experience as a person
on "the inside. "[210]

Wojtyla/John Paul II's anthropological vision from its philosophical and theological standpoint cannot be fully grasped without recognizing his understanding of the personal freedom of the individual person for truth, in recognizing and embracing the truth and to search for it. Weigel opines that JPII's "philosophical project has been to find the both/and—to give proper recognition to the discoveries of phenomenology without renouncing the philosophy of being; to 'make room' for subjectivity within a realist philosophy. "[211]

JPII's work on the German philosopher Max Scheler is invaluable for the over-all system by which he approached *TOB*. Scheler was of the school of Edmund Husserl, who is largely regarded as the father and founder of phenomenology. As a reaction against Kant's ethics of pure duty (duty for duty's sake), Scheler argues for an ethical system based on an ethical emotional value. Wojtyla sees a loophole in both Kant's duty for duty's sake and Scheler's emotional experience of value: while the one does not account for the emotional aspect of the human person, the other does not clarify the human aspiration to value. Therefore, Wojtyla started to work on integrating a self-sufficient Christian ethic, "a reformed phenomenological approach [which] could be integrated with the faith and would greatly aid in bringing the much- needed stamp of subjective experience to the normative science of ethics. "[212] As a University professor, Wojtyla rubbed against the rising intellectual minds of the "Lublin School of Philosophy " who believed that through linking of metaphysics, anthropology, and ethics, a new way of doing philosophy would be born. In various lectures at this time, Wojtyla continued to study and to develop his work around themes like freedom and law, value and duty, experience and ethics, person

---

210   Christopher West, *TOB Explained*, 40.

211   Ibid., 41.

212   Ibid., 36.

and nature, subjectivity and objectivity, all in an effort to arrive at a synthesis of his own vision of an integral Christian ethical system.[213]

Mary Shivanandan does an excellent job of unpacking the inadequacies of Kant and Scheler even as they affect JPII's personalism and ethics. Shivanandan thinks that to understand Wojtyla/JPII's critique of Kant and Scheler, one must read his essay "The Problem of the Separation of Experience from the Act in Ethics in the Philosophy of Immanuel Kant and Max Scheler ", published in the mid-1950s, which analyzes Kant's and Scheler's inability to recognize "the casual efficacy of the human subject in ethical action. "[214] Based on the Aristotelian and Thomistic theory of potency and act, experience and metaphysics, persons experience themselvesas the efficient cause of their own actions, actualizing their will according to the dictates of practical reason. According to Shivanandan, the point of departure includes Kant's rejection of the philosophy of being, which is the basis for Aquinas' theory of potency and act; by doing this, Kant deprives the ethical act of meaning by severing its connection with objective reality. Shivanandan notes further that Scheler, on the other hand,

> .... reinstated sensory experience as a source of knowledge, accepting the essence of a thing exactly as it appears in experience, making no clear distinction between the rational and sensory elements in human knowledge. Both the intellect and emotions are involved in bringing to our consciousness the

---

213   Waldstein, in JPII, *Man and Woman*, 62,locates the point of divergence between Kant's and JPII's versions of personalism in the separation in Kant's dualism between person and nature, which inadvertently allies to his entire philosophical nature and skews his conclusions. Waldstein gives a short summary thus: ".... Kant's anti-trinitarian personalism, which considers sonship the worst slavery and autonomy the only human dignity, exalts the unrelated self. Sex occurs below the level of personhood and threatens personal autonomy. Marriage does the best it can to restore the right one has to one's self. John Paul II's trinitarian personalism exalts the related self that finds itself in the gift of self. Sex does not occur beneath the level of personhood, but is itself an event of personal love, even when it is distorted by being pursued for the sake of mere enjoyment. The natural purpose of sex, children, does not lie outside that love, but qualifies it essentially. "

214   Shivanandan, *Crossing the Threshold of Love*, 27.

essence of a thing, but Scheler gave much greater weight to the emotional aspect both in his theory of cognition and ethics.[215]

In Scheler's phenomenology, reason could understand the *"thingness "* of an object but not its value; emotion, primarily, is able to understand the good. Though these values encountered in the objects are objective, their objectivity is made possible only through emotional experience. Even though Wojtyla is attracted to Scheler's ethics, he rejects it ultimately because in Wojtyla's thought, as translated by Shivanandan, "Only an ethics that has the acting person as the efficient cause is truly an ethics of the person. Emotions are secondary... we experience 'good or 'evil because we experience ourselves as the efficient cause of our own acts. "[216] This apparent discontinuity between Kant, Scheler, and JPII is summarized by Shivanandan aptly thus:

> Whereas Kant has reduced the ethical life to pure reason, Scheler has replaced the mind with emotions as the source of ethical values. But, says Wojtyla, the ethical life cannot be reduced to either pure reason or emotional experience because "ethical experience is a personal whole whose specific properties cease to be themselves apart from this whole. " He believes that a proper understanding of the nature of the will can only be achieved by a thorough analysis of ethical experience and that only the ethics of Aristotle and St. Thomas are based on a proper relation to experience.[217]

Apparently, Wojtyla does not agree with an ethic that denies the subjectivity of the person and in the personal will ordered towards ethical actions (the good). To counter this denial, he had to express the truth about the person in a way that would fit into the categories that contemporary men and women can understand—a philosophy of a person who lives in truth and in love.

---

215   Ibid., 28.

216   Ibid., 29.

217   Ibid.

Wojtyla/JPII's philosophical system is also largely understood to be a reaction against Francis Bacon and Rene Descartes, who sought a return to the primeval condition where the mind has authority over nature. Michael Waldstein aptly describes the Bacon/Descartes task and its implication in the following words:

> Bacon's project of reconstructing the entire order of knowledge in light of the ambition of power over nature is connected with a premise developed earlier in the philosophical and theological current that stands behind the reformation, namely, nominalism: "Late medieval nominalism defended the sovereignty of God as incompatible with there being an order in nature which by itself defined good and bad. For that would be to tie God's hands, to infringe on his sovereign right of decision about what was good. This line of thought even contributed in the end to the rise of mechanism: the ideal universe from this point of view is a mechanical one. "[218] Nominalism, however, did not yet formulate the goal of power as measure of knowledge. Still it eliminated from nature precisely those features that resist its subjection to power, namely, a strong teleology and formal causality. The universe most suited to the goal of power is a mechanical universe, grasped and made ready for use by the mathematical science of mechanics.[219]

The morality of this Baconian program questions its own morality for its lack of control over itself. With the kind of power achieved in technology, and even more so with the weapons and arsenal of mass destruction that nations are stock piling, the earth and humanity itself now need protection which humans seem incapable of providing. Apparently Bacon did not imagine a dynamic where scientific progress

218   Charles Taylor. *Sources of the Self: The Making of the Modern Identity* (Cambridge, MA: Harvard University Press, 1989), 82. Quoted by Michael Waldstein in JPII, *Man and Woman*, 38.

219   Ibid.

can come to mean that all available resources at one's disposal "that can be used will be used. "[220] Waldstein goes further to theorize that theBaconian project took on monstrous proportions when the mathematician/philosopher, the father of modern day scientific and technological project, embraced the theory. Descartes specifically argued for the termination of speculative scholasticism to be replaced with a practical and technological philosophy. In this way, "doing " and "making "would become ultimate reality. This Baconian/Cartesian project of radically aligning knowledge with power over nature makes free will the greatest human good. Waldstein continues, "This apotheosis of the freedom of choice as the greatest human good seems to anticipate already the core of Kant's philosophy of freedom and autonomy. "[221] In direct and opposite contrast to this radical Cartesian metaphysical liberalism, Wojtyla argues in line with Christian tradition, first, that free choice is power subordinated to love because love is a limiting of one's freedom for another's sake.

This mechanistic and scientific domination of nature profoundly affects the meaning of human life within the cosmos. In JPII's *Letter to Families*, he draws attention to the close relation between a scientific picture of the world and utilitarianism:

> The development of contemporary civilization is linked to a scientific and technological progress which is often achieved in a one-sided way and thus appears purely positivistic. Positivism, as we know results in agnosticism in theory and utilitarianism in practice and in ethics. In our own day, history is in a way repeating itself. Utilitarianism is a civilization of production and of use, a civilization of things and not of persons, a civilization in which persons are used in the same way as things are used.[222]

---

220   Ibid., 39.

221   Ibid., 41.

222   John Paul II, *Letter to Families*, 13. As quoted on Waldstein, *Man and Woman*, 42-3

This sort of change in relating to nature by subjugation has resulted in a nihilistic existentialism according to Waldstein, "a certain estrangement between man and the world, with the loss of the idea of a kindred cosmos – in short, an anthropological a-cosmism. "[223] JPII sees this situation as the rise of a new Manicheanism,in which there is a radical opposition between body and spirit; man is no longer subject but object. In this sense, human sexuality becomes manipulable,subject to exploitation; it becomes a commodity to be used, a product to be purchased, totally disconnected from its primordial wonder at creation.

Despite Wojtyla's limited participationas one of the Fathers of the Second Vatican Council, owing to the German occupation of Poland and suppression of the Catholic Church, the Council is nonetheless regarded by many commentators as part of his theological growth and development. The focus of this great council was the question of a new humanism, a development of modernity:how to confront it with almost twenty centuries of Christianity and how to make the Church's message relevant and understood by modern man and woman in their new realities. In his philosophical work *The Acting Person*,[224] Wojtyla tries to make the objective truths about faith an experience to bring within the realm of subjective appropriation. According to Weigel, Wojtyla's most elaborate effort in *The Acting Person* is "to wed the visions of 'person' found in St. Thomas and Max Scheler. His thesis, as the title indicates, is that the irreducible core of the person is revealed through his *actions…* we are not only passive objects, but *acting subjects.* "[225]Because action is interpreted as subjectivity, Wojtyla translates efficacy as "this experience of freedom and subjectivity [where] man begins to experience his own transcendence as a person. Wojtyla believes there is a law of self-giving that defines the person *objectively.* And in the experience of his own freedom, his own ability to act, man comes to experience this truth of his personhood *subjectively.* "[226]

---

223   Waldstein in JPII, *Man and Woman*,43.

224   *The Acting Person* was first published in Polish in 1969 and translated and published in English in 1979.

225   George Weigel in *TOB Explained*. Ibid., 37.

226   Ibid., 38.

Significant to his finding his voice and to his continuous spiritual and intellectual growth is his work in *Signs of Contradiction*,[227] which was born of twenty-two conferences he gave while preaching the papal household and Roman Curia Lenten retreat in 1976(under Pope Paul VI). In the conferences/book, Wojtyla concentrated on the question, "Who is man and how does Christ fully reveal man to himself? " In what he calls the "signs of the times, " Wojtyla envisioned a renewed Church where Christ will be re-introduced to men and women of our age even though the great challenge is that he will be a sign of contradiction. Wojtyla referred to different signs that transmit transcendental realities, but the greatest sign of all is that of man and woman. It is in this relationship that the Church becomes a sign of contradiction, in her sexual ethic. It was in an effort to respond to this that Pope John Paul II penned and gave to the Church what has become perhaps his greatest biblical, philosophical, anthropological, and theological project: The *Theology of the Body* (*TOB*).

For the proponents of JPII's philosophy and theology, what makes *TOB* endearing,if challenging, to modern humanity is the challenge to freedom through the truth. While JPII's work does not impose, the advocates of personal freedom are challenged to understand the "splendor of truth " which according to JPII separates and distinguishes between "knowledge " and "consciousness. " Weigel articulates it thus:

> For a person to be at peace with himself and the world, he must not only know the truth, he must interiorize it, feel it, experience it, and freely embrace it as his own. To do so, he must trust the truth wholeheartedly, have an impassioned love for the objective good and abandon himself to it fearlessly. This is only possible if truth is perfect love, which is only possible if truth itself is a person. Truth is. Truth's name is Jesus Christ.[228]

Herein lies the heart of the matter, at once ontologically true while simultaneously epistemologically impossible for the unbelieving heart.

---

227   Karol Wojtyla. *Signs of Contradiction* (New York: Seabury Press, 1979) also Cf. Lk. 2:34. As quoted in *TOB Explained*, 38.

228   West, *TOB Explained*. 42.

In a rudimentary manner, JPII is asking modern human persons not to limit their experience of the divine to technical knowledge and discernment only. Rather, he asks that modern man and woman engage the *freedom of intellect, will* and *person* to the experience achievable only by the self-donation found in the love of a God who loved us first. Even though we understand concepts with the mind, true love is in the heart. "Ultimate Reality is much more than a concept. It is a Person."[229] This person is Jesus, who brings us from our personal being and existence to the "I" and "Thou"—in our one co-existence and communion with God and with other people.

John Paul II's Biblical and Exegetical Foundations

In all of Wojtyla's/John Paul II's writings, an unbroken thread evidently developed as he himself matured philosophically and theologically. JPII depends on and grounds his foundational thoughts and arguments on biblical tradition and his profound exegetical work with an in-depth tapestry woven by traversing the Old and the New Testaments. JPII's use of proof texts one after the other helps him to situate what is authentically God's plan from the very beginning. Going to *"the beginning"* and finding foundational texts not only give credence to his arguments but also provide an insight into the development of doctrine. His skill at historical critical redactionism makes it possible for him to elucidate scriptural texts upon which doctrines and Christian moral tradition rest.

Even though the historical-critical method has become a common toolfor reading scripture in contemporary times, commentaries on JPII's works do not identify him specifically as a student of the historical-critical method. However, Waldstein thinks JPII's views,as expressed in his comments on the hundredth anniversary of Leo XIII's *Providentissimus Deus* and the 50th anniversary of Pius XII's *Divino Afflante Spiritu*, are overly positive.In these comments, JPII states,

> The Church of Christ takes the realism of the incarnation seriously, and this is why she attaches great importance to the "historical critical" study

---

229   Ibid.

of the bible... [Exegetes must strive] to understand the meaning of the texts with all the accuracy and precision possible and, thus, in their historical, cultural context. The God of the Bible is not an absolute being, who crushing everything he touches, will suppress all differences and all nuances. On the contrary, he is God the creator, who created the astonishing variety of things... God respects them and makes use of them (cf. 1Cor. 12:18, 24, 28). Although he expresses himself in human language he does not give each expression a uniform value, but uses its possible nuances with extreme flexibility and likewise accepts its limitations. That is what makes the task of exegetes, so complex, so necessary, and so fascinating.[230]

Even though JPII seems to see the historical-critical method in a positive light, he nonetheless was not concerned merely about what the text says within a historical context; he is rather more concerned about what a text says to the realities of contemporary times and questions. According to Curran, JPII does not address the use of scripture as a systematician or approach the use of scripture methodologically. Rather, JPII "writes as an authoritative teacher for the whole church on moral issues and questions. "[231] Beyond what the historical text says about contemporary realities, JPII is more concerned about the divine meaning of each text: what God intends to pass along within the wider context of ongoing revelation of the incarnation. The revelation of scripture focuses on the Incarnation, which is the act of

---

230   JPII, *Man and Woman*, Ibid., 18-9.

231   Charles Curran, "John Paul II's Use of Scripture in His Moral Teaching, " *Horizons* 31, no. 1 (Spring 2004): 118. In his book *The Moral Theology of Pope John Paul II*, Curran notes how in various encyclicals and in the *TOB*, JPII starts major sections with scriptural texts as the basis for situating a teaching that is not necessarily of any known scientific method of approaching the study of scripture in current biblical scholarship but from an authoritative, homiletical and catechetical reflection. Cf. 46. Also in the journal article published in *Horizons*, Curran avers, "John Paul II... tends to consider scripture as a unified whole and often develops his understanding on the basis of a meditative and even homiletic reflection on them. This approach is somewhat similar to that used by the writers in the so called patristic age of the early church and to the practice of *lectio divina*—a meditative and contemplative reading of scripture. " 121.

a God who is love. In this light, JPII is able to read historical texts critically and exegetically and make them speak the word of God (love) into the consciousness of contemporary realities and questions. JPII relies heavily on the Gospel of John to situate "the Word that became flesh "; in the Incarnation he is able to point to redemption, thereby establishing for his theological purposes a Christology from above. In Waldstein's opinion, "of all the works of John Paul II, *TOB* is the most direct, profound, and extensive analysis of "what God...wishes above all to transmit to human beings in his WORD. "[232] The foregoing forms a hermeneutical problem for Curran, who states that "the major issue in using scripture in moral theology involves the hermeneutical problem—how one moves from the time and place of the scripture (and recognizing that there are different times and places for the different scriptural books) to the time, culture, and place of today. "[233]

Eduardo Echeverria, while discussing JPII's use of the scriptures to support *TOB* contends that "... in accordance with the biblical hermeneutic of Vatican II's *Dei Verbum*, and in the Church's teaching regarding the unity and reliability of the word of God, he gives 'serious attention... to the content and unity of the whole of scripture' in developing the biblical foundation of the theology of the body "[234] and that "[h]is is a canonical exegesis, which involves placing the individual biblical texts in their immediate literary context, of God's revelation, the context of scripture as a whole, and the living tradition of the Church. "[235] Echeverria sees four hermeneutical approaches to JPII's use of scriptures: first, a hermeneutic of canonical wholeness, unified in such a way that it becomes impossible fundamentally for God to contradict himself. Second, because of the assumption that scripture is of dual authorship, human and divine, JPII's hermeneutical schema necessarily must accede to the unity of historical exegesis and theological interpretation, which means that scripture possesses a "multivalent potential of meaning. " Third, Christ is the unifying

---

232   Waldstein in JPII, *Man and Woman*, 22.

233   Curran, "John Paul II's Use of Scripture, " 122.

234   Eduardo Echeverria, *"In the Beginning...": A Theology of the Body* (Eugene, Oregon: Pickwick Publications, 2011), xxii.

235   Ibid.

principle that makes scripture a canonical whole. Fourth and finally, the interpretation of scripture must be in line with the Church's sacred tradition and within scripture's hermeneutical relevance to the contemporary Church's living experience and understanding.[236]

In constructing his theological anthropology in *TOB*, JPII relies on the "triptych" or the three key biblical verses in the first cycle on which the adequate understanding of the nature of the human person is understood within the three stages of the human drama:stage one is*original man*, "in the beginning" (cf. Mt. 19:3-9); this is the way the human person experienced the self before sin. Stage two is the*historical man* "in the heart" (Mt. 5:27-28), referring to the way the human person experiences the self as affected by sin but redeemed by Christ. The third stage will be*the eschatological man* "in the resurrection" (Mt. 22:23-33), which reflects on humanity's sexual embodiment as it will be realized in the resurrection. These texts, based on the words/ teachings of Jesus, ground JPII's sexual ethics (as well as incorporating the teachings of *Humanae Vitae*) in divine revelation. From JPII's encyclicals, it is easy to see his dependence on scripture as the*primary source of his moral theology. *Veritatis Splendor* is specifically written to reiterate the importance of scripture for contemporary moral theology, and the idea is also referenced in *Dei Verbum*.[237]

JPII creates his theological anthropology of *TOB* around the themes of creation, fall, and redemption. The two accounts of creation in Genesis used by JPII situate the two accounts of creation, establishing humanity as made in the image and likeness of God (from which is derived human dignity),as well as humanity's authority and dominion over everything else in the created order. In this locus JPII sees the original nakedness of humanity in Adam and Eve. In the same Genesis accounts (Chapters 1-4), the account of the fall is narrated. Curran favors an*interpretation of a threefold break in relationship engendered

---

236   Ibid., 95-96.

237   Curran, "John Paul II's Use of Scripture," 119. Curran clarifies this point further here: "John Paul himself implicitly and explicitly calls attention to the primary role of scripture in moral theology. His references to scripture far outnumber any other references made within his fourteen encyclicals, many of which deal with moral life. The encyclical Veritatis Splendor explicitly invokes the importance of the scripture for moral theology."

by the fall; "a break in the relationship of loving dependence of Adam and Eve upon God (Adam and Eve hid themselves); a break in the relationship between man and woman (Adam accused Eve of causing the problem); and a break or struggle within the human person brought about by concupiscence (they recognized their nakedness and covered it). "[238] JPII sees the transition from original nakedness and the fall to redemption as residing in the nuptial meaning of the body, based on a number of scriptural texts other than the Genesis account. According to Curran in the *Horizons* article, "among the texts developed here are 1Cor. 6:15-20 with its emphasis on the human body as the temple of the Holy Spirit and the member of Christ; 1Thess. 4:4 with its call for controlling the body in holiness and honor; and Romans 8:32 with its explicit recognition of the redemption of the body. "[239] JPII's reflections on Ephesians 5 are so central to the entire treatise that it will be discussed under its own sub-heading later on in this work. For now, it suffices to say that the spousal analogy of Christ as the groom of his bride, the Church, is used to teach about the sacramental nature of marriage and the relationship of love that exists between husband and wife as an example of the love of Christ for his Church.[240]

The Pontiff's reliance and insistence on giving his teaching a solid scriptural foundation is a pointer to the idea of a consistent theological Christian moral ethic and an understanding of ontological ethical truths that speaks to constantly a shifting and changing culture, which from different cultures and times, leaves itself open to newer ways of thinking and societal milieus.

"Male and Female, He created them": The Genesis Account

JPII thematically builds his philosophical and theological anthropology of the theology of the body by presenting the ontological meaning of the creation of human persons in their gender differentiation as male and female by going back to the two accounts of the creation of

---

238   Ibid., 128.

239   Ibid.

240   Ibid., 129.

man in the book of Genesis. Chapter 2 of Genesis, verse 18 says, "it is not good that man should be alone, " whereupon the idea of original solitude becomes the grounds for building the idea of original unity. Again, JPII ties this to the beginning, to the original intention of the creator. Key to understanding the idea of original unity is Genesis 2:24: "For this reason, a man will leave his father and mother and unite with his wife, and the two will become one flesh. " Christ appeals to this text in Mt. 19:5 in response to the question of the Pharisee about divorce. Unlike the account of creation in Genesis 1, the Yahwist account in Genesis 2 approaches man in the duality of its sex. According to JPII, "Bodiliness and sexuality are not simply identical. Although in its normal constitution, the human body carries within itself the signs of sex and is by its nature male or female ... *the fact that man is a „body' belongs more deeply to the structure of the personal subject than the fact that in his somatic constitution he is also male or female."*[241] It is for this reason that JPII insists that "the meaning of original solitude, which can be referred simply to 'man,' is substantially prior to the meaning of original unity; the latter is based on masculinity and femininity, which were,....two different 'incarnations,' that is, two ways in which the same human being, created 'in the image of God' (Gen. 1:27), 'is a body.' "[242]

Genesis 2:18-22[243] plays a crucial role in JPII's exegesis of what it means biblically to be male and female, both made in the *imago dei.* The pontiff pays particular attention to the deep sleep *(torpor)*into which Adam falls when God took the rib from his side to create Eve. He contrasts this sleep, induced by God to create the woman from the side

---

241   *Man and Woman,*157.

242   Ibid.

243   It is not good that the man should be alone; I want to make him a help similar to himself. So the Lord caused a deep sleep *(torpor)* to fall upon man, who fell asleep; then he took one of his ribs and closed the flesh again in its place. With the rib the Lord God had taken from the man he formed a woman.

of the man, with contemporary scientific and Freudian psychoanalytic understanding,which emphasizesthe association of the subconscious, such as dreams,with repressed ideas of sex.[244]

For JPII, gender differentiation exists truly only within the prism of the homogeneity of the being of both. Woman made from the rib of man is a metaphoric and figurative way for the ancient people to express the idea of homogeneity in body and the entire somatic structure. JPII claims that this homogeneity is recognized by Adam when he woke up and exclaimed, "This time she is flesh from my flesh and bone from my bones " (Gen 2:23).[245] This joy echoed by the man upon seeing the

---

244   In the footnotes to JPII's *TOB*, Michael Waldstein points out the following interesting contra-distinctions: "In the theology of the Yahwist author, the torpor in which God lets the man fall underlines the *exclusiveness of God's action* in the creation of the woman. The man had no conscious part in it. God makes use of his 'rib' only to emphasize the common nature of man and woman. 'Torpor' is the term that appears in sacred scripture when, during the sleep or immediately after it, extra ordinary events are to take place.... The Septuagint translates [torpor] as „*ekstasis'* (a trance, ecstasy). In the Pentateuch 'torpor' appears once more, in a mysterious context: at God's command, Abraham has prepared a sacrifice of animals, driving away birds of prey from them. 'As the sun was setting, *torpor* fell on Abraham, and a *dark terror* assailed him' (Gen. 15:12). It is at this moment that God begins to speak and makes a covenant with him, which is *the summit of the revelation* made to Abraham... resembles in some way that of the garden of Gethsemane. Jesus 'began to feel fear and distress' (Mk. 14:33) and found the apostles „*sleeping from sadness'* (Lk. 22:445). The biblical author admits in the first man a certain sense of lack and solitude, even if not of fear ('it is not good that the man should be alone,' 'he did not find help similar to himself'). Perhaps this state causes 'sleep from sadness' or perhaps, as in Abraham, '*a dark terror*' of non-existence, as at the threshold of creation: 'the earth was unfirmed and deserted and darkness covered the abyss.' (Gen. 1:2). In any case, according to both texts in which the Pentateuch, specifically, Genesis, speaks about deep sleep, *(torpor)* a special divine action takes place, namely, a 'covenant' filled with consequences for the whole history of salvation: Adam begins the human race, Abraham the chosen people. " Cf. 159.

245   Waldstein makes further interesting allusions to clarify some of the allegories within these texts, "...for the ancient Sumerians, the cuneiform sign used to indicate the noun 'rib' was the same as the one used to indicate the word 'life.' As for the Yahwist narrative, according to one interpretation of Genesis 2:21, God covers the rib with flesh (rather than closing up the flesh in its place) and in this way 'forms' the woman, who thus draws her origin from the 'flesh and bones' of the first (male) man. In biblical language, this is a definition of consanguinity or belonging to the same lineage (e.g., Gen 29:14): the woman belongs to the same species as the man, distinct from other living beings created earlier. In biblical anthropology, 'bones' signify a very important component of the body, given that for the Hebrews there was no precise distinction between 'body' and 'soul'.... 'bone from my bones' can thus be understood in the relational sense, like 'being from being.' 'Flesh from flesh' signifies that, although she has different physical characteristics, the woman has the same personhood that the man has. " Cf. 160.

woman establishes a somatic homogeneity in a reciprocal recognition and affirmation of the second "I, " thereby establishing the original unity from the beginning.

In developing the meaning of "male " and "female, " JPII further asserts that....

> [t]he account of creation of man in Genesis 1 affirms from the beginning and directly that man was created in the image and likeness of God inasmuch as he is male and female. The account in Genesis 2, by contrast, does not speak of the "image of God, " but reveals, in the manner proper to it, that the complete and definitive creation of "man " (subject first to the experience of original solitude), expresses itself to giving life to the *communion personarum* that man and woman form.... Man becomes and image of God not so much in the moment of solitude as in the moment of communion. He is, in fact, "from the beginning " … essentially the image of an inscrutable divine communion of Persons.[246]

In the second creation account, JPII shows that it is in this way the trinitarian concept of the 'image of God' can be understood. "This is obviously not without significance for the theology of the body, but constitutes perhaps the deepest theological aspect of everything one can say about man. "[247] And that in the mystery of creation "… man has been endowed with a deep unity between what is, humanly and through the body, male in him. On all this, right from the beginning, the blessing of fruitfulness descended, linked with human procreation (cf. Gen 1:28). "[248] Gen 2:23: "Then the man said, 'This time she is flesh from my flesh and bone from my bones. She will be called woman because from man has she been taken.' " According to JPII, this verseclarifies the point that the understanding of the person necessarily

---

246   JPII, *Man and Woman*, 531-38.

247   Ibid., 164.

248   Ibid.

passes through masculinity and femininity, two incarnations but the same metaphysical solitude— *"two reciprocally completing ways of "being a body' and at the same time of being human*—as two complimentary dimensions of self-knowledge and self-determination and, at the same time, *two complementary ways of being conscious of the meaning of the body*(emphasis in the original)."[249] JPII argues further that this complementarity/unity of which Gen. 2:24 speaks, "and the two will become one flesh," is expressed and realized in conjugality:

> When they unite with each other (in conjugal act) so closely so as to become "one flesh," man and woman rediscover every time and in a special way the mystery of creation, thus returning to the union in humanity ("flesh from my flesh and bone from my bones ") that allows them to recognize each other reciprocally and to call each other by name, as they did the first time…. Sex, however, is something more than the mysterious power of human Bodiliness, which acts, as it were, by virtue of instinct. On the level of man and in the reciprocal relationship of persons, sex expresses an ever-new surpassing of the limit of man's solitude, which lies within the makeup of his body and determines its original meaning. This surpassing always implies that in a certain way one takes upon oneself the solitude of the body of the second "I" as one's own.[250]

JP II elucidates further that in this intimacy of becoming "one flesh," the conjugal act becomes a mature, conscious choice of the body and persons involved. This conjugal union *carries within itself a particular awareness of the meaning of that body in the reciprocal self- gift of the persons.*"[251] Expounding on this theme, JPII writes,

---

249   Ibid., 166.

250   Ibid., 167-68.

251   Ibid., 169.

In this sense, too, Genesis 2:24 is a future oriented text. It shows, in fact, that in every conjugal union of man and woman, there is a new discovery of the same original consciousness of the unitive meaning of the body in its masculinity and femininity; the biblical text thereby indicates at the same time that each union of this kind renews in some way the mystery of creation in all its original depth and vital power. "Taken from the man " as "flesh from his flesh, " the woman consequently becomes, as "wife " and through her motherhood, mother of the living (Gen. 3:20), because her motherhood has its proper origin also in him. Procreation is rooted in creation, and every time it reproduces in some way its mystery.[252]

In this section of JPII's work, using the accounts of Genesis 2, he establishes that the nuptial meaning of the body shows the human person's capacity to be a gift to the other with deep affirmation, which is lived through the complementarity of the sexes. According to Christopher West, "Man, having first received woman as a gift from God, is disposed towards initiating the gift of himself to the woman. "[253] He avers further that conversely, the woman in receiving this gift leaves herself open to a mutual self-exchange. West calls this "an ever-deepening exchange which in some way reflects the eternal exchange within the trinity. "[254]

The Matthew 5:27-28 Account: In the light of The Sermon on the Mount

"You have heard that it was said, „you shall not commit adultery.' But I say to you: whoever looks at a woman to desire her lustfully has already committed adultery with her in his heart."

---

252   Ibid.

253   West, *TOB Explained*, 128.

254   Ibid.

JPII uses this text almost in the same radical way as with his constant reference to the "beginning ";[255] here he is applying the text within its immediate and more expansive context. This is one of the fundamental teachings of Jesus where he develops and explains the moral ethics of the Decalogue within a newer and stronger exegetical purview. This meta-pedagogy is applied variously to related laws in the Decalogue, such as "Thou shall not commit adultery " and "Thou shall not covet thy neighbor's wife. " These have great implications for personal responsibility, for one's ethos and the interiority of one's subjective acts. In JPII's words, this text from Matthew's Gospel, in the Sermon on the Mount, introduces us to a global context:

> It refers to the following commandments of the Decalogue, in order: the fifth, "You shall not kill " (cf. Mt. 5:21-26); the sixth, "You shall not commit adultery " (cf. Mt. 5:27-32); and the eight, according to the text of Exodus (cf. Ex. 20:7) "You shall not swear falsely, but shall perform to the Lord what you have sworn " (cf. Mt 5:33-37). It is significant that at the end of the passage about adultery the question of the certificate of divorce also appears (cf. Mt. 5:31-32)....[256]

JPII teaches that "adultery in the heart " consists of dwelling on the lustful desire to have sexual knowledge of someone else who is not one's spouse. This is an interior act for men and women expressed through sight and by mere sensory perception. For any moral action that is physically performed, a conscious pre-meditation is required for it to be considered right or wrong. Therefore, adultery necessarily takes

---

255   Ibid., 133. West, in his commentary notes, avers, "Like Christ's words that pointed us to the "beginning, " John Paul says that the Lord's words about lust are pregnant with theological, anthropological, and ethical content. They have a "key meaning for the Theology of the Body, " a "global context, " and an "explicitly normative character. [ ] These words, then, are not only directed towards those who heard the Sermon on the Mount with their own ears. They are directed toward "every man " (male and female) of the past and the future.

256   John Paul II, *TOB: Human Love*, 103

place in the heart before it takes place physically.[257] In this case, JPII argues that it is impossible to keep God's commandments externally only; there is a need for "a vital participation coming from the depths of the heart."[258] It is in this inner world of virtues that each person fights the battle between good and evil, a complex arena of the subjectivity of individual conscience and the sensitivity of the heart. Mastering the heart's interiority prevents legalism or moralism. In this call to a personal ethos and the recovery of the fundamental meaning of the law as ethic, this Sermon on the Mount is rephrased by West thus: "you have heard the objective law and interpreted it *externally*. Now I tell you the subjective meaning of the law – what it calls you to *internally*.... You have heard the *ethic*. Now I speak to you of its proper *ethos*."[259] West clarifies that there is an organic relationship between the law and the teachings of Christ, which must be maintained while any sharp contrast between them must be avoided. This way of approaching a

---

257   Ibid., 126-7. JPII asserts that "[t]he heart has become a battlefield between love and lust. The more lust dominates the heart, the less the heart experiences the nuptial meaning of the body. It becomes less sensitive to the gift of the person, which expresses that meaning in the mutual relations of man and woman.... Violating the dimension of the mutual giving of the man and the woman, concupiscence also calls in question the fact that each of them was willed by the creator 'for his own sake.' In a certain sense, the subjectivity of the person gives way to the objectivity of the body. Owing to the body, man becomes an object for man – the female for the male and vice versa. Concupiscence means that the personal relations of man and of woman are unilaterally and reductively linked with the body and sex, in the sense that these relations become almost incapable of accepting the mutual gift of the person. They do not contain or deal with femininity/ masculinity according to the full dimension of personal subjectivity. They do not express communion, but they remain unilaterally determined by sex..... Manifested as 'coercion *sui generis* of the body,' concupiscence limits interiorly and reduces self-control. For that reason, in a certain sense it makes impossible the interior freedom of giving. Together with that, the beauty that the human body possesses in its male and female aspect, as an expression of the spirit, is obscured. The body remains as an object of lust and, therefore, as a 'field of appropriation' of the other human being."

258   West, *TOB Explained*, 134.

259   Ibid., 135.

new "Christian ethos " is certainly new but not divergent from its Old Testament roots if understood in the sense of fulfillment.[260]

JPII argues that the uniqueness of man is not based on his rationality; to be considered unique to man, among other qualities, is his heart. According to JPII, "the category of the heart is, in a way, the equivalent of personal subjectivity. The way of appeal to purity of heart, as it was expressed in the Sermon on the Mount, is in any case a reminiscence of the original solitude, from which the man was liberated…. "[261] The purity of heart that Jesus reflects upon and which JPII enunciates is a call that is indispensable for holiness and the communion of persons. The words of Mt. 5:27-28 reflect the Beatitude of Mt. 5:8: "Blessed are the pure in heart, for they shall see God. " The war between purity and sinfulness (sometimes referred to as the opposition of the flesh to the Spirit) as it rages in the human heart is a theme that is taken up in the epistles of the New Testament, more so in Pauline writings: "But I say, walk by the Spirit and do not gratify the desires of the flesh. For the desires of the flesh are against the Spirit, and the desires of the Spirit are against the flesh. For these are opposed to each other, to prevent you from doing what you would " (Gal. 5:16-17). Romans 8:5 also says, "For those who live according to the flesh set their minds on the things of the flesh, but those who live according to the Spirit set their minds on the things of the Spirit. " JPII's treatment of this Mathean text seen through the prism of the Sermon on the Mount gives a new pedagogical hermeneutic fora newer way of approaching marital and sexual purity hitherto non-existent in the Jewish scriptures. It also presents a new and dynamic way of understanding the call to holiness required of both the male and female within and outside of marriage.

---

260   Ibid., 135, see footnote. Interestingly, West goes further to show that JPII himself drew on and challenged the phenomenology of Max Scheler. JPII critiques Scheler because he fails to see how for morality to be real to anyone, it must be connected with an experienced value. Scheler failed to recognize subjective responsibility towards objective moral values when his perceptions of value are misguided. According to West, "Christ's words in the Sermon on the Mount, we see the call to purity in one's subjective values. For when man's heart is purified, his subjective values correspond to that which is objectively true, good and beautiful. But even the impure man has a duty toward the objective good. "

261   Ibid., 177.

The Marriage of the Lamb: TheEphesians 5:21-33 Account

This Pauline text is perhaps JPII's strongest connection with other New Testament texts in terms of what, over time, have come to be called the "key words " from scripture used to ground the theology of the body. In this text, we findthe appeal to the "beginning " (Mt. 19:4; Mk. 10:6), the appeal to the human heart from the Sermon on the Mount (Mt. 5:28), and the appeal to the future resurrection of the body (Mt. 22:30; Mk. 12:25; Lk. 20:35-36). In this evangelical outline, JPII sees the author of the letter to the Ephesians[262] as centering his message on the body, ".... both in its *metaphorical meaning*, that is, on the body of Christ which is the Church, and *in its concrete meaning*, that is on the human body in its perennial masculinity and femininity, in its perennial destiny for union in marriage, as Genesis says: 'For this reason a man will leave his father and his mother and unite with his wife and the two will be one flesh' (Gen. 2:24). "[263] JPII's preliminary approach to this text was to reference *Gaudium et Spes*, saying that this text reveals—in a particular way—*man to man himself* and makes his supreme vocation clear (GS. 22:1) as he participates in the experience of the Incarnated One. Mary Shivanandan sees JPII's reflections on Ephesians 5 as reflecting his teachings on marriage and celibacy, the analogy which brings together the great mystery of Christ and the Church, redemption and the spousal meaning of love.[264] In the light of Ephesians 5, JPII approaches the understanding of marriage from the dual dimensions of covenant/grace and the sacramental sign. These two can be approached from the perspective of the mystery of Christ realized in the Church as an expression of the divine plan for redemption, and the Christian vocation of the baptized also seen within the idea of the redemption of the person and of the community as the body of Christ. The text from Ephesians 5 reiterates the communitarian aspect of marriage, not simply as the union of spouses but as the

---

262   In JPII's thinking, there is no doubt that this letter to the Ephesians is genuinely of the Pauline corpus, even if it is imagined by some that it was an idea Paul entrusted to a later secretary. The pope is at variance with biblical scholars who suggest that this letter was a later text adduced to Paul for credibility's sake.

263   JPII, *Man and Woman*, 466-67.

264   Shivanandan, *Crossing the Threshold of Love*, 130.

familial relationship of parents and offspring, and its relationship and obligations with and in the society.

The most contested part of Ephesians 5:21-33 is found in these verses: "Wives, be subject to your husband as you are to the Lord. For the husband is the head of the wife as Christ is the head of the Church, he who is the savior of his body. And as the Church is subject to Christ, so also wives ought to be subject to their husbands in everything. And you, husbands, love your wives.... " JPII's exegesis of this text explains it thus:

> What is at issue here is a relationship with two dimensions or on two levels: reciprocal and communitarian... the reciprocal relations of husband and wife must spring from their common relation with Christ. The text chosen... has a "parenetic " character, that is, the character of moral instruction. The author of the letter wants to point out to the spouses how their reciprocal relations and all their behavior should be formed. He draws the specific indications and directives as a conclusion from the mystery of Christ presented at the beginning of the letter...penetrating their hearts, kindling in them that holy "fear of Christ " (that is *pietas*), the mystery of Christ must lead them to "be subject to one another " ... Husband and wife are, in fact, "subject to one another, " mutually subordinated to one another. The source of this reciprocal submission lies in Christian *Pietas* and *its expression in love.*[265]

The command to love addressed to the husband in this text, and in light of contemporary sensibilities to the idea of the "subjection " of one to the other, takes away any fear that might be created. "Love excludes any kind of submission by which the wife would become a servant or slave of the husband, an object of one-sided submission. Love makes the husband *simultaneously subject* to the wife, and *subject* in this

---

265   JPII, *Man and Woman*, 472-73.

to the *Lord himself*, as the wife is to the husband. "[266] JPII interprets the vision of Ephesians 5 as not merely a discussion of the traditional and ethical bounds of marriage but asexpressing consideration for the reciprocity required by the sacramental nature of marriage and which the Ephesians 5 text demands of spouses. JPII affirms his position by stating that "…the teaching that belongs to this parenetic part of the letter is in some sense inserted into the very reality of the mystery hidden from eternity in God and revealed to humanity in Jesus Christ. "[267] He states further, "In the letter to the Ephesians, we are witnesses, I would say, of a particular encounter of this mystery with the very essence of the vocation to marriage. "[268]

JPII also draws attention to another salient yet equally important parallel that can be instructive to understanding the Ephesians 5 text, the analogy of the relationship that exists between Christ and the Church to the relationship between bride and groom in the spousal bound. In this Pauline analogy, JPII locates a supplementary analogy of the head and the body, which is purely ecclesiological in its ontology. JPII's analysis posits that the text "speaks as if in marriage also the husband were 'head of his wife' and the wife 'body of her husband,' as if spouses also form an organic union. This perspective can find its basis in the text of Genesis that speaks about 'one flesh' (Gen 2:24) …. especially in this passage at the beginning of Ephesians 5:22-23, the ecclesiological dimension seems decisive and predominant. "[269] In Shivanandan's explication, Christ is head, savior, and bridegroom; his redeeming love transforms into spousal love. According to her, "the head-body analogy is primarily of an organic nature implying the somatic union of the human organism, which also includes the psychic and bodily unity of the human person…. It is clear from the Genesis text that the man and woman are 'two distinct personal subjects….' "[270] Then quoting John Paul, she notes that "this analogy… does not blur the individuality of the subjects: that of the husband and wife, that is, the essential bi-subjectivity which is at the basis of the image of 'one

---

266   Ibid.

267   Ibid., 474.

268   Ibid., 474-75.

269   Ibid., 479-80.

270   Shivanandan, *Crossing the Threshold of Love*, 131.

single body.' In the whole passage 'bi-subjectivity clearly dominates.' "[271]

Shivanandan surmises that John Paul's use of the Ephesians 5 text builds the catechesis on marriage and human sexuality on the basis of the following understanding:

> John Paul II calls marriage the "sacrament of creation. " Marriage was created to make visible the invisible plan of God for humanity. The invisible plan or mystery is God's intention for mankind to participate in divine Trinitarian life for all eternity… Redemption in Christ after sin became the source of man's supernatural endowment or gracing…. The mystery of God's spousal love becomes visible in Christ. Since the visible sign of marriage is linked to the visible sign of Christ and the Church, it has from the beginning transferred God's eternal plan of love and salvation into the "historical" dimension.[272]

Sexuality and Marriage in John Paul II's Theology of the Body:

JPII's work in his anthropological, philosophical, and theological expose on the Theology of the Body centers on human sexuality in its core meaning as found in its nuptial understanding. Its method is truly new, especially considering his personalist approach, the attention given to the gift of the self in marriage, and the extensive exegetical biblical foundations. JPII moved away from the traditional focus on the "weakness" of the body (the flesh) and concupiscence to placing greater value on created humanity in the "beginning" and through

---

271   Ibid.

272   Ibid., 132-33.

redemption.[273] The question can be raised if this is a departure from tradition or a development? While the pope's contribution maybe new and even "refreshing, " as some say it is, it does not deviate from Catholic tradition. I agree with Mary Shivanandan when she states succinctly that "John Paul's Theology of the Body and sex is both faithful to the tradition and frees it from certain negative evaluations. Scripture has been his guide in this new interpretation, but he has also been aided by the Aristotelian and Thomistic concept of potency and act and a phenomenological analysis of human experience. "[274]

The Theology of the Body examines questions about human sexuality in light of the totality of the human person; either in the sexuality of the celibate person or the sexuality of non- celibate persons located within the marriage bond and expressed within its conjugality. When JPII teaches about sexuality within marriage, he talks about the ontological and intrinsic nature of the human person as "designed " by the creator from the very beginning. The arguments to support human sexuality within marriage, central to JPII's thesis, hinge on the body as intrinsic to human beings who exist as bodily beings, within marriage;and this body, which is intrinsic to this one person, necessarily exists in a unity of body and soul, making the person a subject of his own moral acts. As a bodily person within the marital union, the conjugal act constitutes the person's bodily, subjective, and moral act. It is in this sense that JPII argues that for the sexual act to

---

273   n the traditional almost Manichean "disdain " for the flesh and a certain sense of "shame " associated with sex seen in Pauline corpus and Augustinian thought, Shivanandan credits JPII for a newer understanding and approach, ibid., 139: "For John Paul II, shame is a boundary experience dividing historical man from original innocence. The sin of Adam and Eve creates a rupture in their perfect communion as male and female. Original sin introduces a tendency towards concupiscence which makes it difficult to accept one another in the fullness of the gift. The body of man, who is made in the image of God, reveals the holiness of creation, but lust, which is the fruit of disordered desire, makes the woman especially an object and not a disinterested gift. The body itself did not become evil, but man lost a sense of its nuptial meaning. Redemption reaches into the interior of the person and makes possible again the 'freedom of the gift.' The Spirit gives a new 'capacity' to the Christian to strengthen interiorly the nuptial meaning of the body, which now becomes a 'task.' Only in marital union is the freedom of the gift possible. The marital act is free from shame when performed in the truth of the language of the body. It is concealed from the eyes of others because its true meaning is only perceived by the spouses themselves in the depths of the heart. Shame towards others outside of the marital union has a positive value in protecting the nuptial meaning of the body. "

274   Ibid., 140.

be morally right, the unity of the person's integrity as a human person in the union of body and soul must exist as an intrinsic good of self-integration. Therefore, through mutual consent and mutual respect, marital intercourse as bodily union becomes a mutual gift between a man and his wife, becoming a communion of persons that is always open to the possibility of procreation, the gift of another life.

At the same time, the sexual union of spouses is intrinsic to the nature of their union as a personal union, which is also directed at friendship and the development of love. According to Echeverria, in JPII's view, "the sexual act is much more than a natural bodily symbol; indeed, it embodies marital union, becoming bodily, or organically complete, and thus one, expresses total self-giving and makes it bodily present... "[275] JPII's claim that all individual persons, because they exist as a union of body and soul, possess the capacity for self-determination, and that it is through the medium of the individual person that human actions take place, that each person establishes his ethics of sex. Echeverria interprets this assertion by JPII in the following context:

> In light of this truth, namely, that the sexual act is the bodily constituent or substratum of that multi-leveled union we call marriage, we can understand the profound significance of John Paul II's theology of the body for the ethics of sex. Given that the human person is a unity of body and soul, it follows that the body is personal. Rather than the body being extrinsic to the person, the subject and the human act, says the pope, or bodily existence being a mere instrument or extrinsic tool in the service of man's consciously experiencing self, the body is the indispensable medium in and through which I reveal myself. Human bodily existence has the character of a subject in and through which my actions are realized as bodily persons. In other words, given man's anthropological unity of body

---

275   Eduardo Echeverria, *"In The Beginning...."*, 249.

and soul, he exercises the capacity for ethical self-determination as a whole man, meaning thereby in and through his body.[276]

In such a case, the sexual act, when it does not bring about the union of spouses, involves merely an objectification for self-gratification. Echeverria, therefore, submits that only marital sex "can constitute a real union of persons... a constitutive element or substratum, a necessary condition, of marriage, which along with marital consent that conjugal intercourse fulfils, succeeds in realizing the fundamental but complex human good. "[277] The goods of marriage that he highlights are "intimate human friendship " ("person-uniting "), procreation (which is "life giving "), and the good of personal integrity, which "entails one's own bodily integrity, for one's body is integral to one's being as a human person. "[278]

In his earlier work *Love and Responsibility*, JPII had clarified, and he re-affirmed in *TOB*, that "the proper foundation for a monogamous and indissoluble marriage is… the personalistic norm together with recognition of the objective aims of marriage. From this norm also derives the prohibition of adultery in the broad sense of the word, and hence the prohibition of pre- marital relations. "[279] This text is essential because it establishes a coherency in thought and lineal agreement

---

276   Ibid., 250.

277   Ibid., 251.

278   Ibid. This view is also found in JPII's encyclical *Familiaris Consortio*, #11. Echeverria reiterates: "… the creator's sexual design for marriage, which is necessarily a bi-unitary bond of a man and a woman, that is, a two-in- one-flesh covenantal union of mutual love… the male and the female must become complementary parts of a single organism making them a two-in-one flesh in which the real good of marriage is realized or participated. That is, the marriage bond is essentially a bi-unity of husband and wife, united as complementary, bodily persons, in a two-in- one-flesh communion. Given that a man and a woman complete each other, they become an organic and thus personal unit. It is literally true that 'they become one flesh' (Gen. 2:24). The inner unity and identity of this bond is typically founded in the conjugal bi-unity of the marital act of sexual intercourse that is realized by bodily communion… This biological matrix is part of, not merely an instrument of, their personal subjectivity, focusing on acts of a reproductive kind are acts that consist in bodily union of reproductive organs of husband and wife, regardless of whether or not reproduction is actually possible. " Ibid., 259.

279   Karol Wojtyla, *Love and Responsibility* (San Francisco: Ignatius Press, 1981), 271.

with magisterial tradition. JPII in the same earlier work avers, "Only a profound conviction of the non-utilitarian value of the person (of the woman for the man, of the man for the woman) enables us to justify fully, fundamentally and irrefutably, this ethical standpoint and try to observe it in practice. "[280]

Critical Evaluations of John Paul II's Theology of the Body

The theology of the body in John Paul II's hermeneutical pedagogy over a period of time has been subjected to scrutiny and critique, as any academic and ecclesiastical/magisterial positions are wont to be. It is noteworthy also that theologies of the body and about the body have begun to spring up in more recent times, particularly since John Paul II's *Theology of the Body*, more than at any other time in history. I will offer what can be considered the basic themes in criticism of JPII's *TOB* to demonstrate the current state of intellectual discourse on the matter. It is worthwhile to note that these critiques themselves serve another purpose: that they sometimes establish that there is "movement " in doctrine because each critique takes off from a point where agreement becomes divergent, meaning that the original thesis forms grounds for contention. To prove the point, the critique will not only have to argue why the thesis is wrong, but by so doing, will have to show tangibly what other thesis is placed alongside, before, or after the original thesis. Putting these arguments side by side makes genuine development possible and visible.

Questions relating to the body, embodiment, sexuality, and marriage in the last couple of decades have become relevant in many fields of study,relating to their meaning both within theological circles and outside of it in scientific scholarship. Even though the following works are not written as a direct reaction to JPII *TOB*, from a purely scientific point of view, they offer nuance to questions about the body or its embodiment and the ways in which they affect knowledge and the experience of the self. In a co-authored article, the authors argue that in centuries of Christian theological thought, the physical body has been viewed as an integral part of personhood, which an entity is functioning in a psychosomatic union of body and soul. However, there

---

280   Ibid.

is an alternative view within the same tradition that emphasizes a radical separation of the soul from the body, associating the sinful nature with the physical body and purity with the soul, and which tries to subjugate the excesses of the sinful body. Using purely empirical data analysis and scientific means, the authors of this work investigate how religious beliefs effect sanctification in people's body image and behavior using four constructs: body satisfaction, objectification, depersonalization, and awareness. The authors surmise that "sanctification is related to a greater investment of time and energy into the sanctified domain of life. Valuing and caring for one's body requires consistent, regular attention, which might result in a lower frequency of feeling disconnected from one's body. "[281] Conversely, they make the claim that "adhering to religiously based negative attitudes towards the body, which accentuate the separation of the soul from the body, might over time result in a greater phenomenological experience of separation from the body consequently... sanctifying the body by viewing it as an integral part of oneself would be related to fewer feelings of dissociation from one's body. "[282] With several analytical graphs and tables they conclude that body theology or embodiment understood from within the Judeo-Christian tradition as sanctification has "potentially beneficial links to how people relate to their bodies, and extends them by demonstrating that sanctification is lined to experiences of the body in addition to behaviors. "[283] Their overriding conclusion is that "the religiously influenced views people hold about their bodies may impact the way they live their lives, their health, and even their psychological well-being. "[284]

In another work, similar to the one previously mentioned, Bonnie J. Miller-McLemore explores what attention theology and practical theologians pay to the idea of embodiment—the physical dimensions of bodies. She argues that the interchangeable use of phrases like *embodied knowing, embodiedness, cultural embeddedness* or *cultural constructions* of

---

281   Heather L. Jacobson, M. Elizabeth Lewis Hall, and Tamara L. Anderson, "Theology and the Body: Sanctification and Bodily Experiences, " *Psychology of Religion and Spirituality* 5, no. 1 (2013): 4.

282   Ibid.

283   Ibid., 14.

284   Ibid.

the body might be the reason for the inadequate attention to physical embodiedness of *bodies*. In stating her objective for writing this essay, she asserts, "I am interested in gaining a greater understanding of how physical (sensual, somatic, visceral, material, carnal, mortal, fleshly, vulnerable...) dimensions of our bodies inform our thought and knowing... What is the relationship between this dimension of human bodies and human knowledge? And how do actual physical bodies shape religious and theological knowledge? "[285] Miller-McLemore is convinced and argues for the position that theology and religion have inadvertently ignored physical bodies. She claims that within Western intellectual cultures, detachment from bodies is often considered a mark of spiritual maturity, of morality, and of science. She states that "late twentieth-century experts on moral and faith development who have had significant influence on pastoral theology... agree with cognitive development theorists that concrete thinking denotes immaturity rather than, for example, an imaginative or philosophically astute way of seeing the world. "[286] She goes on to question if this view "harbors unwarranted prejudice against material religion, bodies, children, laity, ritual, and the knowledge within physical acts of faith. "[287] She is of the opinion that some of the recognition given to the physical body is a recent evolution in theological studies, using an analysis from Sam Gill, a religious studies scholar, who gives the example of the heavily robed and garbed bodies of both professors and clerics as paradigmatic, the academic and liturgical gowns reflecting a deep rooted cultural belief. These garments may be re-translated as a transformation of the human body "into a cloth covered pedestal on which is prominently displayed the all-important head, the domain of mind and spirit. Everything else from the neck down is under suspicion and so its articulation, its sexuality, its fleshiness, is to be covered, suppressed, denied. "[288] She clarifies further that academic institutions themselves discipline the body to sit still and pay attention, with educational architecture and furnishing designed to limit mobility and thus to disembody. Class

---

285   Bonnie J. Miller-McLemore, "Embodied Knowing, Embodied Theology: What Happened to the Body? " *Pastoral Psychology* 62, no. 5 (2013): 751.

286   Ibid.

287   Ibid.

288   Ibid., 755.

room furnishings are designed and bolted to the floor to face in one direction only, the teacher and the chalk board. According to Miller-McLemore, "Academic bodies are not natural bodies; they are bodies disciplined from their earliest days of school to privilege the head part and to develop agnosia with respect to everything from the mouth down."[289] She avers that the intellectual thrill constitutes the relief from entanglement with bodies, what she calls the "monological subject" of the modern scientific mindset-mind operating independently of bodies. She poignantly states in her work, "The hubris of modern mind sustains a certain disdain for our mammalian bodies and the knowledge gained through them. Thus, centuries after Greek Platonic thought shaped early religious history, basic perceptions of bodies remain relatively unchanged. The physical world, like the body, is still 'a place of transit', a temporary and dangerous place to be overcome and transcended."[290]

Her conclusion is not far from that of Jackson et al. when she says, in conclusion, "Theologians have begun to see and analyze the raced body, the disabled body, bodies whose physical attributes matter, bodies whose place in time and space make a difference."[291] Keeping the physical body in tension is paramount for Bonnie Miller-McLemore, and attending to research in the sciences and their investigation of physical bodies as dialogue partners and sources of insight, coupled with the normative hermeneutical resources of the humanities, can guide newer discoveries about the human brain, hormones, genetics, evolution, and the totality of the physical body. She concludes her work by stating, "At the very least, we have witnessed the complexity and necessity of taking physicality, biology, evolution, and neurology more seriously."[292]

Judith Butler theorizes in her work that the materiality of the body is constructed by cultural determinism prediscursive of 'sex' which acts as the reference point or in relation to how socially gender is constructed and produced. Butler argues that the question of the materiality of

---

289   Ibid.

290   Ibid.

291   Ibid., 758.

292   Ibid.

the body is linked to the performativity of gender, a category that is always normative. Sex/gender is a construct which materializes through time, "the regulatory norms of 'sex' work in a performative fashion to constitute the materiality of bodies and more specifically, to materialize the body's sex, to materialize sexual difference in the service of the consolidation of the heterosexual imperative. "[293] In doing her *queer theology*, Butler opines that "The forming of a subject requires an identification with the normative phantasm of 'sex', and this identification takes place through a repudiation which produces a domain of abjection, a repudiation without which the subject cannot emerge. "[294] Butler queries that within the culturally, politically and linguistically constructed gender idea, how and to what ends bodies are constructed (or not constructed), to what ends do bodies that materialize as other support bodies that materialize the norm, then qualify as bodies that matter.[295] Butler goes further to question,

> How does that materialization of the norm in bodily formation produce a domain of abjected bodies, a field of deformation, which, in failing to qualify as the fully human, fortifies those regulatory norms? What challenges does that excluded and abjected realm produce to a symbolic hegemony that might force a radical rearticulation of what qualifies as bodies that matter, ways of living that count as 'life,' lives worth protecting, lives worth saving, lives worth grieving.[296]

---

293   Judith Butler, *Bodies that Matter: On the Discursive Limits of Sex* (London: Routledge, 1993), 2.

294   Ibid., 3.

295   Ibid., 16.

296   Ibid. In Margaret Farley's *Just Love*, she develops theological anthropology of embodiment. In her understanding of social relatedness, Farley agrees with Butler that culture impacts how we perceive the gendered body. However Farley states that the human body is not a passive slate on which society imprints meaning, "created by God, sustained in being by God, offered an unlimited future by the promises of God in Jesus Christ, each human person – embodied and inspirited…the body as well as the soul is engaged by God's grace. " (Cf. Margaret A Farley, Just Love, 131)

Butler rejects the kind of social construct that creates 'bodies' in difference to other 'bodies' in such a way that some bodies matter and become oppressive of other bodies that are marginalized and doe s not matter.

Father Charles Curran is perhaps the foremost theologian known for critiquing and highlighting John Paul II's moral theology and theology of the body. As is evident in his critique of the encyclicals of JPII in Chapter 1 of this work, his expertise will be relied on as an approach to a fundamental theological critique of the theology of the body, especially concentrating on human sexuality within marriage, as well as a platform for a critique of the theological foundations for JPII's theological "building blocks." The first ground of Curran's critique is the argument that JPII's *TOB* is not based on a systematized approach because many areas remain unclear. These deficiencies are explored under the following four headings; first, the idea of the theology of the body, generally, as developed by JPII does not serve as a theology for all bodies. In Curran's view, JPII's *TOB* speaks to heterosexual bodies without addressing whether this is the only meaning of sexuality for the body. There are single people, widowed people, and same- sex couples to whom his theology of the body does not speak, to making it less a theology of the body and more of the nuptial body. Second, Curran believes there is an overemphasis on the lust of the flesh, even though JPII clearly denounces a Manichean dualism between body and soul. JPII continually references and devotes a section to both the passage from the Sermon on the Mount about looking at a woman lustfully and thereby committing adultery with her in one's heart, and Paul's text in 1Cor. 12:18-25,thereby building an idea of a persistent opposition in the heart between the spirit and body. Therefore, the "man of lust " after original sin is unable to subordinate the flesh under the guidance of the spirit as was possible in the state of original innocence. JPII necessarily turns to the question of discipline and self-control against concupiscence and lust. According to Curran, "John Paul II's incomplete discussion of concupiscence, lust and self-control seems too one-sided. Yes, sin affects the body; but it also affects the spirit. Sin does not necessarily bring about an opposition between the higher and the lower parts of the human person.... "[297] He draws the conclusion that there is no absolute necessity for the sexual senses and passion to be controlled by reason as they also have the tendency to point to the good even though they are plagued by sin. He makes the assertion that JPII in his *TOB* gives the impression that passion and sexual pleasure are always in need of taming. "The pope does not seem to acknowledge a fundamental goodness about sexuality... There is just an occasional remark along more positive lines, but the heavy emphasis of the talks remain on the negative reality of sexual passion and the need for spirit and reason to control it. "[298]

Third, Curran questions JPII's understanding of human love. For Curran, because of the lack of a systematized approach mentioned earlier, human love is understood as the contrast between the selfless gift of self and the selfish use of the other for sexual self-fulfillment as if this "self-gifting " does not entail some human fulfilment and sexual pleasure. Curran contends that JPPII is to be commended for developing the idea of marriage as mirrored after the covenant between Israel and God, and Christ and the Church in the incarnation and death of Jesus, commonly interpreted as "agape " love. JPII develops a Platonic and philosophical understanding of "eros " as erotic love and uses the Song of Songs from the Bible to present this love as another form of human love. In this way, erotic love is no longer viewed as something completely negative but a good in itself. Curran's disagreement with JPII stems from what he posits as JPII's inability to develop the mutuality and reciprocity parts of marital love in his talks. Curran avers, "John Paul II does not discuss at length the proper love of self in marriage... the emphasis on love as a sincere gift of self—together with a narrow focus on Genesis—results in a somewhat romantic, narrow, and unreal understanding of marriage in its total life context. "[299] Curran asserts that it is thinking like this from the past that has limited the life, especially of married women, to the sphere of the home solely as wives and mothers without any consideration for their individual existence outside of their roles as married persons/

---

297   Curran, *Moral Theology of John Paul II*, 170.

298   Ibid.

299   Ibid., 172.

bodies. Fourth and finally, Curran comments on the lack of proper treatment of sexual pleasure in JPII talks. He argues that JPII's over insistence on self-control and the control of reason over the "unruly" passions and emotions, and the negative attitude associated with sexual pleasure, makes it difficult for him to develop this aspect of conjugal sexual encounter.

Similar to Curran's critique of JPII's use of scripture in Chapter 1, in this section Curran critiques JPII's use of scriptures on different grounds. With specific reference to the use of scripture in developing the Wednesday catechesis, Curran opines that naturally, JPII uses scripture to support existing Catholic teachings. As an academic metaphysician, he sees in the first account of creation in Genesis a deeply metaphysical content, but here again, Curran believes, he interprets scripture in the light of his own academic interests and presuppositions. Curran points out that in the pope's appropriation of the two texts from the New Testament (Mt. 19 and 1 Cor. 7), he uses only half a text without referring to what later Catholic theology calls the "Pauline privilege, "which gives grounds for remarriage and may be seen as such since it can contradict the pope's position and condemnation of divorce in all cases. Curran accuses JPII of ignoring other sources of moral wisdom and knowledge that have consistently characterized Catholic theological and moral tradition:for instance, lack of the development in the Natural Law theory and contemporary experience, especially in the light of the *sensus fidelium* (the sense of the faithful), which the Church recognizes as valid source of wisdom and truth.

Methodologically, Curran points again to a lack of synthesized historical development and consciousness, which remains a largely static and classicist methodology and which makes Christian marriage the same at all times and in all places by insisting that the words of Christ essentially refer to every man of every time and place. However, historically, it is known that many changes have taken place with reference to marriage even in its acceptance as a sacrament which did not happen until the Second Lateran Council of 1139,becoming explicit with the Council of Verona in 1184.[300] More important is the

---

300   Ibid., 180-81.

issue of the dissolution of marriage, in reference to which Curran uses John Noonan's work *Power to Dissolve* to point out that it was not until the end of the twentieth century, according to Catholic Canon law, that the Church could dissolve five types of marriages.[301]

On the question of virginity and celibacy in the Church, Curran asserts that because JPII bases his understanding on the lives of Jesus and Mary, and orients it to eschatology, the traditional superiority of the celibate life over marriage is necessarily located wholly on its link to the kingdom of God. There seems then to be a division of the Christian community into two camps of those who are "perfect" owing to continence and those who are "less perfect" because they are married and engage in the gift of their conjugality. Curran acknowledges that JPII tries to nuance this position by teaching that perfection comes about in the obedience to the rule of perfect love of God and of neighbor. Vatican II also recognizes a universal call of all Christians to holiness and perfection. Curran summarizes this position as a perception of the fundamental and primary vow of every Christian, like the vow at baptism. All other vows, both at marriage or for religious life, "simply specify the basic baptismal vow and indicate the means by which one is going to strive for holiness."[302] Finally, Curran looks at JPII's understanding and use of complementarity and how it affects women's vocations. Curran states that in the bridegroom-bride analogy, the traditional Catholic belief that women "receive" love in a passive role in gender differentiation is the basis upon which the subordination of women takes place. It is according to this same kind of argument that JPII resists the non-inclusion of women in the

301 Ibid., 182. Curran lists the following five types of marriages as dissolve-able; 1.A marriage that is virginal by vow, agreement or intent, and is contracted by two baptized persons, is dissoluble by religious profession and papal dispensation. 2. A marriage that is sexual in intent, contracted between two baptized persons, and unconsummated by sexual intercourse is dissoluble by religious profession or papal dispensation. 3. A consummated marriage between two baptized persons, but with limited or negative procreative intent, can be declared invalid at the option of the courts. 4. A marriage impermanent by intention, custom or assumption, even though contracted by two baptized persons, and consummated by sexual intercourse, can be declared invalid at the option of the courts. 5. A marriage that is sexual in intent, contracted by at least one baptized person, and consummated by sexual intercourse can be dissolved by the conversion and remarriage of the unbaptized partner in certain cases or by papal dispensation in all cases. (The only indissoluble marriage is one contracted between two baptized persons, which is consummated and into properly.)

302 Ibid., 186-87.

rank of ordained priesthood in the Catholic Church. Curran's second problem with the idea of complementarity as used in JPII's *TOB* is an overemphasis on the "dignity and vocation of women" which is limited to their maternal and family roles. This is found in other encyclicals and writings of JPII, in which attention is not given to possible roles for women in the public sphere.

Thirdly, Curran accuses JPII of putting women on a pedestal far removed from reality and the everyday struggles of life by asking women to rise to their vocation of bringing dignity to conjugal life and assuring the protection of the moral dimension of cultural life. Finally, JPII's treatment of the role of self-giving and service in the life of women (outside of mutual self-donation), Curran believes, places them in a position of self-subservience for life with little or no consideration for their own proper and individual self-love and personal fulfilment in life.

Curran is also quick to acknowledge that JPII was a universal catechist and not a purely systematic theologian. Notwithstanding these critiques, the pontiff's work has moved the tradition forward in many ways, challenging the "Church in the modern world" to explore newer language and narratives to express to contemporary postmodern humanity why the Church teaches what she teaches, especially in the area of ethics and morality.

Even though Mary Shivanandan's work can be considered pro JPPII/*TOB*, she still critiques his treatment and interpretative schema of what it means to be male and female, spouse or parents. She suggests that the difficulty might have arisen because of the emphasis JPII places on each dimension in different contexts. In Shivanandan's view, the Pope sometimes seems to place mother before spouse, which obscures the recognition of woman first as a person, then spouse and then mother. In line with the overall vision of *TOB*, it is in this realization of personhood that the woman can then fulfil her role as spouse and mother. In addition, the first step of realizing the person logically leads to JPII's treatment of Ephesians 5 concerning the mutual roles of bride and bridegroom. Shivanandan's critique on this point is relevant and worthy of note because JPII's *TOB* is considered the first instance in which adequate consideration is placed on personalism.

Susan Ross, among many other contemporary women theologians, speaks up for the feminist position to decry what feminists claim is modern day patriarchy couched in newer theological language, which still fails to take into account the *sacrality* of the feminine body. In her work, Ross takes for her point of departure the inadmissibility of women to priestly ordination in Roman Catholicism and Orthodoxy— the most sacramental traditions in Christian history. This she claims "perpetuates the ontological distinction between clergy and laity (which is also a distinction between the 'male' and 'female' elements in the Church.) "[303] In Ross's view, recent theological efforts influenced by phenomenology, such as the works of Hans Urs von Balthasar, Louis Boyer, and John Paul II, moved away from a sacramental theology of the body which was mainly male oriented and hierarchical. Ross claims, however, that they remain essentially within the frame work of the ontological difference of male/female dichotomy. She calls this theology a retrieval of the metaphysics of activity and receptivity, which remains rigidly traditional. Taking phenomenology as a point of departure, these contemporary theologians perceive male bodies as "source" in generation and the female as "potential." In this symbolism, by linking God to the active source and humanity to the receptive and coupled with the bridal imagery, especially as espoused by John Paul II in his encyclicals, this analogy reinforces the idea of the nature of women as receptive, as stated in John Paul II's encyclical *Mulieris Dignitatem*: "The bridegroom is the one who loves. The bride is loved: it is she who receives love, in order to love in return. "[304] Ross argues that this sort of ambivalence and ambiguity about "bodiliness" on the part of these (male) theologians ultimately result in an ontological dualism which separates reality into opposing spheres that are mutually exclusive of one another.

Feminists note that both incarnational and sacramental theology in Catholic tradition have laid more emphasis on male bodies so as to create a history of "sacramental sex discrimination. "Ross argues that as things stand currently, incarnational and sacramental theology is hollow if the denigration of women's bodies remain, if there is a

---

303   Susan A. Ross, " 'Then Honor God in Your Body' (1 Cor. 6:20): Feminist and Sacramental Theology on the Body, " *Horizon*, 16, no. 1 (1999): 8.

304   Quoted in Ross, "Then Honor God, " 11.

persistent proscription against female bodies in terms of coming into contact with the holy, if women continue to be classified as ontologically different from and consequently inferior to men, and when negative sexual matters continue to symbolize women to men. In which case, the body of Christ suffers a dualism and remains incomplete. Ross also explicitly rejects the idea of "complementarity" because of the ways in which she sees complementarity valued. Quoting Mary Jo Weaver,[305] she posits, "I interpret 'complementarity' as 'completing' or 'mirroring,' which suggest a nature not complete in its own right. It would follow therefore, that complementarity and inferiority are at least subliminally linked. "[306] Interestingly, Ross refers to the work of Naomi Goldenberg, who depends on Freud's psychoanalysis to argue that human beings are essentially physical creatures whose emotional and mental experiences are derived from bodiliness. This way of perceiving the body overcomes the alienation of body and soul caused by the dualism created by Western philosophical and religious thought. Ross quoting Goldenberg states, "In order to stop disparaging the body, we might well have to give up all theism and take our inspiration from ideas which see human beings as nothing more (or less) than human. "[307] The implication here is that Goldenberg sees dualism as dangerous for women's self-understanding; therefore, theism within the Western philosophical and theological understanding must be abandoned to put a stop to this sexual disparagement against women's bodies and create a purely new humanism.

In all of the foregoing, Ross seeks to relocate a feminist theology that reacts against the alienation of the dualism of spirit over matter, male over female and mind over body. To keep this structure in place is to erase the ancient ideas of the Gnostics and Manicheans, and to perpetuate sexism. According to Ross, "What is unspoken in this understanding of the body is its very ambiguity: that is, its toleration of different and even possibly conflicting meanings. "[308] For many feminist theologians, the "self" means the unity of these diverse and ambiguous elements

---

305   Mary Jo Weaver, *New Catholic Women: A Contemporary Challenge to Traditional Religious Authority* (San Francisco: Harper and Row, 1985), xiv.

306   Quoted in Ross, 20.

307   Ibid., 22.

308   Ibid., 23.

of selfhood, the physical and spiritual. She asserts that "[f]eminist theology thus tolerates bodily differences and bodily ambiguity without sacrificing distinctions. Difference is not to be overcome or placed in a hierarchy but valued as distinctive and contributing to the richness and variety of human experience. Ambiguity is not to be dismissed or resolved dualistically, but explored as a way of amplifying and correcting the ways in which human experience is interpreted. "[309] Ross concludes that even though sacramental theology informed by feminism remains largely untried, yet feminists' sacramental understanding and appreciation of the spiritual dimension of the physical reveals some recurring fundamental themes. This understanding of the self is seen as "interrelated, historically situated, and embodied—that constitutes feminist theological anthropology. " She concludes by saying, "What I have described here as a feminist critique of the sacramental tradition's understanding of the body is not a whole sale rejection of any principle of sacramentality. It is rather…a differentiated and historical understanding of the person which includes (or should one say 'incorporates') a concern for the body.... "[310]

John Nelson is widely recognized and acknowledged as one of the foremost contributors to the development of body theology and human sexuality in America. In one of his seminal works,[311] he argues for the position that taking bodily and sexual experiences seriously will help to reshape contemporary understanding of a theology of sexuality. He speaks of how theological perceptions and categories intersect with what it means today to be "a body " within the body of Christ. He offers a historical analysis which locates the churches of the twenty-first century in the Victorian nineteenth century where everything sexual is reduced and located within the inner sanctums of one's privacy. Outside of privatizing the body, Victorian sexuality also privatized the spirit with an interesting twist to the Victorians' understanding

---

309   Ibid., 24.

310   Ibid., 27.

311   John B. Nelson, "On Doing Body Theology, " *Theology & Sexuality* 2 (1995): 38–60.This was a keynote address given at the *Theology & Sexuality* Conference, University of Newcastle upon Tyne. September 22, 1994. Parts of it are also available in *The Intimate Connection* (Philadelphia: Westminster Press, 1989; London: SPCK, 1992), Chapter 6.

of the body-spirit split; there came a dramatic shift in the notion of Romanticism in terms of what it means to be male or female. Women suddenly were no longer viewed as the carnal opposite to men. They were now more spiritual, more religious, and more moral than men. This Victorian habit of putting women on a pedestal was bourgeois, white, upper class, and elitist;it did not include working class women in the "sweat-shops. " Yet they were less rational than men, and their place was still in the private sphere of the home and at most the Church. This privatization has met newer challenges in contemporary sexual issues because individual bodies exist within the public sphere and within the idea of creation and redemption.[312] Nelson writes, "Thankfully, in recent years, mainline churches in the UK, the US, and elsewhere have increasingly recognized the public character of many sexuality issues. "[313] For this reason, "churches have attempted to speak and act on such issues as gender and orientation justice, sexual abuse, commercialization of sex, family planning, population control, abortion, new reproductive technologies, teen pregnancy, pornography, and sexually transmitted diseases, including HIV/AIDS. "[314] It is, therefore, self- evident that questions of sexuality today are no longer a "Victorian secret " or in the private sphere but both public and communal.

Nelson argues further that sexual theology is dialogical because it is born out of a common human sexual and bodily experience that has become part of our public discourse. He advocates for embracing embodiment not "as curse or affliction, nor as incidental to our search for meaning, but as opportunity to learn the poetry of mortal dwelling and, understanding more of that poetry, to live differently. "[315] This, he says, can be done by paying attention to three central Christian affirmations of the way of faith: "the paschal mystery of Christ – incarnation, crucifixion and resurrection. "[316] This model allows theology to speak to a society in which the distortion of sexuality, especially in the light of the subjugation of one gender to the other,

312   Nelson, "On Doing Body Theology, " Ibid.
313   Ibid, 41.
314   Ibid.
315   Ibid., 46.
316   Ibid.

is a question of power, fear and vulnerability. In Nelson's words, this vulnerability "so pronounced in heterosexism and male homophobia – are deeply connected with such sexually transmitted social diseases as violence, racism and environmental deterioration... It may yet be that the conversation of our sexual bodies with the Christic meaning of the cross will illuminate them further. "[317] In this way Nelson imagines a sexuality that encapsulates all bodies, including the body of the created order around us. His vision of an integral sexuality leaves the door wider open and encapsulates the "other " and "things, " thereby challenging the traditional Christian approach to sexuality as limited to humanity with a superior role granted to the male gender over the female.

Conclusion

When either TOB is critiqued directly or questions about the human person, embodiment, sexuality, and marriage are raised, both are volatile and heavily contested battle grounds, and more so in the conversation between postmodern liberal humanism and doctrinal orthodoxy. A careful read of JPII's work shows a passionate yet highly intellectual exploration of matters that are of the utmost significance and importance to both the celestial and earthly domains. John Grabowski summarizes JPII's seminal corpus, *TOB*, and his other works thus:

> The common thread which unites all of John Paul's teaching...is a focus on the human person in the light of the mystery of Christ. While much of the teaching of Paul VI in *Humane Vitae* was based on an appeal to the natural law, John Paul II consistently bases his teaching, not only on the dignity of the person, but on biblical revelation. Thus it is primarily an exposition of various biblical texts which frames the teaching offered within the catechesis on the theology of the body, *Mulieris Dignitatem*, and *Evangelium Vitae*. This is consistent with the Pope's teaching as a whole. Whether grounding his understanding of morality

---

317   Ibid., 55.

within the invitation to discipleship which Jesus extended to the rich young man of Mathew 19 (cf. *Veritatis Splendor*), or his theology of work within the opening chapters of Genesis (cf. the social in *Laborem Exercens*), John Paul II has attempted to make the human person revealed in the light of Christ the basis of the Church's teaching in sexual, social and medical morality.[318]

John Paul II's *Theology of the Body* represents today the current magisterial position on human sexuality, marriage, and sex. There is no doubt that the pope brings a new dimension, a new vision, and a new language into how we perceive and converse on the Church's position and the liberal-modernist position. As it is evident from the last section of this chapter, there is still a lot to unpack and re-investigate, especially in the light of newer moral and ethical questions of our time. Whatever these questions might be, John Paul II has opened a greater avenue to discussing these issues, doctrinally, theologically, philosophically, and with a new humanism.

---

318   John Paul II, *TOB: Human Love*, 20.

CHAPTER THREE

NATURAL LAW, CONTEMPORARY THINKING, AND MARRIAGE AS A BASIC GOOD

This chapter considersquestions of sexuality and marriage in light of natural law, with special attention to Thomas Aquinas and the philosophers/theologians Germain Grisez and John Finnis.The Aristotelian/Scholastic natural law theory vis-à-vis the attempt at reformulation from the new proponents of natural law is too wide a field for extensive study here. Thus,this chapter will be limited to an overview for purposes of situating natural law theory in relation to traditional Catholic doctrine on marital and sexual morality. This material is also reviewed by way ofsupporting the argument that natural law theorists across the ages all agree and perceive that marriage and human sexuality is a basic human good.

Natural law theory has enjoyed a revival[319] in the last few decades in such fields as moral philosophy and theology.The resurgence of the natural law debate inadvertently re-sparked an age old moral discourse which is argued along two major lines: whether the natural law theory

---

319   Some theorists like Leo Strauss, George Sabine, and J.B. Schneewind argue that scholastic natural law theory collapsed entirely and that its resurgence is the birthing of the new natural law theory. However, some others like David Braybrook argue otherwise. Braybrook states, "My contention that the core of St. Thomas' natural law theory survives in a successful natural law theory upheld by the modern authors... in the seventeenth and eighteenth centuries... [But] became secularized as a rationalistic theory before being displaced by an empirical approach to ethics... [It] was superseded and lost from sight; but did not collapse. The empirical foundation proclaimed for it was not a complete innovation, since it was foreshadowed in earlier authors- in St. Thomas... and clearly revived by Hobbes and Locke. David Braybrook, *The Natural Law Modernized* (Toronto: University of Toronto Press, 2001), 17.

needs divine causality or can exist without it.[320] Contested is the question of the relationship between natural law (in the sense in which it is understood within moral philosophy when it gives an account of the human good) and its theological implications. This contention centers on the relationship between faith and reason, and nature and grace.[321] A philosophical and theological controversy on this issue resonates with reformation thinkers like Martin Luther and Calvin. They in turn build their reflections on previous works of Suarez, Grotius and Pufendorf. Intellectualism or voluntarism became a way of exploring the necessity of theism as an essential aspect of natural law thinking; for Luther and Calvin, "morality as such concerns human life on earth. It extends no further... And it can have no hold on God."[322]

---

320   "[Aquinas's] natural law doctrine is embedded in a larger philosophical and theological context. For instance, natural law theory requires a normative view of nature, one that implicitly rejects a purely mechanistic natural science in favor of a philosophy of nature that appeals to formal and final causality. An account of natural law also requires certain metaphysical and theological presuppositions since it presumes that nature is governed by divine providence. " John Goyette, Mark Latkovic and Richard Meyers (eds.), *St. Thomas Aquinas and the Natural Law Tradition: Contemporary Perspectives* (Washington, DC: The Catholic University of America Press, 2004), ix.

321   Ibid.

322   J.B. Schneewind, *The Invention of Autonomy: A History of Modern Philosophy* (London: Cambridge University Press, 1998), 36. Samuel Pufendorf's voluntarism seem to encapsulate Luther and Calvin's later position, as it is stated by J.B. Schneewind, "... voluntarism itself bears on two major aspects of moral theory. It affects both our understanding of the ontological position of morality in the universe, and our understanding of our moral relation to God.

The ontological significance of the doctrine of moral entities is fairly definite. It is a major effort to think through a new understanding of the relation of values and obligations to the physical world. It presents a new response to the developing scientific view of the world as neutral with respect to value. Accepting the concept of a purely natural good dependent on the physical relations of things to humans, [Pufendorf] refuses to see it as the sole kind of value, and insists that moral norms and conventional values of all kinds are conceptually independent of it... Moral entities are inventions, some of them divine, most of them human. Their ontological status gives us no reason to doubt their ability to serve their purpose.

...Only voluntarism leaves God untrammeled... and what makes Pufendorf's voluntarist account of the construction of morality so striking, is that humans are accorded the ability to construct functioning moral entities in just the way that God does, and just as efficaciously. It takes God to get the process started; but God has made us so that constructive willing is part of our normal rational activity... That God keeps watch on his creation does not entail that we should expect any special help from him. " Cf. p. 139-140

Historically, natural law theory (NLT) is traced back to the Stoics, with definite historical links to the pre-Socratic schools, Plato, Aristotle, and other Greek philosophers.Broadly, in Stoic natural law theory we find "concepts of divine governance, of rationality or *logos* embedded in nature, universal human equality and brotherhood... and harmonizing oneself with nature. "[323] Timothy O'Connell avers that Aristotle's *Nichomachean Ethics* in some sense depends on the natural law for its validity, but Aristotle did not use the exact term or anything of its equivalent.In his *Rhetoric*, Aristotle refers to an unchanging universal law,[324] and this passage is often quoted to ground Aristotelian natural law theory.The "law which is binding on all men " seems to establish a foundation for the natural law in Aristotle.Howard Kainz finds Plato ambiguous with regard to the natural law.Kainz states that in the *Republic*, Plato offers an approximation by analogy "in his discussion of the formal idea of justice as 'the just by nature *(to phusei dikaion).*' "[325] Kainz therefore concludes that in Plato,the concept of an ideal abstract "divine " law, existing prior to all human affairs, bears a resemblance to NLT; they are an "adumbration of some higher law, they fall short of an attempt to develop an explicit theory of the natural law. "[326] Stoic philosophers, later explicating Aristotle, developed the theory that they defined as "an objective reality placed on human kind to conform to the giveness of reality. "[327] The Roman civilization, building on preexisting Greek thinking, developed the idea of natural law further as "the law of the natural order and human nature and, in fact, compared and contrasted that law with the other

---

323   Howard P. Kainz, *Natural Law: An Introduction and Re-Examination* (Chicago, Illinois: Open CourtPublishing Company, 2004), 13.

324   "Universal law is the law of Nature. For there really is, as everyone to some extent divines, a natural justice and injustice that is binding on all men, even on those who have no association or covenant with each other... Not of today or yesterday it is, but lives eternal: none can date its birth. Nay, but, an all-embracing law, through the realms of the sky Unbroken it stretcheth, and over the earth's immensity. " Aristotle, *Rhetorica*, as quoted in Kainz, 6.

325   Ibid., 5.

326   Ibid.

327   Timothy E. O'Connell, *Principles for a Catholic Morality* (San Francisco: Harper & Row, 1990), 150.

laws of their experience. "[328] From Cicero[329] to the legal philosopher Gaius and the *Categories* of Ulpian, the Romans distinguished between three forms of law:*jus civile* (civil law), *jus Gentium* (law of the nations) and *jus natural* (the natural law).According to O'Connell, the Roman contribution to structuring the idea of natural law raised two questions: first, is the idea of the natural law to be understood as an obligation (perceived by reason) to conform to nature? Or, second, or is it to be perceived as an obligation (built into nature) to use reason in moral judgement?These questions, according to O'Connell, are the questions succeeding cultures have turned to repeatedly.The Stoics, depending on an Aristotelian framework, created concepts upon which the natural law theory would be defined: the idea of a divine legislator, human rationality, rights and human respect, and coordination with nature.

In Aquinas's*Summa Theologiae*, approaching the natural law can be understood within the framework of nature and the types of law synthesized by philosophy and theology.There is in Aquinas a cryptic separation of divine laws as it is set out in the scriptures and the eternal and universal laws governing the universe and rational beings.Aquinas places this eternal and universal law as workable in a union of nature and grace, thereby situating his definition within a strictly theological frame work.Every other kind of *(jus)* law is based on the natural law, which bears an imprint of the divine legislator on the heart. It follows that because human beings generally are inclined to want to achieve

---

328   Ibid., 151.

329   According to Kainz, Cicero is said to have given the first clear systematic development to the concept of natural law in *On the Republic* where he established the content of the natural law theory on which others would later build on: "True law is right reason conformable to nature, universal, unchangeable, eternal, whose commands urge us to duty, and whose prohibitions restrain us from evil. Whether it enjoins or forbids, the good respect its injunctions, and the wicked treat them with indifference. This law cannot be contradicted by any law, and is not liable either to derogation or abrogation. Neither the senate nor the people can give us any dispensation for not obeying this universal law of justice. It needs no other expositor and interpreter than our conscience. It is not one thing at Rome and another at Athens; one thing today and another to-morrow, but in all times and nations this universal law must forever reign, eternal and imperishable. It is the sovereign master and emperor of all beings. God himself is its author, its promulgator, its enforcer. And he who does not obey it flies from himself, and does violence to the very nature of man. And by so doing he will endure the severest penalties even if he avoid the other evils which are usually accounted punishments. " Marcus Tullius Cicero, *On the Republic*, translated by Charles Duke Yonge (London: H.G. Bohn, 1853), III, 22, as quoted in Kainz, Natural Law, 10-11.

ends congruent to their nature, they thereby participate in the natural law. In Kainz's estimation, natural law in Aquinas "is the actual participation in the eternal law, facilitated by human inclinations to implement the will of the divine legislator. These natural inclinations lead humans to cooperate in divine providence, even though they may not be aware that they are doing so. The primordial springboard for human participation in the eternal law is the fundamental rational apprehension that 'good is to be done and pursued, and evil is to be avoided.' This is the 'first precept' of the natural law. "[330] Natural law is a "dynamic mediating factor, which helps maintain a harmonious relationship between the divine laws on the one hand, and human laws on the other. "[331] Aquinas' contribution to the construction of the natural law theory remains invaluable up till contemporary times. In a later section in this chapter, his philosophical construct will be discussed. The later scholastics viewed natural law as "a participation or reflection of the eternal law, inciting humans at best to a voluntary implementation of the ontological, biological and rational *telos* of human nature.[332] Within Catholic tradition, this is referred to as the scholastic synthesis in the late 19th and early 20th century manuals.

There other natural law philosophers of the 16th and 17th century whose "development " or "adjusting " of Thomistic Natural Law became notable. Our consideration here includes Francisco Suarez (1548-1617), Hugo Grotius (1583-1645) and Samuel Pufendorf (1632-1694), among many others. Westerman identifies these threeas revealing the conceptual fissures underlying the Thomistic tradition are shown.[333]

---

330   Ibid., 20.

331   Ibid., 24. Bruno Schuller, SJ, defines the natural law as follows: "From the side of the knowing subject natural law can be defined as the complexus of all those moral (and legal) norms of behavior knowable to man by reason independently of God's revelation. For without access to revelation man can only rely on the natural humanity of mankind for the validity and meaning of moral commands.... Natural moral law is man's *potential oboedientialis* for the *lex gratiae*. "Bruno Schuller, "Can Moral Theology Ignore Natural Law? " in *Introduction to Christian Ethics: A Reader*, ed. Ronald P. Hamel, and Kenneth R. Himes, OFM (New York: Paulist Press, 1989), 408.

332   Ibid. 31.

333   In this section, I am deeply indebted to the works of Pauline C. Westerman, Howard Kainz, and John Goyette, Mark S. Latkovic, and Richard S. Myers. All their works are carefully referenced in this text.

Suarez's points of departure from Aquinas relate to an altered metaphysical assumption, a critique of Aquinas's proof of God from motion, and Aquinas's distinction between essence and existence.[334] Suarez's differences on these points notwithstanding, he agrees with Aquinas on a host of other issues.For instance, he agrees with the idea of a link between the natural law and Divine and eternal law.These he claims we have knowledge of first, through the natural light of reason and second, through the Decalogue.According to Westerman, Suarez refers to the last seven of the Ten Commandments and St. Paul's teaching in Romans 2:14-15 as demonstrating that God's eternal laws are written on the heart.She asserts further if one is looking for empirical confirmation of the rational application of the natural law, "the 'law of the nations' is the closest approximation to it. "[335] In his book II, *Treatise on Law*,[336] Suarez develops a hierarchy concerning the application of natural law.He differentiates between *lex naturalis* (the law of nature) and *ius naturale* (natural law).Suarez's work opened up questionsabout individual rights and locating the three fundamental inclinations of human nature as individuality, mortality and rationality. This is quite divergent from Aquinas's acceptance of what is common to humanity and all beings and animals.However, he maintains a commonality between grounding these inclinations and Aquinas/scholastic/Aristotelian moral virtues: temperance and fortitude are the same as preserving one's life, chastity parallels the preservation of the species, and prudence is associated with the use of reason to pursue social harmony and spiritual development.[337] Like Aquinas, Suarez accepts civil laws enacted by competent authority to be binding on all in their own right.However, when civil law contradicts natural law, "positive law is superseded, and can even be nullified. "[338] Suarez's effort was not so much to reconstruct scholastic natural law but an attempt to find "how the precepts of natural law can play a role in the

334   Pauline C. Westerman, *The Disintegration of Natural Law Theory: Aquinas to Finnis* (New York: Brill, 1997), 79.

335   Kainz, *Natural Law*, 26.

336   Francisco Suarez, "A Treatise on Law and God the Lawgiver, " in *Selections from Three Works by Francisco Suarez*, Vol. II, ed. James Brown Scott (Oxford: Clarendon, 1944) as quoted in Kainz, *Natural Law*, Ibid.

337   Kainz, *Natural Law*, 28.

338   Ibid, 30.

ius civile as well as in the *ius Gentium.* "[339] Suarez argues overall that human rational nature is the foundation for natural law. The divine will necessarily means that rational nature and perception have obligatory precepts.Suarez advocates rational creatures' adoption of God's laws but, as rational beings, they must exercise some *dominium*, because all law invariably deals with the regulation of humanity's dominium.

Hugo Grotius, a Dutch jurist, is aProtestant lawyer whose work lays out the *modus vivendi* for balancing the competing claims of the emerging nation-states of his time.Westerman claims he "rehabilitated natural law in the Protestant world as the proper basis for international law; he is even heralded as the founder of a new science of natural law. "[340] Grotius's development of natural law theory is seen as furthering Suarez's work, with slight theoretical innovations in the internal and overall structuring of the natural law arguments.His thesis is to reconstruct the notion of "nature " and "divine " differently from the natural law tradition.In Grotius's work, nature is the proximate source of the natural law and its starting point.Westerman states, "By establishing human nature as the intermediate link between God and His laws, he short circuited the discussion about the kind of role God plays in a concept of natural law. "[341] By following this trajectory, Grotius brings together reason, will, and nature as the basis for human nature.In Grotius, there is a distinction between natures ontologically, as understood by the scholastics, and rational nature. A distinction is also made between "volitional divine law "and the law of nature.Based on these distinctions, Kainz asserts that the notion that the natural law can be valid without the idea of God precedes Grotius.However, Kainz thinks that "Grotius made this point more explicitly and forcibly, and is frequently credited with the ground breaking proto-modern attempt to disengage natural law from the question of the existence of a divine

---

339   Westerman, *The Disintegration*, 80. Regarding Suarez's overall ambitious project of reconstruction, Westerman opines, "…. Suarez's theory should be understood as the attempt to rescue natural law from the charge that it infers norms from facts. The three pillars that together form the foundation of natural law are designed in order to avoid the impression that it is only nature (facts), or only nature plus reason (ought-statements) which give rise to moral obligations. In order to turn normative statements into real obligatory norms, additional divine obligation is needed. " 103.

340   Ibid.,129.

341   Ibid., 155.

legislator. "[342] Grotius explains that the separation of the natural law from any essentialist religious or theological links is possible owing to the social nature of *Homo sapiens* and the need to maintain civility among them for maintaining the social order. "Grotius takes the intrinsically social, altruistic nature of rational beings as the pivotal principle on which the dictates of natural law hinge—even if there were no God. " In Westerman's opinion, Grotius' construct is an idealist at the best whose essential traits do not fit harmoniously together. Westerman concludes that there is a profound ambiguity in the definition of the various traits and the relationship between these essential traits of human nature.[343] The differentiation between natural law and natural rights begin to take shape out of Grotius's thinking. In consequent history, the effect of this separation marks a crucial position in international and philosophical jurisprudence.

Samuel Pufendorf, a German philosopher, formulates a set of absolute and conditional principles to situate the human need for society and the attainment of societal equilibrium. Pufendorf's absolute duties include doing no harm to others, valuing and treating others naturally as equals, and being of value to others as long as it can be done conveniently. The "conditional " duties, according to Kainz, "have to do with mutual agreements which results in rules, contracts, and conventions to assure and maintain sociability and mutual trust. "[344] In Pufendorf's work, interpersonal relations requiring belief in God justify the obligations connected with human nature; thereby he was able to arrive at duties to one's self. Pufendorf is regarded as the "mediator " between Grotius and Hobbes without shying away from an "immutable standard on the basis on which positive law can be evaluated. "[345] He distanced himself from those who separate or try to collapse natural law and natural rights. While Suarez argues for nature as part of the foundations for

---

342   Kainz, *Natural Law*, 32.

343   Westerman, *The Disintegration*, 155.

344   Kainz, *Natural Law*, 39.

345   Westerman, *The Disintegration*, 184. This author notes further in this same section: "It seems as if the relationship between Pufendorf and Grotius faithfully mirrors that between Suarez and Aquinas.... So we might say that whereas Aquinas and Grotius emphasize the 'natural' part of the concept of natural law; Suarez and Pufendorf draw attention to the 'law' part of natural law. " 203.

natural law, Pufendorf claims an *impositio* by intelligent beings, God or a human being.In Pufendorf's thinking, on the basis of nature "it is no longer possible to arrive at rational judgements about good and evil. Moral distinctions are the products of a rational *impositio* that comes from *without* and that should be *added* to nature.God imposes moral entities; human beings add norms and values to a physical substratum. "[346] That is, the physical world around us has meaning because human beings add such value to it. Westerman restates Pufendorf's view that human beings do not impose their values upon an empty world, but that "Divine imposition is prior to human imposition.We are therefore not born as mere physical 'substrata' but as human beings…. They are already value-laden by God's imposition. "[347]

In Pufendorf's natural law, all that is known is that man's nature is governed by the law of God, which is not subject to rational inquiry. "Natural law and divine law are ontologically identical.This means that we can only judge or criticize positive law by means of that God-ordained law. "[348] These principles derived from God, which grant the grounds for the notion of *moral* rights, is universal for all human beings. Pufendorf therefore evaluates "positive law, as well as social contract that forms the basis of positive law as consistently informed by this notion of moral rights and the corresponding so-called 'absolute' duties. "[349] The notion of moral rights stabilizes positive law and dispenses a citizen's obligation to obedience or dissent if positive law were to be in conflict with individual or collective moral rights.In the conclusion to this era, the theories of Suarez, Grotius, and Pufendorf provide a key to understanding how the Natural Law Theory of Aristotle, Aquinas, and the Scholastics shifted into neo-liberal and political/jurisprudence natural law theories.Pufendorf's theory is seen as "the last attempt to provide a theory in which an explanation of social phenomena and a justification of these phenomena in the light of universal principles are tied together with one comprehensive theoretical frame work. "[350]

---

346   Westerman, *The Disintegration*, Ibid.

347   Ibid., 207.

348   Ibid., 224.

349   Ibid., 225.

350   Ibid., 227.

Westerman avers that after Pufendorf, two separate branches developed which had nothing in common with the natural law theory but which continue to shape the intellectual world we now inhabit more thoroughly than any natural law theory that preceded it.[351]

With Immanuel Kant and his proposal for a categorical imperative, as well as some work from contemporary natural law theorists, there is an attempt to ground the natural law purely on human reason rather than in nature.These theorists consider "nature to be completely extrinsic to reason and thus of no moral value."[352] Kant tries to account for justifying principles by which he extends the gap between "is" and "ought" on the claim that they are both logically and ontologically different.In this account, "the empirical world is irrelevant to moral discourse.Unambiguously, Kant contrasts the empirical laws of nature with normative laws that can only be supplied by reason.Inclination and passions belong to the realm of nature."[353] Here we note immediately the divergence from Aristotelian-Scholastic natural law.For Kant, hypothetical imperatives can lead to subjective goals as means, not ends, which will be intrinsically good and universally reasonable.Since Kant allows no room for nature, he therefore relies on pure reason. Kant, Bentham, and Locke's influence on this aspect is noteworthy because they influenced the crafting of the "American constitution,

---

351   Ibid. The two branches referenced here are the development of the theory of natural rights and human rights within the 17th century theoretical and political innovations.

352   Kainz, *Natural Law*, 42. Later developments in the Grisez/Finnis new natural law theory will attempt to reshape this position, as Finnis argues, ".... natural law can be understood, assented to, applied, reflectively analyzed without adverting to the question of the existence of God does not of itself entail either (i) that no further explanation is required for the fact that there are objective standards of good and bad principles of reasonableness (right and wrong), (ii) that no such further explanation is available, or (iii) that the existence and nature of God is not that explanation... They are in themselves not practical but theoretical or metaphysical questions... all add significance to the integrating good (in itself self-evident) of practical reasonableness and thus to the moral principles involved in the pursuit of that good. John Finnis, *Natural Law and Natural Rights* (Oxford: Clarendon Press, 1980), 49.

353   Westerman, The Disintegration, 233.

with its emphasis on human equality, and self-evident rights to life, liberty and the pursuit of happiness. "[354]

When "natural law " is referred to in contemporary times, its interpretation will depend largely on the tradition from which it is referenced. The Natural Law Theory has evolved overtime and can indicate the various ways in which morality, religion, politics, and society can interact and inter-mingle. "The expression 'natural law' is a familiar one in several normative contexts. Within the discipline of jurisprudence, for example, it names the most common alternative to legal positivism. In political philosophy it is frequently used to refer to theories of political obligation distinct from the prevailing social contract and natural rights views. In moral philosophy and theology, 'natural law' refers to a distinctive conception of the foundations of moral responsibility. "[355] Within these various fields, there now exist differences in the interpretation of moral and ethical codes within the natural law and theorists. Within these differing positions, the task of the natural law can be summed up as such "that there exist some supervening meta-laws, or as working toward a clarification of such laws, or as the specification of just what the laws are. "[356] Or as clarified further by Kainz, "…as one of a group of theories that emphasize the objectivity of morality…. a subset of moral norms that are not merely the products or creation of subjective intentions, but based in human nature, the nature of society, or evolving nature. "[357] Because of the

---

354   Ibid., 44. These new natural law theorists, by separating nature and reason from the idea of a sovereign divine being, resorted to practical reason. Therefore, the later definition of natural law by Finnis underlies this approach: "A sound theory of natural law is one that explicitly… undertakes a critique of practical viewpoints, in order to distinguish the practically unreasonable from the practically reasonable, and thus to differentiate the really important from that which is unimportant or is important. A theory of natural law claims to be able to identify conditions and principles of practical right mindedness, of good and proper order among men and in individual conduct. " Finnis, *Natural Law*, 18.

355   Joseph A. Komonchak, Mary Collins and Dermot A. Lane, eds., *The New Dictionary of Theology* (Wilmington, Delaware: Michael Glazier, 1988), 703

356   Kainz, *Natural Law*, xiv.

357   Ibid., xv.

varied interpretations given to "law" and "nature," the definition of the natural law is varied and often complex.[358]

One of the major divergent aspects of the natural law is that "some criticize natural law as being too closely connected with religion, in the sense that the magisterium of the Catholic Church and Catholic 'scholastic' philosophers, have traditionally promoted natural law as the paramount moral theory."[359] Within the Aristotelian-Thomist tradition,upon which the natural law theory is built in the Catholic tradition, it is seen as embracing the whole question of morality. "It is understood as the order of things assigned to man by his creator for the development of his human qualities.This order is to be rationally known and used as the basis for free action."[360] The ontological starting point of Catholic natural law theory is found in the nature of man and in the idea that there is a divine thought in the roots of all created being, in the nature and essence of things, which is to be respected by all.This principle demands of every human being a morality which is not merely juridical but is the structure of a moral order which is assigned by God to man in creation and imposed on him as the goal of self-fulfillment.[361]

Since Vatican I, the Catholic Church has continually re-affirmed through various encyclicals[362] and official Church documents that in spite of original sin, human beings "can know the norms of morals and rights independently of the words of revelation; the doctrine of the natural law is one of the foundations which Christians can use to

---

358   Michael Zuckert explains his own definition of natural law as follows, "Natural law thinking is so resilient in part because it combines in a particularly intimate way themes of moral and political philosophy. It is, of course, first and foremost, a moral theory, a theory of moral duty, but it is at the same time a theory of law, of what makes law law and gives it its binding force. Thus, natural law thinking mediates between these two spheres, the moral and legal-political, so puzzling related to each other." Michael Zuckert, "The Fullness of Being: Thomas Aquinas and the Critique of Natural Law," *The Review of Politics 69*, no. 1 (2007): 28

359   Ibid., xiii.

360   Karl Rahner, Cornelius Ernst and Kevin Smyth, eds., *Sacramentum Mundi: An Encyclopedia of Theology.* (Montreal: Herman-Herder-Foundation, 1969), 157.

361   Ibid., xiii.

362   Especially in the encyclical *Humani Generis*.

discuss ethical questions with all men. "[363] This position is clarified and understood to mean that "the ontological basis and the knowability of the natural law gives it universal validity and make it the criterion of all legislations. "[364] The tradition understands that humanity is still discovering the full essence of its being and nature;thus, knowledge of the natural law is also in a historical process that brings new perspectives, which can be more precise or altered.Within this understanding, the Church claims "that there is a true natural law and hence moral duties deriving from the nature of man which are knowable by human reason at least in their fundamental structure. "[365]

Relatively recently, because of the rapid changes in the field of ethical studies, and with greater consideration as well as opposition being directed at the magisterial position on certain issues of sexual, marital, and moral questions grounded in the natural law theory, what is regarded as "The New Natural Law Theory "[366](NNLT)has evolved. This theory offers a comprehensive and philosophically systematized argumentation against contraception, abortion, homosexuality, and other issues along such lines against which the Church has taken a stand. Catholic moralists, ethicists, and philosophers like Germain G. Grisez, John Finnis, Robert Shaw, Robert George, Joseph Boyle, and a host of others are proponents of this position.Grisez, who collaborates often with John Finnis, is generally recognized as the father of the NNLT.[367]

---

363   Rahner et al., *Sacramentum Mundi*, 158.

364   Ibid.

365   Ibid., 160.

366   Kainz, *Natural Law*, 46, states that part of the problem with developing the NLT was the necessity of maintaining the distinction between "values " and "facts " and avoiding a naturalistic fallacy of deriving an "ought " from an "is. " According to Kainz, "In the resultant, conscientious effort at developing a natural-law philosophy which starts with intelligible values rather than facts, and studiously avoids deriving any ethical conclusions from empirical facts about 'human nature,' analytic philosophers German Grisez and John Finnis have taken the lead… has taken the limelight as a new approach to natural law which conforms to prevailing standards for ethical theory. "

367   NNLT is said to be timely because it is regarded as a refutation of the attack on moral realism, which has produced quite a significant clarification of the philosophical deficiencies formerly existing in this school. Working with these philosophical clarifications with sympathizers and collaborators from the early 1960s, Grisez has evolved and can be regarded as the father of the Grisez school of NNLT.

Thomas Aquinas (1225-1274): Natural law theory generally predates Aquinas, yet his contribution to our understanding of this theory remains invaluable.In Aquinas, natural law proceeds from a human being's capacity to live and react as a rational, social, and political animal.For Aquinas, divine laws, God's self-disclosure and intervention in human history, help humanity to participate rationally as a part of a cultural whole, and human beings also make laws to guide the whole.However, he posits that "every law as far as they partake of reason, are derived from the eternal law "[368] and natural law is the "rational creature's participation in the eternal law... founded on human nature which is shared by all human beings.It regards primarily those things which pertain to human nature: .... the preservation of the species, the inclination of the good which is possessed by the human person in accordance with reason. "[369] For Aquinas, the self-evident general principles of practical reason are the primary precepts of natural law, which is theoretic reason; "the good " is the first principle to be comprehended by practical reason.Aquinas states, ".... every agent acts for an end, an end which is pursued as 'the good.' Consequently, the first principle of practical reason is founded on the notion of good, namely that good which all things seek after. Hence, the first principle of natural law: that good is to be done and pursued, and evil is to be avoided. "[370] The Catholic Church re-affirms the gnoseological background given by Aquinas to the understanding of the natural law when in *Gaudium et Spes*, she declares, "Deep within their consciences men and women discover a law which they have not laid upon themselves and which they must obey.Its voice, ever calling them to love and to do what is good and to avoid evil, tells them inwardly at the right moment: do this, shun that, for they have in their hearts a law inscribed by God. "[371] In the *Summa*, Aquinas states,

---

368   Paulinus I. Udozor, *Moral Theology in an Age of Renewal: A Study of the Catholic Tradition Since Vatican II* (Notre Dame, Indiana: University of Notre Dame, 2003), 168-9.

369   Ibid.

370   Ibid., 170 *("bonum est faciendum et presoquendum, et malum vitandum.")* For further readings on Aquinas's first principle of practical reason, among others see also John Finnis, *Aquinas: Moral, Political, and Legal Theory* (New York: Oxford University Press, 1998), 86.

371   Vatican II, *GS*, #16.

Human beings have a natural inclination to accomplish the general ends congruent with their nature, and this inclination is a mark or impression of the eternal law in which they are participating. Natural law thus is the actual participation in the eternal law, facilitated by human inclinations to implement the will of the divine legislator. These natural inclinations lead humans to cooperate in divine providence, even though they may not be aware that they are doing so. The primordial springboard for human participation in the eternal law is the fundamental rational apprehension that "good is to be done and pursued, and evil is to be avoided. "This is the "first precept " of the natural law.[372]

In developing the notion of reason and faith, Aquinas argues that they cannot contradict each other because they have God as their common source.

Key to understanding Aquinas are two approaches to the question of the natural law: first, human reason, which even though crippled by sin is yet capable of knowing the natural law, especially within the nature of the human person. Second, even though natural law is knowledge, which can be independent of divine revelation, it does not follow that it does not recognize divine revelation. Being falls within the ordering of those things apprehended by all, but within the apprehension of practical reason is the good ordered toward action.[373] According to Aquinas,

---

372   Aquinas *ST*, 1a2ae q. 94, a.2, qtd. in Kainz. *Natural Law*, 19-20.

373   I think it is important to note the following comments because of the Derivationist rereading of Aquinas in the hope of a rehabilitation. In ST. I-II Q94.4, Aquinas' natural law directs attention to a normative guidance which exists within a substantive theory of human nature. This knowledge of genuine goods of human life in their proper ordering is self-evident to those who possess the wisdom and capable of discerning truths about our common God- given human nature. Prior to the fall, the eternal law represents God's practical judgement which all could participate in, but because this participation is possible through human rationality, non-participation is also a viable option. For natural law to remain valid, rational human persons need to be able to freely accede to it. According to Aquinas, a true knowledge of conclusion about human goods are not universal, they are often tampered by cultures, and therefore, theoretical inquiry is a way of arriving at practical judgements.

every agent acts for the sake of an end, which has the character of a good, which grounds the first principle of practical reasoning on the notion of good which all rational beings desire:[374]

> Therefore, the first precept of law is that good ought to be done and pursued and that evil ought to be avoided. And other precepts of the law of nature are founded upon this principle…. there is an ordering of the precepts of the natural law that corresponds to the ordering of natural inclinations.
>
> First, man has an inclination toward the good with respect to the nature he shares in common with all substances…Second, man has an inclination toward certain more specific [goods] with respect to the nature that he shares in common with the other animals. Accordingly, those things are said to belong to the natural law which nature teaches all the animals, i.e., the union of male and female, the education of offspring, etc. Third, man has an inclination toward the good with respect to the rational nature that is proper to him… those things are related to this sort of inclination belong to the natural law, e.g., that a man avoid ignorance, that he not offend the others with whom he has to live in community, and other such things related to this inclination.
>
> Insofar as all these precepts of the law of nature are traced back to a single first principle, they have the character of a single natural law.[375]

Aquinas adds and distinguishes three component parts to practical reasoning: *synderesis*, *conscientia*, and *prudential*. In these ways Aquinas is able show how he conceives ways by which individuals deliberate

---

374   *Quod fundatur spra rationem boni quae est.*

375   Thomas Aquinas, *Treatise on Law (Summa Theologiae I-II, Questions 90-108)*, trans. Alfred A. Freddoso (South Bend, Indiana: St. Augustine's Press, 2009), 37-41.

and arrive at virtuous decisions on moral matters, and how these three components affect the legislative process. The "virtuous man " is key to understanding Aquinas's moral theory, one who possesses wisdom, one who acts according to right reason and has well-tempered affections.

Aquinas understands *synderesis* to be that pure part of the soul that is untouched by original sin, that "passive and innate disposition by which we can understand the starting point or 'seed-bed of all subsequent knowledge,' the first principle of practical reasoning. "[376] *Synderesis* is said to be the human power of understanding at its highest peak, known as the "angel's eye. " This is an ability to grasp things at once, a guarantee of non-error; it links human beings with higher creatures and separates them from irrational creatures. It also guarantees choices made in freedom (free will); the ability to freely choose how to pursue and do that which is good.[377] Aquinas avers that *synderesis* also grasps principles; in a first instance, the first principle of the natural law, "good is to be done and pursued while evil is to be avoided, " and in the second instance, he refers to the principles that are natural inclinations in creatures—sociability, self-preservation, and a desire to know God.[378]

Conscientia is the practical application of synderesis to everyday circumstances that arise which is not to be confused with conscience. In Aquinas' thinking, *conscientia* "is associated with some 'inner voice', innate or acquired, that informs us about the moral rectitude of our actions.[379] "Aquinas defines conscientia further as "essentially an activity, the operation through which general rules are translated or processed into more specific rules and eventually into conclusions, which refer to particular cases or circumstances. "[380] Aquinas points

---

376   Westerman, *The Disintegration*, 50.

377   Westerman, ibid., 52-53, comments that in Aquinas, *"synderesis* as the understanding of the first principle helps us to discover truths as well as to judge what we discovered. In the terminology employed by contemporary philosophers of science... the principle grasped by *synderesis* serves both as a regulative principle in the 'context of discovery' and at the same time as a principle that informs our judgement on what has been performed in the 'context of justification'. The first principle indeed serves as both 'departure' and 'arrival' in Aquinas' more imaginative terminology. "

378   Cf. ST. I, II, 13, 3.

379   Westerman, *The Disintegration*, 57.

380   Ibid.

out that the function of conscientia is comparable to synderesis: "The conclusion drawn by conscientia, just like the principles perceived by *synderesis,* play a role in both the context of discovery and the context of justification. "[381] Synderesis and conscientia orient a person in pursuing the good and in the ability to evaluate the choice of that which is good. However, the two do not have the same object:synderesis grasps the major principles, whereas conscientia draws particular conclusions to guide moral choices/behavior in daily living.Aquinas points out that human relationships are variable and contingent; therefore, some flexibility is needed in moral choice making, since the kind of certainty achievable in theoretical reasoning may not always be achievable in the practical domain. "Complete certainty cannot be reached in our conclusions concerning practical affairs, because man's nature, though essentially striving to fulfil its natural inclinations, is— accidentally— variable.Human affairs are contingent, variable, and prone to exceptions.That is why… we should not rely on demonstrations when it comes to practical reasoning. "[382]

By Aquinas' definition of **Prudentia,** "… applying general moral principles to particular conclusions regarding human conduct, "[383] it seems a replication of the function of conscientia and an overlapping of roles.Westerman clarifies that conscientia is purely cognitive while prudentia makes known the moral ideal and the fortitude to put it into action.[384] Aquinas attributes a number of virtues to the function of prudentia, but more important are its component parts/features, which includes acumen, memory, circumspection, teachability, insight, prevision, and reasoning.Westerman asserts that "reasoning " as a component part of prudentia refers to the ability to reason well, which is present in the virtuous man and is the difference between conscientia and prudentia.According to Westerman, conscientia is as different from prudentia as "speaking " is from "eloquence. "[385] She clarifies further that "… just as eloquence can only be valued in respect

---

381   Ibid., 58.

382   Ibid., 61.

383   ST II, II, 47, 6.

384   Westerman, *The Disintegration*, 62.

385   Ibid.

to the degree in which the public is actually convinced, prudentia can only be accorded to those who actually carry out the decisions which are the fruits of their deliberation. "[386] Thus, "prudentia is not only cognitive, but has a link to action as well. The prudent man first 'takes counsel,' then forms a judgement, and finally commands himself to execute his decision. "[387]

Using the analogy of a talented and skillful artist for prudentia, Westerman posits that while synderesis makes it possible to grasp the divine [style],[388] conscientia specifies requirements and prescribes all that is applied to particular situations. But prudentia, applied to moral matters, allows for an imperfect humanity and world, as Aquinas grants a certain freedom for deliberation about how to act in contingent circumstances.[389] In this sense, the three stages of practical reasoning enumerated above include as the first step, *synderesis*, the perception and understanding of divine law; second, *conscientia*, a syllogistic system which helps to determine moral inferences from general principles; and third, *prudentia* as the wisdom that helps the individual and is necessary for the perception of the good and the ability to act virtuously. Westerman, however, asserts we should not over emphasize man's rational capacity, which is limited to the discovery of the main principles but may not always be able to infer indubitable rules from these general principles. The rational being can miss the mark in deductions and thus still fail to grasp divine moral principles.

On the question of whether all acts of virtues belong to the law of nature, Aquinas espouses that because the rational soul is the proper form of a person and every person has a natural inclination to act in accord with reason, this translates to acting in virtue. "Hence, in this sense all the acts of the virtues belong to the natural law, since the faculty of reason proper to each man dictates by nature that he act virtuously. "[390] In Question 94, article 4 of the *Summa*, Aquinas treats

---

386   Ibid., 63.

387   Ibid.

388   Westerman adopts the use of *style* as an aesthetic value to clarify Aquinas' concept of the eternal law. Ibid., 29

389   Ibid., 65.

390   Ibid., 42.

the question if there is a single law of nature for everyone. For Aquinas, the natural law is universal because with respect for the universal principles of either speculative or practical reasoning, there is only one possible outcome; the same truth known naturally to all. Aquinas states,

> Therefore, one should claim that with respect to its first universal principles, the law of nature is the same for everyone both with respect to correctness and with respect to knowledge. On the other hand, with respect to various particular (rules), which are, as it were, the conclusions of those universal principles, the law of nature is the same for everyone in the greater number of cases *(ut in pluribus)* both with respect to correctness and with respect to knowledge, and yet there can be exceptions in a fewer number of cases *(ut in paucioribus)* both (a) with respect to *correctness*, and this because of certain impediments (just as the generable and corruptible natures are defective in a fewer number of cases because of impediments), and also (b) with respect to *knowledge*, and this because the faculty of reason has been perverted in some people by passion or by a bad natural condition.[391]

On the immutability of the natural law, Aquinas argues that the "natural law dates from the very beginning of the rational creature. Neither does it change over time, but remains immutable."[392] However, Aquinas clarifies that through the divine and sometimes by human law, as has been noted in history, certain things useful to human life have been added to the natural law by way of addition. Conversely, with respect to natural law's secondary principal, changes can occur by subtraction but remain always unchangeable with respect to the first principle. Kainz surmises that ultimately, "natural law for Aquinas is a dynamic mediating factor, which helps to maintain a harmonious

---

391   Ibid., 44-45.

392   Ibid., 46.

relationship between divine law, on the one hand, and human law on the other. "[393]

If any set of arguments can be truly construed as a critique of Aquinas, it is generally within the area of teleology in terms of the distinctions between "nature, " "natural, " "unnaturality, " the meaning of "law, " and the idea of perversion. Natural law theorists from Aquinas's era debated the question from a totally different history and context. For instance, Aquinas's natural law theory forms only a part of a larger treatise on law. The entire treatise was an attempt to argue philosophically for the theistic sovereignty of a divine law giver, in whose law every other law participates. Contemporary theorists live in a post-Newtonian world of physics wherein the individual person is understood biologically and structurally, and a shift has occurred from processing the "philosophy of nature " to the "philosophy of mind. " These come from developments in genetic encoding research (DNA), understanding of the physical world around us, and even development in biblical studies as the historical-critical method. From Cicero to contemporary times, the natural law theory has relied on reason as a starting point, with or without reference to God. Most times, "the existence of God and notions of divine law are either inferred with concomitant metaphysical arguments, or taken for granted as a faith commitment complementing the ethical system. "[394] The scholastics, however, understand "natural " as the way in which a human being is born with specific innate characteristics, and morally, "natural " is perceived in the sense of the introduction of that which is extraneous to the human being, especially as it affects ethical questions. For example, the introduction of a prosthetic leg is not natural to the human body, but it is not an ethical choice nor does it prevent the injured member from fully being able to achieve its natural potency. Rather, it supports and

393   Kainz, *Natural Law*, 24. A journal essay by Peter Seipel also clarifies the relationship of the natural law not just with the flourishing of the individual but the entire community by stating, "For Aquinas, the good of justice or practical reasonableness must be protected even if it means rejecting other basic goods because the highest flourishing of the individual is inseparable from the highest flourishing of the community, the latter of which depends upon the good of justice. " Peter Seipel, "Aquinas and the Natural Law: A Derivationist Reading of ST I-II, Q. 94, A.2, " *Journal of Religious Ethics* 43, no. 1 (2015): 28-50.

394   Kainz, *Natural Law*, 88.

enhances it.Conversely, the question of artificial contraception is an "unnaturality "; and "[u]nnatural with a moral connotation has to do with a threat to the exercise of some essential property of human nature (or 'basic value'), the right to which has not been forfeited. "[395] Today, there are hardlyany references to divine laws in political jurisprudence, compared to the Thomistic era.However, Howard Kainz notes that comparing eras still points us to the fact that "progress in theorizing about human nature depends to a great extent on the relative richness of the concept of human nature taken as the starting point. "[396]

Another major disconnect between the Aristotelian-Thomistic tradition and contemporary natural law theorists lies in the conversation about the relationship between mind (soul) and matter (body).The relationship between two physical substances is known as a prime analogate for causality.Quantum mechanics, therefore, challenges the idea of mind over matter simply because the immaterial does not interact with the material. Arguments on this issue are many sided, and volumes have been written on these questions.Kainz gives what can be considered a balanced response to this seeming impasse:

> An argument with regard to natural law might follow a similar path: Possibly the prime analogate for our concept of *law* is not positive law, but the laws of our nature.These laws are expressed in the imperious and ineluctable drive to happiness, which functions as the command of all commands; likewise in the drive for self-preservation, the drive to reproduce, the drives to attain knowledge and freedom.Perhaps these are the source of our primordial experience of authoritative laws whose obedience can put us at peril of losing ourselves.Then, when we encounter laws laid down by the municipality or the state or government, we see something analogous to the imperiousness and ineluctability of our own basic impulses.Or when we see evidence of predictable and calculable tendencies in the material world,

---

395   Ibid., 60.

396   Ibid.

we understand these "laws" by comparison with analogies in our experience.... We must conclude that natural law is "law" only in the same sense that the laws of gravity and thermodynamics are laws... The worst infractions of the natural law would be acts contrary to nature—the perversions. Here one could encounter a bedrock of agreement, concerning things like parent-child incest, pederasty, female genital mutilation, cannibalism, infant sacrifice, genocide, torture; but also inevitable disagreements about other *prima facie* "perversions."[397]

There are also a few "problematic" areas in Thomistic natural law which contemporary theorists argue vehemently for and against.[398] Because the focus here is not to explore the logic of the internal philosophical disputations but rather to situate the state of affairs, some of the issues are broadly delineated,

First, the new natural law theorists consider the "is-ought" question from a metaethical perspective, in which they argue that an "ought" cannot be derived from an "is." Based on the existential nature of the human person, they argue that a deduction with regard to moral values cannot be primarily and simplistic a question of "ought." Second, the new natural law theorists propounda "fact-value" separation to apply to viable ethical theorizing. The distinction made between fact and value in this metaethic is a major value, and "the factual prohibition of disregarding this distinction is considered a valuable directive for furthering progress in ethical theory."[399] In their view, the traditional natural law theory "is susceptible to criticism, especially if the 'nature' referred to with the adjective 'natural' is considered to be something factual in which certain moral values are allegedly imbedded or

---

397   Ibid., 66-67.

398   Charles Curran, however, notes that "outside the Catholic tradition there does not exist the concept of natural law as a monolithic theory or method with an agreed-upon body of ethical content. Many thinkers have referred to natural law, but by no means have they always meant the same thing by it. In addition, they often came to different conclusions about what the natural law called for in human conduct." Curran, *The Development of Moral Theology: Five Strands* (Washington, DC: Georgetown University Press, 2013), 74.

399   Kainz, *Natural Law*, 75.

implicated. "[400] Third, the very popular and commonly pointed at "naturalistic fallacy "is based on classical natural theorists' connection of nature to morality.It is named a fallacy because contemporary natural law theorists argue against defining goods in terms of associated goods of any kind.Kainz clarifies this further: "All of these associations are subject to the 'open question' test--- 'but is x good?' ---which can always be subjected to doubt, since x is not a synonym of 'good.' To maintain that saying 'x is good' is the same as saying 'good is good' is to fall into the naturalistic fallacy. "[401] Fourth and finally, consideration is always given to contrasting the religious versus the secular version of the natural law.At the risk of unnecessary self-repetition, it is safe to conclude that this is the same argument based on ontology/teleology. The difference is between a natural law theory that has God and nature at its foundation and another that relies on human reason and argues for natural rights.

German Grisez, John Finnis and the NNLT School

Natural law theory has enjoyed a re-awakening within the last thirty to forty years, largely owing to what is now popularly referred to as the "Grisez School. " The works of the theologian Germain Grisez in the United States and his contemporary John Finnis in the United Kingdom, along with several other colleagues,are an attempt to respond to the prejudices placed against the traditional Catholic understanding of the natural law theory.These like-minded thinkers have "articulated a highly developed system of natural law built upon a sophisticated account of practical reasoning and a rich and flexible understanding of the human good. "[402] It is generally argued that the Grisez School did not immediately become accepted in mainline Catholic ethical studies due to Grisez's attack on consequentialist theories and popular Catholic "proportionalists. " The Grisez School is a reaction to the perceived inadequacies of the previous natural law theories and the

---

400   Ibid., 76.

401   Ibid., 77.

402   Nigel Biggar and Rufus Black, eds., *The Revival of Natural Law: Philosophical, Theological and Ethical Responses to the Finnis-Grisez School* (Burlington: Ashgate, 2000).

classical moral theology of the Catholic Church, which is an off shoot of scholasticism. The NNLT School argues that scholasticism is overly concerned with the law and classical moral theology's inability to "identify a sufficiently rich conception of a person's well-being (i.e., the good) to which moral principles would direct her. "[403] Grisez opposes what he calls "a logically illicit step " wherein moral theology moves deductively from fact to value, from what is to what *ought to be*.It is the articulation between these two forms of reasoning that is foundational to understanding the ideas behind the systematic application of his NNLT.

Grisez and Finnis argue that the use of theoretical reasoning is to pursue knowledge about aspects of reality while seeking to establish the truth of a proposition by testing the conformity of its content with some prior reality, and that theoretical reasoning can establish this conformity by both deductive and inductive reasoning.[404] The Grisez School develops in its NNLT a virtue ethic which is concerned about human fulfilment and common good.[405] Grisez and Finnis argue for a new approach to re-interpreting Aquinas by eradicating all interpretations from the Neo- Scholastics/Neo-Thomists; the 16th Century Spaniards, Vazquez and Suarez;Protestant contributions to the tweaking of Thomistic natural law found in Grotius, Pufendorf, Culwell, and Clarke; and,finally, the contribution of David Hume,who turned totally away from Aristotelian/ Thomistic tradition to virtue ethics.

Germain G. Grisez,in his re-articulation of what is now broadly known as NNLT, argues that he remains faithful to Thomistic natural theory.He accepts that the natural law consists of intelligible sets of

---

403   Ibid., 3.

404   Ibid.

405   Russell Hittinger is perhaps one of the foremost critics of the Grisez/Finnis school, but on this point he posits that their work constitutes a new natural law theory based on three areas: (1) An attempt to recover Thomistic natural theory which avoids standard objections raised since the enlightenment and any other inherent problems in Aquinas used by contemporary thinkers to tinker with his overall project. (2) They claim to build a systematic and comprehensive status for their position; they contend to have retrieved the systematic core of natural law theory congruent with the tradition which is also persuasive to modern critics. (3) In Grisez's account (but not in Finnis), there is an application of the new natural law theory to moral theology. Russell Hittinger, *A Critique of the New Natural Law Theory* (Notre Dame, Indiana: University of Notre Dame Press, 1987), 5.

propositions of practical reason: first, that good is to be done and evil avoided. Basic human good in the NNLTconsists of eight goods, of which five are existential and reflexive, and which accept deliberation and choice: (i)marriage, (ii) harmony in communal living, (iii) harmony in justice, (iv) harmony within one's self, (v) harmony with God or another source of human meaning and value, like religion. The other three substantive goods, which do not require choice for their existence, include (i) life, health, and reproduction, (ii) appreciation of beauty and knowledge of truth, (iii) leisure and work. These are the modes of practical reason by which everyone weighs a moral decision,without reference to the eventual decision made for right or wrong. As such, they are not moral principles, as they do not help to pre-determine, before choice, what options are morally good or bad. The second set consists of what the NNL theorists refer to as the first principle of morality in its specification or modes of responsibility, which "exclude ways of choosing and acting that ignore, slight, neglect, arbitrarily limit, or damage, destroy or impede a basic human good, excluding as well emotional and non- rationally grounded choices and actions. "[406] Another set consists of moral norms that can be verified in light of the first principle and its mode of responsibility. They identify certain kinds of moral human action which by the object of moral choice within specific alternatives are morally good or bad.

This slight derivative re-reading of Aquinas by Grisez is said to be a movement from natural law principles to specific moral norms. The distinction between the first principle of practical reasoning and the first principle of morality, even though is not directly contradictory of Thomistic natural law, yet provides a Grisez with a newer approach and articulation. In Grisez's thought, practical reason has two dimensions; one reflects on what might be done, and this is the principle of practical reasoning. The other reflects on what ought to be done: this is the principle of morality. The basic principle of morality as re-articulated by Grisez states, "In voluntary acting for human goods and avoiding what is opposed to them, one ought to choose and otherwise will those and only those possibilities whose willing is compatible with a will toward

---

406   Goyette et al., *St. Thomas Aquinas*, 144.

integral human fulfilment. "[407] It from this articulation that Grisez proceeded to the derivation of what he calls "modes of responsibility." According to Robert P. George, these modes of responsibility are formulated in a systematic way by integrating scripture and the writings of Aquinas. "The modes of responsibility are normative principles 'pinning down' the requirements of the first principle of morality. But they are not specific moral norms; that is, they are not normative propositions of practical reason identifying specific sorts of human acts as morally good or morally bad…. "[408] John Goyette and his co-editors conclude,

> …. The integral directiveness of the first principles of practical reasoning, expressed in the first principle of morality that directs us toward the ideal of integral human fulfilment, provides us with a criterion for establishing moral priorities among our interests in the basic goods of human existence. When these goods are considered from the perspective of this integral directiveness, the directiveness of unfettered practical reason, the good of religion, or of harmony between human persons and God or the more-than-human source of meaning and value is seen to have a priority insofar as commitment to this good offers human persons an overarching purpose in terms of which they can order their lives as a whole. Thus a commitment to religious truth emerges as the commitment that can integrate the whole of human life when this is conceived in the light of the demands of moral truth.[409]

---

407   Germain Grisez, *The Way of the Lord Jesus: Christian Moral Principles*, Vol. 1 (Chicago: Franciscan Herald Press, 1983), 205.

408   Robert P. George, ed., *Natural Law & Moral Inquiry: Ethics, Metaphysics and Politics in the Work of Germain Grisez* (Washington, DC: Georgetown University Press, 1998), 13.

409   Goyette, et al., *St. Thomas Aquinas*, 144-5.

In the first principle of practical reasoning, Grisez identifies eight basic forms of human flourishing which serve to identify practically what ought to be done and which he methodologically arranged to correspond to the beatitudes.[410] They include the following: (i) One should not be deterred by felt inertia from acting for intelligible goods. (ii) One should not be pressed by enthusiasm or impatience to act individualistically for intelligible goods.(iii)One should not choose to satisfy an emotional desire except as part of one's pursuit and/or attainment of an intelligible good other than the satisfaction of the desire itself.(iv)One should not choose to act out of an emotional aversion except as part of one's avoidance of some intelligible evil other than the inner tension experienced in enduring that aversion.(v)One should not, in response to different feelings towards different persons, willingly proceed with a preference for anyone unless the preference is required by intelligible goods themselves.(vi) One should not choose on the basis of emotions which bear upon empirical aspects of intelligible goods (or bads) in a way which interferes with a more perfect sharing in the good or avoidance of the bad.(vii)One should not be moved by hostility to freely accept or choose the destruction, damaging, or impeding of any intelligible human good.(viii)One should not be moved by a stronger desire for one instance of an intelligible good to act for it by choosing to destroy, damage, or impede some other instance of an intelligible good.

These eight modes of responsibility help to shape the moral life of a person and to direct moral reflection towards basic human goods by forbidding evil and encouraging the good.Grisez notes that "integral human fulfilment means a single system in which all the human goods would contribute to the fulfilment of the entire human community.... This commitment shaped by the modes of responsibility will be basic in a person's life—that is, it will be large enough to shape his or her whole life. "[411] According to Grisez,

> The eight modes of responsibility together guide action positively towards integral human fulfilment. An ideal rather than a goal, integral human

---

410   Cf. Mt. 5:3-12.

411   Grisez, *The Way of the Lord Jesus*, 222-4.

fulfilment shapes a good life by requiring that one's actions be suited to its realization (if that were possible) and ruling out actions incompatible with this. The third and fourth modes direct one away from a life of sentient satisfaction toward intelligible human goods. The first and eight modes require one to pursue some of the goods and not act against any. The sixth mode excludes a life focused on mere self-satisfaction, and the fifth requires one to treat others fairly. The seventh mode forbids revenge and so conduces to community despite the wrongs people do one another. And the second mode calls for a will towards cooperation with others in genuine community.[412]

All of these constructs in Grisez's new natural law theory aim at creating normative principles by which human beings can rationally determine and judge their own moral actions. This is Grisez's fundamental difference from Thomism; it is a movement from theistic ontology to a purely philosophical ethics concerned with rationality, basic human goods, choices, moral judgements and actions.

John Finnis collaborates with Grisez in an attempt to "rehabilitate " Thomistic natural law. They both attempt to work out a theory of natural law which, unlike the Hobbesian/Kantian revolution, has rights as a starting point.[413] First, Finnis attempts to provide a philosophical framework for the contemporary relationship between morality and

---

412   Ibid., 226.

413   John Finnis met Germain Grisez at Berkeley in 1965, who at the time was developing his new natural law theory though located within the Catholic tradition, it was constructed to be able to speak to contemporary ethical questions. Finnis collaborated with Grisez but took these ideas and applied them to legal jurisprudence. Outside of theses slight differences, their collaboration presents to us today a unified body of work. Also associated with the new natural law school are Robert P. George, Joseph Boyle, William E. May, Gerald Bradley and Russell Shaw, there work and collaboration remains essential in contemporary natural law discussion.

law.[414] This framework should give an understanding of the underlying values on which the principles of competing right claims can be determined. Second, according to Westerman, Finnis tries to articulate common values that are independent of religious orientations, presuming that such values are objective and that they can therefore be argued mainly on a philosophical basis devoid of the idea of religion or God. Third, Finnis sees society as a community with common interests as differing from a society with calculated self-interests. "Finnis shares this criticism of liberal ideology with many contemporary 'communitarian' philosophers.Most of these writers, however, phrase their criticism by means of the alleged contrast between virtue-theories and rights-theories. "[415]Finnis attempts aunification by accommodating rights theories with virtue ethics, by which contemporary ethical and legal questions can be resolved.

Central to Finnis' work is an understanding of the natural law as a normative principle by which persons are able to recognize principles and conditions for practical reasonableness, which establishes proper order among people and guides individual moral conduct.This is based purely on the use of human reason to deduce basic values of human existence and to acquire the needed methodological requirements for practical reasonableness, which leaves no room for inferring from fact to value.Kainz remarks that Finnis' work uses "several thousand words "in arguing the self-evidence of the value of knowledge that does not admit of consensus or feelings of certitude but is based on pure logic and rationality.

---

414   I find S. Adam Seagrave more articulate when he penned the following: "With Finnis' seminal work, a broadly Thomistic natural law was rendered not only compatible with contemporary analytic philosophy and jurisprudence, but foundational with respect to the natural law that defines the liberal tradition. The impact of Finnis' ambitious synthesis of characteristically modern insights with Thomistic natural law, while it has proceeded in connection with a larger movement within post Vatican II Catholicism, has become increasingly relevant to purely secular debates within contemporary liberalism. This impact may be clearly seen in a recent attempt to construct a 'natural law liberalism' which promises to include the core ideas of each tradition within a single, coherent political philosophy. " Cf. Christopher Wolfe, *Natural Law Liberalism* (Cambridge: Cambridge University Press, 2006) as qtd. in S. Adam Seagrave, "Cicero, Aquinas and Contemporary Issues in Natural Law Theory, " *Review of Metaphysics* 62, no. 3 (2009): 491.

415   Grisez, *The Way of the Lord Jesus*, Ibid., 236.

Finnis, like Grisez, starts from the point of practical reasonableness and focuses on a theory that has as its starting point principles that help in decision making on moral matters. This is an attempt to retrieve Aquinas's concept of natural law as a mode of approaching moral principles, which then become a guide for practical acts of decision making. In Finnis, two guidelines are given for natural law as practical reasonableness. First, Finnis speaks of "basic goods" or "basic human flourishing," listing seven (as opposed to Grisez's eight): (i) life, (ii) knowledge, (iii) play, (iv) aesthetics, (v) experience, (vi) friendship/sociability, and (vii) religion and practical reasonableness.[416] In Finnis' thesis, basic goods are "pre-moral" because they serve only as the starting point for moral reasoning. Through the second approach, which moves from a pre-moral starting point to moral judgement making, some formulations are proposed by Finnis: a coherent plan of life, (ii) making no arbitrary preferences among values or persons, (iii) no exaggeration or arbitrary leaving out of any of the basic goods, (iv) fundamental impartiality among human subjects who are partakers of these basic goods, (v) detachment from personal projects in order to avoid fanaticism, with enough commitment to avoid apathy, (vi) pursuit of the good with reasonable efficiency, (vii) respect for every basic value in every act, (viii) diligent pursuit of the common good, (ix), and following one's conscience. These are equal to Grisez's "requirements of practical reasonableness" or "modes of responsibility." It is in the light of these requirements that moral judgements can be reached.[417]

Between Grisez, Finnis, their colleagues and other new natural law theorists, much ink has been spent and many thousand pages scripted in articulating methods and approaches in response to critiques and critiquing others. One finds that even between the two collaborators and "godfathers" of the new natural law movement, there are subtle,

---

416   John Finnis, *Natural Law*, 243-46.

417   Robert P. George, "Natural Law and Justice by Lloyd Weinreb: A Critique of the New Natural Law Theory by Russell Hittinger," *The University of Chicago Law Review* 55, no. 4 (1988): 1394. Robert George, in a journal essay, restates this point thus: "The Grisez/Finnis theory presents a set of general moral principles that, while analytically distinct from the basic practical principles and derived from a still more abstract foundational moral principle, in effect, put the ensemble of basic practical principles to work in concert. The role of these moral principles is to structure and guide human choosing between intelligible goods."

maybe negligible, and yet nuanced differences in their approach to the question of basic goods.[418] Inasmuch as the new natural law theorists try to incorporate theistic ontological natural law theory into legal positivism, they seem to fall short of a tenable conclusion.

Critique of NNLT

In order to consider some salient points that will be discussed again before the end of this chapter we need to look at some of the many critiques and criticisms of the Grisez/Finnis position. Russell Hittinger identifies what he considers the three major components of the new natural law theory of the Grisez/Finnis school.First, practical reason begins with reason's relationship to goods, its contents derived from inclinations, similar to the conventional natural law understanding of primary precepts.Second, basic goods in the new natural law thinking are regarded not only as the *prima principia* of practical reason but also as ends/finalities.They are irreducible objective principles because they are the primary principle of natural law.Third, the Grisez/Finnis account of goods is understood within the prism of total human flourishing and the good of the community.Foundationally, these goods are exhaustive on two grounds: (a) they ontologically constitute the essential goods of humanity, and (b) none of these universal goods can be left out without distorting practical rationality.According to Hittinger, these conclusions are in agreement with the older traditions of the natural law theory.Hittinger asserts, "In establishing their practical axioms, neither Grisez nor Finnis proceeds *ex conditione finis*, nor per force *ex supposione naturae*, where nature is understood to constitute the wider setting in which the *convenientia* between human agents and nature is presupposed. "[419] Contrary to scholastic thinking, according to Hittinger, the NNLT seems not to require a natural theology to mediate between the natural teleology of inclinations and the necessity for a moral command to obey nature. Grisez and Finnis presumed a

---

418   Hittinger, *A Critique*, 9. Russell Hittinger states that the slight difference between Grisez and Finnis are that Finnis does not press his own system into the domain of moral theology. Two, Finnis differs slightly from Grisez on the relationship between religion and practical reason. Third, his mode of moral responsibility is at variance with Grisez's.

419   Ibid., 16.

breakthrough in providing 'natural categoricals' as a new approach to the natural law reasoning.Hittinger, however, doubts if this system actually represents "a constructive advance beyond conventional natural law theory. "[420] Hittinger questions what he perceives as a movement backwards, which attempts to secure the perceptive facet of natural law and the pre-moral natural facet.Hittinger therefore queries, "Is Grisez confused about his own method? "[421] Hittinger argues that the Grisez School wants to stay true to traditional natural law but is unwilling to deploy the theoretical apparatus necessary to sustain it; he calls this a case of wanting to have one's cake and eat it.He argues further that "since Grisez has to bring justifications, *ex supposition naturae*, in through the back door, and since Finnis readily acknowledges that the speculative issues concerning nature place a question mark over the project, it is difficult to understand why neither is willing to make some provision for the employment of speculative rationality. "[422] In the NNLT, the relationship between religion and practical reason is suspect for Hittinger.In natural law, religion is one of the first principles of practical reason, one of the foundational principles of practical rationality.In the new natural law, religion is perceived as "natural religion " and defined by anthropological and cultural traits. Therefore, the good of religion becomes intelligible even if we prescind it from a theistic perspective. Hittinger sees a problem witha principle and its content being posited by intuition: "Despite an agnosticism regarding the bearing of a philosophy of nature or a metaphysics upon practical rationality, a conciliatory gesture is made towards the empirical sciences which, Grisez and Finnis reason, ought to be able

---

420   Ibid., 162-3.

421   Ibid., 164.

422   Ibid., 165. In a journal essay, Robert George also expressed the suspicion held by the traditional Neo-Scholastic natural law theorists regarding John Finnis: "Despite Finnis' explicit warning not to 'confuse the adoption of a set of basic personal or social commitments with the process, imagined by some contemporary philosophers, of 'choosing basic values', his references to 'life plan' (and his citation of Rawls) confirmed the worst fears of certain Neo- Scholastics. They perceive Finnis here as implicitly endorsing value (and therefore moral) relativism. After all, they reasoned, does not the idea that one can choose—free of the constraints of moral norms— 'basic personal and social commitments,' reek of the modernist conception of human liberty against which the natural law tradition has long held out. " George, "Natural Law and Justice, " 1424.

to come up with some 'parallel' list or evidence for the goods. "[423] Hittinger goes further to insist that the Grisez School fails to provide a philosophical justification for moving from this rather casually posited anthropological base to the practical judgements regarding the value of religion and even the question of moral obligation. Hittinger states that "Grisez's philosophical theology does not provide either a speculative or practical basis for a morally significant theistic referent. "[424] Hittinger therefore surmises that,

> .... in the case of religion, there is nothing but the intuition and an ancillary argument from a philosophical theology that seeks to demonstrate by a *via negativa* that God exists—an argument that does not demonstrate any morally significant properties on the part of the deity. Not only is there no basis for obligation with respect to the deity, there is no basis for understanding why there should be any sense whatsoever to religious practices. Atheists and agnostics, as well as theists, are bound by a universal form of the good that is defined simply as a need to establish good relations with unknown higher powers. In *Christian Moral Principles* the problem becomes more acute, for here religion is defined as the good of harmony between the human will and the will of God.... What began as a problem of merely intuitional evidence for a foundational principle of practical reason now becomes a problem of fideism. Because one of the *prima principia* requires the mediation of faith for its intelligibility....arguably the whole of the foundation requires faith in Christian revelation, for Grisez argues that it is only by faith that we have sufficient data to establish the rationality of the eudemonistic motive, and thus of the first principle of morality (as Grisez understands it). We therefore

---

423   Hittinger, *A Critique*, 166.

424   Ibid.

concluded not only that religion is a particular instance of a problem with Grisez's axiology and natural law method, but that it becomes a bellwether for problems with the system as such.[425]

Hittinger proposes three elements to be considered if religion is to be kept on the foundational level of an account of practical reason. First, the basic principle or principles of practical reason must be proven to require propositions concerning humanity's religious nature and or also humanity's relationship with God.On a second level, in taking this to account, there must be evidence to indicate that the omission or suppression of religion distorts, either in whole or in part, the fundamental rationality of practical reason.Third, it must be proven that there is a duty to obey divine commands, or at least participate in some religious practices.These three criteria, Hittinger argues, are the only basis by which a foundational approach to the question can be established.However, "Grisez does not achieve this systematic intention… "[426]

The effort to retain a natural law foundation for practical reason by substitution of intuition as evidence derived from a philosophy of nature, according to Hittinger, does not work.For him this either presupposes or postpones "a philosophical explication of the interrelation between inclinations, goods, and precepts, which in turn presupposes the intricate groundwork, laid in a philosophy of nature and in natural theology. "[427] On a third level Hittinger sees Grisez's structure of human subjectivity as a "tailpiece " of his axiological theory.Here, Grisez's account of the human person is less than clear his account of how or why the self is distinct from the person— or even if this is distinct from the human body.This puzzle, argues Hittinger, is the same one that is prevalent in the irreducibility and incommensurability of Grisez's goods.Here "the topic of moral motivation and values receives a one-dimensional treatment: all agents pursue fulfilments, and all of the basic goods are modes of fulfilment

---

425   Ibid.,167.

426   Ibid., 170.

427   Ibid., 174.

to which we are morally bound. "[428] Hittinger considers that this idea becomes more problematic if viewed through the lens of the role of virtues.Hittinger states, "The goods constituted by Grisez's axiology are curiously Platonic-like forms.He vigorously admonishes scholastic natural law theory for rendering practical reason a mere footnote to the speculative sciences, but Grisez's own understanding of the goods is rather Euclidian. "[429] In the same vein Hittinger continues, "The virtues, on the other hand, are not so readily abstracted from the unity of the self and the unity of the project.The point of the virtues cannot be grasped piecemeal fashion, and therefore an ethics of virtue is forced to deal forthrightly with the issue of selfhood. "[430]

Hittinger thinks that Grisez's effort to recover a natural law system without the traditional approach but by an implicational approach may be applauded if seen as an attempt to reconstruct a virtue ethic.[431] He is cautious, however, because "making sense of the virtues requires something more than making sense of conventions in which the virtues are, at least in part, intelligible. "[432] Hittinger opines that an ethic of virtue done this way is a halfway house that is stranded between a full-fledged natural law theory in the grand tradition and a thoroughly modern rejection of nature as having any constructive bearing upon ethics.For Hittinger, this is a conventionalism that has premodern credentials.[433] Hittinger concludes that the Grisez/Finnis School achieved an impressive overall project by attempting a rehabilitation of traditional natural law theory in their envisioning of a more contemporary approach of practical reason, devoid of utilitarianism and deontology.However, based on the previously analyzed critiques,

---

428   Ibid., 185-6.

429   Ibid., 187.

430   Ibid.

431   Other natural law theorists agree with and acclaim the Grisez/Finnis initiative, such as Robert P. George, who avers, "Grisez has made genuine contributions, first, to the development of natural law theory and, second, to the question of whether there can be specific Christian morality and specific Christian moral norms. " Robert P. George, *Natural Law & Moral Inquiry: Ethics, Metaphysics and Politics in the Work of Germain Grisez* (Washington, DC: Georgetown University Press, 1998), 25.

432   Hittinger, *A Critique*, 188.

433   Ibid., 189.

their NNLT has serious defects.He concludes by stating, "…we are sorry to report that despite the ambition of the Grisez-Finnis project, we are still waiting.What is clear is that there is no way to recover natural law theory by way of shortcuts. "[434]

Pauline Westerman offers four critiques of the new natural law theory in the Grisez/Finnis tradition.First, she asserts that it is based on practical reasonableness, not natural law.Their first principle, which cannot be taken as a precept but regarded as basic orientation for moral issues, is grounded in the pursuance of basic goods. "That means that, strictly speaking, the new theory of natural law neither has anything to do with law nor with nature. "[435] Second, Westerman agrees that the new natural law system deals with the naturalistic fallacy question. Yet, she believes it lacks foundation, stating that the new natural law theorists argue that their older counterparts are wrong based on their own foundation: nature.However, Westerman contends that the alternative offered, self-evidence, is less convincing as a foundation. She continues that for "self-evidence and for this lack of foundation, a theory would be required in which it is argued that man has immediate excess to those self-evident forms of human flourishing.If we are not supposed to rely on nature, a (modern) equivalent of synderesis should be developed. "[436] Such a theory, according to Westerman, is absent.

In her third critique, Westerman asserts that besides the problem of foundation, there is the problem of obligation.The seven basic goods and the presumption that they are valid starting points for moral reasoning are setup as an obligation, which in reality no one is bound to keep.Westerman queries, "Why should we be guided by Finnis' compass rather than by our own sense of direction? "[437] This theory suffers from the dual problems of foundation and obligation, making the Grisez/Finnis' claim that their own theory of practical reasonableness is not natural law to fail and not achieving the aim of broadening the scope of moral inquiry.In Westerman's words, "The extension of one first principle to seven first principles may appear

---

434   Ibid., 198.

435   Westerman, *The Disintegration*, 256.

436   Ibid.

437   Ibid., 257.

to widen the scope for practical reasoning but in fact turns reasoning into a somewhat arbitrary affair. "[438] The scope of practical reasoning is short changed as it does not play any role in deciding which goods are desirable in themselves.

Westerman's fourth critique addresses the necessity to amend the theory of practical reasonableness by explicit references to the *telos* of human nature. In concluding the section of her book on the critique of the NNLT, she posits that the Grisez/Finnis School's "attempt istheoretically interesting... the attempt to unravel underlying objective values on the basis of philosophical argument alone, without assuming the existence of God. "[439] This task Westerman notes can only be "carried out by assigning an important place to the notion of self-evidence. "[440] This self-evidence cannot be embedded within a wider conceptual framework "which might elucidate the kind of rationality required to 'see' this self-evidence and therefore remains unargued. "[441] Concerning Finnis' efforts in his natural law theory to find grounds for the foundation of rights and the critique of liberalism on the grounds of natural law, Westerman opines, "Finnis' theory of natural law exhorts us to be more uncritically law-abiding than any other legal positivist has ever dared to suggest. "[442] The problem adduced by Westerman is that Finnis' theory is a hybrid of two traditions: Neo-Kantianism and natural law theory.Westerman sees the "common good" in relation to rights theory as developed by Finnis as unsatisfactory because itseems to waver between an instrumental and a non-instrumental meaning. The concept of the "common good" in Finnis' work is not clearly explicated, but it seems to be the product of a pre-moral choice. Westerman adds, "It seems to me that human rights are more secure without a foundation than with this arbitrary foundation, especially when the foundation of these rights can be used in order to abrogate these rights, a possibility Finnis' theory allows for. "[443] Westerman

---

438   Ibid.

439   Ibid.

440   Ibid.

441   Ibid., 257-58.

442   Ibid., 283.

443   Ibid., 285.

believes that the arbitrariness and insufficiency of the notion of the common good might be traced to Finnis' neglect of virtues, along with his intention to criticize liberalism without recourse to the virtues-idiom. Therefore, Westerman concludes, "The fundamental ambiguity of Finnis' concept of the common good does not contribute to the attractiveness of his theory as an alternative to 'rights-talk.' "[444]

Lloyd Weinreb, a recognized and respected contemporary voice in the conversation on natural law theory, questions whether it is solely applicable to moral principles *per se*. In Weinreb's opinion it is not, believing that the proper place for the natural law theory is in defense of the moral point of view against skepticism or its modern counterpart, existentialism.[445] He outlines an articulate argument:

> The vitality of contemporary natural law theories is due to their insistence on an objectively valid moral order. Beneath that superficially strictly deontological claim is an affirmation of the reality and significance of human freedom, on which morality depends. (The connection with the older theories is, therefore, genuine; only it is a connection that the contemporary theorists do not want.) Legal positivists generally avoid discussion of the status of morality itself. Although many would deny that there is an ascertainable, objectively valid morality, some would not. They assert only that, whatever its status, morality and law are separate. That separation, however, on which positivists stake their whole case, is a surrogate for the much more fundamental argument that normative order and natural order—freedom and cause—are unbridgeable separate *spheres*. Without acknowledging that it does so, legal positivism rejects the conditions of freedom and, therefore, the possibility of freedom itself. Beneath

---

444   Ibid.

445   Robert P. George, ed., *Natural Law, Liberalism and Morality* (Oxford, England: Oxford University Press, 1996), viii.

the surface of an apparently inconsequential dispute, there lingers the central puzzle of the human situation.[446]

Robert George cautions Weinreb and Hittinger in their criticisms of the Grisez/Finnis NNLT because, from his reading of Weinreb and Hittinger's work, George thinks they have inadequately understood the overall project.He avers, "Perhaps the theory is vulnerable to damning criticism.If so, the basic flaws in the theory are unlikely to be brought to light by critics who have not first achieved an accurate grasp of what is and is not being claimed... "[447] George argues that some texts by themselves invite misinterpretation, but whether or not this is the case with Grisez and Finnis, "it is evident that special care will be needed in the presentation of 'the new natural law theory' if it is to get a fair hearing even among the philosophically most sophisticated, those to whom it is proposed. "[448] Adam Seagrave reaches the same conclusions, stating that "while St. Thomas Aquinas' *Summa Theologica* remains the *locusclassicus* for natural law theory, this theory acquires more force and persuasiveness when it is placed at the summit of a preceding tradition of thought than when it is relegated to the foothills of an emerging one.[449] Seagrave opines that the contemporary transition from traditional natural law is premature, in which case "what is required of current natural law theory is not the abandonment of the more traditional version but rather its further development and application to the pressing problems of contemporary society. "[450]

---

446   Lloyd L. Weinreb, *Natural Law and Justice* (Cambridge, MA: Harvard University Press, 1997), 12. In a journal essay, Weinreb argues, "the separation of ethics from ontology obscures the antinomy of freedom and cause. Yet, this antinomy undercuts the efforts of deontological natural law theorists no less thoroughly than it did those of their ontological predecessors. To obscure the antinomy is not to eliminate it. It reemerges in the form of analogous antinomies of desert and entitlement (in respect of individual justice) and liberty and equality (in respect of justice in the social order) within the concept of justice. Such antinomies are ultimately rooted in the antinomy of freedom and cause (in respect of a putatively normative natural order). " Qtd. in George, "Natural Law and Justice, " 1376.

447   George, "Natural Law and Justice, " 1429.

448   Ibid.

449   Seagrave, "Cicero, Aquinas, " 523.

450   Ibid.

Fulvio Di Blasi thinks that NNLT's failure to understand the *a posteriori* proofs for the existence of God affects their perception of the meaning of nature and the world. Natural law theory is incomplete if it is unable to view and understand the relationship between our world and its creator. According to Di Blasi, "Natural law, before being a philosophical and theological concept, is a cultural and existential truth that belongs to the best dispositions and to the highest moral nobility of the human being. "[451] Di Blasi continues, "Natural law means to look at the world as a marvelous and mysterious fruit of divine intelligence, good and wise above all else, who creates it and governs it according to rules accessible to human minds-minds to whom it primarily and specifically turns. "[452] Di Blasi argues that the mistake with NNLT is that they see facts not beings they replace intelligible meaning with sensory experiences, and by abandoning the possibility of finding intelligibility of moral principles in nature, they turn to practical reason as a guide to moral insights.[453]

Di Blasi opines that the assumption that a non-theistic NLT makes it possible to enter into conversation with an atheistic contemporary world in order to be able to talk about morality generally, is the way to go, such thinking make a fundamental mistake. This conversation has only an open ended possibility since "contemporary atheism has been growing by denying the chief truths and principles of traditional morality, from marriage to the sacred character of human life. Contemporary culture is losing the idea that we are creatures... God is the only medicine to this slippery slope trend- the medicine that some

---

451   Fulvio Di Blasi, "The Role of God in the New Natural Law Theory, " *The National Bioethics Quarterly* 13, no. 1 (2013), 37.

452   Ibid.

453   Di Blasi clarifies his position thus, "This different metaphysical outlook is why NNLT has always been haunted by the naturalistic fallacy. In fact, the naturalistic fallacy, more than anything else, is the reason behind it. The main focus of NNLT has always been to win the battle against the naturalistic fallacy, thus recovering objectivity in moral philosophy. Instead of recovering objectivity by giving back (moral) intelligibility to the world, however, NNL theorists accepted the naïve reduction of the world to facts and took refuge (with Kant) inside practical reason. After Kant, the "objectivity " of practical reason is supposed to replace the "reality " of nature. However, what Kant and the NNL theorists do not understand is that without constantly feeding itself from nature, practical reason gets lost in its own thoughts, and ultimately loses the very objectivity it was supposed to recover. " Ibid. 38-9

Christian thinkers try to avoid. "[454] Di Blasi therefore concludes that the human person admitting it or not, tends towards understanding the overall meaning of existence. This human person who is able to apply intellectual power to the knowledge of the world and God and to see eternal life as the highest truth and final answer to human existence is the same human person the NNL theorists creates as "unable to reach God with his intellect and who cannot have God as the ultimate end. New natural law theory consistently denies the proper role of God at both the metaphysical and moral levels. "[455]

Marriage as a Basic Good in the NNLT School: Crucial and central to this chapter,as well as to the thesis of this entire project, is the argument that marriage, as understood within traditional and contemporary natural law theories, rests on the assumption that the marital union is a basic good for human flourishing.It is interesting to note that whether one ascribes to an ontological theistic tradition or a deontological, there is mutual agreement that marriage between a man and a woman is a basic good with other goods attached, suchas mutuality, conjugality, procreation, and the education of offspring. Within the Aristotelian/Thomistic tradition, there is a rich history of the development of marriage from contract to covenant and its understanding and establishment as a sacrament.In the theology of the Angelic Doctor, marriage is ordered toward a principal end: procreation and the education of offspring.The secondary end of marriage is mutuality and friendship, and in believers, the understanding that marriage is sacramental because it represents the great mystery of Christ and the Church. The work of the two great Dominicans, Albert the Great and Thomas Aquinas, establishes marriage firmly within Catholic doctrinal understanding as a sacrament which confers grace; it is fecund and has an indelible character erased only by death.This became the standard position of the Church structurally, with a few nuances added here and there since Vatican II.

In a section of their work, Salzman and Lawler show marriage to be a basic good within the NNLT.They posit that the NNLT's sexual anthropology is founded on the idea of marriage as a basic good or

---

454   Ibid., 40

455   Ibid., 43

absolute norm, which is developed in both Grisez and Finnis in three steps: (1) heterosexual marriage is a basic good; (2) the marital -sexual act results from that basic good; and (3) every other non-marital sexual act is unnatural, unreasonable, and immoral.[456] In Grisez's work, marriage as a basic good does not depend on, nor is it derived from, other goods of human flourishing.Marriage on its own is a reality having a basic good proper to it.In marriage "[t]his two-in-one-flesh reality is realized by both 'marital consent which conjugal intercourse fulfills'… and bodily communion between the spouses.Marital consent and bodily communion are both required to realize a two-in-one flesh communion between a man and a woman. "[457] Marriage (and by extension sexuality and the sexual act) is such a profound good for human flourishing that Grisez states further, "For couples who are engaged and not yet married, sexual intercourse may realize bodily communion, but it lacks the public consent required of marriage and marital intercourse. "[458] He maintains that without this public marital consent, bodily communion between male and female is not a real but illusory good, an unnatural, unreasonable choice and, therefore, immoral.Salzman and Lawler reemphasize the import of this part of the NNLT, recognizing marriage and marital sexuality as a basic good. "According to NNLT, a foundational moral principle is that 'one may never intend to destroy, damage, impede, or violate any basic human good, or prefer an illusory instantiation of a basic human good to a real instantiation of that or some other human good.'By definition, nonmarital sexual acts cannot be marital acts, and therefore, to engage in such acts is to 'destroy, damage, impede or violate' marriage as a basic good. "[459] They state even more succinctly that

> … in light of the basic good of marriage and two-fold intrinsic meaning of marital acts, NNLT maintains that nonmarital sexual acts are absolutely prohibited because they cannot fulfill the intrinsic meanings

---

456   Todd A. Salzman and Michael G. Lawler, *The Sexual Person: Towards a Renewed Anthropology* (Washington, DC: Georgetown University Press, 2008), 58.

457   Ibid., 59.

458   Ibid.

459   Ibid., 60.

of marital acts and, therefore, cannot activate and achieve the basic good of marriage. Such nonmarital acts include premarital sexual intercourse, artificially contraceptive sexual acts, homosexual acts, natural or nonmarital nonreproductive sexual acts, and masturbation. These acts are unnatural, unreasonable, and therefore immoral.[460]

It is therefore safe to conclude with Grisez and Finnis, in line with the Catholic doctrinal tradition, that it is only within the marriage bond that the sexual act is legitimate. Aimed either at procreation or the union of friendship and love of the spouses, the sexual act constitutes a basic good. David Braybrook suggests that, in the post-modern context, the scholastic tradition does not enjoy a popular following because it prohibits any other form of sexual encounter outside of marriage as self-alienation and an illusory experience of personal gratification. He goes further to explain that outside of the Catholic Church, the tradition is held suspect because it is seen to entail a "subscription to Catholic beliefs about the existence of God… divorce, the status of women, and sexual activity, embracing, in regard to the latter—most notoriously— opposition to contraception and abortion, as well as to fornication and masturbation. "[461]

Conclusion

Thomas Aquinas's philosophy, anthropology, and theology, applied to grounding his theonomic natural law theory, are designed to uphold the idea of ordered ends and their relation to the metaphysical idea of a sovereign God. Human nature is finite and depends on its participation in the eternal uncreated wisdom/law of God. Any movement towards the good is engendered by the human metaphysical dependence on the divine. Westerman argues this position, stating that to suppose a practical doctrine can be fashioned without recourse to speculative metaphysical premises at the apex of such a moral theology is a stretch. "… [I]t would never be possible to develop the normative ethics of

---

460   Ibid., 59.

461   David Braybrook, *Natural Law Modernized*, 5.

natural law doctrine in the absence of its metaphysical requisites. "[462] Westerman concludes by suggesting that the contrast between "the new natural law theory with its praxic, antiteleological tendency, and the classical Thomistic doctrine of natural law, is instructive. "[463] This contrast challenges us all to rediscover and reimmerse ourselves within a tradition of reflection, conscious that the work of Plato, Aristotle, Boethius, Augustine, and Aquinas "is definitive for the tradition of Catholic theology and philosophy. "[464]

Lloyd Weinreb thinks that the vital point of the new natural law theorists is their insistence on an object valid moral order. Even though there is a strictly deontological claim, there is also the recognition and acceptance of human freedom on which morality rests. There is, therefore, a connection between the classicist and contemporary natural law theories that the newer protagonists are unwilling to acknowledge. According to Weinreb, this is the reason why legal positivists avoid discussions about the status of morality itself. They argue rather that there is a distinct separation between morality and law. In Weinreb's assessment, "[t]hat separation, however, on which positivists stake their whole case, is a surrogate for the much more fundamental argument that normative order and natural order—freedom and cause—are unbridgeably separate. "[465] In this way, legal positivism rejects the conditions for freedom and the possibility of freedom. Weinreb says this dispute has more at stake than a mere argumentation on the question of law and morals: "Beneath the surface of an apparently inconsequential dispute, there lingers the central puzzle of the human situation. "[466]

Weinreb refers to order in the universe as being a central force in Thomistic philosophy, political science, ethics, epistemology, psychology, ontology, and theology. The source of unitive order in the universe is Divine Providence initiated by the Creator who ordained everything into one purposeful and coherent end. In working out

---

462   David Braybrook, *Natural Law Modernized*, 5.

463   Ibid.

464   Ibid.

465   Weinreb, *Natural Law and Justice*, 12.

466   Ibid.

the meaning of human freedom and self- determinism, the natural law is Aquinas's way of bringing the human condition within the providential order.Weinreb argues, "Not only is human freedom consistent with the natural order; nature actually requires freedom, without which a rational creature would be frustrated and kept from fulfilling its essence.Yet freedom is directed and limited by nature, lest reason be without responsibility or significance. "[467] Nature and reason are therefore not opposed;rather they co-exist within the unity and coherence of the universal order of the Divine Creator.Time and ages have passed between Aquinas's world and ours, but his world did not doubt as normative the existence of a providential Divine Creator who created the universe in an orderly symbiosis.Aquinas's disputations were not intended to provide arguments to sustain or propup that belief but rather to see how, with the intellectual language of the time, he could make matters of religious faith intelligible to everyone.Weinreb concludes that even if one were to reject Aquinas's premises, one would still recognize his achievement and relevance to the work that has been done in the various theories about the natural law. "If natural law is now presented as a response to the problem of freedom in a morally indeterminate, non-providential universe, one that Aquinas himself could not have contemplated, nevertheless it is associated unavoidably with Thomistic philosophy. "[468]

The problems with contemporary moral theorists are that they are disconnected from traditional Western theistic moral theorizing. Historically, the Western intellectual tradition took root in a theistic foundation which the Enlightenment, post modernity, and a vastly secular and pluralist society have abandoned.[469] We find in the Kantian *Critique of Pure Reason* a separation of moral principles from *nature*

---

467   Ibid., 60-61.

468   Ibid., 63.

469   There are suggestions that contemporary natural law only "borrows " the term but is not really a natural law theory. Once the contemporary theorists moved to deontology, the "natural " in natural law was circumvented. While the traditional theory concerns itself with the question of why a person acts morally from his nature and participation in the eternal divine laws, the new theorists are concerned with the philosophical question of legal jurisprudence, human rights, just and unjust laws, and rationality. This is a subtle yet important question for the entire natural law enterprise.

as untenable against purely human *reason*.[470] Pure reason "like the categorical imperative, they are proposed not as principles of natural law, but *as if* they were... they consider nature to be completely extrinsic to reason, and thus of no moral value. "[471] They therefore, try to use reason only to develop a new objective valid moral system which justifies their own brand of the new natural law theory.Martin Rhonheimer[472] elucidates that theorists who see a disconnect between reason and nature are mistaken.In a journal essay, he expounds on the idea that the basic requirements of Christian morality are intelligible and reasonable.However, they may appear unreasonable, unintelligible, difficult to fulfil, oppressive, unrealistic, and too demanding when perceived outside the prism of religious faith.According to Rhonheimer, "their inherent reasonableness easily converts into unreasonableness of an unattainable ideal, which is therefore unacceptable to most people... people in fact can fully accept these moral demands as practically achievable goals... it is in this context precisely that these moral

---

470   Charles Curran notes that it was Neo-Scholasticism that provided a philosophical frame work for the papacy, the Church and Vatican I a way to respond the question of faith and reason in the 19th Century as both the extremes of rationalism and fideism. According to Curran, "The fideists were wrong because they in positing a primitive divine revelation as the basis for the human knowledge of the first principles of metaphysics and ethics, they denied the proper role and autonomy of reason itself. On the other hand, rationalists gave too much importance to natural reason as providing an intuition of God that can only come from divine grace. Semi-rationalists ... claimed that reason could make true judgements about Christian mysteries. Neo-Scholasticism maintained that reason couldprove the existence of God, know the natural law, and show the credibility of the Christian faith and the Church, but only faith can provide knowledge of the Christian mysteries. " Curran, The Development, 53.

471   Kainz, *Natural Law*, 42.

472   Martin Rhonheimer is a Swiss born Catholic priest who has written copiously on Aquinas and the natural law theory. He writes from his lecturing position at the Opus Dei University in Rome and his works have recently been translated into English. Curran says Rhonheimer understands natural law as a cognitive reality that formally belongs to human reason, embedded in the strivings of the natural inclination and their ends. The first principle of practical reason and moral reason is the precepts of natural law which depend on a natural inclination seen as the goods of reason. In Rhonheimer's understanding of the natural law, it cannot be reduced to simply either human nature or reason. He is a known staunch defender of norms and doctrinal papal magisterial teachings. He is also at the fore front of responding to revisionist theologians like Richard McCormick, Grisez, and Finnis. Cf. Curran, *The Development*, 105.

demands fully recover their reasonableness. "[473] I find Rhonheimer convincing when he summarized his position thus:

> .... Christian morality, to a large extent, throws light on the possibility of living a moral life which fully meets the intrinsic demands of human nature. This means that we can speak of a true specific *Christian humanism* which differs from the purely secular humanism of the non-believer. Thus, what initially appears unreasonable, regains reasonableness through faith, hope and charity. That is how faith in fact rescues reason and reason recovers all its power to make faith both human and effective. Rightly understood, reason therefore needs revelation for being capable of effectively working as moral reason and to maintain the "reasonableness of morality. "[474]

Further on in Rhonheimer's essay, he argues that for Christian humanism in its ecclesiological setting to remain profoundly reasonable, it must retain its full normative validity in its "original moral knowledge, "which is the same as the natural law. Rhonheimer emphasizes his idea as follows:

> .... The basic moral requirements—the human good—contains an intrinsic reasonableness which, in principle, is independent from faith, and in that sense autonomous. Yet, only under the conditions of Christian faith is it possible to comply consistently with a morality which is in full agreement with the "human " and the "truth about man, " because, so I have argued, only when integrated within the context of faith can these requirements be defended and justified – precisely as *reasonable!* .... Thus, I think faith to be a necessary condition of a person's

---

473   Martin Rhonheimer, "Is Christian Morality Reasonable? On the Difference Between Secular and Christian Humanism, " *Annales Theologici* 2, no. 15 (2001): 531.

474   Ibid., 532.

being able both to reconcile the requirements of the human good with his striving for happiness, and therefore also to meet these requirements *consistently*.[475]

This chapter is a broad review of the natural law theory within the Aristotelian-Aquinas-Scholastic-Catholic tradition vis-à-vis its competing non-theistic NNLT and theorists. The natural law specialists have much more to say on the technical and purely philosophical aspects of these varied arguments. This chapter attempts to achieve three aims: one, establish a historical background; two, show how significant the natural law theory is within Catholic moral theology; and three, show that within both the traditional and contemporary natural law theories, marriage, human sexuality, and the sexual act are all seen as constituting a basic human good. Once these have been established, the next chapter will attempt a review of some thinkers who cover a wide range of anthropological, philosophical, feminist, and theological viewpoints to see how they approach and respond to the question of human sexuality and marriage from their own philosophical perspectives or traditions.

---

475   Ibid., 544.

CHAPTER FOUR

INTERACTIONS: SOME CONTEMPORARY THINKERS ON SEXUALITY AND MARRIAGE

In this chapter, I intend to engage contemporary voices that contribute to questions about the morality of the human body as a sexual body, the debates about human sexuality, and the position of the Church with regard to its doctrine on marriage, conjugality and marital sexuality. I have chosen John S. Grabowski, Lisa Sowle Cahill, Margaret Farley, and Mercy Amber Oduyoye as conversation partners. They represent a wide variety of voices and positions that can help shed light on the many perspectives from which these issues are approached. Their Perspectives cover theological, philosophical, cultural, and gender issues from what might be considered a more liberal, postmodern ethical perspectives. These voices, provide us with alternative narratives which affords us an opportunity to appreciate contrasting positions. This appreciation opens the possibility of a dialogic approach aimed at a possible synthesis of traditional and doctrinal position with contemporary theological perspectives.

John S. Grabowski

John S. Grabowski theologizes from a systematic application of biblical and virtue-based categories to questions of human sexuality. He approaches these issues with certain biblical themes, such as covenant, beatitude, and discipleship. Grabowski's theology is grounded in the Thomistic tradition whereby he approaches the subject matter by paying attention to the "person " rather than the law or the sin (i.e., the acts in themselves) as was characteristic of many Catholic moral manuals. Grabowski heavily nuances and applies the virtue ethics of

Thomas Aquinas in his work, a systematic approach which integrates the question of human nature, synthesizing it into a bigger theological method of virtue ethics. Grabowski is an interesting dialogue partner because he comes from the same Aristotelian and Thomistic foundation as the Catholic Church's doctrinal tradition. However, he goes beyond the "traditional" approach to build a newer virtue ethic that points to areas of possible renewal or re-articulation.

Grabowski articulates his specific theological task in his book *Sex and Virtue*, noting that his focus is on a systematic application of biblical and virtue-based categories in sexual ethics for the renewal of moral theology as directed by Vatican II. He acknowledges the work of Lisa Sowle Cahill in this area, stating that while Cahill approaches the same issue from themes such as community, gender, and identification in justice with the marginalized, he approaches these issues from the scripturally based themes of covenant, beatitude, and discipleship to give more weight to virtue itself.[476] Grabowski's aim is to "contend that biblical theology of covenant fidelity wedded to an account of chastity as an integral part of human flourishing can provide a suitable framework for a Christian approach to issues of sexuality in contemporary context."[477]

Grabowski's moral theology centers on the question of how to avoid lapsing into legalism. He is also concerned with how to address the moral and cultural relativism which he believes pervade contemporary life context. In Grabowski argues that a renewal of Catholic moral theology is needed to overcome the heavily legalistic and act-centered morality of the period between Trent and Vatican II. The moral growth of the person, he believes, was not considered, and the manualist utilized biblical "proof texts" were used in isolated ways to ground authoritative laws abstracted from the overall biblical message of salvation and failed to adequately attend to the moral growth of the person.

Grabowski avidly supports Vatican II's call for renewal of moral theology. This renewal, he posits, can be accomplished in three ways;

476   John S. Grabowski, *Sex and Virtue: An Introduction to Sexual Ethics* (Washington DC: Catholic University of America Press, 2003), xiii.

477   Ibid.

first, as delineated in *Dei Verbum*, no. 24, genuine renewal requires that moral theology be immersed in Sacred Scripture which is the "soul " of sacred theology.[478] Second, the focus should be shifted to the human person (as against the previous pre-occupation of focusing on human acts) fully revealed in and by Christ. Quoting *Gaudium et Spes*, Grabowski states that "[t]he 'livelier contact with the mystery of Christ' called for in post conciliar moral theology necessarily brings the human person created for and redeemed by him into sharper focus. "[479] Third, there is a renewed account of the moral dynamism of the person redeemed by Christ and this person's free and personal acts in moral decision making as well as personal growth in moral goodness and holiness.[480]

The seven chapters in *Sex and Virtue* seminally represent the theology of John Grabowski. Grabowski approaches the question of virtue and sexuality from within the milieu of Western culture. He focuses on American Catholicism and the modern-day clash of the idea of sexuality within society and faith, on "a culture which prizes individual autonomy and valorizes sexual expression as integral to personal fulfilment…, confronted with authoritative Church teachings often perceived as hostile to such values and divorced from their own

---

478   In the introduction to his book, *Sex and Virtue*, Grabowski argues that sacred Scripture is integral to the experience of a Christian moral living. Scripture and the sacraments make contact between believers and the mysteries of Christ possible in their lives. Therefore, careful reading and reflection on the sacred texts, either personally or within liturgical settings, are both at the heart of the renewal of moral theology and authentic Christian living. Cf. John S. Grabowski, *Sex and Virtue: An Introduction to Sexual Ethics* (Washington, DC: Catholic University of America Press, 2003), x.

479   Ibid., xi.

480   Grabowski carefully distinguishes between human actions and transcendental freedom, which he says oftentimes is unclear and undercuts the teaching on mortal sin. Grabowski avers, "A better account of the dynamic interplay between moral character and specific moral choices is provided by the recent revival of virtue language and theory… In so far as virtue can uphold the importance of specific moral actions as both illustrating and shaping moral character without reducing the whole of morality to isolated acts, it can make an important and positive contribution to the renewal of moral theology for which Vatican II called… Because premodern moral theology was not divorced from soteriology and spirituality, its moral vision was more closely connected with 'the mystery of Christ' and the life of faith. Likewise, a recovery of virtue theory can offer a wider and more theologically fruitful vision of the moral life. " Ibid., xii-xiii.

experience. "[481] In light of Paul VI's encyclical, *Humanae Vitae*, he looks at thesexual scandals in the Church and the conversation on the perceived struggle between freedom and law as the basis of morality.[482]

Grabowski develops a biblical foundation for understanding conjugality as the sign of a covenantal pledge between spouses. Using the Church's liturgical and sacramental tradition, Grabowski establishes a dynamic exegetical link between the second creation account in Genesis and Israel's Pentateuchal and Prophetic tradition. He traces its newer meaning in the New Testament account in Ephesians 5:21-33 where the analogy of mutual submission in the one flesh is presented as a metaphor for the relationship between Christ and the Church. Applying his key biblical themes, Grabowski then lays the ground work for a covenantal ethic of marital spirituality and marital sexuality based on the invitation to discipleship and the beatitudes. Grabowski proposes a "recovery" of the virtue ethic-chastity from its historical and contemporary impulses, relying on what he refers to as modern psychology and philosophical personalism to provide nuances in the acquisition and expression of the virtue of chastity within the contemporary context.

On the much debated question of gender differentiation, Grabowski views questions of equality or inequality within the dignity of human persons as male or female and the rise of feminism as social, political and cultural phenomena. His work attempts to "locate the equality of the sexes in their possession of a shared human nature, while arguing that sexual difference may be understood as a fundamental relation constitutive of personhood. "[483] Grabowski therefore recognizes and points out threats to the dignity of the sexes such as prostitution,

---

481   Ibid., xiv.

482   Grabowski expounds on this theme further, "All of these developments shed some light on the explosion of bitter disagreement that followed Humanae Vitae. Underlying the fuel provided by the convergence of social and intellectual factors in the twentieth century was the incendiary force provided by centuries of conceiving morality as a struggle between an undirected and privatized freedom and law imposed by external authority. In this case, it was the freedom of individual conscience to avail itself of new sexual opportunities afforded by twentieth century attitudes and technology that were set against the pope's repetition of a seemingly discredited norm merely on the basis of his own authority. The encyclical provided the spark that would ignite both the tinder of new developments and the voluntarist powder keg that lay beneath. " Ibid., 19.

483   Ibid., xv.

pornography, sexual violence/abuse and so on. He takes note of and acknowledges internal revolts and disagreements on *Humanae Vitae*. Unfortunately, the extremely critical inside debates affected a younger generation of Catholics whose understanding of sex and sexuality were largely then informed by an extremely liberalized society whose sexual culture is based purely on individual autonomy and on pleasurable and even "freeing " experiences. As if this were not bad enough, there came the sexual scandals involving priests, further undermining the Church's moral probity to adjudicate matters of sexual conduct. Many cradle Catholics and a greater majority of priests and theologians in the Western world perceived this encyclical as an imposition of papal authority without taking into account people's lived experience. People were then taught to rely on their consciences by theologians and priests who argue that the teaching does not enjoy papal infallibility. Grabowski opposes this trend by stating unequivocally that

> [t]he deformation of morality in its reduction to the dialectic between freedom of conscience over against an external law is at the heart of such a reading of the encyclical and many of the debates that it produced. Yet it was precisely the narrow confines of a morality of obligation that Vatican II sought to challenge in its call for renewal. Much of the controversy following the encyclical is in fact a testimony to the continuing presence of a morality of obligation and the casuistry it breeds within Catholic moral thought. The alienation experienced by many older Catholics in regard to the Church and sexuality can be traced to the impact of such a paradigm. Either they operate within this moral system, in which case the authority of the teaching can be doubted on the grounds of casuistry and conscience. Or, having rejected this paradigm to one degree or another, yet not being given a new way to think about morality, they simply find it

difficult to relate their faith to moral teaching of any
kind. Faith and morality are thus disconnected.[484]

To try to begin resolving this alienation, especially from within the
Church, Grabowski proposes a radical re-thinking of how to present
reasoning about sex devoid of its traditional legalism. The new method
should take into account the sources of moral theology and a better
account of the human person growing in moral excellence. On another
level, magisterial teachings can no longer rely on "authority" but must
be couched in a language that is "compelling enough to offer a cogent
alternative to dominant cultural visions of sex as merely ecstatic release,
personal fulfilment, or a commodity of exchange."[485] Grabowski
advocates for teachings on sexuality that are embedded in the language
of faith but fully aware of and sympathetic to genuine intellectual and
cultural contexts, such as questions concerning the dangers of overpopulation with appalling and unequal distribution of the world's
natural resources. Considering the emerging Western patterns of the
role of women, the changing patterns of sexual mores and behaviors,
and the difficulties parents and religious instructors face in trying to
communicate Christian ethical values to youngsters confronted with
a vastly irreverent, materialistic, and secularized world, Grabowski
concludes that because "no one treatment can fully resolve [these]
issues, some attention must be given to them both on the level of
theory and on the level of concrete moral praxis."[486]

Further, he argues for the primacy of the procreative purpose of
sex and the self-donation that occurs in the couples' sexual act when
performed in chastity, as taught within the Catholic doctrinal tradition.
Grabowski borrows from the Old Testament the idea of enacting
covenants by oath taking, thereby drawing a parallel with the marriage
vow. "Sexual union is thus understood as a kind of anamnesis that
recalls precisely the totality of a couple's gift to one another expressed in
their oath."[487] According to Grabowski, the intensity and exclusiveness
of covenantal relationships remains true in the total self-donation of

---

484   Ibid., 21.

485   Ibid., 22.

486   Ibid.

487   Ibid., 38.

persons in a marital sexual act, and this he claims is the foundation for a theology of sexuality.[488] It is in this self-donation that the covenantal/ oath taken is ratified: "In coition a couple seals their covenant with one another by an embodied enactment of their complete self-giving… sex is thus the embodied symbol of a couple's love and communion in a way similar to that in which liturgy symbolizes and enacts the communion between God and his people through gesture and ritual. "[489] Grabowski concludes, therefore, that the sexual act is genuinely sacramental – however, only for the first time when a marriage is consummated and the two become one flesh.[490] In completing this parallel, Grabowski explains, "Such observations suggest a fundamental analogy between the offering of self to God in the act of worship and the sexual self-giving of spouses to another. Both are liturgical actions that recall and symbolize a covenant relation through bodily gesture of self- donation…. It has an anamnetic quality in that it is a recollection and enactment of what the couple promise in their vows to one another. "[491] This covenantal and sacramental approach can serve as a foundation for the development of a more cogent and compelling vision of sexuality within contemporary theological conversation.

Following the covenantal and sacramental approach, Grabowski situates the ideas of kingdom and discipleship, though not in any particular systematized account of morality. The New Testament strands of Jesus's proclamation of the kingdom of God, his call to

---

488   Grabowski explains that Ephesians 5 uses the term *mysterion* to indicate the relationship of married persons. The same expression is later translated by various ante-Nicene writers in the Latin as *sacramentum*. This term for the Romans of the time implied a sacred oath usually made by soldiers to the emperor. The Romans also understood marriage to be sacred and covenantal; this provided an atmosphere in which the assimilation of biblical theology was possible in spite of some linguistic and cultural difference. Ibid., 43, fn 63.

489   Ibid., 45-6. (It is in this way that JPII describes and seminally names the total self-giving that is communicated within the marriage covenant as "language of the body. " In sexual union, a somatic dialogue ensues wherein the couples speak a language based on their masculinity and femininity.)

490   From my theological reflection, I disagree with Grabowski on this point. The very first consummation of the marital union is as sacramental as at any other time throughout their married lives. Every sexual act within marriage should be a 'sacramental' celebration, an expression of total self-giving.

491   Ibid., 46.

discipleship, his Sermon on the Mount, including the beatitudes, and the general New Testament treatment of Christian moral character can help to concretize the paradigm Grabowski is trying to build. Jesus' proclamation of the kingdom was a call to repentance *(metanoia)* followed by discipleship. The New Testament shows the development of a new approach to understanding covenant, which was re-envisioned at the last supper and constructed on the cross. The "Eucharist is an anamnesis of the new covenant oath made on the cross...analogous to the role of a couple's sexual communion. "[492] The New Testament is filled with references to nuptial imageries even with imagery that transfers the notion of Yahweh as the bridegroom of Israel to the person of Christ. Bridegrooms and wedding banquets proliferate in the inspired authors of the entire New Testament.

The idea of chastity within Christian morality according to Grabowski is "one of the most maligned and misunderstood virtues in contemporary culture... "[493] Such misunderstanding occurs because the word evokes prudery and inhibitions, even dysfunction or neurosis, as opposed to a culture that seeks sexual pleasure as a source of happiness and self fulfilment. As chastity is disdained, fidelity naturally suffers the same fate. Grabowski claims that recent a resurgence and interest in virtues as the basis for the moral life are making a come-back in the works of Alasdair MacIntyre and others. Even within this development, the perception of virtue ethics as rigorist and anti-sex makes its wide acceptance problematic. Grabowski avers, "Further, it is not immediately evident how even the strengths of the classical understanding of chastity can be reconciled with developments in modern thought that focus on the person and his or her cognitive development and specific cultural location. "[494] Through tradition

---

492   Ibid., 54. (Grabowski understands the nuptial meal of the Eucharist in which the bridegroom gives himself bodily to his bridal Church—as the ultimate analogy of the "one flesh " unity of spouses effected by their mutual self-donation in sexual intimacy. Cf. Ibid., 65. In the self-emptying death of Christ on the cross, reveals the *agape* present from all eternity on the trinity. Thus in Grabowski's thinking the cross of Christ is an act of supreme self- gift illumines both trinitarian and spousal self-donation. Or as Grabowski states, "On this basis it can be said that, when fully personal, sexual communion in marriage serves as a created image of the transcendent and spiritual self- giving that is the basis of Trinitarian communion. " Cf. Ibid., 69-70.

493   Ibid., 71.

494   Ibid., 71-2.

and the contributions of medieval authors, Grabowski states that chastity has always been regarded as the virtue which enables mastery over one's sexual urges and desires, especially of the disordered kind. The application of personalist philosophical ethics applied to sexual morality in the works of Dietrich von Hildebrand and Herbert Doms in the 1930-40s helped to clarify a more experiential perspective of marital chastity. Pope John Paul II in his work *Love and Responsibility* later expounds on these ideas—that chastity is not merely mastery over passion but the integration of sexual desires and a wide range of human affectivity. In the single, celibate, and married vocations, "chastity makes it possible for persons to discover the communion for which they were created. "[495]

In an attempt to inculcate the virtue of chastity, Grabowski warns that the complex and far-reaching-effects of cultural influence must be noted, stating, "To some degree or other chastity is a virtue mediated by moral and religious narratives whose acquisition will be shaped by particular cultural contexts and symbols. "[496] Grabowski notes that cultures are different; thus, what one holds sacred may not necessarily be so in another culture. Therefore, he advocates for what JPII calls adopting a "culture of life. "[497] Grabowski argues for engaging culture through critical evaluation, the elaboration of alternative views and practices, the presentation of a more positive vision of human sexuality, and engaging people in specific cultural practices that can allow chastity to flourish. Following and in line with the foregoing, Grabowski explains the connection between "biology" and "environment-culture" or the nurture-versus-nature debate. Grabowski posits that just as in the Trinitarian life of God, wherein "each person is utterly equal in his possession of the divine nature and yet utterly irreducible to one another as persons..., the sexes share a common humanity—the same nature.

---

495   Ibid., 87. Grabowski clarifies the virtue of chastity as having three distinctive forms: First, celibate chastity which is ordered to the gift of one's body and sexuality in nongenital expressions of friendship, love, and service in the Church. Second, conjugal chastity ordered towards fidelity and the total self-gifts of spouses within the marriage covenant. Third, unmarried or widowed single persons, are required the same continence of the celibate except for the widowed person, who can legitimately choose to re-marry. Cf. Ibid., 88.

496   Ibid., 93.

497   John Paul II, *Evangelium Vitae*, #95-100.

Yet they are irreducibly different as persons. "[498] Grabowski's overall marital and sexual ethic, though close to the magisterial position, offers a new method at approaching this important question. Grabowski's position is best summarized in his own words:

> ...a covenantal understanding of sexual fidelity in conjunction with an account of chastity as an integral part of human flourishing can provide a framework for a Christian approach to issues of sexual morality in the present context. This covenantal understanding provides a vantage to critique shallow and distorted views of sexuality in contemporary culture as well as for framing an alternative to them. It is rooted in the mystery of Christ mediated by the biblical witness and the Church's liturgical tradition. It points towards the vocation of followers of Christ to be conformed to him in their capacity to love. Chastity is the virtue that enables this vocation to be realized and lived in a variety of states of life.[499]

In an essay co-authored by Grabowski and Michael J. Naughton, the two authors responded to a previous Charles Curran essay published in *Commonweal* on October 11, 1996. In this essay, Charles Curran accused Catholics of suffering from "schizophrenia" on matters of papal/magisterial sexual ethics. Curran asserts that issues of magisterial teachings on sexual ethics are often times inconsistent because they move from a classicist approach to a more historically conscious and

---

498   Grabowski. *Sex and Virtue*, 110. JPII in *TOB* refers to this unique individuality and oneness of spouses as "the nuptial meaning of the body. "

499   Ibid. 168. Grabowski concludes his book by stating, "...this conceptualization of sexuality to be effective [it] has to be embodied in personal and communal praxis. A full answer to the crisis of sexuality in the contemporary Church and society can only be found in people who by their lives and practices proclaim a countercultural alternative to its trivialization – people's whose masculinity-femininity is a sacramental sign of "the sincere gift of self, " whose sexual practices foster authentic human flourishing, whose sexuality is imbued with virtue. The lived witness of the human vocation to communion within marriages, families, religious vocations, and the single life isboth a sign and a participation in the One whose being is gift and whose life as a Trinity of Persons is an eternal communion of Love. Ibid.

personalist approach. Grabowski and Naughton respond that JPII's position on family life and sexuality is different from the pontiff's approach on social issues. Social issues, Grabowski and Naughton claim, are embedded in constantly changing political and societal dynamics, whereas sexual morality remains within the family context. "The family plays a fundamental role in the procreation and protection of human life through the conjugal union of man and woman in marriage. Because of this role, the family has a more foundational and permanent character than other social institutions. "[500] Grabowski and Naughton continue in their response to Curran by reiterating the importance of family as the locus of other institutions and the human society in its entirety: "The family is the basic cell of every human society; hence society is dependent upon the family. To claim that the family is a more immutable structure than other institutions is not to oppose a 'historically conscious' approach... but to recognize the family's fundamental role in social stability and its rootedness in the permanent union of a man and a woman in the covenant of marriage. "[501]

Grabowski and Naughton insist that the Church's social teachings are more open to historical consciousness than its sexual ethic, because to have it any other way, "the Church would either have to relativize the family or baptize a particular social arrangement—for example, capitalism or socialism. "[502] The authors argue that Curran's charge that because the Church in history has changed her mind on politics, human rights, and democracy, she therefore should be able to change on the question of morality shows a failure on the part of Curran to recognize the basic nature of sexual values and the institutions they embody. In Grabowski and Naughton's view, there is no clash in JPII's teachings as either classicist in sexual ethics or historically conscious in

---

500   John S. Grabowski and Michael J. Naughton, "Doctrinal Development: Does it Apply to Sex? " *Commonweal* 124, no. 11 (June 6, 1997): 2.

501   Ibid.

502   Ibid., 3.

social teachings; rather, "what we do see is an effort to formulate an integrated account of morality that reflects the understanding of the human person as created in God's image. "[503]

In a 2002 *Logos* journal article, Grabowski explores "spirituality " for families in the light of *Ecclesia in America*.[504] Among other issues considered by this post-synodal Apostolic Exhortation, Grabowski pays particular attention to the Christian ideal of conjugal communion and family life, with extra focus on Vatican II's universal call to holiness which then characterizes a spirituality for motherhood and fatherhood. Grabowski's concern is based on what he considers a "dearth of distinctive models of spirituality for families within the tradition. "[505] Alluding to years of the misconceived ideal of the superiority of various forms of monastic spirituality as "watered down " for a second-class married vocation, Grabowski notes that in this tradition, a genuine spirituality for families seems impossible to achieve. His re-reading of *Ecclesia in America* in the light of *Lumen Gentium* and more recent magisterial pronouncements sees the possibility of highlighting numerous resources capable of pin-pointing distinctive and eminently practicable spiritualties for families. These resources will largely include

---

503 Ibid. I find Grabowski and Naughton's conclusion in their response to Curran interesting when they assert, "It must be admitted, however, that there is something in Curran's diagnosis of schizophrenia that rings true. Still, the root of the problem is not a clash between classicist and historically conscious ways of thinking. Rather, it is the endurance of the legalistic morality that dominated Catholic thought in the last four centuries. Because the Catholic manualists held that, strictly speaking, one is only required to avoid evil rather than to do good, many of the positive injunctions of the social tradition were marginalized. So in many cases, Catholic social teaching seems to lack 'teeth' in Church law and in the practice of Catholic organizations. The solution to this legalism is not, however, to equivocate in regard to values of life or sexuality, but to reject the mindset that makes social goods dispensable. As a Church, we must discover ways to describe the binding character of the good without reducing the whole of morality to law. Undoubtedly there is room for deeper understanding and better formulations in all of the strands of Catholic moral teaching. Because the moral life is rooted in the spiritual life, it is always open to growth. But Curran's diagnosis of schizophrenia fails to appreciate the organic unity and integrity of the Church's moral tradition. It also fails to identify the legalism that is the real cause of the schizophrenia hamstringing the application of Catholic social teaching. " Ibid.

504 John S. Grabowski, "Called to Holiness: Spirituality for Families in Light of *Ecclesia in America*, " *Logos: A Journal of Catholic Thought and Culture* 5, no. 4 (Fall 2002): 75–95.

505 Ibid., 75.

biblical and theological themes suited to the vocation of those who have families and encounter society, being called to holiness thereby. Grabowski therefore focuses on biblical themes of family as covenant, as communion, and as domestic Church which participates in the threefold office of Christ as priest, prophet, and king, and as a sanctuary of love and life.

From his position in his journal essay together within the context of *Ecclesia in America* and other contemporary teachings to which he alludes, Grabowski is able to frame a possible model of a comprehensive vision for Christian family life. Of particular significance in Grabowski's thought is the array of social forces that mitigates against families seen and existing as places of *covenant*—a family covenant established through vows, blood, or adoption.[506] In terms of the family as a place of *communion*, Grabowski helps modern persons to see the nature of the family as a foundational expression of the human and Christian vocation to communion. In learning to give and receive love, the couple enter into communion which will invariably embrace their gift of children and family, and embrace the same reason for which humanity was created.[507] Seen and understood as a *domestic Church*, coming out of Vatican II, the family is perceived as a "specific revelation and realization of ecclesial communion or domestic Church " which is both evangelized and evangelizing.[508] Finally, when family life is understood as *a place of sanctuary of love and life*, it is a sacred place of refuge and protection because it is a "holy " place inhabited by human and divine life.[509]

According to Grabowski, powerful social forces are arrayed against the family and its role under these themes. Grabowski, referring to Pope John Paul II, speaks of what JPII calls a kind of "anti-civilization " and "the culture of death. "[510] Grabowski asserts that these influences are evident in a liberal/secularized post-modern world where there is

---

506   Ibid., 80.

507   Ibid., 80-1.

508   Ibid., 84-5.

509   Ibid., 87.

510   Ibid., 88.

[a]n aggressive secularism that banishes an understanding of God from public life and education; unbridled materialism and consumerism that reduce the goal of life to the acquisition of wealth and material goods; contemporary individualism that denies the social nature of the person and reduces his or her freedom to autonomy, various forms of relativism that undermine any account of the truth about the person; anthropological views that reduce human personhood to a level of function and hence deny it to the unborn, handicapped, or elderly; utilitarian views of morality that deny transcendent moral values and reduce people to objects of use; understanding of sexuality that reduce it to a mere biological outlet for pleasure and see children as a burden; and current of thought spawned by instrumental reason that see the created world as mere inanimate matter to be dominated by scientific and technological means.

The family is thus at the fulcrum of the struggle that makes up the drama of our age. The forces arrayed against the family are not fictional beasts sketched by academic theory or ecclesial pronouncement... Given its pivotal role as the sanctuary of life, the family is crucial to the Church's mission in proclaiming the gospel of life.[511]

Grabowski's theologizing sees the family and its spirituality at the front line of an enormous cultural shift. He therefore, in agreement with *Ecclesia in America*, advocates for a renewed evangelization of families, new catechesis, and new pastoral approach to family life. Grabowski's hermeneutic gives weight to traditional magisterial positions, yet he is able to proffer and propose new methods by which tradition can speak to modern society and be intelligible. His work adds a much needed critique and raises profound and related questions for contemporary

---

511   Ibid., 89.

thinking on marriage, family life, and human sexuality and the development of doctrine.

Lisa Sowle Cahill

My second dialogue partner, Dr. Lisa Sowle Cahill,[512] came into the limelight in the 1980s with her studies on gender and sexual ethics. Cahill's work focuses on the complexity of moral issues and the tensions in theological disagreements between the Church and society. She explores sexuality strictly from the hermeneutics of scriptures, gender differentiation, and contemporary Christian ethics. She pays particular attention to how men and women relate sexually, to the rights and wrongs of human sexual relationships, and to what Christian ethics might contribute. In Cahill's own words, "sexuality is morality. It is part of our expressing, for good or ill, relationship to the material world,

---

512   According to William Bole in a 2011 *Commonweal* essay on Cahill, "As a scholar, Cahill finds her footing in the natural law tradition, which affirms the compatibility of faith and reason and the possibility of arriving at objective truths – 'natural' or self-evident truths on which people of all faiths (and no faith) can agree. Natural Law discourse emphasizes public conversation about the social good, and Cahill believes that the Church and other Christian communities can both contribute to this conversation and profit from it, culling truth from a broad diversity of settings and assumptions. Everyone has a capacity for reasonable judgement; no one should be dismissed out of hand. This methodology is front and center in all of her theological investigations. " Cf. William Bole, "No Labels Please: Lisa Sowle Cahill's Middle Way, " *Commonweal* 38, no. 1 (Jan. 14, 2011): 3

Roland Hoksbergen, in his review of Lisa Cahill's 2013 book, *Global Justice, Christology and Christian Ethics*, alludes to Cahill's style of doing theology as follows: "She constructs her argument in full recognition that she is herself embedded in the cultural, intellectual and theological context of her own world, and from that position and perspective works to reconcile opposing theological ideas that have long been in conflict. Among the most prominent contemporary realities that have influenced her, while also calling out for ethical attention, are the increasing acceptance of postmodern understandings, the changing perceptions of the role of women, and our increased global interaction and consciousness, especially the realities of cultural and religious pluralism.... Her writing models the sort of love, reconciliation and hopeful spirit that she would also instil in other Christian hearts and minds. This spirit is amply manifested by the fact that she never really argues against any idea, nor attempts to show that one view is better than another. Instead, she honors every tradition of thought, attempting to extract the positive, to show how opposing views arising from these traditions can be reconciled, and then to push supporters of such views to new syntheses that will get them working together for positive change. This is no small task, but Cahill makes good progress. " Cf. Roland Hoksbergen, "Lisa Sowle Cahill, Global Justice, Christology and Christian Ethics, " *Studies in Christian Ethics* 27, no. 3 (2014): 340-382

to other life forms, to the self, and to other persons, including God. "[513] Arguably, Cahill succeeds in finding a pathway by balancing extreme positions in locating a Christian ethic of equal gender relationality. Her work gives a balanced and fair critique to Catholic moral theology and secular non-religious contemporary voices. Cahill works from a feminist perspective which she claims is "simply a commitment to equal personal respect and equal social power for women and men. "[514] In this expose of Cahill's theological assumptions, attention is given to three of her books: *Between the Sexes: Foundations for a Christian Ethics of Sexuality* (1985); *Sex, Gender and Christian Ethics* (1996); and *Family: A Christian Social Perspective* (2000), they pay particular attention to questions about family and sexual ethics from within the Catholic tradition and therefore align with the trajectory of the central thesis of this book.

In *Between the Sexes: Foundations for a Christian Ethics of Sexuality* (1985), Cahill claims that her work specifically is focused on "the 'rights and wrongs' of relationships between women and men ...it is about sexual ethics and the ethics of male and female cooperation. "[515] As in most of her other works, Cahill's thesis relies on four reference points for her Christian ethics, (1) the Bible/Scripture as foundational text for the faith community, (2) the community's faith tradition, (3) theology, praxis, and philosophical accounts of ideal humanity (normative to human experience), (4) and a descriptive account of what is common to human experience. Cahill opines that "fidelity to these four mutually correcting sources, and success in judiciously balancing them, is a standard by which we can measure the adequacy of various positions and traditions, including our own. "[516] Further on, she contends that our reading of the Bible should respond to the mores of our culture, and that the standard of an adequate Christian theology and ethics of sexuality "is precisely the dialectical and complementary relationship of Bible, tradition, and normative and descriptive accounts

---

513   Lisa Sowle Cahill, *Between the Sexes: Foundations for a Christian Ethics of Sexuality* (Philadelphia: Fortress Press, 1985), 2.

514   Lisa Sowle Cahill, *Sex, Gender & Christian Ethics* (Cambridge, UK: Cambridge University Press, 1996), 1

515   Cahill, *Between the Sexes*, 1.

516   Ibid., 6.

of human existence. "[517] Cahill warns against the presupposition that a philosophical account of sexuality is enough to define the essential and ideals of the meaning of sexuality. Actual historical distortions and adaptations, she maintains, show philosophy's limitations. Cahill proposes that sexuality may be understood better as an affirmation of the character of interpersonal relationships, procreation, and the equal dignity worthy of both women and men. Cahill's project ultimately is to be able to offer what she calls the two criteria by which the Christian community can approach questions of family and sexuality: commitment and procreative responsibility. Cahill, however, reiterates, "Particular sexual acts and relations can realize these values in different ways and in different degrees… Not all Christian interpretations of these criteria should continue to determine moral analysis of sexuality. "[518] It is in this way, according to Cahill, that Christian ethics become dynamic and ordered in fidelity to the Christian symbols of beneficent Creator, righteous Judge, gracious Redeemer, and transforming Spirit. "These symbols require us to attend to our own experience of God and community as the beginning point of reconciliation of body and spirit, self and others, and humanity and God. "[519]

Cahill presents as central to the Christian tradition a communal aspect which serves reproductive acts, civil and religious communities, and even the love of the spouses, all of which are located within the service of same communitarian focus. Cahill locates this social dimension in Augustine, Aquinas and Luther. In her estimation, the main stream of Western moral philosophy since the enlightenment has relied on autonomy, rationality, and freedom of the individual, as exemplified in John Locke's liberalism that is common to North American society and politics. In this liberalist autonomy, the individual is concerned about personal interests and needs, and only paralleled by the competing rights of others in the pursuit of the same ideal.[520] In sexuality, liberalism tends to support the autonomy of consenting adults to any

---

517   Ibid., 9.

518   Ibid., 11.

519   Ibid.

520   Ibid., 140.

liaison without necessarily acceding to religious or political control. Cahill perceives and warns about liberalism and autonomy, stating, "Still, liberal individualism and relativism in sexual ethics stand to be corrected by the traditional service-oriented and communal ideals against which contemporary personalism arose as a modification. "[521]

Cahill accedes that in both Testaments of the Bible, the institutionalization of heterosexual, monogamous, permanent, and procreative marriage is favored, such that procreative marriage is cohesive with the continuity of the body politic, the Church, and family. Biblical texts are also explicit in condemning deviations from these general norms because they are understood to be incompatible with the life of faith in the covenant community. Among the unacceptable acts in sexuality are included adultery, fornication, *porneia*/sexual immorality and homosexuality.[522] Cahill immediately proceeds to raise some questions in an attempt to clarify if normative scriptural texts are universal and have unquestionable authority. The questions include whether "the authority of the 'norm' of heterosexual monogamy differs in any crucial sense from a 'norm' such as patriarchy whose decisiveness for Christian faith, practice and theology is dubious? "[523] Referring to these as less unclear, she nonetheless asks if "the prohibitions that biblical authors derive from monogamous, heterosexual, and procreative meanings of sexuality unfailingly indicate specific relations and acts that decisively fail to embody those goods that meaningful sexuality is said to realize? "[524] Cahill notes that the Bible itself provides for an occasional exception whose status does not contradict the norm against which they are defined, questioning if "divorce of some sort was permitted by Mathew and Paul. On the biblical model, the question of exceptions appears to be an open one. How then shall the viability of proposed exceptions be determined? "[525] With increasing data on the study of the etiology of homosexual phenomenon, Cahill again cautions,

---

521   Ibid., 141.

522   Ibid., 143.

523   Ibid., 144.

524   Ibid., 144-5.

525   Ibid., 145.

No simple definitions of what is morally "normative, " or even what is "healthy, " in human sexuality will be available from sheer empirical investigations, even though the latter augment reflection immensely. It must be remembered that even empirical "data " are organized and interpreted with the help of categories that are themselves not wholly "value free. " ... Empirical evidence can be appropriated meaningfully in Christian ethics only if interpreted in the light of other, complementary sources: Scripture, tradition, and normative, as distinct from descriptive, accounts of the human.[526]

Cahill accepts a nuanced departure from the traditional Christian central ethics of sexual norms which accommodates certain variant ways of living out these norms, proposing, first, that the Christian community "should formulate criteria that define fidelity to the essence of this norm, while allowing variance in the way it is fulfilled. "[527] Second, she observes that "it is necessary to contemplate true departures from norms as well as unusual applications of them, though the vast majority of 'exceptions' fall into the latter category. "[528] These possible exceptions, while tolerable, must be rare, with the understanding that "fixation of attention on the outer limits of applications and departures is not a perspective on sexuality congruent with the biblical one... "[529] Cahill calls for a "responsible " application of sexual moral norms by Christians in situations where "strict adherence to the norm of procreative, heterosexual monogamy is inappropriate, difficult or impossible. "[530] Cahill includes in these situations, questions about remarriage after divorce, committed but premarital ("preceremonial ") sex, avoidance of conception in marital conjugal sex, and committed homosexual relationships. Cahill acknowledges how difficult the sexual morality subject has been, but she remains hopeful that despite

---

526   Ibid., 148.

527   Ibid.

528   Ibid.

529   Ibid.

530   Ibid., 149.

all the differences in opinion, positions held as untrue can be held sincerely and conscientiously and that the presumed position, held and believed deeply, may from time to time stand in need of revision. In Cahill's words, "Shifts in sexual milieus do not necessarily mean that Christian ethics needs to be re-written entirely, but may require radical reappropriation of the images by which it is formed. "[531]

In *Sex, Gender and Christian Ethics,* Cahill calls for a feminist critique of what it means to be male and female while upholding the insights of traditional Christian ethics of conjugality, commitment, and parenthood as the hallmark of human relationships. This unitive component of marriage is an ideal which for Cahill is not an absolute norm. Gender equality must entail dignity of persons, mutual respect, and equality of social power, excluding any kind of patriarchy. In response to communitarian proponents of Christian morality and feminist critics of oppressive gender and sex norms, Cahill posits that there is a need for an effective intercultural criticism of unjust structures with a moderate defense of moral objectivity.[532] Cahill argues that feminists' deconstructions of moral foundations "creates a normative vacuum which cripples their political critique....they allow values like autonomy and freedom, tracing to Enlightenment roots, to slide in as tacit universals, operative without intercultural nuancing or explicit defense. "[533] Cahill pursues a different path:

> Human embodiedness, as to some extent structuring
> our social relations, need to be reintegrated with
> freedom. All must be elements in a Christian ethics
> of sex and gender which is committed to equality,
> to intercultural discernment of real goods and evils,

---

531   Ibid., 151.

532   Lisa Sowle Cahill,   "Renegotiation Aquinas: Catholic Feminist Ethics, Postmodernism, Realism, and Faith, " *Journal of Religious Ethics* 42, no. 2 (June 2015): 193-217. In this journal essay, Cahill clarifies feminist ethics specifically as "committed to improvement of the human condition – especially the condition of women – within whatever opportunities the political realities provide in specific times and places. Feminist theological ethics goes beyond philosophy to ground its hope in the breaking reign of God proclaimed by realist gender justice ethicists, and in the mystery of infinite being whom the postmodern gendered faith ethicists invoke. " Ibid., 213.

533   Cahill, *Sex, Gender,* 2.

and to the human and moral interdependence of sexual desire and pleasure, sexual commitment, and responsibility.[534]

In the conversation about sexual morality between revisers and traditionalists, the primary interpretative norm should be relationship and fulfilment. These norms, according to Cahill, are both valid but must always be placed "in a deeper and more nuanced social context, with better attention both to the familial ramifications of sexual partnerships, and to differences and similarities in cross-cultural experiences of sex, gender and family."[535] Cahill opines that for Christian sexual ethics to be meaningful for contemporary times, "it must ground sexual freedom and fulfilment in some account of the human goods at stake in sex and in the relationships built upon it."[536] It also must develop a system that can speak to and listen to multiple moral traditions, each in their own cultures. "This will require meeting the postmodern critiques of rationality and moral value, and reconstructing some recognizable foundations for sex and gender ethics."[537] Cahill also points out an interesting contemporary line of division in Christianity that must be overcome:

> I believe that a cautious but essentially realist ethics is necessary to avoid the social ineffectiveness of moral relativism. I also believe it is warranted by the way practical moral debate and negotiation actually take place.... It also can escape the pitfalls of rigidity and abstraction to which both Kantian minimalist universalism (often in Protestant theological forms) and neo scholastic casuistry (a Catholic development) have been liable, and which have contributed to the retreat of many Christian ethicists into communitarianism.[538]

---

534   Ibid., 3.

535   Ibid., 10.

536   Ibid., 11.

537   Ibid., 12.

538   Ibid.

Sex, Gender and Christian Ethics, strives to place in context, what sex, gender and marriage should mean in contemporary times based on what it has meant historically. According to Cahill, pre-modern cultures of fourth century migrants into Europe and Christianity set a high priority on the social functions of marriage and family and perceived gender from a hierarchical point of view. Sex was understood with regard to its purely reproductive functions, family and parenthood by their socio-economic functions. Cahill avers that "sexual intimacy was structured patriarchally, and sexual pleasure was not linked to the mutual affection of the reproductive partners, so much as to the accomplishment of reproduction itself, whose requirements it always exceeded. Hence sex's reputation as unruly and dangerous to its own social role. "[539] Cahill claims that it was not until modern times that the Church's theology of marriage presented its interpersonal dimensions as the primary goal of the union. Nonetheless, Christians in most cultures approach marriage from that deep personal commitment of love and family above socio- economic needs or function. According to Cahill, "Sex, interpreted in light of the individual's intersubjective experience, is valued for allowing intimacy as reciprocity, and as supplying mutual pleasure which enhances intimacy. "[540]

Cahill thinks that women's status has improved worldwide in contemporary times owing to "increased access to education, healthcare, and family planning measures. "[541] Notwithstanding, Cahill is quick to point out that there is a continued societal permissiveness towards men's sexual behavior which re-entrenches gender inequality. Cahill clearly challenges the current state of things:

> The connection between sex, love and babies cannot
> be apprehended, much less credibly advocated, in
> any individualist or act oriented concept of sex,

---

539   Ibid., 166. Dr. Cahill's position, valid as they are seem not to take in to consideration non-western cultures and their understanding of marriage, sex and family life which times are often connected to the idea of community of the ancestors, the living and the yet to be born. I believe that such considerations gives a more wholesome overview of these issue

540   Ibid., 167.

541   Ibid., 206.

becoming a parent, or making a commitment. A strength of Catholic tradition is its strongly social vision of these realities. They now require re-visioning toward a personalized and gender equal paradigm, which recognizes the biographical and diachronic context of sexual and parental meaning and hence of sexual morality. To rehabilitate the parental significance of sexuality within such a paradigm, it may be necessary to give up specifying those purposes which fulfill sexual activity in the immediate experience of participants – where, in the event, procreation is rarely the dominant conscious aim – and to reposition reproduction in the social context which has for so long been so important in constituting its human meaning. The parenthood of the individual should be placed in the context of relationship to one's co-parent; conceiving, birthing, and parenting a child should be placed within the family, both nuclear and extended; and the family must be seen, neither as a "haven " from the world, nor as a nexus of social control, but as a school for critical contribution to the common good. To place parenthood in social context would also mean, from a Christian standpoint, to ask how Christian values transform, the family, and shape the family's contribution to society.[542]

Even in light of this modern critique of commitment and inter-subjectivity in both the Protestant and Catholic traditions, Cahill argues that "a post-modern reticence about moral foundations has made it difficult for many social critics—Christian and otherwise—to argue convincingly that equality, reciprocity, and respect should function as cross-cultural norms. "[543] She goes further to proffer that liberal assumptions about the priority of freedom have made it equally difficult "to complement the importance of these values with a more

---

542   Ibid., 207.

543   Ibid., 255.

complete consideration of human embodiment, its social dimensions, and its function in defining human goods and suggesting human moral values. "[544] Therefore, there is a need for a consistent commitment to embodiment and the redefinition of marriage, parenthood, and family in which gendered sexuality is re-imagined. Cahill avers, "The Roman Catholic commitment to (provisional) objectivity in moral evaluation, and to the ideal unity of sexual expression, and shared parenthood, can contribute to a more complete Christian ethics of sex as an embodied social reality. "[545] Contemporary Catholic theological ethics needs to draw from people's cultural experiences to be able to redefine its concrete moral obligations. The Church must recognize and take to heart culturally shared moral norms and critique commonalities for mutual criticism and improvement to develop. Cahill concludes that Christian discipleship transforms sex, family, parenthood, and gender by recognizing and upholding the embodied and social aspects, the personal and intentional perspectives of persons, for discipleship to become transformative. "Christian sex and gender ethics... builds but reforms human cultural practices so that they better represent the Christian values of incarnation, community, solidarity, fidelity, compassion and hope that moral and social change are possible. "[546]

In another piece published in *Theological Studies* (2003), Cahill notes that JPII's post synodal Apostolic Exhortation and *Theology of the Body*, which developed a hermeneutic of marriage as an interpersonal expression of communal family life, may not be adequate for confronting and challenging the social realities of postmodern and societal approaches to marriage today. She points to a new approach by a new generation of Catholic scholars "who write from a culture and for an audience pervaded by transience of relationships, trivialization of sex, and exploitation of just about every area of human meaning by market capitalism. "[547] These new scholars, according to Cahill, seek to make a credible case for marriage without naiveté and undue romanticization about marriage, sex, and interpersonal love and the

---

544   Ibid.

545   Ibid., 255-6.

546   Ibid., 267.

547   Lisa Sowle Cahill, "Notes on Moral Theology: Marriage, Developments in Catholic Theology and Ethics, " *Theological Studies* 64, no. 1 (2003): 78-105.

ways in which they are woven into a dense web of social relations. These scholars avoid absolutes, and do not engage official positions as "problematics " to be solved. Cahill states, "Their views cannot easily be categorized along 'conservative' and 'liberal' or 'orthodox' and 'dissenting' lines. Their attempt to formulate a fresh perspective in a different voice is of special significance in understanding the nature and future of catholic debates about the theology and ethics of marriage. "[548] These emerging scholars are sensitive to the cultural and socio-economic conditions and gender equality which remains a bedrock to the success of any marital commitment. Cahill elucidates further, "Their primary concern is to find resources for resistance of cultural trends toward family fragmentation and consumerism, and to do so by exploring in a realistic way their own experiences of sexuality, marriage, parenthood, and social connectedness. "[549] In this sense, Cahill sees a new challenge but a positive one that can help move the Catholic tradition further and closer toward becoming intelligible for a largely postmodern Catholic theologians/scholars and young people.

In *Family: A Christian Social Perspective* (2000), Cahill attends to the public conversation on a renewed approach to understanding "family " and "family values. " Cahill acknowledges two schools of thought among social theorists of the 1990s in North America. These schools of thought understand and diagnose these phenomena quite differently: on the one hand, some see the widespread disintegration of traditional family life as a result of unfettered autonomy, individualism, hedonism narcissism and moral laxity. On the opposing side, others perceive the newer understanding of pluralistic family forms as a breakaway from the traditional patriarchal nuclear family unit. Cahill argues in support of the second position stating that although family, "created by kinship and marriage is the most basic family form or definition of marriage, it is not the only or exclusively legitimate form. "[550] According to Cahill, "There are other types of human alliance.... for mutual economic and domestic support, as for reproduction and child rearing, that are analogous to the basic kin- and marriage-based family. These need not

---

548   Ibid., 81.

549   Ibid., 80.

550   Lisa Sowle Cahill, *Family: A Christian Social Perspective* (Minneapolis: Fortress Press, 2000), xi.

entail biological kinship or male-female marriage. "[551] Cahill argues further that the outer boundaries of what family life means are difficult to define because its analogous forms arise according to specific circumstances and needs. Therefore, it would be imprudent to set definitive limits on what is strictly meant by family. However, Cahill proposes to advance an inclusive interpretative model which can both hold up the traditional male-female understanding and at the same time not exclude "single parent families, divorced families, gay and lesbian families, blended families, or adoptive families. "[552] To show a true Christian ideal of what it means to be family, Cahill posits that the focus should be on function rather than on the regularity of form since these other forms of "families " often, given the necessary support, can function as well as the traditional ones. Cahill clarifies her position in this book as follows:

> My thesis is that strong family, spousal, and parental relationships are important, but that these very ideals are undermined by condemnatory and punitive attitudes and policies toward nonconforming families.... In my view, the Christian family is not the nuclear family focused inward on the welfare of its own members but the socially transformative family that seeks to make the Christian moral ideal of love of neighbor part of the common good.... Unfortunately, however, so-called Christian ideologies of family life are at least as likely to sanctify injustices of gender, class, and race as they have been to challenge and reform them. The term, *Christian family* is ambivalent. Often the family is preserved at the expense of any real Christianity, while "family values " rhetoric becomes a means of reinforcing social inequalities.[553]

---

551   Ibid.

552   Ibid.

553   Ibid., xi-xii.

"Families " according to Cahill, are in trouble, and the crisis is different for men as compared to women, for whites as compared to people of color, for the chronically under educated, the unemployed compared to middle-class workers, and for teenaged or single parents. This crisis has "other social and economic roots that are just as truly matters of Christian moral concern as are narcissistic individualism and unwillingness to make and keep commitments. "[554] The plight of contemporary families gives ground to three convictions expounded by Cahill. First, human beings are intrinsically social in nature. Based on the human's natural capacity for empathy, intimacy, and altruism, and coupled with technological advancement in communication media, human families can grow by enhancing their capacity for inclusive social communications and cooperation. Second, the reality of sin allows humans to conceive violence, which can permeate and affect large numbers of peoples. Third, Christianity, in its symbols, traditions, practices, teachings, and theological endeavors over the centuries needs to ensure that the "Christian family will begin to transform civil society and all the other co-arising institutions through and in which Christians exist with others on this planet. "[555]

Cahill concludes her reflection on the family by proposing what she refers to as "five constructive recommendations for Christian family life. " These recommendations address the nature, functions, and values of families and the Christian conversion of family bonds and roles. First, Christian families should be grounded in human relationships that promote general wellbeing. Second, Christian families should educate and promote the social, economic, and political participation of its members to engender the common good. Third, kinship families, integrated and relativized by Christianity's inclusive nature, should reach out to new families who are especially wearied and heavily burdened by exclusivity to welcome them into the body of Christ. Fourth, given the Church's social role of the *preferential option for the poor*, the institutionalizing of just treatments and access to goods must be first and foremost in importance whenever people are faced with conflicting practical claims. Fifth and last, Christian families must

---

554   Ibid., 1.

555   Ibid., 17.

train the moral commitment and imagination to see human beings and relationships in the light of the reign of God. So that Christian social sins call equally to forgiveness which is slow to judge but quick to offer support. Cahill states that the "Christian family is not the perfect family but one in which fidelity, compassion, forgiveness, and concern for others, even strangers, are known. In striving to embody these virtues, however imperfect its success, a family lives in the presence of God and begins to transform its surroundings. A Christian family is such a family. "[556]

Cahill's moral foundation, she applies a critical realism based on practical, intercultural, reasonable, and prudent human experience while drawing on the works of Aristotle and Aquinas. Again, in this book, Cahill depends on Scripture (particularly the New Testament in this case), for her model of community, solidarity, compassion, and inclusion of those who are socially and economically pushed to the margins of society.

Ted Peters, in commenting on Cahill's work states that she is aggressively engaged in the task of "philosophically and theologically grounding Roman Catholic ethical thought in an emerging postmodern and pluralistic culture. "[557] Peters states further that Cahill's work argues with an apologetic force and compassionate sensitivity for a natural law ethic that places the standard Roman Catholic tradition in conversation with contemporary voices to secure a solid foundation by which she establishes her sexual and family ethic. Peters opines that Cahill offers "a most penetrating and edifying analysis of the Christian tradition regarding the relationship between reproduction and companionship in marriage. "[558] Cahill's work is distinctively

---

556   Ibid., 136-7.

557   Ted Peters, S.A., "Feminist and Catholic: The Family Ethics of Lisa Sowle Cahill, " *Dialog* 35, no. 4 (1996): 269

558   Ibid., 270. Peters quotes Cahill verbatim on the question of reproduction and marriage, referring Cahill's essay titled, "Catholic Sexual Ethics and the Dignity of the Person " in *Theological Studies, Vol. 50* (1989), states, "If the prophetic message of today's Church is to be that sexual expression should arise from personal commitment which, barring extra ordinary circumstances, is open to and responsible for children, it will have to find a language to ground the meaning of sex and parenthood convincingly in the personal devotion of the partners. " Ibid., 270.

feminist, situated within the natural law and Roman Catholic tradition but sensitive to Catholics and non- Catholics alike.[559] Cahill's focus as a feminist theologian is on a vision of the human good by which transformatory action can take place. Cahill identifies several contexts and cultures involving the exploitation of women: oppressive marriage customs, patriarchal domination and subjugation of women, poor and uneducated women in developing nations, genital mutilation, human trafficking for commercial sex trade, and hierarchical structures that exclude women within the Church. For Cahill, no consistent feminist critique of injustice can achieve any transformatory project if it still assumes matters of sex and gender as reducible to social constructs that are subject to relativity of values.[560]

Cahill's theological method and overarching project are structured on a universal retrieval and re-application of the Thomistic natural law

---

559   Peters sums up her universality and inclusivity thus, "The fundamental task Lisa Cahill takes up in her recent scholarly work is to ground the ethics of marriage in a concept of natural law that, on the one hand, benefits from the cross-cultural sensitivity and passion for justice on behalf of women demanded by deconstructionist postmodernism while, on the other hand, not surrendering to a pluralistic relativity that forbids lifting up a universal vision of what constitutes human flourishing. The value of postmodernist philosophy is that it provides us with the hermeneutic of suspicion, and this suspicion permits unintimidated rethinking of the tradition; it permits a critical reassessment of the pre-conscious patriarchal and oppressive cultural forms perpetuated by the tradition. It also encourages a retrieval of the fundamental egalitarian commitments inherent in the Christian gospel. Cahill's feminist ethic, committed to social equality of men and women, works with a critical dialectic between the patriarchal and egalitarian (sub) traditions within Christianity. And to adjudicate between these two sub-traditions within the Christian tradition she appeals to the human universal experience of embodiment and its articulation in her own version of natural law. The result is an ethic of marriage and nuclear family relations within which sexuality contributes to human flourishing through procreation and companionship. Ibid., 270.

560   Ibid., 271.

theory.[561] She envisions a natural law ethic that engages the human goods of sex, love, and procreation for human flourishing, an ethic which, she argues, cut across cultural contexts and common universal human conditions. Cahill understands the family and reproduction as essential to the propagation of the human race and expansion of communities unto the next generation. Therefore, sex, birth and family are intrinsic to the human condition, and outside of this perceived genetic self-perpetuation, human beings naturally create relationships, which cross culturally are the same everywhere and can be apprehended through reason and experience. Therefore, Cahill's ethical theologizing does not remain ideally on the level of foundations but includes "a middle axiom, " common, yet central to Cahill's project: she proposes moving from theorizing about ideals to people's lived experiences. Cahill's middle axiom philosophy therefore equips her to ask the fundamental question which guides her philosophy and theology of marital sexual ethics: does the traditional biological basis for the recognition of a family remain necessary in the light of contemporary prevalence of non- traditional family units? This includes homosexual unions, divorced and remarried persons who have children that do not belong biologically to both of them, and single parent homes.[562]

561   In another essay, Cahill expounds on her own approach and re-interpretation of what the natural law is: "In the postmodern period, conceding the historical contextualization of all thinking and knowledge, a credible natural law method cannot claim to provide absolute certainty over all particular cultures and historical perspectives. Yet it can hope for the gradual reduction of cultural bias by means of a critical interaction of experience and reflective thinking. Defined broadly, a natural law ethical approach is one that depends on reasonable and critical reflection on experience and that aims at as broad as possible a consensus about the good life or flourishing (in Aristotelian terms) for human beings. " Lisa Sowle Cahill, "Women, Marriage, Parenthood: What are Their Natures? " *Logos: Philosophic Issues in Christian Perspective 9* (1981), 11 as quoted in Ted Peters, "Feminist and Catholic: The Family Ethics of Lisa Sowle Cahill, " 272. Peters then avers that this natural law thinking sums up Cahill practical project: "…to establish a foundation for normative ethics in the universal human experience of embodiment as it manifests itself in sexuality and family relations, a trans-historical and trans-contextual human experience the appeal to which constitutes a form of natural law ethics. " Ibid., 272.

562   Peters clarifies Cahill's position further by expounding on the idea of a more generic notion of family that is not necessarily nuclear or biological by positing, "Even if there is room in Cahill's ethics for non-genetic inheritance, this non-biological bond would still draw energy with the biological bond. She is drawing a picture of the family in general-a picture of the ideal family-without rendering a negative judgement about specific families that include non-biologically connected members. Building a family around adoption, for example, is a laudable thing for Cahill; but it draws its energy from the biological family it mimics. The biological tie remains essential. Ibid., 274.

Cahill's middle axiom theory and basis for her theologizing stands or falls on this fundamental foundation. This is a common thread in Cahill's expansive corpus of work.

Cahill's sexual and marriage ethics can be summed up broadly along these lines: advocacy for equality of the sexes and full reciprocity in the marriage union. While she is in agreement with the Church on the question of abortion, she decries as at least patriarchal and oppressive the manner in which it seems the Church uses abortion to limit a woman's role to that of a mother in the home. Cahill endorses unitive personalism in marriage and acknowledges the good of procreation. She also argues against any social, economic, political, cultural or religious structures that jeopardize women's welfare around the world. Peters thinks that Cahill's theological method of family and sexuality is centered on the woman's worth, which has to do not only with motherhood but also her personhood,

> A theology that restricts sexuality and marriage to biological procreation reinforces the oppressive weight of poverty. Poor health, physical exhaustion, the unending struggle to provide materially for her children, when combined with submission to her man, leaves the woman of the underclass little access to personal joy beyond that offered by motherhood. The Christian social message that Cahill wants to deliver is this: Full reciprocity between women and men in loving marital bonds will create families that will be genuine schools of transforming values. In this school of transforming values, she adds, the Christian family should teach inclusive love for the outsider, for the marginalized, for those beyond our kin connection.[563]

Margaret Farley Margaret Farley, a religious nun of the Sisters of Mercy proposes a framework for a Christian sexual ethic which takes into account the question of justice. She carefully recounts the harm,

---

563   Ibid., 277.

violence, stigma and unjust actions perpetrated against others daily and worldwide in the name of sexuality. In two major works, *Personal Commitments: Beginning, Keeping, Changing* (1986) and *Just Love: A Frame Work for Christian Sexual Ethics*, (2008), we find most of Farley's thought on the ethics of gender, sexuality, and marriage. In most of her writings, Farley tries to propose various means for rethinking the ways we approach issues of sex and sexuality. Interacting with western cultures of the past, Farley reconstructs how we can now envision embodiment, gender, sexuality, love, and desire. She concludes that the key to understanding ourselves, given our new awareness, lies in the justice of our loves, our desires, and our actions. She opines that the role of the academic theologian is to ask questions so as to come up with new insights, anchored in tradition yet able to address the future. Farley's *Just Love: A Frame work for Christian Sexual Ethics* (2006) was censured by the Congregation for the Doctrine of the Faith (CDF) which judged her views as being in direct contradiction to traditional Catholic teaching. The CDF noted that Farley's position showed a "defective understanding of the objective nature of natural moral law…,[is] in direct contradiction with teaching in the field of sexual morality…,[poses] a great harm…, [and] cannot be used as a valid expression of Catholic teaching either in counselling and formation, or in ecumenical dialogue."[564] Nonetheless, Farley's work adds great value to this conversation, in so far as she logically addresses questions of sexuality by raising further questions which cannot remain uncritically challenged. She invites everyone to take a second look at the problems faced by Christians in their relationships and to find ways by which the Catholic magisterium can justly acknowledge and accept them.

In *Personal Commitments*, Farley sets out a frame work by which she approaches the question of marriage, family life, and sexuality from a key concept of the question of personal commitment. She asserts that for every individual's experience, personal commitments are always a social question and that social contexts shape people's personal commitments. Farley is convinced that the discernment and interpretation of experience deserves clarity in moral concepts and

---

564   Laurie Goodstein and Rachel Donadio, "Vatican Scolds Nun for Book on Sexuality, "published June 4, 2012, accessed May 12, 2014, http://www.nytimes.com/2012/06/05/us/sister-margaret-farley-denounced-by-vatican.html.

reasoning. In what Farley refers to as the era of rebellion from the 1950s through to the 1970s, engendered by a new focus on commitments to peace movements, civil rights, and social concerns of all kinds, the traditional understanding of commitments to entities like family, church, and country were questioned. These traditional perspectives were perceived as rigid, narrow, superficial, complacent, and uncritical obedience to structures and institutions. The traditional beliefs were demythologized by rapid changes in a socio-culturally rapidly evolving world in which personal and permanent commitments were looked at from another angle. Various studies at the time pointed to a new sociology of a kind of "Protean Man" characterized by "self-process." This new face of humanity was studied by psychologists, sociologists, and philosophers who came to the conclusion that long term or permanent commitments are not only impossible but also unwise because human freedom is incapable of controlling the future. Turning to the idea of commitment in which one person claims to love another, Farley argues that since love cannot be bound or obligated, it is impossible to predict if love will last. According to Farley, "Love is too easily stifled by the very idea of being obligated. Indeed, the binding of love may be what destroys it—destroys the spontaneity that makes us want to keep loving and doing the deeds of love."[565] Farley however, recognizes and acknowledge that personal commitments are generally perceived as being deeply connected with our deepest religious concerns, deeply woven into the fabrics of our existence "that they inevitably touch our most fundamental convictions and our most fundamental loves. And some commitments not only intersect with these beliefs and loves; they are expressions of them."[566]

Farley equates commitments with a gift, a pledge, which belongs to the giver but is then held in trust by the one to whom the pledge was made. It then establishes a claim on faithfulness and constancy because, in Farley's words, "Much of the time 'all' that we give is our word—not money, not rings, not special tokens that 'stand for us' us.

---

565   Margaret A. Farley, *Personal Commitments: Beginning, Keeping, Changing* (San Francisco: Harper & Row, 1986), 5.

566   Ibid., 9.

We stand in our word. Still, when we give just our word, we search for ways to 'incarnate,' to 'concretize,' to make tangible, the word itself. "[567] Farley understands "commitment " as

> .... a new relation in the present—a relation of binding and being-bound, giving and being-claimed. But commitment points to the *future*. The whole reason for the present relations as "obligating " is to try to influence the future, to try to determine ourselves to do the actions we intend and promise.... I give to the [other] person the power to limit my future freedom. The limitation consists in the fact that I stand to lose what I have given in pledge if I fail to be faithful to my promise.... The essential elements of interpersonal commitments are an intention regarding the future action and the undertaking of an obligation to another regarding that intended action.[568]

According to Farley, the commitment to love is a resolution and not a prediction, the giving of one's word as promise, to act faithfully as best as one can. All that it entails is an obligation undertaken to do what is promised. Farley points out that in a real sense, people commit themselves to a "framework " of love, to whatever one believes to be essential to this framework in such relationships as friendship, marriage, family and membership in communities of various sorts. To be present to one's commitment is to be committed to a future in a promise that was made in the past. Farley asserts, "If we are to be 'present' to our commitments, we must find a way to hold together their past and their future. We must find a way for free choice to prevent the loss of our love to the past and to sustain its engagements (even its spontaneous response) in the future we have promised. "[569] The heart of the matter for Farley, then, is the question of what moral obligation or duty lays claim on the one who makes such a commitment; what is the content

---

567   Ibid., 17.

568   Ibid., 18.

569   Ibid., 68.

and basis of this moral obligation? "Just love " is Farley's prescription for sorting out competing claims and responsibilities for discerning obligations and faithfulness to commitments.

Farley posits that goodwill and altruism notwithstanding, there are experiential situations where people are unable to keep their promises or commitments and might justly need a release from it. Farley explores four categories that might be considered valid for a release from commitments:

1. If and when the original meaning of the commitment was not true in itself, such as if the capacity to fully comprehend the nature of the commitment one was making; the one making the commitment "must have the *capacities* ordinarily required for free choice – hence, not to be too young, or mentally incompetent, not to be coerced by force or fear or fraud, not to be seduced...and not to be ignorant of factors that essentially change the nature of the commitment-relation. "[570]

2. A second condition is a "release by the promise "; this is a situation whereby a claim to commitment is waived or relinquished by the recipient or is simply mutually dropped.

3. The third condition is constituted by impossibility of fulfilment, which naturally leads to the conclusion that the said obligation does not hold.

4. The fourth condition is a situation where there are competing obligations, which Farley explains thus: "The claim I have given to someone by my promise always points in the direction of an obligation, but other claims (even claims from other commitments) may actually determine a different obligation in a given situation... the obligation not to harm persons (even myself) may take priority over the obligation to keep a promise. "[571]

The commitment to love, for Farley, means to love justly: "It is to a new claim, to undertake a new level of obligation, for loving and for a way of loving according to the content of our commitment. "[572] Farley

---

570   Ibid., 75.

571   Ibid., 76.

572   Ibid., 80.

expounds further on the theme of just love: "... the norm for a right love is the concrete reality of the beloved, of whoever or whatever is loved. "[573] To be bound or released from a commitment one makes, one needs to take into account the seriousness and urgency of the needs of those who lay claim to one's love and the overall implication of the good involved. Farley concludes that the "incapacities of the human heart may indeed break human hearts, but they need not destroy their loves. The clue to this truth is not outside of but within the meaning of commitment. As we have seen, in lives stretched out in time, there can be no absolute fullness, no utter once and for all yielding of love. "[574] Farley's conclusion: "commitment, therefore, is love's way of being whole when it is not yet whole, love's way of offering its incapacities as well as its power. "[575]

In Farley's *Just Love*, while developing and drawing on themes from *Personal Commitments*, she creates a frame work for patterns of relationships with particular focus on marriage, family, sex, and sexuality. In contemporary times, owing to the proliferation of the various forms of "family life, " a "seismic " shift in practice has evolved, with deep implications for how we now see and interpret marriage, family, and sex. According to Farley, because this shift contradicts cultural and religious traditions of relationships between families, the rearing and education of children, inheritance rights, and the reinforcing of gender roles, this newer understanding precludes the ability of providing newer perspectives. In expounding on the idea of religious and traditional marriage, Farley states, "A primary determinant of marriage was the need of families to gain in-laws, to establish or secure political and economic alliances between and among families. Yet the history of the functions of marriage is a complex one that cautions us against too hasty interpretations of the past or its relation to the present. "[576] Within Western civilization, the new trajectories of marriage and family have

---

573   Ibid., 82.

574   Ibid., 134.

575   Ibid.

576   Margaret A. Farley, *A Framework for Christian Sexual Ethics* (New York: Continuum Publishing Group, 2008), 247.

changed in a most profound way in the "motivation for marriage and who regulates its forms, and in the patterns of gender relations within both marriage and family. "[577]

In Farley's estimation, the major shift in the evolution of western marriage from family dominated arrangements to interpersonal love and changes in gender relations took place over four centuries of history. The role of Christianity in shaping the political and cultural under- pining of marriage and family is complicated and substantial, especially the idea of monogamy. Farley asserts that "monogamy was incorporated more broadly into early Christian beliefs and theologies—in terms of its potential symbolic significance for understanding the relation of Jesus Christ and the Church, and in terms of its amenability to Christian understandings of neighbor- love. "[578] Within this Christian influence, Farley points out three negative attitudes from antiquity that have affected the idea of marriage and family life: first, a seeming rejection of family ties where the Christian message became a sword of division (Mt. 10:34-39); second, the demand on adherents of the faith to leave everything behind—father, mother, children, etc. (Mt. 12:25); third, an apocalyptic anticipation of the dawning of a new age which enhanced a desire for martyrdom and which meant that marriage and family life were not a necessity. In response, the early Church fathers tried to counter this trend by providing what Farley calls "the Pauline household codes. "[579] However, Farley does not see these codes in a good light; based "on an imperial model for the subordination of all in a household to the *paterfamilias*, the codes supported slavery and reinforced patterns of the domination of husbands over wives. "[580] Farley insists that the message of the early Christian Church was largely ambiguous and ambivalent at the very least. "Attitudes of rejection, substitution, and affirmation regarding marriage and family continued in tension…. Through many centuries, the Christian church continued to affirm marriage as good, although celibacy was considered better. "[581]

---

577   Ibid., 248.

578   Ibid., 252-3.

579   Cf. Col. 3:18-4:1; 1 Tim. 2:8-15; Eph. 5:22-33; 1 Pet. 2:11-16; Titus 2:2-10. Farley, *A Framework*, 256-7.

580   Ibid.

581   Ibid.

Farley points out the ambiguity and disparity between the understanding of marriage and celibacy, noting that the affirmation of the family was based on its functional role, the propagation of the race and the socializing of children. Farley argues further that while marriage was raised, in the twelfth century, to the dignity of a sacrament, it was still not seen to be on the same level with celibacy. Farley locates a significant shift in emphasis from the fourteenth century when Renaissance humanists introduced a change of focus: from otherworldliness to social responsibility, from sexual renunciation to self-discipline, and the combination of family and productive labor. The Protestant reformation (especially Luther and Calvin) re-articulated the attitude towards marriage, sex, and family life, though acknowledging and accepting whatever was perceived traditionally to be wrong with sexuality to be part of human nature after the fall.[582] The reformation tradition inadvertently also led to the separation between the private world of the family and the public world of productive labor. In this new cultural matrix, "femaleness" became associated with the private and domestic sphere.[583]

In reflecting on relationships, Farley insists that the framework of justice is the ethical governing principle that should guard every relationship. Therefore, since there are various forms of "families" as we now understand it, the same norm of justice should apply to all. Farley questions how we approach the varied forms of socially understood and accepted families in justice, "… single-parent… same sex individuals, partners or spouse, with children? Blended families following divorce and remarriage? Families with parents whose children are not genetically related but also not legally adopted. Families where parents are not legally married but who raise children together? "[584] Farley refers further to, "families where there are multiple 'mothering' or 'fathering' of children not only by biological mothers and fathers but also by grandparents or aunts or uncles or cousins or close friends? Families that do not live together at all? Nuclear families and extended

---

582   Ibid., 258.

583   Ibid., 259. There seems to be a lacuna in Farley's development of this historical account. The woman's role has always been locked between motherhood and the domestic, I therefore wonder why her historicity locks this down to this specific point in time?

584   Ibid., 261.

families? "[585] Like many ethicists, Farley advocates inclusiveness in the understanding and acceptance of what is recognized as "family" today. Farley asserts,

> We do need not only to support but to celebrate every configuration that 'works', that functions reasonably well in facilitating and undergirding a life for people together in mutual affection and flourishing, perhaps especially when it comes to the rearing of children.... What limits there are have to do less with our preferences for, or idealization of, a 'best' model, than with the justice and love that a model makes possible.[586]

Farley consistently disagrees with any marriage that excludes the framework of just love, if it be inequality between spouses by the stipulation of roles such as "breadwinner" and "helper." Farley rejects misleading language which grounds male hegemony in the marital structure, where there is talk of "total self-gift" or of two halves who come to complete each other. For Farley, it is only in slavery that there is a totality of self-giving and to talk of halves completing each other is to exclude those who do not marry as never becoming sufficiently whole. Because interpersonal love grounds the sphere of marriage, its goal must be the goals of love, "embodied and inspired union, companionship, communion, fruitfulness, caring and being cared for, opening to the world of others, and lives made sacred in faithfulness to one another and to God."[587] In Farley's opinion, "Christianity has not always been a good articulator of this."[588] Farley therefore calls attention to the rhetoric about marriage and family which needs to be realistic and cautious—neither too high sounding nor skeptical because the goals of both marriage and family are difficult to realize fully through life. "Hence, in everyday life, our choices to ratify our commitments, our effort to grow in simple patience, kindness, forms

---

585   Ibid.

586   Ibid., 262.

587   Ibid., 268.

588   Ibid.

of presence, forgiveness, and the 'little by little' of welcoming love: these can be part and parcel of the 'in between' of lives marked not just by success and joy but by failure, irritation, confusion, and the need for radical hope. "[589] In this book, Farley concludes her theological reflections on marriage, family and human sexuality thus:

> In the end, I have… attempted to contextualize and illuminate our understandings of sexuality and its possibilities for human fulfilment… to sort out the multiple meanings and goals of sexuality, sex, gender, and embodiment. Above all, I have asked and tried to respond to the question of when sexuality and its expressions are appropriate in human relationships. I have proposed a sexual ethic grounded in and specified by concerns for justice. Justice, I have tried to show, is not a cold notion apart from love; it is what guides, protects, nourishes, and forms love, and what makes love just and true. It concerns our loves and our action; it concerns the sort or persons we want to be.… It is not an easy task to introduce considerations of justice into every sexual activity. But if sexuality is to be creative and not destructive, then there is no substitute for discerning ever more carefully whether our expressions of it are just.[590]

James M. Gustafson, in an essay responding to Farley's constructual framework for a just love and personal commitments, offers a single criticism while applauding most other aspects of Farley's work. Gustafson notes that Farley's position tends to perceive love and commitment from the perspective of the primary agent involved, instead of the two agents involved. Whereas Farley's argument may be understood to support one agent only, her same argument is applicable to the other agent as well. According to Gustafson, what he finds missing in Farley's position is "a development of obligation and commitment in such a way that the rights and interests of each party receive some

---

589   Ibid., 269.

590   Ibid., 311.

protection from the vagaries of human desire, the tendencies to deceive and exploit one another, the propensity to neglect the other out of indifference and heedlessness. "[591] Gustafson concludes his critique by stating that commitments are like dikes against the flood of immediate desires and actions which "violate the well-being of the beloved and properly establish the grounds for claims for loyalty, for fidelity, and for obligations. They are necessary for the preservation of order in human society. "[592] Gustafson states his belief that Farley's view of commitment includes the propriety of such a claim. However, Gustafson differs in the degree in which he would emphasize the more sordid aspects of human propensities in a philosophy of the person.

Luke Timothy Johnson reviewed *Just Love* in *Commonweal* magazine edition in January 2007. He praised Farley's overall project as an effort which does not emphasize any particular conclusion but encourages a responsible reflection towards conclusions. Though Johnson agrees on many points with Farley, he points out three areas where he finds her work lacking. First, the framework Farley constructs as an ethical structure is lacking in terms of the "Christian" dimension mentioned in the book's subtitle, thereby paying little attention to the ecclesial dimension of sexuality. Johnson queries Farley's work thus: "How does the church's standard of holiness with respect to the body come into play? How might the church as a community play a role in discerning appropriate codes of personal behavior? And how can this discerning activity (which properly puts emphasis on human experience) negotiate the often difficult declarations of the magisterium? "[593] On a second level, Johnson questions Farley's person-based sexual ethics based on a justice which resonates with Christian ethics, but which Farley never distinguishes as distinctive of the Christian identity or Christian commitment. Third and lastly, Johnson notes that Farley's just love framework lacks an in-depth and robust engagement with Scripture. Johnson states, "I would have appreciated a more robust engagement

---

591   James M. Gustafson, "Response to Margaret Farley, " *The Journal of Religion* 58 (1978): S156-159.

592   Ibid., S159.

593   Luke Timothy Johnson, "What's Justice Got to do With It? " *Commonweal* (January 22, 2007), accessed August 13, 2015, https://www.commonwealmagazine.org/whats-justice-got-do-it.

with both the problems and possibilities offered by biblical witness; Farley's method as a scholar ends up giving more space to the Samoans than to scripture. "[594] Despite the critique, Johnson concludes his article by crediting Farley's *Just Love* as a work which does not attempt to provide all the answers to questions of sexual ethics, yet lays a solid framework by which reflections on these questions can be carried out.

Amber Mercy Ewudziwa Oduyoye

Amber Oduyoye's theology is done from the African-feminist and post-colonial Christian studies perspectives. She is also known to have made massive contributions to the field of Christian ecumenical work. Central to her theological reflection is the question of how African religions and cultures influence the experiences of African women in marriage, sex, family and society today. She also focuses on the effects of economic oppression of African women. Her work raises some questions about the role of African women but even more so about women impoverished by stagnated cultures from different developing nations of the world. Her work is examined here for its focus on women's sexuality from inside a traditionally patriarchal society and the role of women in the battle against HIV/AIDS in economically impoverished societies, with consideration for the narratives of African women who are marginalized by a male dominated and controlled culture, oppressive marriages, sexual subjugation and violence, and the residual effects of colonialism.[595] In chronicling her life story, Oduyoye

---

594   Ibid.

595   Kwok Pui-lan, in her journal essay "Mercy Amba Oduyoye and African Women's Theology" using the idea of post-colonial experience of African women states the situation thus, "The issue of gender featured prominently in the cultural debates between the colonizers and the colonized. The encounter between Western colonizing culture and indigenous cultures raised thorny issues pertaining to women's roles and sexuality, such as polygamy, child marriage, veiling, female circumcision, and widowhood. The subordination of women was often cited as symptomatic of the inferiority of indigenous cultures, and saving colonized women from oppression, ignorance, and heathenism became an integral part of the colonialist discourse. Shuttled between tradition and modernity, indigenous women were seen either as victims of male aggression or as pitiful objects of Westerners' compassion. To reclaim that they are subjects in charge of their own destiny, African women have to fight against patriarchy in their traditions, on the one hand, and the complex legacy of colonial feminism, on the other. " Cf. Kwok Pui-lan, "Mercy Amba Oduyoye and African Women's Theology, " *Journal of Feminist Studies in Religion* 20, no. 1 (Spring 2004): 8.

emphasizes her opportunity to obtain a Western education. She was one of the first to study in the UK after Ghanaian independence. She was at the forefront, or as she expresses it, the "first fruit"" in a field that prior to her time was dominated mainly by males. Oduyoye remarks, "With theology came the passion for justice and dignity. With teaching came also all my involvements in humanization and with this, an interest in the development of characters in African novels, especially those by women. "[596] Oduyoye's style and approach to building this feminist- theological system is two pronged, involving inculturation and liberation.[597]

In the collection of essays *African Women, Religion and Health*,[598] the African women theologians who celebrate the life and work of Mercy Amba Oduyoye eulogize her immense insights into women issues in Africa. In her piece contributed to this corpus, Nyambura J. Njoroge reflects on the ability to name the African woman's pain, suffering, and indignity. Through the advocacy of Oduyoye, African women theologians for over two decades have continue to study and attempted to "name " these challenges and courageously address them "in ways that are healing, transforming and life giving. "[599] Reflecting on Oduyoye's childless marriage, Njoroge is able to name the indignity associated with childlessness in African marriage, which brings indignity and suffering upon many African women. Copiously referring to Oduyoye's reflections on this topic, Njoroge, in Oduyoye's

---

596   Mercy Amber Oduyoye, *Beads and Strands: Reflections of an African Woman on Christianity in Africa* (Maryknoll, NY: Orbis Books, 2004), xiv.

597   Elizabeth Amoah, writing the preface to the collection of essays in honor of Mercy Amba Oduyoye reflects on how Oduyoye's work has influenced many African women theologians and resulted in the creation of "The Circle " and the "Institute of African Women in Religion and Culture. " Through some of these agencies, Oduyoye continues to mentor and nurture these women by sharing her life experiences which contributes to the main foci of her theological work; First, thinking on post-colonial Christianity in Africa, second, women, African tradition and the gospel. Thirdly, global issues as it affects African women's integral development. Cf. Elizabeth Amoah, "Preface, " in *African Women, Religion, and Health: Essays in Honor of Mercy Amba Ewudziwa Oduyoye*, ed. Isabel Apawo Phiri and Sarjini Nadar(Maryknoll, NY: Orbis Books 2006), xxi.

598   Ibid.

599   Nyambura J. Njoroge, "Let's Celebrate the Power of Naming, " in *African Women, Religion, and Health: Essays in Honor of Mercy Amba Ewudziwa Oduyoye*, ed. Isabel Apawo Phiri and Sarjini Nadar(Maryknoll, NY: Orbis Books 2006), 60.

voice avers, "The issue I have been addressing may have only marginal relevance for feminists, womanists, and mujerista theologians, the theological sisterhood in the Western world; but in a community of women- centered theologians, where one hurts, all should hurt. "[600] She further expatiates that in the context of a liberating eschatology, to raise a question so personal and so "old fashioned " that it may embarrass even African women, Njoroge quotes Oduyoye in questioning the "child factor in African marriage and family life as… complex, and its public faces are daunting; but nothing is more oppressive than the ordinary meanings imposed on the absence of children in a marriage. " Njoroge summarizes this unjust decimating African narrative against women in marriage thus:

> As African women theologians, our celebration is complete only when we hear and respond to Mercy's central cry for creating a life-giving theology of procreation and eschatology… we hear an unambiguous, yet intense voice, calling us as African women theologians to create a life-giving theology… that addresses the trauma women undergo in the quest for a child of their own… Put simply, Mercy passionately calls us to assist Churches to formulate teachings, counselling methodologies, and materials that help women, men and their families to realize that there is more than one way of being fruitful in the eyes of God.[601]

In her famous book, *Beads and Strands*, Oduyoye critiques the socialization, internalization, or domesticating of cultural norms which juxtapose poverty and motherhood in Africa. She sees as fundamental to this sort of thinking a dramatic change in the economic systems of African nations. This system deliberately excludes women from opportunities to generate wealth, and in this individualistic and competitive culture, having children can also be a source that leads to poverty. Oduyoye expounds further on this line of thinking by saying that all of these are antithetical to the moral norms, family values, and sense of community

---

600   Ibid., 62.

601   Ibid., 63.

traditional to African cultures. Children are children and are assets as
long as they belong to their community and nation. This poverty that
Oduyoye speaks about is compounded when a woman is perceived to
be "single " even if her home is filled with children she must provide
for in all ways. Oduyoye sees Western influence in this matter and
sees a situation where "The criteria is not the welfare of women and
children, but their relation to the androcentric laws by which most of
humanity is ordered and governed. These androcentric legal provisions
have difficulty recognizing mothers as heads of households but choose
to invent names like 'single mothers', suggesting they have stepped
outside the norm of submitting to male authority. "[602] She argues for a
contrary position where in African pre-colonial incursion, there was no
such thing as a single parent, woman or man, as they are understood
to be integral to family life. In contemporary times, women who head
homes do because of events beyond anyone's control, such as migrant
workers prevented by the laws of the country where they work from
bringing in those closest to them, including spouses and children.
Wars, political unrest, and natural disasters that displace people may
also force women to be heads of homes.

The impoverishment of African women is the economic
impoverishment instituted by a world order that is patriarchal.
According to Oduyoye, this aspect of impoverishment in Africa is
ignored and undisclosed. Oduyoye, reflecting on the impoverishment
of African women, observes that

> [i]n Africa, socio-cultural impoverishment is more
> evident as western technological culture intensifies
> its claim to be the human culture and imposes its
> norms of what is legal and ethical on the rest of
> the world. Women in Africa do not fall into the
> category of the under-employed, if anything, they
> are over- employed as none can claim a 40-hour
> week.... [They suffer] the phenomenon of being
> taken for granted, of not having one's labor enter
> the statistics of national production....

---

602   Oduyoye, *Beads and Strands*, 59.

The impoverishment of women that has resulted from the joint effects of Western Christianity and Islam, Arabic and African cultures, is still being overlooked. In conflicts of cultural values, women's culture and women's welfare have always taken second place. The real roots of the impoverishment of women, socially, economically, are to be found in the materialistic Western culture with its androcentric laws and perspectives, for these reinforce African ones and together suppress and often eliminate women's welfare from their provisions.[603]

This institutionalized impoverishment continues to date, according to Oduyoye, because androcentricism has certain needs that women fulfil, whether knowingly or unknowingly. These needs keep patriarchy in power and women in subjugation:

> The androcentric world needs to have a continual flow of human beings, to carry patriarchal names and other naming systems... needs children to be born and socialized into citizens who will even lay down their lives for their country. This androcentric world expects women to be the producers of human beings, but the experience of women is that their own development and perception of humanness and the human community has to be set aside in order to be 'good women', serving the system. Material and economic poverty are the experience of many mothers. What makes the latter thoroughly

---

603   Ibid., 60-1. Kwok Pui-lan, in citing some other writings of Oduyoye expounds on the misconceptions of Western women as they approach the questions African feminism contends with: "Oduyoye often laments that people outside Africa, including many Western feminists, tend to focus on the religio-cultural oppression of African women, through polygamy and genital mutilation, for example without paying equal attention to African women's suffering under economic injustice... Western women have a tendency to define feminism by focusing solely on sexuality, but African women understand feminism to be more comprehensive and multifaceted, including socioeconomic, religious, and cultural aspects. " Pui-lan, "Mercy Amba Oduyoye, " 11.

unacceptable is that the system often shields the fathers from the 'poverty' that could be associated with their paternity.[604]

This androcentricism and its exploitation of women, in Oduyoye's thinking, also account for the exploitation of nature for pure gain which tries to exclude others. Along these same lines, Oduyoye recognizes the exploitation of poorer countries still at the very beginning of development by the richer and more advanced countries. It is exploitation, according to Oduyoye when poor countries have to export more to already rich countries in order to support industrialization in the North rather than safeguarding what mothers need to feed their children in the South. These same economic measures are used ideologically to entrench the "anti-baby economy of the North. "[605] Oduyoye explores the idea of young women in Africa seeking work in formal sector who are required to show that they are on 'anti-motherhood drugs.' This she sees as one of the conditions placed before African women to challenge their access to wealth and independence; "So the message is clear, if you do not want to be poor or become impoverished, do not become a mother. "[606] Oduyoye therefore strongly advocates for a "better management of creation, the earth, the human community, the nation and the home, by both women and men, rich and poor, North and South... Mothers give our race the guarantee of survival. Mothers are not only to be honored, they are to be empowered. "[607] The misconceived notion embedded in African minds that a woman necessarily needs a suzerain, and that a woman who is "single " and "independent " and manages her affairs well without a man is an affront to masculinity, must be overcome in all texts, according to Oduyoye's theology. Paradoxically, women in their familial and public roles are expected to be mothers or not, depending on if it serves the status quo, without regard or respect for womanhood.

---

604   Oduyoye, *Beads and Strands*, 61.

605   Ibid., 63

606   Ibid., 63

607   Ibid.

The Church is also one such locus of the mental and physical impoverishment of the African woman, done knowingly or unknowingly, through the agency of post colonization[608] or just mere cultural hegemony. Oduyoye states unequivocally,

> Liberation for women must also happen in the Church. It was a 'church father' (Augustine of Hippo, a city in ancient Africa), who declared that a woman apart from a man is not made in the image of God, whereas a man apart from a woman, is. Furthermore, it was a 'protesting' monk, pastor, and theologian, Martin Luther, who declared that women were fit only to go to church, to work in kitchens and to bear children. So, who defines the humanity of woman? Is it the male, or is it God? If it is God, how do we get at the God-originated definition of womanness? Is family life a vocation, a demand of biology, or a convenient base for organizing human society? Patriarchal systems often forbid questions of this genre.[609]

Oduyoye that this kind of exclusion predates the coming of missionaries to Africa. She points to the history of many African traditional religions where some women were in charge of shrines and cultic centers. However, in Oduyoye's words, "it is also observable that there are more women in secondary roles of mediums and cultic dancers, than there are women who serve as high priests of shrines or as healers. "[610] At the same time, Oduyoye points out that women clients of these

---

608   Oduyoye's analysis of what she calls "crossroads Christianity " its fluidity and border crossing shows the breeding of a post-colonial experience of the hybridization of Christianity, the extension of the gray area in-between defying easy categorizations and boundaries. Cf. "Mercy Amba Oduyoye, " 12.

609   Oduyoye, *Beads and Strands*, 69-70.

610   Ibid., 79.

cults and shrine outnumber men.[611] Oduyoye therefore concludes by warning, "When examining the role of women in religion in Africa – whether speaking of Christianity, Islam, or traditional religions – we must face two fundamental questions: What responsibilities do women have in the structures of religion? How does religion serve or obstruct women's development? "[612]

In Oduyoye's book, *Hearing and Knowing*, she provides two critiques of assumptions which relegates women to the background within the Church. First, she points to the assumption "that the greater includes the lesser. Since man is said to include woman, maleness has been made to stand for humanness, and female means either to be supportive of or to tamper with the male norm. "[613] Second, she addresses the "linguistic assertion that male pronouns include the female and that the term *man* includes woman. Some languages, English for one, confuse the issue further by the use of 'man' as both specific and a general term. "[614] Oduyoye challenges and calls for a change of thinking for all forms of religion in Africa that calls in question women's sexuality and the birthing process. She argues that the time has come to throw out the idea of pollution owing to menstruation or childbirth. In marriage, "women are persons-in- communion, not persons who 'complete' the other.... We may need to re-orient our thinking so that we see communion as a relationship devoid of hierarchical relations and power seeking. "[615]

---

611   This is also true today in Christian Churches all over the face of the continent. Most Churches therefore rely on the women for financial support and for the catechesis of its young members. Oduyoye, however, warns that "[t]he Church must shed its image as a male organization with a female clientele whom it placates with vain promises, half-truths, and the prospect of redemption at the end of time. Wider vistas of human living are needed here and now. " *Beads and Strands*, 99.

612   Ibid.

613   Mercy Amba Oduyoye, *Hearing and Knowing: Theological Reflections on Christianity in Africa* (Maryknoll, NY: Orbis Books, 1986), 127.

614   Ibid.

615   Ibid., 88.

Conclusion

The exploration of these divergent contemporary voices on the questions of marriage, family, gender and sexuality, remains essential to this project. These voices help to clarify that there is an understanding that the traditional Judaeo-Christian understanding of family life remains cogent even for our time and variant cultures. Some contemporary social and cultural situations call our attention to and advocate for an expansion and inclusion of the expanding understanding of family life outside of the traditional, nuclear male-female-child understanding. All these thinkers agree that for the propagation of the human species, the traditional marriage system remains crucial and central to our understanding of family life. Crucial also to the Christian faith is its ability to transform its message (doctrine) to accommodate the ever changing cultural and moral landscape of the postmodern human community. The work of John Grabowski that I have reviewed in this chapter, while appropriating covenant and sacraments with a focus on personalism challenges a re-think of traditional Catholic understanding of marriage, sex and family life. Lisa Cahill's hermeneutics based on scriptures, gender differentiation and contemporary ethics calls attention to the need for a reappropriation of the meaning of what can be considered as 'family' in the light of contemporary thinking. For Cahill, family today, once it entails communality, compassion and solidarity must not be limited to monogamous forms of family life. Margaret Farley approaches the question of family, marriage and sex from a just love position. Wherein personal commitment and personal love becomes the hallmark of unions which includes all forms of family life and love. Amber Oduyoye, challenges the patriarchy and economic oppression of women in Africa and impoverished nation, as a way to re-imagine and appropriate the justice that should exist in married life. These contemporary voices and the challenges they present to the Church, nuances ones again the viability of the possibility and the necessity for a development in doctrine.

CHAPTER FIVE

ENGAGING VARIOUS CONTEXTS FOR CONTINUED THEOLOGICAL AND PASTORAL IMPLICATIONS

This final chapter contains four sub-sections. The first explores what "development of doctrine " means, taking into careful consideration the works of John Henry Cardinal Newman, Jan Hendrik Walgrave and Christopher Kaczor. The second section pays particular attention to engaging two contemporary pastoral questions and contexts in order to tease out their theological and pastoral implications within the wider context of contemporary Christian sexual ethics and the development of Christian doctrine. First, I will engage a variety of sources onquestions concerning HIV/AIDS, sex, and the use of condoms within the conjugal act in the marriages of discordant Catholic couples, especially in Africa and in other developing areas around the globe. This issue relates to the lived experiences of the peoplewhom the Churchleads, teaches, and instructs.It pushes to the heart of this book in so far as it challenges the idea that norms in doctrine must remain the same because of the ever-new questions to which the Church must respond.In this way, the all-important question of development in doctrine comes into focus again. The second question addressed is same-sex unions whether they are equal to heterosexual and monogamous marriage. This question is the ultimate pastoral challenge, as many countries in the Western hemisphere either have already written homosexual unions as marriages into law or are coming close to passing such laws. Again, the Church will have to provide clear and unambiguous clarification on where she stands doctrinally on the definition of marriage, what it entails within Christian tradition, and what the Church understands marriage to be. In the third sub-section, borrowing the idea of "matter " and "form

" from sacramental theology, I will apply this notion as a descriptive tool to understanding the nature of the development that is possible in doctrine. In the fourth section, the works of Josef Pieper, Orlando Espin, and Stephen Bevans among other contemporary thinkers are reviewed to situate the idea that the development of doctrine exists within a paradigm of faith that becomes tradition, which continues to exist in time as a faith that is traditioned. The conclusion contains some pastoral and theological evaluations with some proposals for a theological engagement in dialogue on questions of tradition, development, doctrine, cultures, and post modernity.

The Development of Doctrine

"In the past God spoke to our ancestors many times and in many ways through the prophets, but in these last days he has spoken to us through his Son " (Heb. 1:1). In this text, scripture makes clear the progressive nature of God's self-revelation, which culminates in Christ. That which pre-existed the epiphany of the Lord, the Old Testament, is a form of preparation to receive the fullness of revelation. Jesus says of this, "I have come not to abolish the law and the prophets but to bring them to fulfilment " (Mt. 5:17). In another text, Jesus says, "All things have been delivered to me by my Father, and no one knows the Father except the Son and anyone to whom the Son chooses to reveal him " (Mt. 11:27). In Jesus' life, ministry, death, and resurrection, he reveals all that is necessary for salvation. After the ascension, the Holy Spirit will continue the work of revelation to the apostolic age and the Church. "Those who do not love me do not obey my teaching. And the teaching you have heard is not mine but comes from the Father who sent me. I have told you this while I'm with you. The Helper, the Holy Spirit, who the Father will send in my name, will teach you everything and make you remember all that I have told you. " (Mt. 14:24-25) What Jesus revealed to the apostles made them privileged and authentic witnesses, who could carry on these revealed truths into the new age of the Church. *The Sacramentum Mundi* states,

This process of authentic interpretation of the message of Jesus, through inspired meditation on the saving acts of the Lord, and hence not restricted to human insight but aided by revelation, is restricted in time to the age of the apostles and of the primitive apostolic Church.... We must sharply distinguish between the foundation period of the Church (apostolic age) and its subsequent history.[616]

Apparently, the apostles themselves clearly saw the task of preserving the purity of these revealed truths as the Gospel of Jesus, deposits of faith which may not be adulterated or added to but faithfully preserved (cf. 1 Tim. 6: 20, 2 Tim.1:13ff). In the first Council of Jerusalem, the task of "development " is faced by the infant Church of the apostles. The decision to accept gentile converts into the community of faith, with or without circumcision, is resolved and within the text, a theological position is arrived at: "And God, who knows the thoughts of everyone, showed his approval of the Gentiles by giving the Holy Spirit to them, just has he had to us... No! We believe and are saved by the grace of the Lord Jesus, just as they are " (Acts 15:8, 11).

The next generation of the Apostolic Fathers carried on the tradition because of their belief that this uncorrupted message must be carried on from generation to generation and until the end of the ages. Their duty is not only to preserve the deposit of revealed truths "but also to interpret it, authoritatively setting forth its content. "[617] These deposits of the faith must always be rooted in what is revealed as the word of God and must be demonstrably grounded in it because only then can the Church present these truths as dogma born of *intellectus fidei*(theological reflections about God). This coupled with *sensus fidei*, the consciousness and sense of the faithful "founded on the grace-

---

616   Karl Rahner, ed., *Sacramentum Mundi: An Encyclopedia of Theology*, Vol. 2(New York: Herder & Herder, 1968): 99.

617   Ibid., 100. It must be said that any message that goes through various cultures, languages and epochs in history have the tendency to lose something of its nature. It is the responsibility of the Church to continually find ways to keep the essential purity of the deposit of faith true to its foundational revelation, for all times and all places.

given connaturality of this sense with the objects of faith, "[618] inspires the entire Church in the development of doctrine, in the Church's infallibility and rebuttal of errors. The "dogmas" formulated by the Church as a whole, reflecting on the changing cultural horizon of different times and places, attempts to present living doctrines that are firmly rooted in faith in Jesus, based on Scripture and tradition. According to Richard McBrien—following up on revelation, scripture, and adherence to tradition in Catholicism—a configuration of values exists in a special way which is specific to Catholicism. This includes a "sense of sacramentality... its principle of mediation... a sense of communion... its drive towards rationality and critical realism... respect for history, tradition and continuity... a radical notion of sin... appreciation of grace as well as for conscience and freedom; indeed its fundamental openness to all truth and to every value – in a word,

---

618   Ibid., 101. These decisions about the faith, while they do not contradict reason, at the same time cannot be subject purely to empirical verification. Dogma in the apostolic period was applied to common and general Christian belief and how the Church teaches these truths. In terms of distinguishing between what is authentically Christian belief and what is not in precisely formed statements, *The New Dictionary of Theology* says, "In this historical context, the meaning of dogma was modified. The meaning it had attained in its previous contexts was never denied, but its new connotation prevailed and remains so to this day. In its attempt to stem the tide of rationalism engendered by the enlightenment, the Church not only emphasized that revelation is a source of truth, that authoritative decisions flow from the Church's reception of God's revelation, but did so in the currency of its time, the proposition. It was at this time that dogmatic statements became identified with syllogistic reasoning propositionally expressed. This understanding of dogma grew in direct proportion to the development of the theology of the papal magisterium, a theology also conditioned by the Enlightenment... It must be emphasized that to be considered dogmatic a proposition must be set forth explicitly, and must pertain to divine, public, and official Christian revelation, that is, sacred scripture and tradition. It should be noted that although dogmatic propositions are expressions of revelatory truth, they are neither commensurate with the totality of truths, divine mystery, nor are they primarily juridical or legal statements. They are intended, as the early Church knew so well, to communicate truth to the Church in order that the Church as a community and each person within the community could become existentially engaged with God's truth." Cf. Joseph A. Komonchak, Mary Collins, and Dermot Lane, eds., *The New Dictionary of Theology* (Wilmington, Delaware: Michael Glazier, 1988), 295.

its catholicity. "[619] The Catholic Church subsisting in its catholicity therefore recognizes that there is a true development of doctrine pieced together by Fathers of ecumenical councils, episcopal conferences, and the college of bishops working in tandem with the papal office continuously to draw out the understanding of the deposit of faith given to the Church by Christ and the apostles.

John Henry Cardinal Newman(1801–1890),was an important figure in the 19th century and the religious history of England. Prior to his conversion into the Roman Catholic Church, Newman was an Oxfordacademic and priest in the Church of England who became attracted to the High-Church tradition withinAnglicanism. He became a leader and an able polemicist within theOxford Movement. This was a radical and controversial group of Anglicans who wished to return to many of the Catholicbeliefs and liturgical rituals that had been lost in theEnglish Reformationwithin the Church of England. Newman's contribution to the idea of development of Christian doctrine is perhaps the first monograph on the topic. In his book on the reality of development in Christian doctrine, published in 1846, Newman argues as follows:

> It is not a great assumption, then, but rather mere abstinence from the wanton admission of a principle which would necessarily lead to the most vexatious and preposterous, to take it for granted that the Christianity of the second, fourth, seventh, twelfth, sixteenth, and intermediate centuries, is in its substance the very religion which Christ and his apostles taught in the first, whatever may be the modifications for good or evil which lapse of years,

---

619   Richard P. McBrien, *Catholicism*, Vol. 2 (Washington, DC: Winston Press, 1980), 1183-4.

or the vicissitudes of human affairs, have impressed upon it.[620]

Newman, who was a major player in the great debates about orthodoxy in the mid-1800s, was not unaware of the major shifts in the universities, culture, and evolving "theologies" of the time, especially in the climate of post reformation Anglicanism, a State owned Church and arch- enemy of Roman papacy. Within the three hundred years prior to the 1800s, Christian doctrines had faced all sorts of scrutiny along with philosophical and polemical argumentations that had engendered infidelity, controversies and varying positons. Therefore, for Newman, "[t]he facts of revealed religion, though in substance unaltered, present a less compact and orderly front to the attacks of its enemies, and allow of the introduction of new conjectures and theories concerning its sources and its rise. "[621] Newman goes on to explain that while Sacred Scripture contains the letters (and spirit) of doctrines, they cannot remain merely written words. Using the example of the

---

620   In 1845 Newman, joined by some of his followers, left the Church of England, as well as his teaching position at Oxford University, and was received into the Catholic Church. He was ordained a priest and continued as an orator and influential religious leader, based in Birmingham. In 1879, he was created a cardinal by Pope Leo XIII in recognition of his services to the cause of the Catholic Church in England. He was a founding father of the Catholic University of Ireland which later became University College, Dublin, and is today regarded as the largest university in Ireland. He is highly respected for many literary contributions to theology, both as an Anglican and later on as a Catholic. John Henry Newman, *An Essay on the Development of Christian Doctrine* (New York: Appleton & Company, 1846), 11. In a later section, Newman reiterates that "[n]o one will be disposed to deny that the body of doctrine which at this day goes by the name of Catholic is at once the historical and logical continuation of the body of doctrine so called in the eighteenth, in the seventeenth, in the sixteenth and so back in every preceding century successively till we come to the first. Whether it be corrupt development or a legitimate, conducted on sound logic or fallacious, the present so-called Catholic religion is the successor, the representative, and the heir of the religion of the so-called Catholic Church of primitive times. Neither can anyone, I think, deny... that the doctrines of which the present Catholic religion consists are *prima facie* the correct, true, faithful, legitimate developments of the doctrines which preceded them, and not their corruptions; that a very strong case ought to be made out against that religion, to prove that it is materially corrupt, and not in its substance Apostolic... It was said, then, that a truedevelopment retains the *essential idea* of the subject from which it has proceeded, and a corruption loses it. " Ibid., 98.

621   Ibid., 19.

biblical phrase "the word became flesh, " Newman demonstrates that making this phrase intelligible to people's minds involves a process of investigations that naturally lead to development. In Newman's process, a multitude of propositions result "which gather round the inspired sentence of which they come, giving it externally the form of a doctrine, and creating or deepening the idea of it in the mind. "[622] In scriptural revelation, the idea of prophecy is put into play by Newman, in which he argued that these various prophecies could have been given definitively and without dependence or connections, yet they are "pregnant " texts, types, wherein one gives birth to another. According to Newman, "it is not that first one truth is told then another; but the whole truth or large portions of it are told, then their rudiments, or in miniature, and they are expanded and finished in their parts, as the course of revelation proceeds. "[623] The entire Bible is written based on the principle of development, prophetic announcements, predictions, and injunctions of doctrine. They all have had "that development which has really been given them, first by succeeding revelations, and then by the event, it is probable antecedently that those doctrinal, political, ritual and ethical sentences, which have the same structure, should admit the same expansion. "[624]

In a review of the transition from the "old dispensation " to the very end of Jesus' ministry and into the beginnings of the apostolic period after the ascension of the Lord, Newman ascertains that "we shall find ourselves unable to fix an historical point at which the growth of doctrine ceased, and the rule of faith was once for all settled. "[625] Newman further explicates:

---

622   Ibid., 50.

623   Ibid., 53. Expounding on this same theme, Newman added, "Nothing can take place without age, and all things wait their time... it is for a while rudimental and unformed, till by degrees tempering its own age, it is matured into mildness of flavor. So too righteousness, for there is the same God both of righteousness and of creature, was at first, in its rudiments, a nature fearing God; thence, by the gospel, it burst forth into its youth; and now, by the Paraclete, it is fashioned into maturity. " Ibid., 165.

624   Ibid.

625   Ibid., 55.

It may be added that, in matter of fact, all the definitions or received judgements of the early and medieval Church, rests upon definitive, even though sometimes obscure sentences of scripture… while scripture nowhere recognizes itself, or asserts the inspiration of those portions which are most essential, it distinctly anticipates the development of Christianity, both as polity and as a doctrine… From the necessity then of the case, from the history of all sects and parties in religion, and from the analogy and example of scripture, we may fairly conclude that Christian doctrine admits of formal, legitimate, and true developments, or of developments contemplated by its Divine author.[626]

Newman concludes therefore that development in Christian doctrine is a larger part of God's work:

And there is a plan for things beforehand laid out, which, from the nature of it, requires various systems of means, as well as length of time, in order to the carrying on its several parts into execution. Thus, in the daily course of natural providence, God operates in the very same manner as in the dispensation of Christianity, making one thing subservient to another; this, to somewhat further; and so on, through a progressive series of means, which extend, both backward and forward, beyond our utmost view. Of this manner of operation, everything we

---

626   Ibid., 56.

see in the course of nature in as much an instance as
nay part of the Christian dispensation.[627]

In his work, Newman focuses on the gradual consolidation of
Christian doctrine and ritual, examining the processes by which this
development is achieved. These different principles of development
and continuity remain valid as long as they remain subservient to the
divine author, revelation, faithfulness to tradition without corruption
and without the latter contradicting the former or vice versa. Newman's
work was a repudiation of the various schisms and counter accusations
of schism between the Church of England and the Roman Catholic
Church of the eighteenth century. Newman concludes that "the
tradition of eighteen centuries becomes a chain of indefinitely many
links, one crossing the other; and each year, as it comes, is guaranteed
with various degrees of cogency by every year which has gone before
it. "[628]

Jan Hendrik Walgrave is a renowned specialist/theologian whose
work in the area of the development of doctrine remains a *tour de
force*. Walgrave has authored a book on Newman that focuses on
the development of dogma. In his seminal work, titled *Unfolding
Revelation: The Nature of Doctrinal Development*, Walgrave argues

---

627   Ibid. 58. Newman makes an interesting allusion to the "battles " the Church
has had to face through the ages: "If then there is now a form of Christianity such, that it
extends throughout the world, though with varying measures of prominence or prosperity
in separate places; -- that it lies under the power of sovereigns and magistrates, in different
ways alien to its faith; -- that flourishing nations and great empires, professing or tolerating
the Christian name, lie over against it as antagonists; -- that schools of philosophy
and learning are supporting theories, and following out conclusions, hostile to it, and
establishing an exegetical system subversive of its scriptures; -- that it has lost whole
Churches by schism, that it is now opposed by powerful communions once part of itself;
that it has been altogether or almost driven from some countries; -- that in others its line
of teachers is overlaid, its flocks oppressed, its Churches occupied, its property held by
what may be called a duplicate succession; -- that in others its members are degenerate and
corrupt, and surpassed in conscientiousness and in virtue, as in the gift of intellect, by the
very heretics whom it condemns; --that heresies are rife and bishops negligent within its
own pale; -- and that amid its disorders and fears there is but one voice for whose decisions
its people wait with trust, one Name and one See to which they look with hope, and that
name Peter, and that see Rome; -- such a religion is not unlike the Christianity of the fifth
and sixth Centuries. " Ibid., 150.

628   Ibid., 172.

for the position that development of doctrine is the ongoing effort of the church to consistently try to fit the expressions of faith into contemporary patterns of thought, retouching, recreating, and guiding the progressive movement of Christian belief by which faith is constantly and continuously reincarnated in human culture and giving it new meaning within a developing human history. Walgrave attempts, as precisely as possible, to investigate what can be considered a legitimate development in doctrine, what is organic growth that is perceivable in the original deposit of faith, and therefore "what is warranted extension of the primitive discipline of the Church, and what, on the other hand, is accretion, additive increment, adulteration of the deposit, distortion of true Christian discipline. "[629] Walgrave approaches the question of development in doctrine from the standpoint of systematized historicism to elicit a way of explaining and justifying the history of several dogmas,[630] which exist in a world of constant cultural evolutions. For the Church to be able to penetrate this world, "the Church itself must become world, must translate its life into forms of human culture. "[631] Walgrave insists that "... the Church must also become history, not in some of the aspects of its life but in all of them, including the doctrine and the language of the Church. "[632]

Definitionally, development for Walgrave is interchangeable with evolution; therefore, it is a "gradual process or action of bringing out something concealed or latent in whatever way from another thing

---

629   Jan Hendrik Walgrave, *Unfolding Revelation: The Nature of Doctrinal Development* (Philadelphia: Westminster, 1972), xii.

630   Walgrave states, "Consequently, the theological question of development can only be stated as a special question, on the acceptance of a number of presuppositions resulting from a certain conception of the nature of revelation and faith. The theologian has to explain how a revelation, if its truth must be expressible in human language, maybe objectively closed at a fixed period of history and nevertheless admit of further development not only by way of subjective penetration but also by way of objective understanding. " Ibid., 6.

631   Ibid., 16.

632   Ibid. Referring to the opposing positions within the ecclesial community, Walgrave notes, "The basic opposition, the opposition of principle, between theological conservatism and progressivism has to be overcome. There is no danger in a dialectical rivalry between conservative minded and progressive minded groups in the Church. Such competition is part of the very structure of history. But if these cease to understand and accept one another, if they are separated by a radical split based on opposing first principles, the consequences may in the long run become disastrous. "

or a previous state of the same thing. "[633] There are two approaches to the idea of *doctrine* in Walgrave's thought: doctrine as theology and doctrine as dogma. In Walgrave's summation, Christine doctrine consists of the official teachings of the Church which voice apostolicity; as such, doctrine is *semper eadem* handed down one generation to another. Viewed in this light, as an undisturbed historical continuity, it becomes a living tradition.[634] Rephrased, Walgrave states that "the vague traditional expression *development of doctrine* may be narrowed down to its true meaning by the expression *development of dogma* and then restored to its full meaning by the expression *development of tradition.* "[635] In the "development "of theology in the Anselmic dictum, *"fides quaerens intellectum"* guides theologians to find the balance between faith and reason, or to affirm dogma and the discoveries of new science as the products of man's restless intelligence. "Theology is the leading link between Christian tradition ruled by authority and autonomous human thought trying to understand and to order by its own means the continuous stream of new experiences and thought. "[636] Walgrave opines,

> Theology never ceases to be creative. However much it may depend on the history of the past, its true nature is not historical but systematic. It always tries to fit the expression of faith into the patterns of contemporary thought, and to influence in return the products and movement of the modern mind. Its attitude toward contemporary thought is at once assimilative and critical. Theology, then, guides the progressive movement of Christian belief within the Church. It is the instrument by which faith is continuously incarnated and reincarnated in

---

633   Ibid., 17.

634   Ibid., 39. Walgrave clarifies further: "Tradition, then, is a process of living continuity. In its course new aspects of the reality in which faith is living come into sight. It is like a stream, always the same from its source to its mouth, but rising and widening through the influx of fresh waters as it runs through different landscapes. "

635   Ibid., 40.

636   Ibid., 41.

human culture, assuming and purifying its earthly historical body.

It follows, then, that theologians' study is the intellectual work house in which the development of doctrine is ultimately achieved... Theology incessantly copes with the new problems, discusses them, clarifies them; and some of its fruits are gradually recognized by the Church as true developments of its divine deposit.[637]

Walgrave understands revelation as a part of the unveiling of history which is also the gradual self-revelation of God. The idea that the revealed will gradually take form, in time, in the mind of the Church, is the basis for understanding the Church's consciousness of historicity. Walgrave cites the works of the Patristics—Irenaeus, Tertullian, Origen and others—to support the gradual nature of development and God's self-revelation according to the "growing receptivity of man, which is itself a work of divine education."[638] The problem of development and immutability, according to Walgrave, was not much of a concern for the Scholastics. "The 'authorities' of antiquity were not viewed in their historical settings and succession, but only as building blocks for their dialectical constructions or doctrinal systems."[639] It was in this manner that without working out any specific theory of development, the Scholastics laid out all the building blocks, the concepts and distinctions that will be applied to the logical theories of development that later arose. This method was also based on the argument, according to Walgrave, that "[e]very doctrine of faith

---

637   Ibid.

638   Ibid., 55. Walgrave gives another perspective, another window by which 'development' could be understood: "It is important to note from the very beginning that the same general principles by which Irenaeus and Origen, Tertullian and Gregory the Great, Hugh of St. Victor and Thomas Aquinas justify a development in revelation may be invoked as well to anticipate that between the first and the second coming of Christ too there may be a development of doctrine. Origen explicitly states that although Christ is the fullness of revelation the real fullness is not found in His humble Incarnation but is awaited in His glorious manifestation. The period between the two advents is the reign of the Spirit, who is the main gift of the glorified Lord to His Church. It is the Spirit, then, who guides the Church towards the final stage of divine revelation." Ibid., 62.

639   Ibid., 115.

accepted by Christians must be equally as true to a message of the past as to the present appearance of saving truth in the light of faith. We cannot appeal to the present appearance of truth against anything that is clearly intended by the *traditioconstitutiva.* "[640] Within the gamut of Catholic sources of doctrine (scripture, magisterium, conciliar formulas, dogmatic definitions, etc.) is an underlying belief that the Holy Spirit inspires them. "Therefore it may be rightly said that the later dogmas are included in the *sensus plenior* or the full sense of the scriptures. "[641]

Walgrave, in a very dense but carefully thematized treatise, argues that there is development in Christian doctrine from within the Church, sometimes as a reaction to internal schism or to fight heresy. Other times, the response is to movements, shifts, and changes in cultures, society, and behavioral patterns outside the Church. Walgrave concludes his work thus:

> The development of doctrine is a social phenomenon. All factors at work in the history of Christianity are also at work in the history of its self-understanding and self-interpretation. This implies that the negative factors of one-sidedness and passion, leading to division and disruption, are as active in the history of Christian thought as in that of humanity in general. If, the, a definite truth, historically determined by God, has to be preserved in the process of its divergent interpretations, the idea of an institutional authority, equally determined by God and enabled by Him to settle controversies of interpretation, is as natural to the mind as the idea of an historically revealed truth itself.[642]

Reflecting on the moral theology of John Paul II and piecing together a variety of sources from his works, **Christopher Kaczor** established a decent theory of development of doctrine. Paying particular attention to

---

640   Ibid., 381.

641   Ibid., 391.

642   Ibid., 394.

John Paul II's encyclical, *Veritatis Splendor*, Kaczor situates development in relation to a post conciliar Church. Kaczor affirms that John Paul II acknowledges multiple factors that influence the formulation of newer insight, especially in questions on faith and morals. Advancements in science, new philosophical insights, and cultural and societal changes that challenge and enrich the Church's need to respond by providing newer ways of explaining the ontological realities of dogma and revelation. The process of expounding, explaining, and communicating newer approaches to evangelization and catechesis is part of the process of development in doctrine. According to Kaczor's reading of John Paul II, a proper and legitimate process of development retains the content and meaning of the original teaching, while it finds perhaps, a new language or method of re-communicating these truths without deviation. Kaczor summarizes his position thus,

> Authentic development of doctrine, in John Paul's view, must always be a fuller expression of previously proclaimed truth and must never be a reduction or elimination of essential elements of the Christian patrimony. Authentic development includes the fullness of faith, a retention of the meaning of dogmatic formulas, and a proposing of Christian truths, even if not commonly understood in a particular cultural context.[643]

Condomized Sex within Sacramental Marriage

The first question to examine here now arises frequently: whether Catholics in the medical field, Catholic aid agencies, professionals in counseling and education, and clergy may suggest the use of condoms within marriage to reduce the possibility of transmitting the HIV virus

---

643   Christopher Kaczor, "John Paul II on the Development of Doctrine, " *Nova et Vetera* 11, no 4 (2013): 1178.

to an uninfected spouse?[644] Vatican II stresses the importance of an authentic conjugal love in marriage and the divine laws pertaining to the responsible transmission of life, which must be harmonized as acts proper to conjugal love and in accord with human dignity.[645] These issues present a modern day ethical dilemma for the Church because on both sides of the debate, one finds equally plausible yet mutually exclusive arguments, valid yet conflicting reflections from biblical and theological points of views on the use of condoms in the conjugality of monogamous unions of discordant Christian couples, among many other contemporary ethical questions. Julie Hanlon Rubio expresses the discordancy question quite succinctly: "Is condom use morally evil, or can it be justified by double effect, the lesser of evils, compassion or justice? "[646] Rubio speaks to what she considers a more fundamental problem within the controversy: "Still it seems that underneath these attempts to find an exception that will save lives is an affirmation of the important place of sex in marriage. "[647] Rubio sees as equally important and questions "[w]hether couples should be required to sacrifice sexual pleasure in order to comply with the moral duty to be open to life... whether the good of ongoing sexual practice in marriage must be forgone. "[648]

Theologians have argued for and against condomized sexual encounters for married people using various theological principles,

---

644   One of the earliest documented official positions that mentions the use of a "prophylactic " to avoid further infection is found in a document prepared by the United States Catholic Conference administrative board, titled "The Many Faces of AIDS: A Gospel Response. " A short paragraph in the Appendix addresses what a health worker might be permitted to do, practically speaking: "On the more personal level of the healthcare professional, the first course of action should be to invite a patient at risk, or one who already has been exposed to the disease, to live a chaste life. If it is obvious that the person will not act without bringing harm to others, then the traditional Catholic wisdom with regard to one's responsibility to avoid inflicting greater harm may be appropriately applied. " Cf. James F. Keenan, ed., *Catholic Ethicists on HIV/AIDS Prevention* (London: Continuum, 2002), 21.

645   Pope Paul VI, *Gaudium et Spes: Pastoral Constitution on the Church in the Modern World*, published December 7, 1965, accessed February 5, 2016, https://www. ewtn.com/library/COUNCILS/v2modwor.htm, #51.

646   Julie Hanlon Rubio, "Family Ethics: Beyond Sex and Controversy," *Theological Studies* 74, no. 1 (2013): 149.

647   Ibid.

648   Ibid.

from the principle of double effect to the principles of *epikeia*, lesser evil, and so on. The United States Catholic Conference (USCC) in 1987 proposed what they called the principle of toleration. They stated clearly their opposition to any kind of advocacy for the use of condoms but, in a casuistic approach, proffered toleration of the use of condoms to deter the spreading or infecting of others as a viable alternative. This, according to the USCC, was a recommendation that does not endorse contraception or illicit sexual activity or a quick fix. Rather, a recommendation that the condom in this case was to be seen as prophylaxis. It is not intended to prevent conception (as a contraceptive) but to prevent harm.[649] Demographics show that the pandemic of HIV/AIDS is of global proportions with a particular focus on the developing nations of the world. Our attention must be drawn to people who live on the margins, who are minorities in impoverished countries and who are more vulnerable to the scourge of this disease. According to James Keenan, moral questions are shifting from an "analysis of the individual set against social forces to those which weigh the balance of goods and benefits for various groups in society."[650] Keenan states further that since the most sophisticated treatments in technologically advanced nations do not provide a cure for this infection, the "primary prevention of HIV infection must become the focal point of our reflection. This reflection must occur with adequate attention to the concrete realities which shape the day-to-day experience of vulnerable populations."[651]

Many countries in Africa, among other developing nations of the world, are the epicenter of the battle to save lives from a disease that is decimating populations, especially the poor, in unprecedented numbers.[652] Current data from the joint United Nations Programme

---

649   Keenan, *Catholic Ethicists*, 22-4.

650   Ibid., 38.

651   Ibid.

652   Margaret A Farley, "Hope for the Future," *Journal of Feminist Studies* 28, no. 2 (2012): 137. Here, Farley points to developments in understanding the etiology of the disease, the demographics around the peoples most at risk of infection, possible prevention, and treatment of infected persons. There is recognition that to stop the spread of this dreadful disease, multiple factors enter in, "a paradigm that incorporates studies of gender and religion." She argues that based on the work of African women theologians, especially those of Sarojini Nadar and Isabel Phiri, empirical work on HIV and AIDS

on HIV/AIDs provide statistics showing that instances of infection

remains deficient if they continue not to take into account a "fourfold development out of a conviction that health cannot be understood without including gendered and religio-cultural aspects of health; to a prioritization of contexts over universal principles; to an opening in concern for women but also for men; to an 'active,' critical but transformative, mode of research and its deployment for behavioral change " Ibid., 138. Farley agrees with the predominant school of thought that low, middle-income countries in sub-Saharan Africa, East Asia, and parts of Latin America, less than half the population has access to antiretroviral therapies. These countries depend on the largesse of other countries outside of their own regions for programs, medication, therapies, and treatments. Farley, like many other theologians, sees and supports the necessity of shifting from a predominantly regional preoccupation with HIV/AIDS to a more central global vision and discourse. Ibid., 140.

In another piece, in response to the role of religions and religious leaders who were attending a summit on HIV/AIDS and the impact of world religions, Farley wrote, "…. I was also confused by the relative lack of attention given to some questions directly related to the substance of religious traditions themselves. Are there, for example, any ways in which religion has shaped beliefs, attitudes, and practices that either contribute to or prevent the spread of HIV? Little was said about the impact of religious teachings on sexual practices, the status and roles of women, and the connections among gender, race, and poverty in the context of AIDS. Perhaps implicit in the whole summit was a recognition of the relevance of such questions, yet explicit attention to them was largely missing. The words spoken about compassion raised little controversy; words about sex, the place of women, and a gendered analysis of poverty might have been controversial. " Margaret A. Farley, "Partnership in Hope: Gender, Faith and Responses to HIV/AIDS in Africa, " *Journal of Feminist Studies in Religion* 20, no. 1 (2004): 134. Farley cautions against inertia, by positing,

> If religious traditions have anything to say that is healing word, a strengthening and promising word, in such situations, it must be a word that is embodied in deeds. Short of this, religious traditions will be, as they have all too often been in relation to the spread of HIV, more a part of the problem than a part of any remedy. The first response of most persons who stand in religious traditions and have any understanding at all of the AIDS pandemic is compassion. But compassion is an empty word unless there is a clear-sighted recognition of what compassion requires. All the major world religions have had something to say in response to the large questions of people's lives, including the question of suffering. Far from being completely irrational, religions have helped to 'make sense' of parts of life in relation to wholes, of aspects of life that philosophy alone has not been able to fathom. In so doing, they have given meaning to both ordinary and extraordinary experiences of persons, and they have shed light on our responsibilities to one another…. Faith communities must also critically review their role in shaping beliefs, constructing attitudes, and reinforcing behaviors that have contributed to the spread of AIDS. Just as religious traditions are profoundly influenced by the cultures in which they are embedded, so cultures are shaped and reinforced by the religions that are part of them. " Ibid., 138.

Farley concludes that "sometimes the response within religious traditions is simply to reiterate moral rules prohibiting behaviors that happen also to put persons at risk of infection. Such a response has often not been very successful. Indeed, it has all too often heightened the shame and stigma associated with AIDS, and it has prevented behavioral changes that might be preventives against the disease, such as the use of condoms and the achievement of greeter freedom of choice on the part of women. " Ibid., 139.

droppedremarkably between the years 2000 and 2015. Nonetheless, according to UNAIDS current data and facts sheet, in 2014, 36.9 million people were living with HIV and the numberscontinue to increase, in large part because there are more people globally accessing antiretroviral therapies and as a result are living longer, healthier lives. As of June 2015, 15.8 million people were accessing treatment. Despite obvious amelioration, the number of new HIV infections and AIDS-related deaths occurring globally each year is unacceptably high. According to this UNAIDS report, in 2014, around 2 million people were newly infected with HIV and 1.2 million people died of AIDS-related illnesses.

UNAIDS states that

[n]ew HIV infections have fallen by 35% since 2000 (by 58% among children), and AIDS-related deaths have fallen by 42% since the peak in 2004. The global response to HIV has averted 30 million new HIV infections and nearly 8 million (7.8 million) AIDS- related deaths since 2000....Ensuring access to antiretroviral therapy for 15.8 million people is an achievement deemed impossible 15 years ago. In 2000, fewer than 1% of people living with HIV in low- and middle-income countries had access to treatment. In 2014, the global coverage of people receiving antiretroviral therapy was 40%. But HIV continues to shine a harsh light on the inequalities of the world. AIDS is unfinished business.[653]

UNAIDS agrees that the case for change is compelling and commanding especially in developing nations and poorer populations. In these places, significant gaps and shortcomings in the response must be rectified. UNAIDS makes the claim that accelerating the AIDS response in low- and middle-income countries could avert 28 million new HIV infections and 21 million AIDS-related deaths between 2015 and 2030. "The next phase of the AIDS response must account for

---

653   UNAIDS, *AIDS Epidemic: Enduring the Urban AIDS Epidemic, Data and Facts Sheet, 2015*, accessed Dec. 17, 2015, http://www.unaids.org/en/HIV_data/report.

new realities, opportunities and evidence, including a rapidly shifting context and a new sustainable development agenda. "[654] As I have stated earlier, the UNAIDS fact sheet concurs that in 2014, there were about 25.8 million (24.0 million–28.7 million) people living with HIV in sub-Saharan Africa, of which more than half arewomen.In 2014, there were an estimated 1.4 million (1.2 million–1.5 million) new HIV infections in sub-Saharan Africa, even thoughthis number represents a decline of 41% in new infections between 2000 and 2014. In sub-Saharan Africa, which accounts for 66% of the global total of new HIV infections, approximately 790,000 (670,000–990,000) people died of AIDS-related causes in 2014. - Between 2004 and 2014, the number of AIDS-related deaths in sub-Saharan Africa fell by 48%. The numbers show that impoverished people of developing nations, especially women and children, are most vulnerable to HIV infection. The reasons are many, butmainly poverty, illiteracy, and economic imbalance in poor countries are key causes.Many women are exposed to illicit sexual affairs to make ends meet, and through conception, many children are exposed to infection.It is owing to this unjust social imbalance that the question of condomized sex by discordant couples becomes pertinent.

The disagreement on the use of condoms by discordant persons among theologians has been has gone one of two ways. Some maintaining that condomized sex should be permissible between infected sacramentally married couples. Others maintain that it may not be permitted as condoms will always interfere with the natural intention of sexual intimacy within marriage and thereby contradict doctrinal tradition.Surprisingly, the Catholic magisterium to date, has not given an official position on this matter.Often times, people who deal with this question of discordancy in pastoral settings, especially in regions widely affected by HIV/AIDS, are in a quandary in terms of providing adequate pastoral counseling and advice. Somewhat disconcertingly, various published and unpublished positions can be found among episcopal conferences, theologians, pastoral agents and some agents who work in advocacy. Often, bishops, theologians, and aid agents in heavily affected areas, which are usually also poor areas, seem to see a practical utility in an exemption for the use of condoms

---

654   Ibid.

between discordant couples to prevent the spread of HIV to the uninfected partner or even to prevent conceiving a child.[655]

Dr. Margaret A. Ogola speaks in an urgent and cogent way to the situation of HIV/AIDS patient in Africa, with particular focus on women and children. Ogola is a pediatrician and director at the Cottolengo Center for Children with HIV/AIDS in Kenya. In her many years of working generally with HIV patients, she states that about half of the infected patients who come to the health center are discordant couples who often times go to a second level of re-infection and then to a third level of co-infection. Ogola avers, "The nature of this virus is such that it changes its face... An individual may start an HIV journey with one strain and end up with several strains. "[656] She notes that there has been a significant shift in the risk group for infections. Previously, the highest infection rate was among young women aged 15 to 24. Now, there are more infections among women living in relatively stable marriages. In this cultural matrix, the women are mostly powerless. As the virus mutates and more strains of the virus are discovered, infection by spouses, re-infections, co-infections, and drug resistant strains put more people at risk. According to Ogola, "Women in Africa have few if any sexual rights, particularly married women who are socialized to give in to sexual demands. Sixty percent of all HIV cases are women... women in marriage are in a different situation all together because they are owned; in much of Africa the

---

655   In research carried out in Ghana and published as a journal article, the authors, James Yamekeh Ackah and Benjamin Spears Ngmekpele Cheabu, point to the example of the US Catholic Bishops Conference in 1987 in a document in which they argued for a look at educational programs to be given out as accurate information about prophylactic devices or relevant means proposed by medical experts to prevent the spread of the disease. Ackah and Cheabu also alludes to Archbishop Boniface Lele of Mombasa and Bishop Kevin Dowling of South Africa who stated clearly that the use of condoms for discordant couples should be encouraged to reduce reinfection. However, like Bishop Kirima of Nyeri Diocese, they are quick to point out that the best way to prevent infection or spread is through chastity and abstinence. James Yamekeh Ackah and Benjamin Spears Ngmekpele Cheabu, "Humanae Vitae and Birth Control: Practices and Perspectives from the Ghanaian Catholic, " *Research on Humanities and Social Science* 4, no. 28 (2014): 51-2.

656   Margaret A. Ogola, "Looking Back and Looking Forward at HIV/AIDS in Africa: Serodiscordant Couples, Re- infection, the Role of Women, and the Condom, " in James F. Keenan, ed., *Catholic Theological Ethics Past, Present, and Future: The Trento Conference* (Maryknoll, NY: Orbis Books, 2011), 201.

dowry men pay when marrying represents a purchase price. "[657] Ogola challenges the Catholic Church to courageously look at the plight of poor African women who should not be left to their fate,

> This journey has taken twenty-five years. I must confess that twenty-five years ago I was in the forefront of burning condoms, which indicates something about the journey I have had to make to be able to make this statement today: In view of the fact that people are living together, the need to rethink the condom as a prophylactic is inescapable. As a church we have to look at this issue with greater clarity.
>
> I worked for Kenyan bishops for over ten years and have helped write pastoral letters and strategic plans. Yet we are still arguing over the issue, leaving service providers who are actually dealing with patients on the front line in a fuzzy limbo over what to do with couples who come for advice... As people live longer and couples live longer, they cannot be abandoned to their fate... Statistics show that that *(virucidal)* jellies give a protection rate of 50 percent. Condoms, with all that has been said against them, provide a protection rate of 80 percent. In my view, both condoms and jellies may protect African women from their vulnerability to HIV and AIDS.[658]

Ogola is convinced and concludes that the condom is the cheapest and most accessible and effective way to keeping infection rates low, especially among vulnerable women. In which case, it cannot be argued that it is anti-life as in the case of condom use as contraception. When combined with antiretroviral medications, it reduces infections significantly. Ogola opines that the one thing the scourge of HIV/AIDS has been able to do is to "remove us from our comfort zones

---

657   Ibid., 204.

658   Ibid.

and un-thought-out dogmas. "[659] She avers further, "Unless one wishes to continue in acceptable levels of casuistry, the inescapable conclusion is that latex rubber saves lives. "[660] Here, and again, the Church is confronted with the existential and personal experiences of people who encounter the "really-real, " people who are on the side of the Church and understand a problem from a purely scientific, yet theological dimension. Not to listen carefully to voices like this is tantamount to impetuousness and arrogance.

Fr. Martin Rhonheimer, phenomenologist, philosopher, and new natural law theorist, supports the idea of condomized sex for discordant couples. The moral dimension to this use in conjugality is strictly limited to preventing the transmission of the HIV virus. Rhonheimer agrees with the magisterial position that contraception is intrinsically evil and therefore wrong. Condoms, in Rhonheimer's philosophizing, are not necessarily evil in themselves; rather, they can be used for good even while they have a contraceptive effect.[661] In his thought, the discordant couple is not employing an evil means to achieve a good end; hence, the contraceptive part of the use of condoms would be merely an undesired side effect and thus would not contravene the Church's position on contraception. Fr. Rhonheimer argues for a caveat for promiscuous persons such as prostitutes and sexually active homosexuals to show responsibility by using condoms to reduce the risk of infecting others and spreading the disease. While not arguing that this is morally right, he states that it is less vicious. Fr. Rhonheimer agrees completely that married couples who are in good health may never resort to any form of contraception, devices or chemicals.[662]

Luc Bovens opines that marital relations between discordant partners[663] are not a normal circumstance and that, thus, the principle

---

659   Ibid., 205-6.

660   Ibid.

661   Martin Rhonheimer, "A Debate on Condoms and AIDS, " *The National Catholic Bioethics Quarterly* 7, no. 2 (2007): 40-8.

662   Ibid.

663   In this essay, Luc Bovens consistently uses the phrase 'partner' which makes the application unclear. Whether this term refers strictly to discordant sacramentally married people or is inclusive of partners in other forms of sexual situations remains amorphous and unclear.

of double effect may be applied to justify the use of condoms in such circumstances. According to Bovens, "the good outcome of condom usage is that the healthy partner will not become infected. This is clearly a sufficient weighty reason relative to the absence of procreation. So long as one intends only *not to infect one's partner*, and one does not intend to thwart procreation, neither as a means nor as an end…, "[664] Bovens argues, the fear of condoning the use of condoms based on the possible negative impact on public morality is not enough grounds to deny discordant persons the possibility of continuing to consummate their marriage licitly. Bovens clarifies further that there are cases where the intent to thwart procreation is non-existent, like having sex when conception cannot naturally take place, such as in circumstances of infertility, post-menopausal women, or the use of contraceptive pills for therapeutic reasons, as contained and approved in the encyclical *Humanae Vitae*. Arguing against the position that the use of condoms in conjugal sex interferes with the completeness of the act, where the sperm is not deposited into the vagina, making it a non-unitive act, Bovens responds that the interference of the condom in the sex act cannot be considered a moral difference:

> …. [S]uppose that we can work up some sympathy for the position that a couple really cannot become truly one unless genitals actually touch and seminal fluid make contact with vaginal secretion. Becoming a *we* is still not a binary issue – that is, there is a continuum between forming a shared *we* and fully remaining separate selves. And so we may not *fully* succeed in fusing with one another now that there is a piece of latex between us. We may lose some of the *we* in love making. But then the question remains, would our HIV-discordant couple retain more a sense of a *we* through committing themselves to perpetual abstinence? Is this little bit of unitive function that is thwarted by latex really more worrisome for the *we* than a cold bed would be?[665]

---

664   Luc Bovens. "Can the Catholic Church Agree to Condom Use by HIV-Discordant Couples? " *Journal of Medical Ethics*, 35, no. 12 (2009): 743-746.

665   Ibid., 745-6.

Bovens concludes that the argument that the accessibility of condoms my increase promiscuity among the general population is not important enough as to deprive discordant persons of a great good within their marriage.

Simon Aihiokhai,[666] while acknowledging the Catholic Church as the largest global care giver through many of her social agencies for those infected or affected by the HIV virus, nonetheless accuses ecclesiastical authorities of not doing enough, especially for discordant couples in Africa.Aihiokhai decries the lack of specificity in the Church's official pronouncement concerning discordancy.The often articulated position, including the comments of Pope Benedict XVI while visiting the Cameroon in 2009, constantly reiterate and emphasize responsible sexual mores and the fear that the use of condoms will bring about greater moral decay.Aihiokhai states, "This view of the pope does not address the African situation.Sexual promiscuity is not the only cause of HIV infection among discordant couples. "[667] He further maintains that "not to call attention to the need for an approach that will address the situation faced by discordant couples is to miss a pastoral opportunity. "[668] He argues for using the principle of *epikeia*[669] as a hermeneutical tool that allows for the use of condoms within the context of a sacramental, monogamous, and Catholic marital relationship.

Aihiokhai submits that since there is no canonical or juridical/ sacramental legislation that bars discordant couples from sacramental marriage in the Church, especially given the framework of Africa's economic, social and cultural practices (which, in itself isdisadvantageous), the Church needs to change her narrative and be more pro-active in confronting these problems.Alluding to *Humanae*

---

666   Simon Mary A. Aihiokhai, "A Case for the Use of Condom as a Therapeutic Means by Discordant Couples in the Roman Catholic Moral Tradition, " *International Journal of African Catholicism* 4, no. 2 (2013).

667   Ibid. 86.

668   Ibid. 87.

669   Epikeia requires that an individual act beyond the words prescribed by law, and having determined the intention of the legislator (not the intention which is expressed in the words of the law, but rather that which constitutes an exception or a contradiction to those words), to deviate from the course clearly prescribed by the words of the law, on the basis of the belief that the lawmaker in enacting the law benignly excluded from it the case at hand.

Vitae, no. 15, Aihiokhai has challenged the episcopal conference in Africa[670] to be more prophetic and to speak to the reality of the suffering and pains of their people.[671] Aihiokhai points out that discordant and sacramentally married couples are at a crossroad in their marital obligations to each other. The total self-giving between married people—physically, emotionally, spiritually, sexually and otherwise—all ought to be life affirming. According to Aihiokhai, this self-giving should be "such that each partners' health is nourished and not jeopardized. Thus, actions that are life denying ought to be avoided. In this case, unsafe sex will amount to life denying.... It is important that a distinction between medical necessity and promiscuity be made when referring to the use of contraceptives. "[672] In his final comments, he argues that moral theology should engage authentic human wisdom, share ideas that are relevant to bettering the lives of people in disadvantaged places, and properlyapply the notion of "epikeia to moral dilemmas faced by the people. "[673] Similar arguments have been raised based on the principle of double effect,offering that the use of condoms within marriage is the lesser of two evilswhen the other choice is to risk infecting the un-infected partner. So far, the Roman Catholic Church has insisted on what she refers to as a "heroic self-sacrifice in abstinence " in the case of discordant couples.

On the opposing side of the conversation, Janet E. Smith's response to Fr. Martin Rhonheimer's essay is useful. She is among those who side with Church teaching in maintaining that no condom use is permissible whatever the situation, and she offers, succinctly and

670 According to Aihiokhai, "Since the majority of new HIV infections are in Africa, one would think that there will be a consensus among the African catholic Bishops, who constitute part of the hierarchy of the Roman Catholic Church, in their efforts to tackle this epidemic. They have been divided on the approach to preventing HIV. Generally, most of them have accepted the general magisterial position; that any form of the use of condom is a false approach to managing and preventing the disease. " Aihiokhai, "A Case, " 90. Elsewhere, Aihiokhai challenges the Church in Africa: "The task of priests and bishops, as well as nuns and those with pastoral responsibilities in the African Catholic Churches ought to reflect a pragmatic approach to tackling the situation faced by discordant couples. It will be injurious to these persons if the pastoral agents simply recite to them what the official position of the magisterium is – one that does not address specifically of discordancy and HIV infections. " Ibid., 110.

671 Ibid., 109.

672 Ibid., 110.

673 Ibid., 111.

clearly, a precise, theologically sound argument. Smith states that the difference in position between herself and Rhonheimer (Grisez, Finnis and Ralph McInerny) is a question of how to determine the object of a moral act, what constitutes the "end" of an act, what the "practical reason" is, and the role of "nature" in the evaluation of any moral act. Smith explains that condomized[674] sex, in general, is wrong but differentiates between homosexual and heterosexual condomized sex. Homosexual condomized sex, according to Smith, is devoid of any kind of procreative meaning while heterosexuals (including infertile couples) thwart the procreative meaning of the sexual act by using contraception. Smith explains the state of infertile couples thus:

> It is certainly true that the infertile cannot remove fertility from acts that have no possibility of being fertile.... They can still perform actions that per se have a contraceptive *telos* or meaning... that is why marriage between the infertile is permitted: because they can engage in actions that by their nature, by their intrinsic potency, are ordained to procreation even though they cannot actualize that potency. If their acts can have that *telos* in a per se way and can express the meaning of sexual intercourse, it would seem that it is possible for them to do things that would violate that telos or meaning. If they fail to do or to give to each other what is minimally necessary for an act of sexual intercourse to be per se apt for procreation, they would be falsifying the meaning of the act. Condom use prevents them from doing or giving what is necessary for an act to be per se procreative of its kind.[675]

---

674   Smith makes an interesting clarification on "condomized" thus: "I use the neologism 'condomized' because I understand the suffix "-ized" to mean something that is characterized by a noun that has been made into a verbal adjective and that it refers to an action that shares in the nature of the thing named: on the analogy with 'marginalized' I think 'condomized' is correct. 'Condomistic' seems to me to be parallel with 'hedonistic' which suggests 'sharing something in common with' but not necessarily 'being an instance' of the named reality." Cf. Janet E. Smith, "The Morality of Condom use by HIV-Infected Spouses," *The Thomist* 70 (2006): 30.

675   Ibid., 44.

Condomized heterosexual sex in all situations, according to Smith is not only non- consummating, it is also non-unitive.Smith uses the analogy of condomized sex as "simply two bodies rubbing against each other or, in fact, rubbing against latex. "[676] Smith submits that "condomized sexual intercourse shares in the essential characteristics of *coitus interruptus* or withdrawal and mutual masturbation more than in an act of expressive of complete self- giving.*Coitus interruptus* is wrong not only because it is contraceptive but also because it is not unitive. "[677] The analogy employing the idea of *coitus interruptus* in Smith's argument is because the male leaves nothing of himself which defeats the purpose of union.In such a case, the penetration alone does not complete the act but the depositing of the semen in the vagina.[678]

To support her argument that the use of condoms within the sexual act always carries a contraceptive intent for heterosexuals, she appeals to the moral tradition of the Church. Here, the Church uses the terms *finis operantis/agentis* and *finis operis/actus*,the former meaning

---

676   Ibid., 48.

677   Ibid.

678   In supporting her argument, Janet Smith clarifies that she does not intend to debate the effectiveness of the use of condoms or how they can reduce the transmission of disease. Smith states that her focus is on the question of the morality of condom use as a means of reducing the transmission of the HIV virus. Smith's arguments is based solely on the contemporary Catholic understanding of marriage and human sexuality—that the sex act is located only within marriage, open to procreation, and unitive—using the essential terminologies of traditional Catholic moral analysis, which often the characteristically Aristotelian/Thomistic metaphysic developed into such principles as the principle of double effect. This will be used to ground her position that "the use of a condom prohibits a heterosexual act of sexual intercourse from being unitive and that the use of a condom by heterosexuals is always contraceptive. " Ibid., 31. Smith therefore refers to John Paul II's *Theology of the Body*, stating, "Pope John Paul II's theology of the body significantly deepens our understanding of the unitive meaning of marriage. He speaks of the nuptial meaning of the body, by which he means that the body itself expresses that human beings are essentially meant to be in relation with each other. H speaks of Adam's 'original solitude' that is overcome by the 'original unity' that he enjoys with Eve before the fall. One supposes that had man not fallen each of us would have been in a monogamous spousal relationship—we all would have had matches made in heaven! The desire that many experience for multiple sexual partners and the difficulty of sustaining marital unions are results of the fall. Fidelity and indissolubility would surely have characterized prelapsarian marriages. The Church's understanding of marriage as a symbol of Christ's love for the Church serves to illuminate the unitive meaning of marriage. The procreative meaning of the sexual act is not accidental to the unitive meaning; it is, in fact, part of its deepest essential structure. " Ibid., 35.

the intention, end, or motive of the agent, and the latter meaning the "end, ordination, meaning, or character of an act that is inherent in an act and so intrinsic to it or 'embedded' in it that one cannot choose that action without also choosing that end along with any further ends the agent might have. "[679] Any moral act, therefore, either meritorious or sinful, includes both *finis operantis* and *finis operis*, and if the act is to be meritorious, both must be ordered to right reason. Smith, therefore, insists:

> I maintain that the use of a condom by those seeking to reduce the transmission of the HIV is the object and means of the action and as object has its own end/meaning (the *finis operis*) – namely, the prevention of procreation – and the "intention to reduce the transmission of the HIV " is the end (the *finis operantis*) of the action, that is, it is the intention of the agent... I maintain that even though something is not intended as the end of the agent, the *finis operantis*, if it is chosen as a means to the end of the agent, it too is an essential component of the act and enters into the moral evaluation of the action. It is "beside " the primary intention of the agent but nonetheless has its own *telos* or end or meaning, and insofar as it is chosen as an essential element of the larger action, its inherent *telos* is part of that action: it is not undertaken *per accidens* but is essential to the action. To apply this principle to the action at hand, a condom used by fertile heterosexuals has its own inherent ordination or telos, the intentionality of preventing the deposit of semen and the prospect of a sperm fertilizing an egg. Thus, whether the spouses use a condom to prevent pregnancy or the transmission of the HIV they cannot fail to intend the intrinsic telos of the condom in an act of heterosexual sexual intercourse.[680]

---

679   Ibid., 55.

680   Ibid., 56-7.

This argument supports the idea that an agent's act, even if the agent does not desire a specific probable outcome (*finis operis/actus*), is a choice for a bad effect, not simply as a side effect, but as an intrinsic part of the object or means.Smith accepts that the original intention is an attempt to reduce the risk of transmitting HIV, but the means of achieving this is by contraception, "choosing to do something immoral for the sake of something moral. "[681] Smith closes her essay noting that those outside of Catholic tradition may not be persuaded by these arguments. However, the accusation that the Church is somewhat complicit in the spreading of the disease by rejecting the distribution of condoms (especially in poor countries) is, at the very least, puzzling.According to Smith, the Church stands behind its rule of chastity before marriage and fidelity after marriage as the real solution to stopping further spread and infection.

Anthony Fisher questionswhether the Church has any real argument for insisting that every sexual act "must be completed by *seminatio intra veginam* and so be *per se aptum ad generationem* in order to be a *conjugal* act. "[682] Fisher attributes the Catholic understanding and arguments to a long history and dependence on tradition.Following in the Thomistic tradition, Fisher sees sex as *fides, proles* and *sacramentum*(spouses' commitment to each other, to their family and to God). The Second Vatican Council teaches that conjugality in marriage must "preserve the full sense of mutual self-giving and human procreation " in which subjective intentions cannot make right what is objectively wrong.[683] Conjugality in this sense must both be unitive and procreative, and the inseparability of these two aspects makes other forms of sex morally wrong, even when done lovingly by spouses.Fisher establishes that the Church's position is the consequence of a long Catholic tradition, standing, and established sound philosophical anthropology, canon law and moral theology.Consequent upon this logic, Fisher asserts that "even HIV-discordant married couples may not engage in

---

681   Ibid., 59.

682   Anthony Fisher, "HIV and condoms within marriage," *Communio: International Catholic Review* (Summer 2009), 3, accessed Oct. 3, 2015, http://researchonline.edu.au/theo_article/67.

683   Choon-Leong Seow, *Homosexuality and Christian Community* (Louisville, Kentucky: Westminster John Knox Press, 1996), 144-5.

condomized intercourse. "[684] This tradition is in dissonance with the viewpoint of modern persons, who lack the sensibilities of chastity and sexual discipline that characterized previous generations.In agreement with others who hold the same opinion on condomized sex, Fisher argues that suchis not plausible because the act does not end in the couple'scomplete giving of themselves to each other. These arethe same principles, according to Fisher, that make homosexual and extra-marital sexual acts impermissible. Fisher states that this position is not popular because modern minds think this teaching is opaque.Fisher leaves room for a possible scenario for condomized sex, which he favors as the "use of a condom to reduce the risk of HIV transmission and not with a view to preventing conception.In such a case I think they would have no contraceptive object or will and their acts would not be contraceptive. "[685] Fisher adds that in some instances, even for fertile couples, condomized sex is possible. He bases his supporting argument on the section in *Humanae Vitae* thatpermitsoral contraceptives on therapeutic grounds if such is needed, "foreseeing that that it has a contraceptive side-effect: the lack of a contraceptive will or intention means this is not an act of contraception. "[686]

In his work, Fisher devotes a good number of pages to dealing with the role of Catholic relief agencies and their position in advocacy for or against training in the use of, educating about,or distributing condoms.Fisher opines that "despite some impressive psycho-linguistic gymnastics, efforts to characterize distributing and encouraging the effective use of condoms as merely material cooperation in extra-marital intercourse fail. "[687] Thus, the official policies of Catholic relief agencies all over the world are constant: they insist that they do not finance, distribute, promote, urge, or even suggest the use of condoms.

> Much more might be said about the appropriate response to the HIV crisis, including the best means of prevention.Beyond promoting behavioral change, including delaying onset of sexual activity, reducing

684   Fisher, "HIV and condoms, " 4.

685   Ibid., 6.

686   Ibid.

687   Ibid., 7.

partners and above all promoting chastity, there are many issues to be addressed such as attitudes to the body, Third World disadvantage, relations between sexes and moral relativism.... I conclude that distribution and promotion are clearly ruled out and that even information programs are morally problematically cooperation in extra marital sexual activity.[688]

When it comes to the question of possible reasons for cooperating in informational programs aimed only at HIV-discordant couples, Fisher articulates some of the salient points arguing against this position as follows:

- Programs such as this creates a false sense of security which supports "behavioral disinhibition " or "risk compensation, "still putting them at risk of infection.

- This gives the false impression that contraceptive sex or extra- (non) marital sex is permissible.

- Immediate damage is done to those affected physically, psychologically, in their relationship with God, the Church and with others.

- The Church's traditional position, which is already misunderstood, stands to be further misconstrued by a mixed message of exceptions to the rule, which may be a fatal compromise to the life of faith.

- Consequently, a consistency in magisterial and papal teachings will be compromised with regard to marriage, sexuality, and family life.

- This may also exacerbate widespread moral decline, widespread use of contraception and all sorts of defiant sexual behaviors that will aid the continuous spread of the disease.

Fisher therefore concludes that it is wrong for any Catholic agency to cooperate in the promotion of condoms, even if by merely participating in "factual " information dissemination for any kind of option, even

---

688   Ibid., 11. It is interesting to note that Jon Fuller, a Jesuit physician and scientist has presented three studies that demonstrate a significant reduction of infection in a study carried out for a period of two years. Cf. Jon Fuller, "AIDS Prevention: A Challenge to the Catholic Moral Tradition, " *America* 175 (1996): 13-20.

when such information is seen to be restricted to HIV-discordant couples. Ultimately, Fisher thinks that abstinence from sexual intercourse is possible within marriage, as it is a free and responsible choice that married people have to make at various times and various reasons.Sometimes, this abstinence extends for considerable lengths of times and maybe the only prudent option left at the time.According to Fisher, by this kind of prudent abstinence, "spouses affirm rather than undermine their marriage as a communion of persons which has chronological and moral priority over its one-flesh expression. "[689] In Fisher's opinion, "abstinence is clearly the safest course for HIV-discordant couples. "[690] For discordant couples who may have to abstain from sexual intercourse within their marital life, Fisher advocates for counselling, education, and spiritual support.Both the Church and society have a moral obligation to support single people as they strive to live the virtue of chastity; "so too, many married couples need more help in dealing with sexual frustration and other challenges in the physical-emotional side of their marriage. "[691] This position, which has remained constant in Catholic tradition, professionals and agencies will open them to severe criticism and "at odds with the powers and wisdom of the age. "[692]

Benezet Bujo is a renowned and eminent African theologian, a priest of the diocese of Bunia in the Democratic Republic of Congo, and

---

689   Ibid., 10.

690   Ibid. Further on, Fisher makes a strong classic argument: "As I intimated earlier....many proponents of 'harm minimization' and 'safe sex' strategies seem to presume a rather low view of the human person: that HIV-infected person are 'going to have sex no matter what', that they are beyond reason, influence or conversion, and that the best we can offer is damage limitation. Such fatalism is alien to the Catholic confidence in the persuadability of the mind to truth, the convertability of the will to virtue, and the efficacy of good human and spiritual support. The Church is mandated to give witness to the life transforming and perfective power of divine grace and so must always hold out hope to individuals that they are capable of chastity, virtue, holiness; if we imply that we expect less, we should not be surprised when people fulfil our low expectations. The witness of unmarried individuals who abstain from sexual intercourse in order to protect the good of life, health, marriage and love, must be honored and supported. Likewise the witness of individuals and agencies who focus on compassion, care and chastity helps to evangelize a culture desperately in need of alternatives to its heart-breaking and health-breaking permissiveness. "

691   Ibid.

692   Ibid.

a professor of Moral Theology and Social Ethics at the University of Fribourg, Switzerland. On the question of HIV/AIDS and discordancy, Bujo acknowledges that this scourge is afflicting great numbers of people in Africa. Bujo notes also that the efforts of the Church to proffer a solution to this problem is brought about by an attempt to remain committed and defend the goodnews of Jesus. Bujo avers that this moral positon of the Church oftentimes seems too rigorous and does not speak realistically to the lived experience of those who are affected by this scourge. Condom use as a response to HIV/AIDS, in Bujo's opinion, was raised in the West as a panacea. This is in conflict with the traditional teaching of the Church which sees contraception as intrinsically evil, and evil cannot be tolerated as a means to achieving a good. Based on this logic, discordant couples may not resort to the use of condoms but rely on permanent abstinence. Having acknowledged this official teaching and position of the Church, Bujo draws attention to the specificity of the African situation. Bujo asserts, "Despite the contrary view of the Catholic Church in Africa, many believe that right now condoms are the only means to protect the population from complete extermination. "[693] Bujo states further that experience has shown that absolute continence usually fails, leading to wider spread of the disease and the infection of a hitherto uninfected partner and most likely the newly born child. Bujo therefore advocates "a context in which the principle of the lesser evil *(manus malum)* or the application of the principle of double effect *(actus cum duplici effectui)* should be applied. "[694] In order to clarify his point Bujo reiterates: "it must be clearly stressed that the use of condoms is to be understood as a lesser evil *(minus malum)* or avoiding the use of condoms as a lesser good *(minus bonum)*, only as long as no better option is available. "[695] In proposing an "interim ethic, " Bujo sheds greater light on his position by re-emphasizing the difference between *what is*, and *what ought to be*:

> ... the principles of lesser evil and of double effect
> urgently require us to seek a more adequate solution:
> that is, it is legitimate to endorse an "interim ethics

---

693   Benezet Bujo and Michael Czerny, eds., *AIDS in Africa: Theological Reflections* (Nairobi, Kenya: Paulines Publications Africa, 2007), 66.

694   Ibid.

695   Ibid., 67.

" only until something better comes along. The real and fundamentally valid solution, however, involves a change in behavior and demands a new lifestyle, an inner renewal of one's approach to sexuality, rather than naively trusting technical solutions. Such behavioral change concerns not just the individual; it is essential, rather, that the whole of society contribute to it.[696]

Recalling the 1994 Synod on Africa, in which the Bishops of Africa adopted "family " as a model for the Church in Africa, Bujo sees this model as apt and appropriate, an African understanding of family which encapsulates the living, the dead, and the yet to be born. In light of the various problems faced in Africa, Bujo appeals for a pragmatic use of this family model: "it is more urgent than ever to develop a community morality that corresponds to the Church as family according to the African model. "[697] Bujo insists that checking HIV/AIDS in Africa is a common project between communities, the Church, and the international community, and that the situation will not improve until "the world community is ready to address all issues—particularly in relation to the people of the South, first and especially in Africa the most exploited—with justice and letting love prevail. "[698]

---

696   Ibid., 68-9.

697   Ibid.,76.

698   Ibid., 77. An aspect of the various issues involving the international community, which Bujo addresses, is the question of the wide distribution of condoms without expounding on the underlying ethical issues. Bujo queries whether "massive condom advertising, as has been experienced above all in the Third World, can only lead to the trivialization of sexuality. It can give the impression that, with a condom, anything is allowed.... One might ask, for instance, whether the spread of condoms in sub-Saharan Africa has to do with a desire to protect people from disease or whether it leads to more problems? As in the case of gun running, business interests can thrive at the expense of the poor and the dead; the highest aim not being human health but rather condom exports and cash. " Ibid., 68. Arguing along this same line of thought, Cameroonian theologian, Elias K. Bongmba asserts that "the African Church needs to continue its fight against the disease in collaboration with other groups who are waging a war against HIV/AIDS. The medical community will continue to deepen our understanding of the disease, but Churches at the local, denominational, and ecumenical levels have a vested interest in exploring the broader social context in which HIV/AIDS occurs and in working out new intervention strategies. " Cf. Elias K. Bongmba, *Facing a Pandemic: The African Church and the Crisis of AIDS* (Waco, Texas: Baylor University Press, 2007), 7.

In another essay, Bujo calls attention to the efforts of Basic or Small Christian Communities (SCC)[699] to support those afflicted by HIV/ AIDS. These communities act as a healing community whose presence offers comfort, counseling, and help. Their ministry is not limited to the Church but includes every one of every faith and ethnicity. Because this ecclesial ministry offers "real " presence, Bujo calls for a renewed look at "the administration of the sacraments of the Eucharist, penance and the anointing of the sick. "[700] Many contemporary African theologians are of the opinion that women suffer the most in the HIV epidemics, as care takers, care givers, those most often infected, and so on. Bujo characterizes the situation thus: "In Africa, there are so many women in the service of those infected with HIV/AIDS that the phrase 'feminization of ecclesial identity' was coined, which could give to our ecclesiology a new dynamic. This outstanding presence of women in the service of the sick renders the question of administration of the sacraments even more complex. "[701] Bujo therefore poses the question,

---

699   Ronald Kamara, while reflecting on the work of the SCC in Uganda, notes that their work "at the heart of the Church's evangelization strategy in communities [has] played a big part in spreading the Church' message of HIV prevention in communities. Specifically the following are some of the undertakings by SCCs in HIV prevention: Initiating behavioral change campaigns in communities, awareness development and health education, linking people with facility services, advocating to bring services nearer to the people especially HIV counselling and testing, fighting stigma and discrimination especially among and within families, supporting out of school youth to engage in meaningful and gainful activities like sports, crop and animal husbandry, bringing people in communities to pray and worship together. " Cf. Ronald Kamara, "The Role of Small Christian Communities in the Fight Against HIV/AIDS with Specific Reference to Uganda " in Marco Moerschbacher et al., eds., *A Holistic Approach to HIV and AIDS in Africa* (Nairobi, Kenya: Paulines Publications Africa, 2008).

700   Benezet Bujo, *Plea for Change of Models for Marriage* (Nairobi, Kenya: Paulines Publications Africa, 2009), 168.

701   Ibid. In stating this argument, Bujo makes the case that "...the African Church as family and as sacramental presence of Christ is fully made present by the small Christian communities and by each and all their members. This service to HIV/AIDS patients makes visible the comforting presence of Christ, who, by dying on the cross, sealed with his blood the foundation of his Church. Women have a special position and a task that is of great importance from an African perspective. Women in Africa are symbols of life per excellence. Serving the sick and those deprived of their rights, they are giving a new dynamic to life, and even giving new birth to it. It is women who personify, in a unique and special way, Jesus' words, 'I came so that they may have life and have it more abundantly.' " (Jn. 10:10).

"Would it not be good to rethink the traditional theology of the two sacraments, reconciliation and anointing of the sick, in the context of Africa today regarding the ministers of the sacraments? "[702]

In terms of Bujo's proposal for the active role of the Church that is based on the family structure as model, solidarity and common responsibility must be the Church's watchword.Surprisingly, Bujo makes a bland and open-ended statement that is un-nuanced: "This concerns, after all, and especially, husband and wife… being members of Christ's, they must live out their marriage knowing fully their responsibility to one another, and because of HIV/AIDS, *avoid any risks* to themselves "[703] (emphasis mine). Bujo appeals for better education in both schools and catechesis, to curb illiteracy and the kind of ignorance that makes poor people turn away from modern-

---

702   Ibid. 169. I also find Agbonkhianmeghe E. Orobator's take on the role of women in the fight against HIV/AIDs in the African Church very instructive both in the logic and in the argument proposed. Orobator states,
When AIDS comes to the Church, it affects the entire body or communion of faith, its self-understanding and mission… These situations require a multi-sectoral approach, precisely because they create a field of participation open to all sectors of the social and political spectrum, including the Church…. The Church is multi-sectoral community in solidarity with 'the people of our time', in particular those living with HIV and AIDS. This solidarity translates not only into a feeling, but also into a variety of ministries within the Church, aimed at those infected and affected by disease… Ministries, however, do not spring from chaos; they are an ordered response, in different situations, of the community called Church 'guided by the Holy Spirit'. They are not a prerogative of the few, but a function of the entire community… Healing, as an ecclesial function in the context of AIDS, seeks to actualize the virtues of compassion, hospitality and solidarity characteristic of all the stories of healing in the gospel… In the context of AIDS, the face of the Church as a multi-sectoral, ministering and healing community has a distinctly feminine profile. This profile or face embodies an important aspect of the Church's identity and mission, namely Church-as- mother. 'Holy Mother Church' is a venerable appellation that dates back to Christian antiquity (cf. Gal 4:21-31). Within the situation of AIDS, this maternal title allows us to discover a rich dimension of the nature of the Church. While more women than men suffer the affliction of AIDS and the associated condition of poverty, our analysis of this situation falls short if it overlooks the equally striking fact that more women than men are working individually and collectively in Church based or Church sponsored organizations responding to HIV and AIDS. It would seem reasonable to see this as conforming an age-old insight into the maternal identity of the Church… In the time of AIDS, we need to probe… and propose a more adequate interpretative framework for the maternal face of the community called Church, the feminization of ecclesial identity. Agbonkhianmeghe E. Orobator, "When AIDS Comes to Church, " in Benezet Bujo and Michael Czerny, eds., *AIDS in Africa: Theological Reflections* (Nairobi, Kenya: Paulines Publications Africa, 2007), 120-8.

703   Bujo, *Plea for Change*, 182.

scientific medicine and technology (where available) to consulting with necromancy and mystical visionaries.

Paulinus Ikechukwu Odozor is another well-known African theologian whose contribution to the conversation on HIV/AIDS in Africa and the situation of discordancy approaches the question with an appeal to casuistry.In Catholic theology, casuistry as a principle is an aspect of moral theology that is applied to moral singular facts in the face of moral conflict.Casuistry is employed to find practical solutions that preserve all intrinsic values.Experience shows that rules/laws have limits because they are sometimes not self- interpreting and do not naturally resolve ambiguities and conflicting moral principles. According to Odozor, humans formulate values that will help communities to flourish, but sometimes these values are incomplete in their expression— "thus, the need for constant revision of some of the norms that govern human conduct.Casuistry is an important way of effecting these revisions, which may lead to the abrogation of particular norms, the enlargement of some others or the refinement of yet others. "[704] Reflecting on the question of contraceptive intercourse, Odozor while acknowledging the magisterial position, also questions whether, where HIV/AIDS is concerned within discordancy, condomized sex can be seen simply as contraceptive. Following those who think that in discordancy the use of condoms is not contraceptive, Odozor agrees with them in seeing it as an example of the ordering of the hierarchy of values found in casuistry:

> Life and marriage are here seen as higher values to be preserved when faced with this rather regrettable choice.Thus, when faced with AIDS and its consequences, the community is forced to rethink its moral principles and presuppositions.The goal is not to abandon the result of many years of communal wisdom taught authoritatively by the magisterium of the Church.Rather, it is to find imaginatively creative ways of understanding or coming to terms with the community's ethical commitment in the face of

---

704   Paulinus Ikechukwu Odozor, *Casuistry and AIDS: A Reflection on the Catholic Tradition*, in Keenan, *Catholic Ethicists*, 297.

this entirely new and devastating phenomenon.... Catholic moral casuistic tradition has always paid attention to circumstances, principles, and the individual conscience in the search for solutions to the problems which new phenomena raise for the individual and society.[705]

While Odozor does not commit either to supportingor not supporting the use of condoms for discordant couples, his statement, like Bujo's, is un-nuanced and therefore open to reader translation. Odozor opines that in the casuistic tradition, a special value is placed on human life.Therefore, "solutions that are in favor of life are more in keeping with the best insights of our moral tradition. "[706] Odozor supports the casuistic tradition, in which an unusual situation may call for extraordinary action.These insights in Odozor's reflection "are present in the casuistic tradition and can be used *mutatis mutandi* to treat HIV/AIDS related cases. "[707] Odozor thinks that the application of casuistry to the problem of HIV/AIDS and the use of condoms can help to find the balance between moral idealism and reactive rigorism. The application of casuistry, in Thomistic terms, is helpful when prudent people react to diverse persons and situations, draw from past experiences to make judgements about future possibilities to arrive at sound conclusions about ethical problems, including HIV/AIDS and the use of condoms in discordancy.

While a lot more ink can be expended on various approaches and arguments for and against, one thing is sure: The Church needs to make a definitive statement on the matter of condomized sex in discordancy. Clearly, this matter challenges prior teaching and creates an avenue for a development in doctrine. Pope Benedict XVI appointed a commission to study the possibility of permitting the use of condoms for discordant couples, and to determine under which theological ethical principles this might be permissible.Surprisingly, years later, the Church remains silent about the outcome of the commission's work and remains silent on an official magisterial and doctrinal position.Two events make the

---

705   Ibid., 298-9.

706   Ibid., 301.

707   Ibid., 302.

situation more troubling in the light of a lack of an official position. The first is a situation that is now often referred to as a classic example of a "double down " by Pope Emeritus, Benedict VXI, when he made comments that male prostitutes (and all who engage in dangerous sexual activities) are better off using condoms to prevent the spread of disease. The second case involves religious missionary nuns travelling to work as missionaries in the Congo during the civil war years of the early 1960s. Because they were in danger of rape, they received permission to use contraceptive drugs as a form of protection. The technical aspects of each case is long and unnecessary at this point. The import of both events is well summarized in Lisa Sowle Cahill's response the nuns/Congo case which I believe applies also to the Pope Benedict/male prostitute case. In a journal essay Cahill writes,

> The debate was important, instead, because it presented the possibilities that practical problems could challenge the accustomed ways of thinking about contraception, and because it joined respected theological voices in a re- examination of the prohibition on it – although it is revealing of racial attitudes that these particular circumstances were required to raise the question in the European mind. The debate was one of several movements in the Church which together, at the time of Vatican II, were to sponsor a hope among both theologians and laypersons that the traditional strictures on control of conception would be revised.[708]

Cahill's position resonates because to seek solutions (even if temporary) to the problem of HIV/AIDS in Africa and developing poorer nations around the world, there is the necessity for a closer study of cultural problems, marriages rites, rites of young adult initiations and passage, and the sexual mores of different societies. These varied contexts make it often more realistically difficult to navigate or to proffer one single solution as one size fits all. It is even more dangerous for the Church to remain silent on how to respond a disease that is

---

708   Lisa Sowle Cahill, "Catholic Sexual Ethics and the Dignity of the Person: A Double Message, " *Theological Studies* 50, no. 1 (1989): 129.

taking the lives of huge numbers of poor people as a lack of concern or show of empathy.God forbid that banners like "Black Lives Matters " ever show up as a reaction against the Church on this issue. For now, the Church offers the argument that since scientifically we do know that even condoms are not always 100% safe, discordant couples are encouraged to embrace abstinence even if indefinitely; "by so doing spouses affirm rather than undermine their marriage as a communion of persons which has chronological and moral priority over its one-flesh expression.They must find other ways of demonstrating love and experiencing physical and emotional intimacy together. "[709]

Same Sex Unions

The second pastoral problem to be examined is the question of same sex unions, a situation where we have two equally committed Catholics who believe they have taken the moral highroad and are expressing the will of God in their same gender relationship. This peculiar pastoral and contemporary problem needs to be thoroughly engaged, scrutinized, and re- articulated within the magisterial tradition. Many countries, especially within the Western hemisphere have recently legalized same sex unions. Many more countries around the world are debating legislation on the same matter, and it appears that it is only a matter of time, likely sooner than later, until the legalization of same sex unions will be widely acceptable. This represents a locus where a dramatic change in society and culture comes in direct headlong collision with the established magisterial and traditional position on the meaning of marriage and family life. Because of the nature of the Christian understanding of marriage, that it is strictly between a man and a woman, this new form of same sex unions has created an impasse. This sort of impasse creates a break in communion, communion as unity in the body of Christ and communion as coming to partake at the Eucharistic table. In this second section of my final chapter, same sex unions of baptized Catholics and the question of admission to Eucharistic communion and the universal communion of the people of God is part of a larger theological and pastoral problem with far-reaching implications for the Christian Church in contemporary times

709 Fisher, "HIV and Condoms, " 10.

more than at any other time in the history of Christianity. Based on what the Church sees as the norm, which is a definitive scriptural condemnation of homosexual acts, this needs careful attention.

Choon-Leong Seown avers that "…. there are those of us convinced that the authenticity of the Church is in question if it is unchanging and exclusivistic…. In this scriptural tradition, the Church is unfaithful if it turns its back on those who are marginalized in various ways by society or if the Church itself excludes people on the basis of their race, gender or sexual orientation from full participation in its life and leadership. "[710] And while arguments range on both sides of the divide on the morality or immorality of the homosexual act,[711] Charles Curran notes that "since the 1980s many more Catholic moral theologians have entered the discussion about homosexual relations, but for the most part the methodological and substantive positions do not depart from the earlier positions.Most of the new voices argue in favor of homosexual relations in a committed relationship, but defenders of the existing hierarchical teaching continue to write. "[712] Homosexuality and the question of same sex unions are often argued from a theological and ethical perspective.However, the inferences drawn by these questions have wider implications for all sources of moral theology; "scripture, Church teaching, reason, experience, and the data of human sciences. "[713] More than this, I agree with Choon-Leong Seow's articulation of a more profound dilemma, "The issue of homosexuality is not merely a question of what the ancient text meant.It is, more importantly, a hermeneutical issue, a question of how we understand the texts and appropriate them for our specific contexts. It is, further, a theological-ethical issue, a question of how we as Christians think about ourselves and our conduct in relation to God. "[714]This dialectic is the basis for my exploration questions pertaining to same sex unions and their greater pastoral implications for what it means to be Church, to be in

---

710   Choon-Leong Seow, *Homosexuality*, ix.

711   For a condensed and precise summary of the major arguments for and against, cf. Charles Curran, *Catholic Moral Theology in the United States: A History* (Washington, DC: Georgetown University, 2008): 191-3, 195-9.

712   Ibid., 197.

713   Ibid., 195.

714   Seow, *Homosexuality*, ix.

communion with the Church, and to be able to go to the table of the Eucharistic communion. Certain questions arise: are we reading the texts right? Are we legislating rightly about who we include and who we exclude? Even in a more simplistic kind of way, one may ask, "What would Jesus do?

The Church has been consistent in her teaching and position on homosexuality. Homosexual orientation, while not a sin, is yet an "objective disorder because it is ordered to an intrinsically moral evil. "[715] The Church makes a distinction between *orientation* and *homosexual acts*: "The homosexual orientation is 'objectively disordered' while the homosexual acts are 'intrinsically disordered.'[716] These terms have been translated into an indictment on the personhood of homosexual persons. However, according to Zalot and Guevin, this misunderstanding is based on a lack of understanding of the philosophical language as based on the natural law theory. These authors refer to the understanding that God created male and female in complementarity for a union of life and procreation. "Because homosexual acts are deficient—notice again, we speak of deficiency, not sin—in their ability to bring forth new life, they are deemed to be contrary to the natural ordering of creation. They are in this sense, 'disordered.' "[717] Further clarification is made that every human person suffers a certain kind of disordered inclination, be it to cowardice, gluttony, gossip, theft, etc.; these simply remain inclinations and are not sinful until one willingly acts on them, at which time they become moral evil. Within the same logic, homosexual orientation is not sinful, but to engage in homosexual acts is. Central to the Church's teaching on this matter is the centrality of the male-female marital relationship, and the call of all Christians to chastity in whatever state of life they choose to live. For homosexual persons, the Church calls on all to see in such persons the image of God, to afford them the dignity due to them, to fight any discrimination against them, to love them as brothers and sisters in Christ. When this position on homosexuality

---

715   Congregation for the Doctrine of the Faith (CDF), "Letter to the Bishops on the Pastoral Care of Homosexual Persons, " 1986, www.vatican.va/congregations/cfaith/documents/rc_con_cfaith_doc_19861001_homosexual- persons_en.html.

716   Jozef D. Zalot and Benedict Guevin, *Catholic Ethics in Today's World* (Winona, MN: Anselm Academic, 2011), 276.

717   Ibid.

is put side by side the Church's position on marriage, the picture on the future possibility in the development of doctrine in this area seems to be a completed project. The catechism of the Catholic Church and the code of canon law state unambiguously, "The matrimonial covenant, by which a man and a woman establish between themselves a partnership of the whole life, is by its very nature ordered toward the good of the spouses and the procreation and education of offspring; these covenant between baptized persons has been raised by Christ the Lord to the dignity of a sacrament. "[718]

Within the New Natural Law Theorists' enclave, in this instance, relying on John Finnis' work, we find a total rejection of same sex unions based on the logic that homosexual and heterosexual non-reproductive sexual acts are unnatural, unreasonable, and for this reason immoral. Finnis and his colleagues argue in favor of heterosexual marriage and the conjugal act employing three arguments. First, marriage between a man and a woman is a basic good; second, sex also is a basic good of marriage; and third, every other non-marital sexual act is unnatural, unreasonable, and immoral. In line with Catholic tradition, NNLT accepts the two intrinsic and inseparable inner meanings of marriage: procreation and unity (friendship). Finnis and his colleagues maintain that homosexual acts do not fulfil or achieve these two intrinsic values as such homosexual acts (as well as those of non-married persons, sodomites, masturbators, contracepting couples, those who perform oral sex, and all who violate the intrinsic meaning of the marital act) cannot achieve the basic good of marriage:

> But the common good of friends who are not and cannot be married (for example, man and man, man and boy, woman and woman) has nothing to do with their having children by each other, and their reproductive organs cannot make them a biological (and therefore personal) unit. So their sexual acts together cannot do what they may hope and imagine. Because their activation of one or even each of their reproductive organs cannot be an

---

718   *Catechism of the Catholic Church*, 2nd ed.(The Vatican: Libreria Editrice Vaticana, 2000), #1601.

actualizing and experiencing of the *marital* good –
as marital intercourse (intercourse between spouses
in a marital way) can, even between spouses who
happen to be sterile – it can do no more than provide
each partner with an individual gratification... their
choice to engage in such conduct thus dis-integrates
each of them precisely as acting persons.[719]

The NNL theorists claim that homosexual acts are unnatural
since they do not have any possibility of a reproductive telos, and
the two persons' reproductive organs fail to create the natural desired
complementarity. Finnis states that "the biological union of the
reproductive organs of a husband and wife is part of, not an instrument
of, their personal reality... sexual acts are not unitive in their
significance unless they are marital... "[720] The NNL theorists therefore
conclude that since homosexual acts are not a marital act, they damage
and impede a major moral principle, violating a basic human good. In
addition, since marriage is a basic human good, homosexual acts are
unnatural, unreasonable and immoral.

The work of Todd Salzman and Michael Lawler questions the
presumption that all homosexual acts are intrinsically evil and see a
distortion of tradition. Both writers argue that the Church understands
and accepts in finding theological truths the input of sound theological
exegesis, application of scientific data where applicable, history,
culture, and experience. This is a complex process involving patient
dialogue, research, discernment, and time. Carefully examining these
foundations (borrowed from the theology of Cardinal Josef Ratzinger),
Salzman and Lawler submit that by following this principle of holistic
complementarity, not all homosexual acts can be judged to be morally
wrong. From a biblical perspective, Salzman and Lawler argue that
since the Bible itself is subject to history, there can be no absolute norms
on any kind of sexuality which can be broadly applied across varying
cultural contexts. Contemporary theology today, therefore, cannot rely

---

719   Todd A. Salzman and Michael G. Lawler, "New Natural Law Theory and
Foundational Sexual Ethical Principles: A Critique and a Proposal, " *The Heythrop Journal*
47, no. 2 (2006): 184; cf. also John Finnis, "Law, Morality and Sexual Orientation, " *Notre
Dame Law Review* 69, no. 5 (1995): 301.

720   Salzman and Lawler, "New Natural Law, " 185.

on abstract biblical texts from a different epoch and cultural context. Reflecting on the natural law argument employed by the magisterium, Salman and Lawler aver that "[h]omosexual acts are 'natural' for people with a homosexual orientation just as heterosexual acts are 'natural' for people with heterosexual orientation. "[721]

Both writers understand the interpretation of "natural" to be socially constructed. Therefore, "as such, what is 'natural' in sexual activity, which is an expression of the sexual person, will vary depending[722] on whether or not the person's sexual orientation is homosexual or heterosexual. " They make the case against the objection that the homosexual act is non- procreative, arguing that permanently or temporarily non-reproductive heterosexual acts are essentially different since they also are non-procreative. Again, based on human experience, Salzman and Lawler posit that "homosexual couples manifest 'the gift of life' in their sexuality through embodied interpersonal union... both fertile and infertile, manifest 'the gift of life' in their sexuality in their embodied interpersonal union. "[723] Therefore, what constitutes morally good sexual acts for both heterosexual and homosexual couples is embodiment and interpersonal union. Against the complementarity argument, they state that "abundant social-scientific data to support the claim that personal, unitive complementarity is experienced in committed, stable, and justly loving homosexual relationships... and in the case of homosexual parents, these complementarities facilitate both parental complementarity and the positive nurture of children. "[724]

Salzman and Lawler challenge the Church and ask for a revision of the current magisterial position which teaches that all homosexual acts are intrinsically immoral. Both authors call for a more systematic approach based on sound biblical exegesis, scientific data based on experience and the best of magisterial teaching on human sexuality. For them, the consensual sexual act between two persons, heterosexual

---

721   Todd A. Salman and Michael G. Lawler, *Sexual Ethics: A Theological Introduction*(Washington, DC: Georgetown University, 2012), 170.

722   Ibid.

723   Ibid., 171.

724   Ibid., 174-5.

or homosexual should not be a means of objectifying, dominating, or exploiting another; any sexual violence in either heterosexual or homosexual union is never justified. In their conclusion, they state their position clearly:

> Heterosexual orientation is an innate, deep-seated, and stable orientation to, predominantly, persons of the opposite sex; homosexual orientation is similarly innate, deep-seated, and stable orientation to, predominantly, persons of the same sex. Ethics can have for its object only acts that are free, acts that can be imputed to personal responsibility. Whatever is determined, insofar as it is determined, is neither moral nor immoral' it simply is. Sexual orientation is neither chosen nor readily changeable; it simply is. It is, therefore, in itself neither moral nor immoral. The sexual behaviors that flow from it, however, may be moral or immoral.[725]

Stephen J. Pope agrees with Salzman and Lawler's position that recent scientific findings lend credence to the concept of the naturalness of homosexuality and therefore examine what impact this claim may have on contemporary natural law ethics. Pope sees the Church as traditionally using the natural law argument to prohibit homosexual acts. The natural law argument has been used to reinforce the idea of human nature in a singular dimension—the divinely intended or sanctified person, characterized for the heavenly kingdom. Pope argues that this image does not acknowledge a broader range of human flourishing, which includes a natural desire for the good. According to Pope, "This tendency goes hand-in-hand with the tendency to isolate its *theological* interpretation of the descriptively human from *empirical* interpretations of the descriptively human. "[726] As a result, the natural law theory separates the "normatively human from scientific information and insights regarding the descriptively

---

725   Ibid., 178-9.

726   Stephen J. Pope, "Scientific and Natural Law Analyses of Homosexuality: A Methodological Study, " *Journal of Religious Ethics* 25, no. 1 (1997): 109.

human. "[727] Pope identifies the normative human as crucial within the Church's application of its sources for theology and in its excursion in finding moral truths; scripture, tradition, human experience and magisterial authority in translating and interpreting what constitutes genuine human flourishing. According to Pope, "Human flourishing is conceived much more strongly in affective and interpersonal terms than strictly natural terms. Interpersonal love is here the locus of human flourishing. "[728] Pope sees a relationship with a Thomistic understanding of practical reason which arrives at ethical principles by generalizations based on judgements or the understanding of virtuous persons who experience connaturality with the good. Pope insists that despite all the works of biblical scholars and Christian tradition, which clearly condemn homosexual sex, the conversation is by no means ended, "but it does imply that the burden of proof must be borne by those who would argue for the legitimacy of some kind of homosexual covenant. "[729] Pope calls for a more precise and comprehensive account of what truly constitutes human flourishing according to a natural law ethic, which "as a moral tradition offers neither timeworn prohibitions nor vague platitudes but genuine moral wisdom. "[730] For Pope, what trumps the natural law argument is the affective complementarity of two people of the same sex who are living in a committed and loving relationship.

Matter and Form: A Hypothetical Frame Work

The complexity of the subject matter requires a dialogical and cross fertilizing of differing theological and non-theological positions, taking into account the historical, revisionist, contemporary, philosophical, and anthropological foundations of the Church's understanding of marriage and human sexuality. Here, I intend to apply "Matter " and "Form " as a descriptive tool for understanding the essentials of the development of Catholic doctrine. As I have referenced several times earlier on, doctrine can include revealed truths, Scripture, sacred

727   Ibid.

728   Ibid., 111.

729   Ibid., 119.

730   Ibid., 121.

tradition, definitions, or even ongoing synodal formulations of the magisterium. Within the doctrinal tradition, a dogmatic definition or teaching proclaimed infallibly has greater weight than other teachings not so defined. All doctrines proposed by the magisterial tradition require adherence from the entire Church, yet the weight of one proclamation differs from that of another. No one encapsulates this idea better than John Cardinal Newman who spoke eloquently to this situation thus:

> ...certainly some rule is necessary for arranging and authenticating these various expressions and results of Christian doctrine. No one will maintain that all points of belief are of equal importance. There are what may be considered minor points, which we may hold to be true without imposing them as necessary; there are greater truths and lesser truths, points which it is necessary, and points which it is pious to believe. The simple question is, "How are we to discriminate the greater from the less, the true from the false...."

> If the developments, which have above been called *moral*, are to take place to any great extent, and without them it is difficult to see how Christianity can exist at all, if only its relations civil government have to be ascertained or the qualification for membership with it defined, surely an authority is necessary to impart decision to what is vague and confidence to what is empirical, to ratify the successive steps of so elaborate a process, and to secure the validity of inferences which are to be made the premises of more remote investigations.[731]

To approach the fundamental question of my thesis, I here appropriate the idea of "matter" and "form" in the sacramental theology of the Church employed as a metaphor, or an analytical tool, or a hypothetical framework to try to explain the converging point of

---

731   Newman, *Essay on the Development*, 59.

the disagreeing positions. I suggest that understanding possible changes or shifts in the doctrinal position on human sexuality can be better explored borrowing the idea of matter and form from sacramental theology. Using matter and form as metaphors helps to delineate the difference between theological essentials and incidentals, between its subjective and objective components.

The form/matter distinction has a long standing history in theology, with roots in both Aristotelian/Thomistic science and philosophy. It is applied to the sacraments in contemporary Catholic liturgical theology:

> The nature of each sacrament is explained in terms of its distinctive form and matter. Thus the "matter" of baptism is the pouring of water…. The "form" is the saying of the accompanying words "I baptize you in the name of the father and of the son and of the Holy Spirit." This gives religious meaning to the material gesture and makes the composite act an efficacious supernatural sign of grace… Although this form/matter analysis is not the only or the exhaustive explanation of the full meaning and reality of the sacraments, it is a very illuminating one as far as it goes, and it would be difficult indeed to dispense with it entirely.[732]

The form in sacramental theology is often the word of Jesus, while the matter consists of the operative materials used, as handed down by sacred Scripture and Christian tradition. Sacraments are enacted in symbolic **acts** and **words**, matter and form, and I am adapting this analogy to try to explain the nature of marriage within the Christian tradition. There are certain aspects that remain unchangeable and can be seen as the form of its sacramentality, whereas the Church's response to newer questions that need re-interpretation and re-articulation can be seen as matter, which has changeability. Therefore, we can trace shifts in the teachings concerning conjugality between married couples, questions concerning artificial birth control and natural birth control

---

732   Joseph A. Komonchak et al., eds., *The New Dictionary of Theology* (Wilmington, Delaware: Michael Glazier, Inc., 1988), 403-4

etc., leading to raising further questions about discordant couples and even the question of same sex unions.

I argue that since the Church, through the actions of the Holy Spirit, is itself a sacrament of salvation, so are her teachings. Therefore, while the teaching on sexuality as *form* remains historically and doctrinally the same, its *matter* evolves and will continue to evolve as society and cultures evolve.[733] The imagery that sacramental symbols evoke for the Church are clearly mediated to the Church's mission of teaching. Sebastian Madathummuriyil posits that even though emphasis is shifting from the power of language and symbol to the activity of the Holy Spirit, this agency of mediation can be "described in terms based on the double and complementary missions of the word and spirit... explained only in terms of the originary giveness of the spirit, who mediates Christ through the language and symbols of the sacraments. "[734] JPII makes copious references to the sacramental dimension of sexuality, a point that will be highlighted and addressed below, though there is variance in the perspectives.[735] Morton and Barbara Kesley note that "a sacrament is an outward and visible sign of an inner and spiritual grace.... Sexuality is at its best is an outer, visible, physiological sign of the inner and spiritual grace of love. "[736] The Kesleys state that not all forms of sexual behavior fit into this definition but that when it does

---

733   Komonchak, Ibid. The promise of the Paraclete to the apostles is to confirm them in the truth, (in **all** truths), since the Church is in all places and at all times, Holy and Apostolic, the message she carries must necessarily be inspired. For the message to remain valid, it must have in itself ontological truths that are valid for all times and in all places. Otherwise, the claim to inspiration is false and empty, devoid of the Spirit of God. It is this unchanging and always true aspect of the message (dogma) that I apply the hypothesis, 'form' to, while other important but less critical aspects of the message (doctrine) are 'matter' since they do not detract from the originality of the message even when they are re-adapted for a new situation and culture.

734   Sebastian Madathummuriyil, "The "Dative Subject " of the Sacrament: An 'East-West' Perspective, " *Studia Liturgica* 43, no. 1 (2013): 115, 121.

735   JPII devotes a good deal of time on reflecting on the sacramental nature of marriage. Starting with Ephesians 5, he builds the sacramentality of marriage as the Pauline and Johannine analogy of Christ who is the groom of his Church bride, and that this sacramentality effectively points to its redemptive meaning.

736   Morton Kesley and Barbara Kesley, *Sacrament of Sexuality: The Spirituality and Psychology of Sex* (Rockport, Mass: Element Inc., 1986), 3.

fit, human sexuality becomes a living symbol or sacrament of love—
"a window into the self-giving love of God, a spiritual experience, a
communion with love or God. "[737]

Arguing along the same line of thought, Longfellow and Nelson posit
in their book that a Christian understanding of sexuality is a "far more
comprehensive matter, broader, richer and more fundamental to our
human existence than simply genital sex. "[738] They contend that human
sexuality, as intended by God, is neither incidental nor detrimental to
our spirituality; rather, it fully integrates this dimension of our being.
They argue further that human sexuality is "more fundamentally and
inclusively…., who we are as body-selves who experience the ambiguities
of both 'having' and 'being' bodies. Sexuality embraces our ways of
being in the world as persons embodied with biological femaleness or
maleness and with internalized understandings of what these genders
mean. "[739] They posit that "sexuality, " based on its etymology from the
Latin, suggests an incompleteness that constantly seeks connection and
wholeness, "a physiological and emotional grounding of our capacity
to love. "[740] My conclusion is to insist that the core of doctrine[741]
does not change because of its normativity, but incidentals that relate
to contemporary challenges need the attention of the Magisterium,
theologians, and secular society to study and dialogue carefully with
mutual respect in a listening environment, and to give answers that are
ethical and respect human beings and lead to life.

---

737   Ibid.

738   James Nelson and Sandra Longfellow, eds., *Sexuality and the Sacred: Sources
for Theological Reflection* (Louisville, Kentucky: Westminster/John Knox Press, 1994), p.
xiv.

739   Ibid.

740   Ibid.

741   A distinction is made which clarifies this position further concerning "… the
distinction between dogma and doctrine…; in ordinary conversation the two words are
often used interchangeably. Technically, however, there is a difference. Dogmas relate the
truth of revelation. Doctrines explain and teach how a particular dogma maybe understood.
There may be several acceptable explanations or doctrine surrounding a single dogma. For
example, it is Christian dogma that Mary is the Mother of God. Theological explanations of
this dogma are doctrines. It is on the level of doctrine that the Church admits of pluralism,
not on the level of dogma. " Komonchak, *New Dictionary of Theology*, 295.

Many theologians, ethicists and general commentators agree that there is an impasse as well as a large gap between teachings from the Church's magisterium and their reception by the lay faithful as well as the secular or public sphere's opinion on these matters.[742] It is therefore worthwhile to continue the conversations that will close this gap, either by insistence on the coherency of doctrine or an acknowledgement that there is a need to change certain aspects of this position. While it is possible in conscience to dissent to the non-infallible teachings of the Church, Vincent Genovesi warns that when it comes to moral discourse, an appreciation and understanding of the difficulties and struggles of the lay faithful need to be acknowledged by the magisterium. In this way, the lay faithful are more open and less antagonistic to what the Church teaches as doctrine, as revealed truths. "Clearly the magisterium, as the authentic teaching body in Roman Catholicism, enjoys the presumption of truth in its pronouncements, so that if ever a Catholic is inclined or impelled to disagree with an official Church teaching, this may never be done lightly or facilely but only cautiously, conscientiously, prayerfully, and respectfully. "[743] Therefore, while the Church has a moral duty to adhere to, and insist on the normativity of her role as *"mater et magistra, "*[744] the individual Catholic and Catholics collectively, as a faith- confessing people, must be open to nurturing

---

742   "Questions of sexual morality are among the most volatile issues in the Roman Catholic Church today. They are also among the most vital... Equally well known is the great discrepancy between official Catholic teaching and Catholic practice.... There is only one prevailing consensus: a serious rift exists between official teaching about sex and the lived reality of Catholics.... A deep and pervasive legitimation crisis exists. Elevating the level of this crisis in recent years has been the sexual abuse scandal traumatizing American Catholic Church. This has sent its credibility into a free fall. And the response of officials to the scandal has merely served to reinforce the very problems that they purport to solve. " Kieran Scott and Harold D. Horell, eds., *Human Sexuality in the Catholic Tradition.* (New York: Rowman & Littlefield Publishers Inc., 2007), 3. The writings of Charles Curran and Richard McCormick treats in depth the question of magisterium and reception. Theologians who support the Curran and McCormick position argue that without adequate reception from the faithful, magisterial authority has no footing. Opponents of their position, in turn, argue that not to have reception is an anomaly since the entire process of pronouncing a teaching is a process which includes the faithful, and that having the backing of divine authority behind her teachings, the lay faithful acknowledge and accept what the Church teaches.

743   Vincent J. Genovesi, *In Pursuit of Love: Catholic Morality and Human Sexuality,* 2nd ed. (Collegeville, Minnesota: The Liturgical Press, 1996), 11.

744   Mother and teacher.

and the possibility of engaging the Church in a truthful exposition of their lived experiences as married Christian spouses and parents.

Christopher Roberts, reflecting on the impasse between contemporary secular voices on matters relating to the Church's position on sexuality, marriage, and sex, states that these two voices do not agree as secularists deviate from the traditional categories of Christian theology and anthropology and the Church's historic confessions of faith on these matters. For him "arguments about sexuality that dispense with theological logic and that are premised on human autonomy and experience are incongruous in debates within the churches. "[745] He further states that such liberal and secularist arguments are "glossed with appeals to justice or love...[and that] such liberal arguments suggest that we can know ourselves sufficiently apart from revelation and doctrine, as if there were parts of life removed from God's grace, address, vocation, command, judgment or teleology. "[746] Likewise, the disparity between these two positions is highlighted further by lay theologians Jon Davis and Gerald Loughlin when in their edited work they observe,

> In contrast to the traditional-reticent view of sex is the liberal view, which sees the body and its sexuality as the central location of the "self, " and which sees any repression or restriction of the self and its sexual appetites as a denial of human being. This is the view that promotes and celebrates the plasticity of the body's sexual energies.... Sex is like food, a commodity, and the culture in which it is bought and sold a veritable pornotopia. It is the culture in which we live.[747]

Claims such as the foregoing—of deviation from "traditional" categories of Christian confessional faith, theology, and anthropology—are always where the battle line is drawn among those who insist on "tradition "

---

745   Christopher C. Roberts, *Creation and Covenant: The Significance of Sexual Difference in the Moral Theology of Marriage* (New York: Continuum, 2007), 3.

746   Ibid.

747   Jon Davies and Gerald Loughlin, eds., *Sex These Days: Essays on Theology, Sexuality and Society* (Bloomsbury: T&T Clark, 1997), 8.

as static and unchanging, and those who insist that tradition must be fluid, flexible, and malleable.

Faith, Tradition and Traditioning the Faith

According to Terrence Tilley in his seminal work, *Inventing Catholic Tradition*, the problem is that many participants in religious debates presume a supernatural origin of tradition, especially ritual tradition, passed as a whole from one generation to the other. He argues that historically known shifts in practices and beliefs have hitherto been accepted as a given. He surmises that "[i]f that which is passed on as tradition has to be passed on 'unchanged and uncorrupted' over long periods of time, then there are no concrete traditions that will pass the test. "[748] For Tilley, "...traditions, to endure, seem to require reconstruction, revision, and reinvention as circumstances change. "[749] However, and in agreement with my position, Tilley states, "we can concede that tradition can change in *accidentals*, but you haven't shown it changes in *essentials*."[750] For Tilley, traditions are fluid not fixed.

Josef Pieper, in explaining what he considers the basic elements of tradition, asserts that tradition involves two partners, one of them transmitting and the other receiving what is transmitted. The latter *(traditum/tradendum)* can belong to a wide range of human experience. All of these bodies of knowledge *(tradita)*, in whatever way they are communicated, end up as a teaching. According to Pieper, "Is not tradition, in so far as we mean by that word the handing on of truth, basically the same as the communication of what is known by teaching from generation to generation? In brief, are not the words 'tradition' and 'teaching' synonyms? "[751] To accept tradition either as a teaching

---

748   Terence W. Tilley, *Inventing Catholic Tradition* (Eugene, Oregon: WIPF, 2000), 28.

749   Ibid., 29.

750   Ibid., 32 (emphasis mine).

751   Josef Pieper, *Tradition: Concept and Claim* (Wilmington, Delaware: ISI Books, 2008), 12. Pieper says about the process of transmitting tradition: "No one who wants to hand down a tradition successfully should talk about 'tradition.' He must take care that the content to be handed down, 'old truths', if they are really true, be kept really alive and present – for example and before anything else, by means of a living language; through creative rejuvenation and sloughing off the old skin like a snake, so to speak; through a continual confrontation with the immediate present and above all with the future, which in

or something that is handed down, involves belief, because receiving tradition is to accept a claim based on someone else's insight. The process of tradition is not just a teaching, instruction or handing down. It is also a process of reminding. Pieper opines that "[h]uman existence can come to grief not only because people neglect further learning, but also because people forget and lose something indispensable."[752]

Tradition, especially where belief is involved, includes the idea of authority; "*traditum*" stands or falls based on the trust of the person standing at the end of the line of reception, who is trusting that the process goes back to the person who stood closest to the origin of *traditum*--because that first person, closest to the origins, can testify and vouch for its authenticity. Therefore, "this closeness to the origin of the tradition provides proof and basis for the authority of the one who is handing down tradition—the authority, of course, not the penultimate in line, but of the first."[753] This authority of the "ancients" is not based on age, the elderly or those with snow-white hair; Pieper states that the essential element and what constitutes the ancients is their proximity to the origin, the very beginning of tradition:

> ...there is hardly any question that there is at least a profound analogy between this description of the "ancients" and the definition by which Christian theology characterizes the "prophets," the "hagiographer," the charismatic called by God, someone who is "inspired" in the strict sense, the author of a sacred book. The common element, for which "analogy" is perhaps too weak a term, consists in the fact that both of them, the "ancients" and the "prophets," are thought of as the first recipients and transmitters of a *theios logos*, a divine speech, a word of God... Naturally, in the "wisdom of the ancients" ... the decisive element is not that

the human realm is the truly real. When you do this, you will see clearly what a demanding the act of tradition is... In truth, the activity of the living transmission of a *traditum* is highly dynamic business. Ibid., 15.

752   Ibid., 23.

753   Ibid., 24.

it comes "from old, " but that it has its origins from a divine source. The ancients do not just stand at the beginning of time. They are the earliest in the chain of the succession of tradition, the first recipients of tradition.[754]

Pieper surmises that it is logical to say, therefore, that Christianity conceives the divine proclamation given to the apostles as new and the very beginning of the sequence of tradition. The apostles are the primeval "ancients " who are linked ultimately to the very source; the incarnated Logos. Pieper then alludes to a nexus, the connection of theology with the transmission/development of Christian doctrine: "In so far as theology is understood as the interpretation of revelation, theology cannot even exist legitimately without presupposing the reality of revelation. "[755] In this sense, "*tradition* "must always be linked to truth, "[i]t must be thought of as something definitive; that is, in principle, no human thinking can make it obsolete, in so far as people are convinced that what it transmits goes back ultimately to a divine speech, therefore to revelation strictly speaking. "[756] For Pieper, as long as these links exist and are maintained or kept in sync, sacred tradition continues, linking the present to the past, indeed to the very source and origin of tradition.

Orlando Espin sees the process of "traditioning " as more significant than arguments about tradition. For Espin, "without 'traditioning'— the transmission of Christianity across generations and across cultural boundaries—there would not be a Christian religion in the twenty first century. "[757] This process of traditioning is found in *lo cotidiano*[758] (daily human experiences)— "an epistemological womb within and through

---

754   Ibid., 29.

755   Ibid., 31.

756   Ibid., 32.

757   Orlando O. Espin, "Traditioning: Culture, Daily Life and Popular Religion, and their Impact on Christian Tradition, " in *Futuring Our Past: Explorations in the Theology of Tradition*, eds. Orlando O. Espin and Gary Macy (Maryknoll, New York: Orbis Books, 2006), 2.

758   A Spanish expression Espin uses, which means the daily life and lived experiences of people as they actually exist, willful, sinful, damaged, and healing all at once.

which all of daily reality is produced and reproduced. "[759] Traditioning across these various cultures and centuries, within the *sensus fidelium*, "acts as inculturation and transculturation of revelation, making it possible for the latter to become understandable and received by the people (thus empowering ongoing evangelization and conversion), "[760] He concludes that the means of traditioning is always traditioning something whereby "there is no traditioning, then, without tradition. " To assume that the content of Christianity that is traditioned is part of tradition is to acknowledge that whatever is traditioned is shaped, presented, and received within the social position, gender, and culture of those who transmit and receive the good news across time and cultural boundaries.[761] It is this sort of social and cultural traditioning that Nancy Pineda-Madrid alludes to in saying that "... experience is viewed as social, then traditioning, an inherently social idea, entails processes of interpretation that necessarily and invariably create community... These processes take place ad infinitum.[762] For her, traditioning "occurs through a process of interpreting our past toward a hope-filled future in the context of our present... "[763] Pinedad-Madrid's thinking re- asserts and re-enunciates the social aspect and condition of the traditioning process already stated by Espin. This position gives credence to the idea that traditions evolve as the social milieu in which they are found evolves.

Stephen Bevans provides another key set of frameworks by which tradition, society, and culture intermingle with theology to provide a living tradition and doctrine that speaks to contemporary hearts. Bevans sees tradition as the faith atmosphere in which the entire Church engages in the work of theology, a collection of "classics " which fuels and inspires theologians to understand their faith based on the wisdom of ancients. According to Bevans, *tradition* as derived from its Latin etymological roots is a handing on, handing down, or handing

---

759   Ibid., 7.

760   Ibid., 10.

761   Ibid., 15.

762   Nancy Pinedad-Madrid,   "Traditioning: The Formation of Community, the Transmission of Faith, " in Espin and Macy, *Futuring Our Past*, 204.

763   Ibid.,. 222.

over, done within a community suffused with humanity, which in itself is traditioned and hands on in turn its own traditions. Theology is, therefore, a result of this traditioning process. Human life itself and community are possible only because of tradition and traditioning. For Christian tradition specifically, Bevans opines that it

> .... is the way that the faith we believe today is the same faith that Christians have always and will always believe—that our faith today is the faith of the "apostles, " .... Who despite the various changes in the faith's content and expression throughout history and through its encounters with various cultures, nevertheless preserves Christian faith in all its integrity and freshness.[764]

According to Bevans, there are various sources, objects, or monuments of tradition *(loci theologici)*, which provide Christian tradition with an essential link to the wisdom of the past, which, in turn, sets parameters to which the Church today must conform. These "classics " as enumerated by Bevans include the sacred Scriptures of the Christian Church (both Old and the New Testament); the patrimony of the fathers (and mothers) of the Church; the liturgy—not merely as participation but more in the sense of *lex orandis, lex credenda* (the law of prayer is the law of belief)—a *theologia prima*; the magisterium, which remains one of the most respected means of articulating the Church's tradition through the ages; and then the art, architecture (and music) of the various periods, which are also harbingers of tradition. In agreement with Espin and Pinedad-Madrid, Bevans states "we are not maintaining tradition if we simply parrot formulas or transmit ideas that have not been appropriated. Tradition as the legacy of the Church's faith is something alive, something that, like ourselves, changes while ever remaining the same. "[765] Bevans offers the over-arching argument that

---

764   Stephen B. Bevans, *An Introduction to Theology in Global Perspective* (Maryknoll, New York: Orbis Books, 2009), 92-3.

765   Ibid., 99.

[t]o be Christian, in other words, means to be faithful to the Christian tradition. But that fidelity— given the plurality of tradition—has to be a *creative* one. Sometimes—and this is the particular task of theologians—for the sake of the tradition, we need to "abandon " the tradition and prove our fidelity to it by creative reinterpretation.[766]

Therefore, for Bevans, the question of the possibility of doctrinal development is not only possible, it is essential to the nature of the Church for her to remain faithful to her mission and to the ministry of proclaiming the good news. Every culture and every religion thrives because it builds and grows on a tradition; otherwise it becomes deformed and derailed from its foundations. Contemporary and post-modern persons pride themselves on their civility by keeping to "high class culture " in the arts, music, literature, etc., but then frown on religious adherence to tradition. When the Church recognizes what is true within her sacred traditions, she has the responsibility to transmit these truths uncontaminated.

Amoris Laetitia: A Case for Development in Doctrine.

The very much anticipated post synodal exhortation of Pope Francis was finally signed on March 19th, 2016 and was officially released on April 8th of the same year. After two synods on the family in 2014 and 2015 respectively, the exhortation has enjoyed a flood of quick responses, positively and negatively. *Amoris Laetitia* (The Joy of Love) is cryptically referred to by some critiques as vague, polyvalent, puzzling and undecisive in many passages. Others who support the document see it as monumental and an epochal shift from the traditional position on marriage, which was heavily couched in a juridical-philosophical age and language of Trent. Whatever position one adopts, a close reading of the text is striking because of the document's breadth, depth and attention to details. Pope Francis relies on various sources in crafting this exhortation which includes various aspects of the final reports of the two synods. Various patristic traditions and documents,

---

766   Ibid., 104.

the teachings of previous popes, application of various documents of episcopal conferences around the world, and his own catechesis on the family. Francis refers also to contemporary figures such as Dr. Martin Luther King, Erich Fromm and uses lines from the motion picture "Babette's Feast. "

Right from the introductory paragraphs, Francis states clearly a desire to move away from a traditional model of "one size fits all " in seeking to respond to the complexities of newer moral question faced by the Church. While Francis recognizes as a multifaceted gem and a polyhedron the role and intervention of the synod Fathers, he however posits that it is not all doctrinal and moral issues that needs to be settled basically by magisterial intervention. Pope Francis warns that care be taken to avoid a juxtaposition between a sterile demand for change and the application of general abstract norms. On this point, he avers,

> The debates carried on in the media, in certain publications and even among the Church's ministers, range from an immoderate desire for total change without sufficient reflection or grounding, to an attitude that would solve everything by applying general rules or deriving undue conclusions from particular theological considerations.[767]

In the broader ecclesial conversation, Francis proposes a vision where each country, region, or episcopal conferences will be empowered to seek solutions suited to its own culture and sensitive to particular traditions and local needs. Francis clarifies and articulates this further by stating, "For cultures are in fact quite diverse and every general principle... needs to be inculturated, if it is to be respected and applied "[768] It is only by following this principle of inculturation problems are addressed outside of dogmatically defined doctrines which through magisterial authority are universally binding on the Church.

In chapter one of *Amoris Laetitia*, Francis starts his reflection based on the sacred scriptures, with a meditation on the Jewish wedding liturgy in Psalm 128 and applyies this to Christian marriage. Focusing

---

767   AL #2

768   AL #3

on the many stories in the bible about families, births, love stories and even dysfunctionality in families, Francis points at the reality of family, not an abstract ideal, but one that is confronted with the reality of sin. The word of God thus become a source of comfort and companionship. (cf. AL 8-16) In chapter two, while grounding marriage in the reality of its lived experiences, the Pope focuses on the multifaceted challenges faced by modern families. Concreteness, which is key to this pastoral exhortation and the reality of daily living is applied to questions of legal dismantling of families, violence against women, the loss of respect for the elderly, inadequate attention to persons with disabilities, pornography and the abuse of minors, lack of proper housing, migration, the ideological war of denial of difference between gender and the culture that breeds anti-birth mentality with the negative impact of biotechnology that adversely impact natural procreation. Within the prism of the realities, Francis calls for a Church that listens to the movement of the Spirit and not to insist on abstract artificial theological idealism about marriage. In chapter three, the Pope focuses at length on certain essential elements of the Church's magisterial teaching on marriage as a vocation according to the gospels. Francis re-affirms unequivocally the long standing tradition of indissolubility, the sacramental nature of marriage, the transmission of life and education of children. While making constant references to *Gaudium et Spes*, *Humanae Vitae* and *Familiaris Consortio*, Francis also recognizes and calls pastors to take into account the complexities of various situations and to be attentive to the families' experience of distress and how they try to endure problems they encounter within the family.

Drawing on the Hymn to Love found in St. Paul's first letter to the Corinthians, 13:4-7, in chapter four the Pope carefully reflects on a theological exegesis of this Pauline text. Francis approaches human love concretely with careful attention to the psychological, erotic and emotional world of spouses. In *Amoris Laetitia* # 122-3, Pope Francis makes real his ideal for an ethic of human experience when he wrote, "There is no need to lay upon two limited persons the tremendous burden of having to reproduce perfectly the union existing between Christ and the Church, for marriage as a sign entails a dynamic process… one which advances gradually with the progressive integration of the gifts of God. "[769] In this section, Francis reflects on what he terms the "transformation of love "; where due to longer life span, the initial decision constantly needs renewal so that as the focus shifts from the physical to togetherness and mutuality, they may continue to enrich each other in a shared vision and life project. In chapter five, Francis' focus is on love's fruitfulness and procreation, welcoming new life, the love of parents, the 'fruitfulness' of adoption. Francis calls society back to family life in a broader sense which includes uncles, aunts, cousins, relatives and friends. Because of the social nature of the family, Francis lays emphasis on the relationship between the young and the old, between brothers and sisters as a testing ground for relating to others. In chapter six, titled "Some Pastoral Perspectives ", the Pope reflects on pastoral practices aimed at fostering solid families according to God's plan. Towing traditional teachings from the work of the two synods, the works of Saint John Paul II and his own catechesis, he reminds the Church not only to evangelize families but families also are called to be evangelizers. Families, he avers, should be involved in the psycho-affective formation of men preparing for the priesthood and ministry. He then turns his attention to the preparation of the engaged for married life and the accompaniment needed in the early years of marriage. This includes accompaniment for responsible parenthood, the abandoned spouse, separated or divorced persons, persons in mixed marriages or disparity of cult and the application of the new policies for the process of annulment. In the final sections of this chapter, Francis calls the Church to encourage and support families with members who have homosexual tendencies. These persons are to be treated with respect and dignity. Francis condemns all acts of discrimination, aggression and violence towards people of the HGBLTQ community. It concludes with the accompaniment needed for when families experience the 'sting' of death through the loss of loved ones.

In the seventh chapter, the Pope reflects on the education of children in their ethical formation. In particular treats discipline (which can include punishment), sex education, handing on of the faith and the achievement of self-autonomy recognizing that the entire family life is a place of foundational education for children. Chapter

---

769   AL #122

eight is perhaps the most poignant because its invitation to mercy and pastoral discernment. Relying on the themes, *guiding*, *discerning* and *integrating*, the chapter addresses the fragile and often times complex realities of marriage.

Addressing pastors, the Pope calls for a 'gradualness' in discernment of Church norms and mitigating circumstances in pastoral care which Francis refers to as "the logic of pastoral mercy. " *Amoris Laetitia* #s 192-312 in my opinion is where Pope Francis lays down the outcome of the synods on the family. Here, Francis again calls the Church a field hospital where all who come must receive help. Francis then speaks to controversial issues providing a consistent teaching nuanced with mercy. In reaffirming the Church's position on what marriage is, he avers, "some forms of union radically contradict this idea, while others realize it in at least a partial and analogous way.... (the Church) does not disregard the constructive elements in these situations which do not yet or no longer correspond to her teaching on marriage. "[770]

In all irregular situations, Pope Francis advocates for the avoidance of judgements which does not "take into account the complexity of various situations,

> .... all these situations require a constructive response seeking to transform them into opportunities that can lead to the full reality of marriage and family in conformity with the Gospel. These couples need to be welcomed and guided patiently and discreetly. That is how Jesus treated the Samaritan woman (cf. Jn 4:1-26): he addressed her desire for true love, in order to free her from the darkness in her life and to bring her to the full joy of the Gospel.... The way of the Church is not to condemn anyone forever; it is to pour out the balm of God's mercy on all those who ask for it with a sincere heart... For true charity is always unmerited, unconditional and gratuitous. Consequently, there is a need to avoid judgements which do not take into account the complexity of various situations and to be attentive, by necessity,

---

770   AL # 292

to how people experience distress because of their condition. It is a matter of reaching out to everyone, of needing to help each person find his or her proper way of participating in the ecclesial community and thus to experience being touched by an unmerited, unconditional and gratuitous " mercy. No one can be condemned for ever, because that is not the logic of the Gospel![771]

In clarifying how to understand *Amoris Laetitia*, Francis states,

If we consider the immense variety of concrete situations such as those I have mentioned, it is understandable that neither the Synod nor this Exhortation could be expected to provide a new set of general rules, canonical in nature and applicable to all cases. What is possible is simply a renewed encouragement to undertake a responsible personal and pastoral discernment of particular cases, one which would recognize that, since "the degree of responsibility is not equal in all cases ", the consequences or effects of a rule need not necessarily always be the same.[772]

Francis grounds his appeal on relationships and discernment through the insights of Thomas Aquinas. According to Francis' translation of Aquinas, general rules are set as a good which should not be disregarded but with the understanding that the formulation of these rules cannot provide for all particular situations absolutely. Practical discernment in contextually also cannot be raised to the level of a general norm. According to Francis, the logic of pastoral mercy is to show understanding in the face of an unusual situation without dimming the light of the fuller ideal put forth by the magisterium as the teaching of the Lord himself. Otherwise, Francis warns, "At times we find it hard to make room for God's unconditional love in our pastoral activity. We put so many conditions on mercy that we empty

---

771   AL # 292-7

772   AL # 300

it of its concrete meaning and real significance. That is the worst way of watering down the gospel. "[773] In the ninth and final chapter, Francis draws on the spirituality of marriage and family life which he calls 'thousands of small but real gestures.' Francis calls for a spirituality of care, consolation and incentive which entails shepherding in mercy. Francis concludes the exhortation with a prayer to the holy family.

Various commentators have expressed concern over what many perceive as the ambiguousness of *Amoris Laetitia*. Others are worried with a special focus on chapter eight of the document which deals with the Holy Father's proposal for accompaniment, discernment and integrating weakness. At the root of the opposition either to the document or specific sections is the question of whether fundamental pastoral practices can change while doctrinal sacramental theology remains unchanging? It becomes a conflicting, cheek in tongue kind of situation since pastoral practices are born of application of theological and doctrinal teachings.

For instance, Roberto de Mattei of the Lepanto Foundation opines that upon Pope Francis' invitation of Cardinal Walter Kasper to introduce the themes of the two synods, Kasper's thesis was for a change in the Church's traditional matrimonial practices. This, according to de Mattei became the *leit motiv* of the two synods and it also impacted Francis exhortation. Mattei falls back on some of the comments of the Synodal Fathers who warned that there must remain a consistent and intimate coherence between the Church's doctrine and its practices. Mattei sees as suspect the re-interpretation of St. Thomas Aquinas in this document, from a Hegelian dialectic, making the document a text "that is not ambiguous, but clear – in its vagueness.[774] *Amoris Laetitia* in responding to the most serious questions faced at the synod; married, divorced and remarried persons, Matteo insists that the Pope did not condemn or approve any specific solutions. Focusing on the question of 'irregular' situations in marriage, Mattei clarifies further,

---

773   AL # 311

774   Roberto de Mattei. The Post-Synod Exhortation, Amoris Laetitia: First Reflection on a Catastrophic Document. (First Publsihed on Rorate Caeli), Available at http://rorate-caeli.blogspot.com/2016/04/de-mattei-post-synod- exhortation-amoris.html, 1.

According to Catholic morality, circumstances, which comprise a context wherein an action is carried out cannot modify the moral nature of the acts, thus rendering right and just an intrinsically evil action. Yet the doctrine of absolute morality and of the *intrinsece malum* is neutralized by *Amoris Laetitia*, which is conformed to the "new morality" condemned by Pius XII in numerous documents and by John Paul II in *Veritatis Splendor*. Situation ethics allow the circumstances and, and in the final analysis, the subjective conscience of man, to determine what is good and what is evil. Extramarital sexual union is not considered intrinsically illicit, but in as much as it is an act of love, assessable according to the circumstances. More generally, evil does not exist in itself, just as grave or mortal sin does not exist. The leveling-out between people in a state of grace (regular situations) and people in a state of permanent sin (irregular situations) is not only linguistic: it seems to be subject to the Lutheran theory *simul iustus et peccator*, condemned by the decree on justification at the Council of Trent (Denz- H, nn. 1551-1583).[775]

Mattei therefore surmises,

.... The exhortation, Amoris Laetitia, offers an answer: open the door to the divorced and remarried, canonize situation ethics and begin a process of normalization of all common-law cohabitations.

Considering that the new document belongs to the non-infallible ordinary Magisterium, it is hoped that it is the object of an in-depth analytical critique, by theologians and pastors of the Church, under no

---

775   Ibdi., 3

illusion of applying "the hermeneutic of continuity
" to it.[776]

Sandro Magister, in the immediate flurry of reactions to the public publication of *Amoris Laetitia*, penned what he considered the immediate deficiencies of this exhortation with particular reference to chapter eight of the document. Magister's argument stems from what he perceives as a slap in the face for the Catholics who have been obedient and persevered until now in marriage. This exhortation, in Magister's opinion, is mercy for all except the obedient children of the Church. Magister states that this document is a triumph in casuistry, execrated with words which gives the impression that every sin is excusable because of the varied extenuating circumstances of people. Thereby applying itself to a "meadow land of graces " even in the context of grave sin and irregular marriage situation. This then makes it possible for those in irregular unions to have access to the Eucharist. Magister accuses the text of duplicity in the application of certain footnotes (of particular concern is FN #329) which is dubiously applied to the exhortation to support bringing into communion those in irregular situations through the private forum.[777]

The Italian Professor of philosophy, Rocco Buttiglione who is re-known for his in-depth study of John Paul II's works, in an interview in *La Stampa* asserts that Pope Francis' *Amoris Laetitia* is a step in the direction marked by the pontificate and teaching of John Paul II. Buttiglione, while affirming Francis' exhortation, states, "It seems to me to be a great effort to speak the word of faith within the context of today's world. Which was also the biggest concern of John Paul II: the real man, the existing man, the man of reality, not the one described in the books or the one we would wish him to be. "[778] Within sacred tradition on questions about marriage, Buttiglione is of the opinion that while the moral and doctrinal teaching on indissolubility remains intact and unchanging, yet the pastoral discipline is changing. Buttiglione

---

776   Roberto de Mattei. Op.Cit., 3-4

777   Sandro Magister. On the Carousel of Comments. Available at http://chiesa. espresso.republica.it/articolo/1351273?eng=y, posted on April 12, 2016, 3.

778   Andrea Tornelli (Interviewer) in "La Stampa" Available at http://www.lastampa. it/20116/05/013/vaticaninsider/eng/enquiries-and interviews/amoris-laetitia, 1

clarifies the difference between subjectivism from human subjectivity based on Thomism as applied in the exhortation; when there has been a moral failure but the acting person may not be able to assume the full cognitive and rational recognition of what they have done. Buttiglione refutes the claims that *Amoris Laetitia* is situation ethics which John Paul II and Benedict XVI thoroughly rejected. He acknowledges that there are pastoral risks involved in the explication of this document, however, living in a pansexual world with less evidence of morality, this document serves as a pastoral accompaniment and guidance.[779]

Lamin Sanneh of Yale Divinity School sees Francis' apostolic exhortation as a way of letting the Church grow and thrive in contemporary times. The exhortation signals an important shift in how the Church traditionally approached those living in 'irregular' situations, divorced persons and gay Catholics. According to Sanneh, Francis is calling the Church back from depending on the spirit of the law, to a Church that goes out to meet people where they are rather than throwing laws and regulations like stones from a distance. The exhortation represents, and in Sanneh's words, "The initiatives Pope Francis has unveiled fall short of the demand of divorced Catholics and gays and women for full inclusion, but by design there is a crack in the door. There is a Catholic spring in the air in which consensus will now have to reckon with the need for generosity and mutual care. "[780] According to Sanneh, what seems a devolution of power to the local Churches is not much of a break away from tradition as it is an engagement with the world the Church encounters today. This devolution will also help local pastors in meeting the needs of their people.

Amoris Laetitia of Pope Francis in this context, in this book, is not so much of reflecting on the issues to which it tries to respond. What is offered here, is not a pointed review in order to weigh the points and counter points of those who agree with it or disagree. Rather, the effort here was aimed at supporting my argument for how doctrine develops. This document, essentially supports and grounds my fundamental

---

779   Ibid., 4

780   Lamin Sanneh. Francis is letting the Church Grow and Thrive. Available at http://www.ncregister.com/daily- news/amoris-laetitia-a-tale-of-two-documents, April 3, 2016, 1

argument for the processes of doctrinal change. That there are issues within doctrine which in and of itself cannot and do not change. And that there are other issues that needs re-clarification, maybe modification or outright change. Pope Francis may have applied what most social interpreters sees as a hermeneutic of continuity with adequate attention to the reality of peoples' lived experiences. Yet, even that is not new or original to Francis' pontificate. John Paul II in his *Theology of the Body* already reminded the Church of the acting person and the challenge to move from the scholastic "what ought " to "what is. " *Amoris Laetitia* represents the constant struggle that ensues in the face of socio-cultural changes, Christian doctrine, orthodoxy and magisterial authority. I like to imagine this interaction and liken it to the idea of an object in motion (society and culture) and a solid immovable mass (Christian doctrinal tradition). Pope Francis' exhortation, is an example of how these two spheres are brought into interplay. Newer questions demand newer answers.*Amoris Laetitia* is one of the ways in which the Church in the modern world attempts to soften this impact to avoid wreckage.

Conclusion

Considering how volatile the conversation on human sexuality generally has become, especially since the 1960s, and how in particular, sexuality within marriage, its attendant and related problems are still being argued, perhaps this conversation can be seen as a form of dialectic towards a renewed hermeneutic for our time. The idea of a church that is fossilized can never be applicable to any Church of Christ that is alive in the Holy Spirit. The Church in all times and places must always engage different cultures and situations and must be willing to open herself up so that people can encounter Christ in their socio-historical consciousness and times. Lisa Sowle Cahill, referencing the Cameroonian theologian Eloi Messi Mesongo, noted that the Church's tradition is always "undergoing adaptation, indigenization, inculturation, liberation, reconstruction', and sometimes distortion or perversion in the name of 'mastery' or fear. "[781] While society relies

---

781   Lisa Sowle Cahill, "Catholic Feminist and Traditions: Renewal, Reinvention, Replacement, " Journal of the Society of Christian Ethics 34, vol. 2 (2014): 28.

on logic, experience, and history, the Christian Church goes a step further to rely on divine revelation to sustain various communities of faith. These various communities, differing in language, culture, and traditions must find ways by which what has been passed on is not only interpreted in a way that is undistorted but is essentially the same, with the coloring of the diverse cultures the faith nurtures. Janet Soskice ascribes preeminent authority to sacred Scripture; what is "handed on " is in the sacred texts. Soskice states, "... any crude contrast between scripture and tradition is self-defeating. The first Christians were Jews or proselytes who identified with Judaism. They received as 'handed on' the scriptures of the Jewish people. "[782] What the Christians of the New Testament experienced of Jesus did not cause them to reject the Old Testament books but to reread them. Soskice thereby concludes that

> [t]radition, even in its more central received form of scripture, is given but it is not static – scriptures are always open to being reread or reperformed. The process of "rereading " ... was documented in the book of Acts, but it is already evident in the Hebrew Scriptures. The book of Hosea recalls for its readers the book of Exodus. The later chapters of Isaiah reread the earlier chapters in the light of the exile. It appears that what is "passed on " has always been reread in the light of God's new actions in the world... To stand in tradition is not to stand still but to stand in the deep, loamy soil that feeds further growth.[783]

Alasdair MacIntyre agrees with Soskice that what we inherit is a part of the past that constitutes our present. One thus becomes a part of history, a bearer of tradition transmitted through many generations. Therefore, "[a] living tradition then is historically extended, socially embodied argument, and an argument precisely in part about goods

---

782   Janet Soskice, "Tradition, " in *Tradition and Modernity: Christian and Muslim Perspectives*, ed. David Marshall (Washington, DC: Georgetown University, 2013), 27.

783   Ibid., 28-9.

which constitute that tradition. "[784] MacIntyre maintains that an adequate appreciation of tradition provides the possibility of grasping those things of the future made possible by the past for the present. "Living traditions, just because they continue a not-yet-completed narrative, confront a future whose determinate and determinable character, so far as it possesses any, derives from the past. "[785] Central, therefore, to this reflection is to come to terms with which religious tradition is affected by post modernity, and the many ways in which humans understand the social construct. The dialogue that continually takes place between the sacred space, theology, and magisterial authority with the shared space of the secular society must find a middle ground of mutual understanding.

I find Rowan Williams, the Archbishop of Canterbury, instructive in his comments to the symposium of Christian and Muslim dialogue (Building Bridges) which he conveyed in May 2010 and was held at Georgetown University, Washington DC, where he stated that what is considered "modern" is itself tradition, a set of habits and beliefs handed down and accepted as meaningful, a history that is real and complex. Williams believes that "this does not mean either an acceptance that traditional claims to truthfulness are empty or that 'modern' accounts of knowledge and certainty are to be taken as beyond criticism. "[786] Rather, it means that the location of a belief against a backdrop of its social condition does not determine its truths. While 'modern' is not to be feared, where there is no assumption that "there is one and only one socially and intellectually credible way of arriving at a belief, and that this is essentially through unaided observation on the part of the individual ego. "[787] Williams asserts that people of faith are who they are because they participate, they take time to believe. "They assume that what is spoken about and explored in a share *imaginaire* over time is worthy of trust on the basis of a range of criteria that are not easily

---

784   Alasdair MacIntyre, "MacIntyre on Tradition, " in Marshall, *Tradition and Modernity*, 154-5.

785   Ibid.

786   Rowan Williams, "Afterword, " in Marshall, *Tradition and Modernity*, 224.

787   Ibid.

reduced to 'modern' terms. "[788] Tradition, according to Williams, can appear ambivalent when perceived as having been kept away from the corrosive influence of modernity. Tradition can be profoundly positive if it is understood as the human embeddedness in a world that is fluid through time and language. "For the believer, that language itself is ultimately grounded in God's own movement outward to what he has graciously made; and that is where our gratitude finds it terminus. "[789] In other words, tradition is the womb from which our present exists; this present will then be "traditioning " the future, in this movement we all learn to co-exist.

---

788   Ibid.

789   Ibid., 225.

GENERAL CONCLUSION

At the beginning of this book, my foundational thesis was to explore the core contents of doctrinal development within the Catholic tradition. Using John Paul II's Theology of the Body as a frame work, the focus for locating doctrinal development was a view from the lenses of human sexuality. Within this context, to dissect and expound on why and often times the Church is perceived by many to be archaic and out dated in her teachings and doctrinal position on questions of sexuality, marriage, sex and family life. I believe that a close examination of this work provides a coherent and logical sequence of argumentation that supports my thesis. I have argued that in the question of the Church's doctrinal position, there are teachings that by their very nature (with or without magisterial definition) are essential to the core of Christian doctrine (when it is known as dogma) that are unchangeable. Further, that there are aspects of the Church's teachings that are flexible, malleable and changeable as they respond to newer questions in the historical changes in society and cultures. By no means are my reflections in these chapters "the answer ", rather, these reflections, as I will expound on later, are only a contribution to a question that needs constant tinkering and thinking to arrive at the mind of Christ for His Church.

In my first chapter, I present a time line of a hundred years of magisterial and papal teachings on various aspects of sexuality and family life. Within these encyclical tradition, there are obvious developments in various aspects of the Church teachings. For instance, In Pope Leo XIII's encyclical, *Arcanum*, and Pius XI's *Casti Connubii*, marriage was understood as a contract. However, when we encounter John Paul II's 1981 synodal apostolic exhortation, *Familiaris Consortio* and all other subsequent writings, the language shifts to understanding marriage as a covenantal bond. In the second chapter, while reviewing

John Paul II's Theology of the Body, we find a new language which places companionship and lifelong commitment at the center of marriage. This language is different to the hitherto teaching that places procreation first in the order of the goods of marriage. In the third chapter, the review of the history and development of the Natural Law Theory is given consideration. This study is extended to the New Natural Law theory and theorists. I consider this study central to the overall argument because the Church traditionally has relied on defending her positions on human sexuality fundamentally on arguments based on nature. The Church has faced criticism based on arguments from nature, which explains why Grisez, Finnis and others have tried to construct a deontological new natural law theory. Within the historical development enunciated in chapter three, there are major historical shifts from Cicero and the Greco-Roman thinkers, to the Stoics who philosophize from an Aristotelian background, then Thomas Aquinas who synthesized a natural law theory that prior to his time was purely philosophically based by grounding it in theism. Scholasticism thus took over the natural law theory and made it foundational to Catholic deontologism. The resurgence of the natural law theory in the 16th and 17th Century gave rise to thinkers like Francesco Suarez, Hugo Grotius, Samuel Pufendorf, Immanuel Kant, Jeremy Bentham and John Locke. The tradition of the natural law theory continues to expound to date in the work of Germain Grisez, John Finnis and their other collaborators under the title of the New Natural Law Theory. This historical excursion is aimed at achieving two goals; one, to grasp the importance of this argument and its impact on the history of thinking. Second, to see how the theory is applied from a purely philosophical (and often times applied to political jurisprudence) and its impacts on theological thinking from scholasticism to date. The disparaging attacks and opinions against arguments from 'nature' by revisionists and non-theists does not contend well in the face of such historical analysis.

These first three chapters are the basis on which I presume the conclusion that I have successfully proven my thesis. The importance of this topic lies on the fact that at the rate in which secularism is growing in the West and the idea of religious faith symbolized by a Church not all together free of internal problems, it is necessary to separate proverbially, 'the wheat from the darnel.' I believe it is the responsibility of theologians to try to articulate and make comprehensible, the logic of theological presuppositions. Arguments can dialogically become meaningful and useful if both parties, in this case, liberal and secularist society and the Church, can understand the basis and foundational starting points on which both proceed to argue their different positions. What I perceive as a problem within the ongoing conversation is the inability or even the unwillingness of both conversation partners to try to learn and understand the background to the other's position. From my studies, I can say confidently that the problem is more on the part of a liberal and secular world. Society seem to challenge the Church to change its position and teachings as if all of these teachings are made up by a committee. Therefore, can be revised and changed to fit into newer and ever changing socio-cultural circumstances. I see within the Church, some 'theologians' and revisionists whose argument seem to exclude the divine aspect of the message the Church carries and teaches. While I am quick to point out that not all revisionists and theologians can be lumped into this group, it seems the larger parts of revisionists have an agenda of always trying to re-write the history of doctrinal teachings.

The aim generally can be perceived to be an altruistic desire to be welcoming and loving to all. They are quick to quote the popular refrain that 'God loves the sinner but hates sin.' Within their self-acclaimed progressive ideology, they make a caricature of past errors in the Church, often times demonizing popes, prelates and people who do not fit into the scheme of the 'new Church', a Church of the future they envision which will accommodate individual preferences. I perceive a schism that will be of epic and cataclysmic proportions in western civilization as secularists and revisionists attempts a re-write of these cultures devoid off its Christian history, intellectual growth and cultural heritage. Beyond the ill-advised dependence on pure reason of Descartes and Kant, the new humanisms propounded without religious ethic looks only inwards, it is selfish and can only lead to an implosion. There is a broad innovation of the ways in which moral theology is seeing to have shifted from its traditional prohibitive and manualist approach. The new understanding in the 20th and the 21st century, the person centered approach, a personal interiority, the flourishing of the acting person in a search for moral truths is the new approach. Here the shift is from external actions in the pursuit of the good to one's disposition in acting according to conscience. The Church agrees, Pope John Paul II is at the fore front of seeing the „*acting-person*' play a leading role in making moral decisions, the difference only being that this person acts according to the commands of Christ and according to the mind of the Church.

The implications for this sort of impasse is almost irreconcilable at this time. The forces on both sides of the discourse are like two parallel lines that can never converge. While liberal- secularist modernity challenge and ask for change in what traditionally the Church has always proposed as an official and doctrinal position, the conservative traditionalists ask for faithfulness to tradition. One of the most difficult questions of our time is how to approach same sex unions, to be seen and accepted on the same level as the traditional understanding of Christian marriage. Based on scriptural evidence, and sound biblical exegesis, it is clear that within the Christian tradition, heterosexual marriage is the norm. In line with apostolic tradition, heterosexual marriage has existed from the beginning of the Christian Church of the first millennium and has been extended to the Church of today in a continuity of tradition. There are specific texts, (that we have alluded to several times in this work) from the gospels which are ascribed to Jesus, elucidated on later especially within the Pauline corpus (especially Ephesians chapter 5: 21ff), which establishes the 'man' and 'woman' gender differentiation and complementarity as a necessity for the ontological basis of Christian marriage. This gender differentiation, its unitive and sexual complementarity, the reproduction of offspring and formation of the individual human family sets the basis by which the good of Christian marriage can be received. In an effort to clarify what is at the heart of the question here, I approach Christian marriage within Christian tradition to be 'form' – which means in its sacramentality, not even the magisterium is capable of changing its fundamental meaning. Having said this, I must acknowledge that this immutability cannot totally be immuned to the possibility of cultural adaptations. A case in mind will be the various instances where the Christian missionary enterprises have come in contact with polygamists or polyandrist cultures and the ways in which this encounter took place and the ways in which the

Church had to be creative and allow for an encounter that includes these 'others' within the Church and at the table of the Lord. This, in a sense, is another theological implication; is this question of same sex unions a question of contextualization or historicity?

The Church continues to exist and continue to speak to the men and women of different times, places and cultures. As the world grows and evolves, for good or bad, the Church must learn to live in this world and not be of this world. The Church must connect with the world with the mercy of God and the courage that comes from the way, the truth and the life. This question of 'mercy' must be nuanced and understood carefully from its theological basis. Pope Francis' appeal to mercy (and the proclamation of a jubilee year of mercy) must not be re- interpreted and hijacked by a media only interested in subterfuge. The questions that are seriously under contention in the contemporary Church are no longer theological disputations over creedal formulas. They are no longer about reformations, and not even seriously about Patriarchates and bishoprics. In our time, our doctrinal disagreements are over the newer ways in which society is redefining its understanding of sexuality as experienced in marriage, the sexual act and family life. Moral theologians and ethicists –moral and medical, continue to study and proffer suggested solution for the different problems within the area of human sexuality. From pre-marital sex, pre-marital cohabitation, trial unions with cohabitation, pre-marital teenage pregnancies, single parenthood, divorce, extra-marital affairs, to same sex unions – the list continues; theology and theologians continue to argue and debate the foundations, ontology and teleology of these issues. While those who argue in favor of traditional magisterial position on marriage, sex and family life see an impasse, those who are revisionists seek grounds by which historicity and contextualization be a yardstick for judging new sexual ethics. While there has been a shift from 'nature' to persons and their experiences, I see a need to combine these sources at arriving at moral uprightness and healthy development in doctrine.

In my previous review of what I proposed as two ways by which an understanding of the Church's arguments are based; the question of same sex unions, seen as equal to heterosexual sacramental marriage, and the question of condomized sex for discordant couples especially in economically disadvantaged arears of the world; I made allusions to the possibility of change in 'matter' and unchangeability in 'form.' Both examples are not defined dogmatic teachings of the Church that enjoys infallibility *„ex cathedra.'* However, both teachings are subsumed under the ordinary magisterial infallibility of the Church acting collegially in union with the *sensus fidelium.* When these two issues are viewed, putting into consideration the contextualized, historically conscious and reflecting on the lived experience of Christians around the globe, I think it is safe and logical to conclude that the question of same sex unions to be accepted as being on the same level with traditional sacramental marriage is at best a theological oxymoron. Now, whether this sort of 'union' can be translated as a newer form of way of life, or whether it is even possible within the Church to reference same gender unions as 'sacrament' or 'marriage', that is another kettle of fish all together. This question at this time, in my opinion, has brought the Church to the burning bush that is not burnt. It requires of all of us, a humbling, a need to take off our shoes, for the grounds on which we stand is a hallowed ground. Here, like Moses, we must encounter God anew and allow him to speak His **word** to us. The entire Church needs the wisdom of the "I AM WHO AM " to be able to act mercifully and justly with each other.

However, I have a benign prejudice in favor of the question of the possibility of condomized sex in discordant situations; one, it does not in any way contradict sacred doctrine (dogma) or challenge defined ecclesial position. This is an event in time that requires a definitive magisterial declaration and teaching, even if it is a temporary fix. It is clear that the Church is careful in her teachings and public statements so that no one stands to be misled into error. In this case, the Church needs to be present in the suffering of those infected with the dreadful HIV/AIDS disease. The Church is already present to them in the many programs, health care and pastoral provisions which the Church is at the fore front and leads especially in economically impoverished places.

Whatever arguments one may proffer; one thing is sure: the Church needs to make a definitive statement on the matter of condomized sex in discordancy. This matter challenges prior teaching and creates an avenue for a development in doctrine. Pope Benedict XVI appointed a commission to study the possibility of permitting the use of condoms in discordancy, to determine under which theological and ethical principles this might be permissible, and years later, the Church is still silent about the outcome of the commission's work, and provides no official magisterial and doctrinal position. Three events in the Church make the situation more troubling; the first is involves religious missionary nuns travelling to work as missionaries in the Congo during the civil war years of the early 1960s. Because they were in danger of rape, they received permission to use contraceptive drugs as a form of protection. The second case is a situation that is now often referred to as a classic example of a "double down " by Pope Emeritus, Benedict VXI, when he made comments that male prostitutes (and all who engage in dangerous sexual activities) are better off using condoms to prevent the spread of disease. The third and final one is the recent comments of Pope Francis on the question of either taking the option of abortion or the prevention of conception in the light of the most recent question of the Zika virus.[790] While the Pope is reported to have strongly opposed abortion as always evil in and of itself. In the case of the Zika virus, Pope Francis references *Humanae Vitae* and the nuns in the Congo scenario, and with clarification later on by Fr. Lombardi, the Holy Father's spokesperson, Lombardi tries to clarify, "Pope Francis asserted that in cases of emergency women in good conscience may consider the use of contraceptives as a legitimate alternative for choice. "[791] The world media have immediately translated this to mean that the Pope has endorsed the use of contraceptives in emergency cases and based on the decision of the woman when acting according to the dictates of her conscience. The import of these events is well summarized in Lisa Sowle Cahill's response to the nuns'/Congo case which I believe applies also to the Pope Benedict/male prostitute case and Pope Francis' 'off the cuff' remarks in the Zika virus case. In a journal essay Cahill writes,

> The debate was important, instead, because it presented the possibilities that practical problems could challenge the accustomed ways of thinking

---

790   On Pope Francis' return flight from Mexico while chatting on board with reporters travelling with him, the question of how to deal with sexual intimacy between a husband and wife was raised in the light of the Zika virus.

791   E. Christian Brugger, "Pope Francis and Contraception: A Troubling Scenario, " National Catholic Register, published Feb. 24, 2016, accessed Feb. 28, 2016, www. ncregister.com/daily-news.

about contraception, and because it joined respected theological voices in a re- examination of the prohibition on it – although it is revealing of racial attitudes that these particular circumstances were required to raise the question in the European mind. The debate was one of several movements in the Church which together, at the time of Vatican II, were to sponsor a hope among both theologians and laypersons that the traditional strictures on control of conception would be revised.[792]

Cahill's position resonates because to seek solutions (even if temporary) to the problem of HIV/AIDS in Africa and developing poorer nations around the world, there is the necessity for a closer study of cultural problems, marriage rites, rites of young adult initiations and passage, and the sexual mores of different societies. These varied contexts make it often more realistically difficult to navigate or to proffer one single solution as one size fits all. It is even more dangerous for the Church to remain silent on how to respond to a disease that is taking the lives of huge numbers of poor people as a lack of concern or show of empathy. God forbid that banners like "Black Lives Matters " ever show up as a reaction against the Church on this issue.

However, to respond from the peoples' places of suffering is to become a Church that speaks in mercy, without fear of misunderstanding; it is to adapt to a new perspective that is life giving and not death dealing. All the faithful in the Church wait in great obedience and hope for a clarified position. One cannot but recall the words of the great St. John XXIII at the opening of the second Vatican council on October 11, 1962, reminding the council Fathers of their principal duties,

> The major interest of the Ecumenical Council is this: that the sacred heritage of Christian truth be safeguarded and expounded with greater efficacy. That doctrine embraces the whole man, body and soul. It bids us live as pilgrims here on earth, as we journey towards our heavenly homeland... If this

---

792   Cahill, Lisa Sowle, "Catholic Sexual Ethics and the Dignity of the Person: A Double Message, " *Theological Studies* 50, no. 1 (1989): 129.

doctrine is to make its impact on the various spheres of human activity – in private, family and social life – then it is absolutely vital that the Church shall never for an instance lose sight of that sacred patrimony of truth inherited from the Fathers. But it is equally necessary for her to keep up to date with the changing conditions of this modern world, and of modern living... This... Council... is to give to the world the whole of that doctrine which, notwithstanding every difficulty and contradiction, has become the common heritage of mankind –to transmit it in all its purity, undiluted, undistorted... And our duty is not just to guard this treasure, as though it were some museum-piece and we the curators, but earnestly and fearlessly to dedicate ourselves to the work that needs to be done in this modern age of ours, pursuing the path which the Church has followed for almost twenty centuries... What is needed is that this certain and immutable doctrine, to which the faithful owe obedience, be studied afresh and reformulated in contemporary terms. For this deposit of faith, or truths which are contained in our time-honored teaching is one thing; the manner in which these truths are set forth (with their meaning preserved intact) is something else... In these days... it is more obvious than ever before that the Lord's truth is indeed eternal. Human ideologies change. Successive generations give rise to varying errors, and these often vanish as quickly as they came... The Church has always opposed these errors, and often condemned them with the utmost severity. Today, however, Christ's Bride prefers the balm of mercy to the arm of severity. She believes that, present needs are best served by explaining more fully the purport of her doctrines, rather than by publishing condemnations... The great desire, therefore, of the Catholic Church... is to show herself to the world as the loving mother of all mankind; gentle, patient, and full of tenderness and sympathy for her separated children... She unseals the fountains of her life-giving doctrine, so that men, illumined by the light of Christ, will understand their true nature and dignity and purpose. Everywhere, through her children, she extends the frontiers of Christian love, the most powerful means of eradicating the seeds of discord, the most effective means of promoting concord, peace with justice, and universal brotherhood.[793]

While attentively listening to the words of John XXIII, Catholics are expected to acquiesce in obedience to the processes of a greatly hierarchical and magisterial Church, they are also advised to look deep into their consciences – where God speaks to every man and woman in the depths of their being. For a Church in full communion, consideration should be given to reviewing and rearticulating what ought to be done in the case of discordancy within marriage, and the use of condoms as prophylactics. This in my opinion does not distort the Church's teaching on the prohibition of contraceptives, it does not diminish in anyway the sanctity of marriage, conjugality or family life. The mandate of the Church is to teach, guided by the Holy Spirit. The Church has a sacred trust to remain faithful to the message of Jesus Christ as found in sacred scripture, as it was handed down within the tradition of the apostolic Church, in collegiality and subsidiarity. Working with the theologians of the Church, the joint reflections of the entire Church must always lead us back to the truths of the faith, without curtailment or compromise. The Church must remain courageous 'in' and 'out' of season to insist on the teachings of Christ even at the possibility of alienation by society. St. Paul's words remain instructive to the Church of all times,

I solemnly urge you to preach the message, to insist upon proclaiming it (whether the time is right

---

793   John XXIII, "Address to at the Opening of Vatican Council II, " October 11, 1962 (Washington, DC: TPS Press, 1964), accessed on Feb. 20, 2016, www.catholicculture.org/culture/library/view.cfm?recnum=3233.

or not), to convince, reproach, and encourage, as you teach with all patience. The time will come when people will not listen to sound doctrine, but will follow their own desires and will collect for themselves more and more teachers who will tell them what they are itching to hear. They will turn away from listening to the truth and give their attention to legends. But you must keep control of yourself in all circumstances; endure suffering, do the work of the preacher of the Good News and perform your whole duty as a servant of God. "[794]

The Church must also be courageous to move away from traditions that are either moribund or are no longer applicable to contemporary time and age. The Church cannot maintain silence interspaced by 'off the cuff' remarks, disjointed and uncoordinated statements about questions that affects people at the deepest parts of their being and existence. In the light of the pontificate of Pope Francis and his call to a jubilee year of mercy, the Church must lead this march of mercy and justice. In Francis' Bull of Indiction for the Jubilee year of mercy titled, *Misericordia Vultus*, he states,

Jesus Christ is the face of the Father's mercy. These words might as well sum up the mystery of the Christian faith... The Church is commissioned to announce the mercy of God, the beating heart of the gospel, which in its own way must penetrate the heart and mind of every person... wherever the Church is present, the mercy of the Father must be evident. In this Holy Year, we look forward to the experience of opening our hearts to those living on the outmost fringes of society: fringes which modern society itself creates. How many are the wounds borne by the flesh of those who have no voice because their cry is muffled and drowned out by the indifference of the rich! During this jubilee

---

794   2Tim 4:2-5

year, the Church will be called even more to heal these wounds, to assuage them with the oil of consolation, to bind them with mercy and cure them with solidarity and vigilant care... Let us open our eyes and see the misery of the world, the wounds of our brothers and sisters who are denied their dignity, and let us recognize that we are compelled to heed their cry for help... this extraordinary Jubilee Year dedicated to living out in our daily lives the mercy which the Father constantly extends to all of us... The Church feels the urgent need to proclaim God's mercy. Her life is authentic and credible only when she becomes a convincing herald of mercy... The Church is called above all to be a credible witness to mercy, professing it and living it as the core of the revelation of Jesus Christ.[795]

The mercy that Pope Francis advocates for is not a frivolous and irresponsible transmitting on of revelation, doctrine and dogma. Rather, it is a call to expound on the meaning of these sacred truths and making it intelligible to modern women and men. Following the example of St. John XXIII, the Church is encouraged not to be quick to invoke anathemas or hand down interdicts. The arms of mercy of the Father must be the first recourse and must be explored to its furthest possible. Making a case for discordant couples and stating an official position is clearly one of the ways in which mercy can be pursued. In the gospel of Mark, Jesus warns against juxtaposing human made traditional constructs to replace what is the commandments of God. Mark quotes Jesus who referenced Isaiah, "These people, says God, honor me with their words, but their hearts is really far away from me. It is no use for them to worship me, because they teach human rules as though they were my laws! You put aside God's command and obey

---

795   Pope Francis, *Misericordia Vultus*, Bull of Indiction of the Extraordinary Jubilee Year of Mercy, April 11, 2015, accessed March 14, 2016, https://w2.vatican.va/content/francesco/en/apost_letters/documents/papa-   francesco_bolla_20150411_misericordiae-vultus.html

human teaching. "[796] Within the broad framework of human sexuality, the Church must find adequate ways to respond to the exigencies of the 21st century. The modern theologian cannot afford to gloss over the witness of the apostolic fathers and of the early Church to the work of the living Jesus among the people of his time. We cannot do theology as if there is no Holy Spirit to lead us to all truths. Theology becomes a pure intellectual work if it does not want to work with the authority granted to the apostles by Christ and subsequently to the Church. In all things of faith and Christian doctrinal tradition, it must all lead back to the mind of Christ. This is the task with which we are faced in our time, as in all times of the past and of the future. One must acknowledge that within the locus of sexuality alone, there are still many questions the Church must respond to. Hopefully, the outcome of the Synod on the family will answer or shed light on these question. As long as humanity continues to evolve, there will be new developments, good and bad that will continually need to be faced. In the words of John Cardinal Onaiyekan, the Cardinal Archbishop of the Metropolitan Archdiocese of Abuja, Nigeria, speaking about the Church and the fears of many about the criticisms from within and outside the Church on the questions about sexual morality, marriage and family life, the cardinal states, "No need for panic. The boat of Peter maybe in turbulence. But it will never sink. It will always arrive at its shores because Jesus is in it. "[797]

---

796   Mk. 7:6-8

797   John Cardinal Onaiyekan, "Marriage in our Contemporary World: Pastoral Observations from An African Perspective, " in *Eleven Cardinals Speak on Marriage and the Family*, ed. Winfried Aymans (San Francisco: Ignatius Press, 2015), 63.

Bibliography

Ackah, James Y., and Benjamin S. N. Cheabu. "Humanae Vitae and Birth Control: Practices and Perspectives from the Ghanaian Catholic. "*Research on Humanities and Social Science* 4, no. 28 (2014): 51.

Aihiokhai, Simon Mary A. "A Case for the Use of Condom as a Therapeutic Means by Discordant Couples in the Roman Catholic Moral Tradition. "*International Journal of African Catholicism* 4, no. 2 (2013): 79–117.

Amoah, Elizabeth. "Preface. " In *African Women, Religion, and Health: Essays in Honor of Mercy Amba Ewudziwa Oduyoye*, edited by Isabel Apawo Phiri and Sarjini Nadar, xvii- xxii, Maryknoll, NY: Orbis Books, 2006.

Anderson, Carl A., and José Granados. *Called to Love: Approaching John Paul II's Theology of the Body*. New York: Doubleday, 2009.

Aquinas, Thomas. *Treatise on Man*. Translated by James F. Anderson. Englewood, NJ: Prentice- Hall Inc., 1962.

Aymans, Winfried. *Eleven Cardinals Speak on Marriage and the Family: Essays from a Pastoral Viewpoint*. San Francisco, CA: Ignatius Press, 2015.

Bevans, Stephen B. *An Introduction to Theology in Global Perspective*. Maryknoll, NY: Orbis Books, 2009.

Biggar, Nigel, and Rufus Black. *The Revival of Natural Law: Philosophical, Theological, and Ethical Responses to the Finnis-Grisez School*. Burlington, VT: Ashgate, 2000.

Blasi, Fulvio de. "The Role of God in the New Natural Law Theory. "*The National Catholic Bioethics Quarterly* 13, no. 1 (2013): 35–46.

Bongmba, Elias K. *Facing a Pandemic:The African Church and the Crisis of AIDS*. Waco, TX: Baylor University Press, 2007.

Bovens, Luc. "Can the Catholic Church Agree to Condom use by HIV-Discordant Couples? "*Journal of Medical Ethics* 35, no. 12 (2009): 743–6.

Braybrooke, David. *Natural Law Modernized*. Toronto: University of Toronto Press, 2001.

Brown, Peter. *The Body and Society: Men, Women and Sexual Renunciation in Early Christianity*. New York: Columbia Press, 1988.

Brugger, Christian E. "Pope Francis and Contraception: A Troubling Scenario. "*National Catholic Register*, Feb. 24, 2016. Accessed March 14, 2016.www.ncregister.com/daily- news.

Bujo, Bénézet. *Plea for Change of Models for Marriage*. Nairobi, Kenya: Paulines Publications Africa, 2009.

Bujo, Bénézet, and Michael Czerny. *AIDS in Africa: Theological Reflections*. Nairobi, Kenya: Paulines Publications Africa, 2007.

Butler, Judith. *Bodies that Matter: On the Discursive Limits of "Sex."* New York: Routledge, 1993.

Buttiglione, Rocco. *Karol Wojtyła: The Thought of the Man Who Became Pope John Paul II*. Grand Rapids, MI: Eerdmans, 1997.

Cahill, Lisa Sowle. *Between the Sexes: Foundations for a Christian Ethics of Sexuality*. Philadelphia: Fortress Press, 1985.

———."Catholic Feminists and Traditions: Renewal, Reinvention, Replacement. "*Journal of the Society of Christian Ethics* 34, no. 2 (2014): 27–51.

———. "Catholic Sexual Ethics and the Dignity of the Person: A Double Message. "*Theological Studies Theological Studies* 50, no. 1 (1989): 120–50.

———.*Family: A Christian Social Perspective*. Minneapolis: Fortress Press, 2000.

———."Notes on Moral Theology: Marriage: Developments in Catholic Theology and Ethics. "*Theological Studies*. 64, no. 1 (2003): 78.

———."Renegotiating Aquinas: Catholic Feminist Ethics, Postmodernism, Realism, and Faith. "*Journal of Religious Ethics* 43, no. 2 (2015): 193–217.

———.*Sex, Gender, and Christian Ethics*. Cambridge: Cambridge University Press, 1996.

———."Women, Marriage, Parenthood: What are their 'Natures'? "*Logos: Philosophic Issues in Christian Perspective* 9 (1988): 11–35.

Callahan, Daniel. "Contraception and Abortion: American Catholic Responses. "*The Annals of the American Academy of Political and Social Science* 387 (1970): 109–17.

Carlen, Claudia. *The Papal Encyclicals*. Wilmington, NC: McGrath Publishing Company, 1981.

Catechism of the Catholic Church. Vatican City: Libreria Editrice Vaticana, 2000.

Catholic Theological Society of America. *Human Sexuality: New Directions in American Catholic Thought*. New York: Paulist Press, 1977.

Cicero, Marcus Tullius. *On the Republic*. Translated by Charles Duke Yonge. London: H.G. Bohn, 1853.

Clark, Elizabeth, ed. *St. Augustine on Marriage and Sexuality*. Washington, DC: The Catholic University of America Press, 1996.

Cahill, Lisa Sowle, Hille Haker, and Eloi Messi Metogo, eds. *Human Nature and Natural Law* (*Concilium* 2010/3). London: SCM Press, 2010.

Curran, Charles, E. *Catholic Moral Theology in the United States:A History*. Washington, DC: Georgetown University Press, 2008.

———.*The Development of Moral Theology: Five Strands*. Washington, DC: Georgetown University Press, 2013.

———.*The Moral Theology of Pope John Paul II*. Washington, DC: Georgetown University Press, 2005.

Davies, Jon, and Gerard Loughlin. *Sex These Days: Essays on Theology, Sexuality and Society*. Bloomsbury: T&T Clark, 1997.

de Mattei, Roberto. The Post-Synod Exhortation, Amoris Laetitia: First Reflection on a Catastrophic Document. (First Published on Rorate Caeli), Available at http://rorate- caeli.blogspot.com/2016/04/de-mattei-post-synod-exhortation-amoris.html

Doherty, Dennis, ed. *Dimensions of Human Sexuality*. New York: Doubleday & Company, 1979.

Dwyer, John C. *Human Sexuality: A Christian View*. Kansas City, MO: Sheet & Ward, 1987.

Eccheveria, Eduardo J. *"In the Beginning...": A Theology of the Body*. Eugene, Oregon: Pickwick Publication, 2011.

Espín, Orlando O. "Traditioning: Culture, Daily Life and Popular Religion, and their Impact on Christian Tradition. " In *Futuring our Past: Explorations in the Theology of Tradition*, edited by Orlando O. Espín and Gary Macy, 1-17, Maryknoll, NY: Orbis Books, 2006.

Farley, Margaret A. "Hope for the Future. "*Journal of Feminist Studies in Religion* 28, no. 2 (2012): 137–41.

———.*Just Love: A Framework for Christian Sexual Ethics*. London: Continuum, 2008.

———."Partnership in Hope: Gender, Faith, and Responses to HIV/AIDS in Africa. "*Journal of Feminist Studies in Religion* 20 (2004): 133–48.

———.*Personal Commitments: Beginning, Keeping, Changing*. San Francisco: Harper and Row, 1986.

Finnis, John M. *Aquinas: Moral, Political, and Legal Theory*. New York: Oxford University Press, 1998.

———.*Fundamentals off Ethics*. Washington DC: Georgetown University Press, 1983.

———."Law, Morality and Sexual Orientation. "*Notre Dame Law Review* 69, no. 5 (1994): 11– 39.

———. *Moral Absolutes: Tradition, Revision, and Truth*. Washington, DC: The Catholic University of America Press, 1991.

———.*Natural Law and Natural Rights*. Oxford: Clarendon Press, 1980.

Fisher, Anthony. "HIV and Condoms within Marriage. "*Communio: International Catholic Review* 3 (Summer 2009): 329–359.

Fremantle, Anne. *The Papal Encyclicals in their Historical Context: The Teachings of the Popes from Peter to John XXIII*. New York: New American Library, 1963.

———.*The Papal Encyclicals in their Historical Context*. New York: New American Library, 1956.

Fuchs, Eric. *Sexual Desire and Love: Origins and History of the Christian Ethic of Sexuality and Marriage*. New York: The Seabury Press, 1983.

Fuller, Jon. "AIDS Prevention: A Challenge to the Catholic Moral Tradition. "*America* 175, no. 20 (1996): 13–20.

Genovesi, Vincent J. *In Pursuit of Love: Catholic Morality and Human Sexuality*. 2nd ed. Collegeville, MN: Liturgical Press, 1996.

George, Robert P. "Natural Law and Justice by Lloyd Weinreb: A Critique of the New Natural Law Theory by Russell Hittinger. "*The University of Chicago Law Review* 55, no. 4 (1988): xx

————.*Natural Law, Liberalism, and Morality*. Oxford: Oxford University Press, 1996.

————.*Natural Law and Moral Inquiry: Ethics, Metaphysics, and Politics in the Work of Germain Grisez*. Washington, DC: Georgetown University Press, 1998.

Goldingay, John. "The Bible and Sexuality. " *Scottish Journal of Theology* 39, no. 2 (1986): 175– 188.

Goodstein, Laurie, and Rachel Donadio. "Vatican Scolds Nun for Book on Sexuality. "*New York* Times, June 4, 2016. Accessed Sept., 10, 2015. http://www.nytimes.com/2012/06/05/us/sister-margaret-farley-denounced-by- vatican.html?hp.

Gorospe, Vitaliano. "The Church and the Regulation of Birth: After *Humanae Vitae. "Philippine Studies* 17, no. 3 (1969): 556–85.

Goyette, John, Mark Latkovic, and Richard S. Myers. *St. Thomas Aquinas and the Natural Law Tradition Contemporary Perspectives*. Washington, DC: Catholic University of America Press, 2004.

Grabowski, John S. "Called to Holiness: Spirituality for Families in Light of Ecclesia in America. "*Logos: A Journal of Catholic Thought and Culture* 5, no. 4 (2002): 75–95.

————.*Sex and Virtue: An Introduction to Sexual Ethics*. Washington, DC: Catholic University of America Press, 2003.

Grabowski, John S. and Michael J. Naughton. "Doctrinal Development: Does it Apply to Sex? "*Commonweal* 124, no. 11 (1997): 2ff

Grisez, Germain. *Contraception and the Natural Law*. Milwaukee: Bruce Publishing Company, 1964.

————.*The Way of the Lord Jesus: Christian Moral Principles*. Vols. 1& 2. Chicago, IL: Franciscan Herald Press, 1983.

Grisez, Germain, and Russel Shaw.*A Grisez Reader for Beyond the New Morality*. Edited by Joseph H. Casey.Washington, DC: Catholic University of America Press, 1982.

————.*Fulfilment in Christ: A Summary of Christian Principles*. London/: University of Notre Dame Press, 1991

Gustafson, James M. "Response to Margaret Farley. "*The Journal of Religion* 58 (1978): S156-9.

⸻. *The Sixties: Radical Change in American Religion*. Philadelphia: American Academy of Political and Social Science, 1970.

Hamlon, John S. *A Call to Families: Study Guide and Commentary for Familiaris Consortio*. Collegeville, MN: Human Life Center, St. John's University, 1984.

Handren, Walter J. *No Longer Two: A Commentary on the Encyclical Casti Connubii of Pius XI*. Westminster, Md.: Newman Pr., 1955.

Hanigan, James P. *What Are They Saying About Sexual Morality?* New York: Paulist Press, 1982.

Hardon, John A. *Catechism on the Splendor of Truth*. Bardstown, KY: Eternal Life Publications, 1996.

Hittinger, Russell. *A Critique of the New Natural Law Theory*. Notre Dame, IN: University of Notre Dame Press, 1987.

Hoksbergen, Roland. "Lisa Sowle Cahill, Global Justice, Christology and Christian Ethics. "*Studies in Christian Ethics* 27, no. 3 (2014): 340–4.

Holloway, Carson. *The Way of Life: John Paul II and the Challenge of Liberal Modernity*. Waco, Tex.: Baylor University Press, 2008.

Jacobson H.L., M.E.L.Hall, and T.L.Anderson. "Theology and the Body: Sanctification and Bodily Experiences. "*Psychology of Religion and Spirituality* 5, no. 1 (2013): 41–50.

John Paul II. *Man and Woman He Created them: A Theology of the Body*. Boston, MA: Pauline Books & Media, 2006.

⸻.*The Theology of the Body: Human Love in the Divine Plan*. Boston, MA: Pauline Books & Media, 1997.

⸻.*Gift and Mystery: On the Fiftieth Anniversary of My Priestly Ordination*. New York: Doubleday, 1996.

Johnson, Luke Timothy. "What's Justice Got to do with it? "*Commonweal*, January 22, 2007.2- 25 literature Resource Center EBSCOhost

Kaczor, Christopher. "John Paul II on the Development of Doctrine. "*Nova Et Vetera* 11, no. 4 (2013): 1173.

Kainz, Howard P. *Natural Law: An Introduction and Re-Examination*. Chicago, IL: Open Court Publishing, 2005.

Kamara, Ronald. "The Role of Small Christian Communities in the Fight Against HIV/AIDS with Specific Reference to Uganda. " In *A Holistic Approach to HIV and AIDS in Africa*, edited by Marco Moerschbacher, Joseph Bitole Kato and Pius Rutechura, 13-16. Nairobi, Kenya: Paulines Publications Africa, 2008.

Keenan, James F. *Catholic Ethicists on HIV/AIDS Prevention*. New York: Continuum, 2002.

Kelsey, Morton T.,& BarbaraKelsey. *Sacrament of Sexuality: The Spirituality and Psychology of Sex*. Rockport, MA: Element, 1991.

Knust, Jennifer Wright. *Abandoned to Lust: Sexual Slander and Ancient Christianity*. New York: Columbia University, 2006.

Komonchak, Joseph A., Dermot A. Lane, and Mary Collins. *The New Dictionary of Theology*. Wilmington, DE: Michael Glazier, 1988.

Lee, Patrick. "The Human Body and Sexuality in the Teaching of John Paul II. " In *John Paul's Contribution to Catholic Bioethics*, edited by Christopher Tollefson, 107–120. Amsterdam, Netherlands: Kluwer Academic Publishers, 2004.

Lusvardi, A. R. "The Law of Conscience: Catholic Teaching on Conscience from Leo XIII to John Paul II. "*Logos - Journal of Catholic Thought and Culture* 15, no. 2 (2012): 13–41.

MacIntyre, Alasdair. "MacIntyre on Tradition. " In *Tradition and Modernity Christian and Muslim Perspectives.*, edited by David Marshall, 151-7, Washington, DC: Georgetown University Press, 2013.

Mackin, Theodore. *The Marital Sacrament: Marriage in the Catholic Church*. New York: Paulist Press, 1989.

Madathummuriyil, Sebastian. "The 'Dative Subject' of the Sacrament: An 'East-West' Perspective. "*Studia Liturgica* 43, no. 1 (2013): 111–32.

Magister, Sandro. On the Carousel of Comments. Accessed on April 13, 2016 Available at http://chiesa.espresso.republica.it/articolo/1351273?eng=y, posted on April 12, 2016.

May, William E. "Veritatis Splendor: An Overview of the Encyclical. "*Communio: International Catholic Review* 21, no. 2 (1994): 1–23.

McBrien, Richard P. *Catholicism*. Minneapolis, MN: Winston Press, 1980.

McCormick, Richard A. *The Critical Calling: Reflections on Moral Dilemmas since Vatican II*. Washington, DC: Georgetown University Press, 1989.

Meilaender, G. "Veritatis Splendor: Reopening Some Questions of the Reformation. "*Journal of Religious Ethics* 23, no. 2 (1995): 225–38.

Milhaven, John Giles. "Thomas Aquinas on Sexual Pleasure. " *Journal of Religious Ethics* 5, no. 2 (1977): 157–18.

Miller, J. Michael. *The Encyclicals of John Paul II*. Huntington, IN: Our Sunday Visitor, 1996.

Miller-McLemore, B. J. "Embodied Knowing, Embodied Theology: What Happened to the Body? "*Pastoral Psychology* 62, no. 5 (2013): 743–58.

Moore, Gareth. *The Body in Context: Sex and Catholicism*. London: Continuum, 1992.

Nelson, James B. *Body Theology*. Louisville: Westminster/John Knox Press, 1992.

———.*Embodiment: An Approach to Sexuality and Christian Theology*. Minneapolis, MN: Augsburg Publishing House, 1978.

———."On Doing Body Theology. " *Theology & Sexuality* 2 (1995): 38-60.

Nelson, James B., and Sandra P. Longfellow. S*exuality and the Sacred Sources for Theological Reflection*. Louisville, KY: Westminster/ John Knox Press, 1994.

Newman, John Henry. *An Essay on the Development of Christian Doctrine*. New York: Appleton & Company, 1846.

Njoroge, Nyambura J. "Let's Celebrate the Power of Naming. " In *African Women, Religion, and Health: Essays in Honor of Mercy Amba Ewudziwa Oduyoye*, edited by Isabel Apawo Phiri and Sarjini Nadar, 59-76, Maryknoll, NY: Orbis Books, 2006.

O'Connell, Timothy E. *Principles for a Catholic Morality*. San Francisco, CA: Harper & Row, 1999.

Odeyemi, John Segun. *Catholics and Human Sexuality: The Humanae Vitae Questions*. Iperu- Remo, Nigeria: The Ambassador Publications, 2004.

Odozor, Paulinus Ikechukwu. *Moral Theology in an Age of Renewal: A Study of the Catholic Tradition Since Vatican II*. Notre Dame, IN: University of Notre Dame Press, 2003.

————.*Sexuality, Marriage and Family*. Indianapolis, IN: University of Notre Dame Press, 2001.

Oduyoye, Mercy Amba. *Hearing and Knowing: Theological Reflections on Christianity in Africa*. Maryknoll, NY: Orbis Books, 1986.

————.*Beads and Strands: Reflections of an African Woman on Christianity in Africa*. Maryknoll, NY: Orbis Books, 2004.

Ogola, Margaret A. "Looking Back and Looking Forward at HIV/AIDS in Africa: Serodiscordant Couples, Re-Infection, the Role of Women, and the Condom. " In *Catholic Theological Ethics, Past, Present, and Future: The Trento Conference*, edited by James F. Keenan, 201-8, Maryknoll, N.Y.: Orbis Books, 2011.

Onaiyekan, John Cardinal. "Marriage in our Contemporary World: Pastoral Observations from an African Perspective. " In *Eleven Cardinals Speak on Marriage and the Family: Essays from a Pastoral Viewpoint*, edited by Winfried Aymans, 63-72, San Francisco, CA: Ignatius Press, 2015.

O'Riordan, Seán. "The Synod on the Family, 1980. "*The Furrow* 31, no. 12 (1980): 759–77.

Orobator, Agbonkhianmeghe E. "When AIDS Comes to Church. " In *AIDS in Africa: Theological Reflections*, edited by Bénézet Bujo and Michael Czerny , 120-8,Nairobi, Kenya: Paulines Publications Africa, 2007.

Pagel, Elaine. *Adam, Eve and the Serpen*t. New York: Random House, 1988.

Peters, Ted. "Feminist and Catholic: The Family Ethics of Lisa Sowle Cahill. "*Dialog* 35, no. 4 (1996): 269–77.

Pieper, Josef. *Tradition: Concept and Claim*. Wilmington, DE: ISI Books, 2008.

Pinedad-Madrid, Nancy. "Traditioning: The Formation of Community, the Transmission of Faith. " In *Futuring our Past: Explorations in the Theology of Tradition*, edited by Orlando O. Espín and Gary Macy, 204-226, Maryknoll, NY: Orbis Books, 2006.

Pope, Stephen J. "Scientific and Natural Law Analyses of Homosexuality: A Methodological Study. "*The Journal of Religious Ethics* 25, no. 1 (1997): 89–126.

Pui-lan, K. "Mercy Amba Oduyoye and African Women's Theology. "*Journal of Feminist Studies in Religion* 20 (2004): 7–22.

Rahner, Karl, Cornelius Ernst, and Kevin Smyth. *Sacramentum Mundi: An Encyclopedia of Theology*. Montreal, Canada: Herman and Herder, 1969.

Reiterman, Carl. "Birth Control and Catholics. "*Journal for the Scientific Study of Religion* 4, no. 2 (1965): 213–33.

Rhonheimer, Martin. "A Debate on Condoms and AIDS. "*The National Catholic Bioethics Quarterly* 7, no. 2 (2007): 40.

———."Is Christian Morality Reasonable? On the Difference between Secular and Christian Humanism. "*Annales Theologici* 15, no. 2 (2001): 529.

Robertson, C. K., ed. *Religion and Sexuality: Passionate Debates*. New York: Peter Lang, 2006.

Roberts, Christopher Chenault. *Creation and Covenant: The Significance of Sexual Difference in the Moral Theology of Marriage*. London: Continuum, 2007.

Ross, Susan A. " 'Then Honor God in Your Body' (1 Cor. 6:20): Feminist and Sacramental Theology on the Body. "*Horizons* 16, no. 1 (1989): 7–27.

Ross, Susan A. "The Bride of Christ and the Body Politic: Body and Gender in Pre-Vatican II Marriage Theology. "*The Journal of Religion* 71, no. 3 (1991): 345–61.

Rubio, Julie Hanlon. "Family Ethics: Beyond Sex and Controversy. "*Theological Studies* 74, no. 1 (2013): 138–61.

Salzman, Todd A., and Michael G. Lawler. *Sexual Ethics:A Theological Introduction*. Washington, DC: Georgetown University Press, 2012.

———.*The Sexual Person: Toward a Renewed Catholic Anthropology*. Washington, DC: Georgetown University Press, 2008.

————."New Natural Law Theory and Foundational Sexual Ethical Principles: A Critique and a Proposal. "*Heythrop Journal* 47, no. 2 (2006): 182–205.

Sanneh, Lamin. Francis is letting the Church Grow and Thrive. Accessed on April 5, 2016. Available at http://www.ncregister.com/daily-news/amoris-laetitia-a-tale-of-two-documents, posted on April 3, 2016,

Schmitz, Kenneth L. *At the Center of the Human Drama: The Philosophical Anthropology of Karol Wojtyła/Pope John Paul II*. Washington, DC: Catholic University of America Press, 1993.

Schneewind, J. B. *The Invention of Autonomy: A History of Modern Philosophy*. London: Cambridge University Press, 1998.

Schuller, Bruno. "Can Moral Theology Ignore Natural Law? " In *Introduction to Christian Ethics: A Reader*, edited by Ronald P. Hamel and Kenneth R. Himes, 407-12, New York: Paulist Press, 1989.

Scott, Kieran, and Harold Daly Horell. *Human Sexuality in the Catholic Tradition*. New York: Rowman & Littlefield Publishers, 2007.

Seagrave, S. A. "Cicero, Aquinas, and Contemporary Issues in Natural Law Theory. "*The Review of Metaphysics* 62, no. 3 (2009): 491–523.

Seipel, Peter. "Aquinas and the Natural Law: A Derivationist Reading of ST I-II, Q. 94, A. 2. "*Journal of Religious Ethics* 43, no. 1 (2015): 28–50.

Seow, C. L. *Homosexuality and Christian Community*. Louisville, KY: Westminster John Knox Press, 1996.

Shivanandan, Mary. *Crossing the Threshold of Love: A New Vision of Marriage in the Light of John Paul II's Anthropology*. Washington, DC: Catholic University of America Press, 1999.

Smith, Janet E. "The Morality of Condom use by HIV-Infected Spouses. "*The Thomist* 70, no. 1 (2006): 27-69.

Soskice, Janet. "Tradition. " In *Tradition and Modernity Christian and Muslim Perspectives*, edited by David Marshall,25-30, Washington, DC: Georgetown University Press, 2013.

Spinello, Richard A. *The Encyclicals of John Paul II: An Introduction and Commentary*. Lanham, Md.: Rowman & Littlefield Publishers, 2012.

Suarez, Francisco. "A Treatise on Law and God the Lawgiver. " In *Selections from Three Works of Francisco Suarez*, edited by James Brown Scott, Vol. 2, 3-20, Oxford: Clarendon Press, 1944.

Sullivan, F. A. "The Doctrinal Weight of Evangelium Vitae. "*Theological Studies* 56, no. 3 (1995): 560-565.

Taylor, Charles. *Sources of the Self: The Making of the Modern Identity*. Cambridge, Mass.: Harvard University Press, 1989.

Thomas Aquinas. *Treatise on Law (Summa Theologiae)*. Translated by Alfred J. Freddoso. South Bend, IN: St. Augustine's Press, 2009.

Tilley, Terrence W. *Inventing Catholic Tradition*. Eugene, OR: WIPF& Stock Publishers, 2000.

Tornelli, Andrea in "La Stampa " Accessed on April 23, 2016. Available at http://www.lastampa.it/20116/05/013/vaticaninsider/eng/ enquiries-and interviews/amoris- laetitia.

Twomey, Vincent. *Moral Theology After Humanae Vitae: Fundamental Issues in Moral Theory and Sexual Ethics*. Portland, OR: Four Courts Press, 2010.

UNAIDS. *AIDS Epidemic: Enduring the Urban AIDS Epidemic, Data and Facts Sheet - 2015*. Accessed Feb. 28, 2016.http://www.kff.org/ hivaids/facts-sheet/the-hivaids-epidemics.

Urbine, William, and William N. Seifert. *On Life and Love: A Guide to Catholic Teaching on Marriage and Family*. Mystic, CT: Twenty-Third Publications, 1993.

Walgrave, Jan Hendrik. *Unfolding Revelation:The Nature of Doctrinal Development*. Philadelphia: Westminster, 1972.

Watson, Francis. *Agape, Eros, Gender: Towards a Pauline Sexual Ethic*. Cambridge: Cambridge University Press, 2000.

Weaver, Mary J. *New Catholic Women: A Contemporary Challenge to Traditional Religious Authority*. San Francisco, CA: Harper and Row, 1985.

Weinreb, Lloyd L. *Natural Law and Justice*. Cambridge, MA: Harvard University Press, 1997.

West, Christopher. *Theology of the Body for Beginners: A Basic Introduction to Pope John Paul* II's *Sexual Revolution*. West Chester, PA: Ascension Press, 2004.

————. *Theology of the Body Explained: A Commentary on John Paul II's "Gospel of the Body."* Boston, MA: Pauline Books & Media, 2003.

Westerman, Pauline, C. *The Disintegration of Natural Law Theory: Aquinas to Finnis.* New York: Brill, 1997.

Wilkins, John. *Considering Veritatis Splendor.* Cleveland, Ohio: Pilgrim Press, 1994.

William E. May. "Pope John Paul II: Moral Theology, and Moral Theologians. " In *Veritatis Splendor and the Renewal of Moral Theology*, edited by J. A. DiNoia and Romanus Cessario,211-240. Chicago, IL: Midwest Theological Forum, 1999.

William, Bole. "No Labels Please: Lisa Sowle Cahill's Middle Way. "*Commonweal* 38, no. 1 (2011): 9–15.

Williams, Rowan. "Afterword. " In *Tradition and Modernity Christian and Muslim Perspectives.*, edited by David Marshall, 221-27, Washington, DC: Georgetown University Press, 2013.

Wojtyla, Karol. *Love and Responsibility.* San Francisco, CA: Ignatius Press, 1981.

Wojtyła, Karol. *The Jeweller's Shop: A Meditation on the Sacrament of Matrimony, Passing on Occasion into a Drama.* Translated by Bolesław Taborski. San Francisco: Ignatius Press, 1992.

————.*Sign of Contradiction.* New York: Seabury Press, 1979.

Wolfe, Christopher. *Natural Law Liberalism.* New York: Cambridge University Press, 2006.

Zalot, Jozef D., and Benedict Guevin. *Catholic Ethics in Today's World.* Winona, MN: Anselm Academic, 2011.

Zuckert, Michael. "The Fullness of Being: Thomas Aquinas and the Modern Critique of Natural Law. "*The Review of Politics* 69, no. 1 (2007): 28–47.

Encyclicals and Other Church Documents

Benedict XVI. *Caritas in Veritate*.Vatican, June29,2009. Accessed March 14, 2016.http://www.vatican.va/holy_father/benedict_xvi/ encyclicals/documents/hf_ben-   xvi_enc_20090629_caritas-in-veritate_en.html

———. *Deus Caritate*. Vatican, December 25, 2005.Accessed March 14,   2016.http://www.vatican.va/holy_father/benedict_xvi/ encyclicals/documents/hf_ben-   xvi_enc_20051225_caritas-in-veritate_en.html

———. *Spe Salvi*.Vatican, November 30, 2007. Accessed March 14, 2016. http://www.vatican.va/holy_father/benedict_xvi/encyclicals/ documents/hf_ben- xvi_enc_20071130_spe-salvi-en.html

Pope Francis. "The Vocation and Mission of the Family in the Church and the Contemporary World. "Homily atXIV Ordinary General Assembly. Libreria Editrice Vaticana, October 4, 2015.

———.*Misericordia Vultus*. Bull of Indiction of the Extraordinary Jubilee Year of Mercy. April 11, 2015. Accessed March 14, 2016. https:// w2.vatican.va/content/francesco/en/apost_letters/documents/ papa- francesco_bolla_20150411_misericordiae-vultus.html

Pope Francis. *Amoris Laetitia*. Vatican, March 16, 2016. Libreria Editrice Vaticana. Accessed on May 28, 2016 at htpp://www.vaticanstate. va/content/vaticanstate/en.html.

John XXIII. "Address to at the Opening of Vatican Council II, " October 11, 1962. Washington, DC: TPS Press, 1964. Accessed on Feb. 20, 2016.

John Paul II. *Evangelium Vitae* [The Gospel of Life]. Vatican City: Liberia Editrice Vaticana, 1995.

———.*Familiaris Consortio: Apostolic Exhortation on the Christian Family in the Modern World.* N0v. 22, 1981. Accessed March 14, 2016.http://www.vatican.va/.../apost_exhortations/documents/ hf_jp- ii_exh_19811122_familiaris-consortio_en.html

————. *Gratissimam Sane*. Vatican, February 2, 1994. Accessed March 14, 2016.http://www.vatican.va/holy_father/john-paul- ii/letters/documents/hf_jpii_let_02021994_families_en.html

————. "Letter of John Paul II to Women. " Vatican, June 29, 1995. Accessed March 14, 2016.http://www.vatican.va/holy_father/john_paul_ii/letters/documents/hf_jp_ii_let_290 61995_women_en.html

————. *Veritatis Splendor* [The Splendor of Truth]. Vatican City: Libreria Editrice Vaticana, 1993.

Paul VI. *Humanae Vitae: Encyclical Letter on the Regulation of Birth.* Vatican, 1968.Accessed March 14, 2016.http://www.vatican.va/holy_father/paul_vi/encyclicals/documents/hf_p-   vi_enc_25071968_humanae-vitae_en.html

Pius XI. *Casti Conubii*. Vatican, December 31, 1930.Accessed March 14, 2016. http://www.vatican.va/holy_father/pius_xi/encyclicals/documents/hf_p- xi_enc_31121930_casti-conubii_en.html

Pontifical Council for the Family. "Charter of the Rights of the Family. " Vatican, October 22, 1983.Accessed March 14, 2016. http://www.vatican.va/roman_curia/pontifical_councils/family/documents/rc_pc_family_ documents_19831022_family_rights_en.html

————. "Family, Marriage and De-Facto Unions. "Vatican, November 9,2000. Accessed March 14, 2016. http://www.vatican.va/roman_curia/pontifical_councils/family/documents/rc_pc_family_doc_20001109_de-facto-unions_en.html

Pontifical Council for the Laity. "Men and Women: Diversity and Mutual Complementarity, "Study Seminar. Vatican, Jan., 30-31, 2001. Accessed March 14, 2016. Summary at http://www.vatican.va/roman_curia/pontifical_councils/laity/laity_en/pubblicazioni/rc_pc_laity_doc_20040901_notiziario-9-2004pc-laici_en.html#Women_and_men:_diversity_   and_mutual_complementarity_

Sacred Congregation for the Doctrine of the Faith. "Considerations Regarding Proposals to Give Legal Recognition to Unions Between Homosexual Persons. " Vatican, June 3, 2003. Accessed March 14,   2016.http://www.vatican.va/roman_curia/congregations/cfaith/documents/rc_con_cfaaith_doc_20030731_homosexual_unions_en.html

Sacred Congregation for the Doctrine of the Faith (CDF). *Letter to the Bishops on the Pastoral Care of Homosexual Persons*. Vatican, October 1,1986. Accessed March 14, 2016. http://www.vatican. va/roman_curia/congregations/cfaith/documents/rc_con_cfaith_ doc_1 9861001_homosexual-persons_en.html

Sacred Congregation for the Doctrine of the Faith.*"Persona Humana:* Declaration on Certain Questions Concerning Sexual Ethics. " Vatican, December 29, 1975. Accessed March 14, 2016.http:// www.vatican.va/roman_curia/congregations/cfaith/documents/ rc_con_cfaith_ doc 19751229_homosexual-persons_en.html

The Papal Encyclicals. Compiled by Claudia Carlen. Vol. 2, 1878-1903. Wilmington, NC: McGrath Pub. Co., 1981

United States Catholic Bishops. "Between Man and Woman: Questions and Answers about Marriage and Same-Sex Unions. " USCCB, November 2003.Accessed March 14, 2016.ttp://www.usccb.org/ issues-and-action/marriage-and-family/marriage/promotions- and-defensse-0f-marriage/questions-and-answers-about- marriage-and-same-sex- union.cfm

———. "Marriage: Love and Life in the Divine Plan " USCCB, November 17, 2009.Accessed March 14, 2016.ttp://www.usccb.org/issuess- and-action/marriage-and- family/marriage/love-and-life/upload/ pastoral-letter-marriage-love--and -life-in-the- divine-plan.pdf

———. "Statement on Same Sex Marriage. " USCCB, July 1993. Accessed March 14, 2016.ttp://old.usccb.org/laity/marriage/ samesexstmt.shtml

Vatican II. *Gaudium et Spes*. Vatican, December 7, 1965. Accessed March 14, 2016.http://www.vatican.va/archive/hist_councils/ii_vatican_ council/documents/vat- ii_decl_19651207

www.ingramcontent.com/pod-product-compliance
Lightning Source LLC
Chambersburg PA
CBHW021703120626
46545CB00004B/1373